RESETTING THE SCENE

Contemporary Approaches to Film and Media Series

A complete listing of the advisory editors and the books in this series can be found online at wsupress.wayne.edu.

SERIES EDITOR

Barry Keith Grant
Brock University

RESETTING THE SCENE

CLASSICAL HOLLYWOOD REVISITED

EDITED BY PHILIPPA GATES AND KATHERINE SPRING

WAYNE STATE UNIVERSITY PRESS
DETROIT

Library of Congress Control Number: 2020944681

ISBN 978-0-8143-4779-9 (paperback)
ISBN 978-0-8143-4780-5 (printed case)
ISBN 978-0-8143-4781-2 (e-book)

On cover: *A Star Is Born* (Wellman, 1937). Wisconsin Center for Film and Theater Research, used with permission by Daniel Mayer Selznick representing Selznick International. Cover design by Lindsey Cleworth.

Wayne State University Press rests on Waawiyaataanong, also referred to as Detroit, the ancestral and contemporary homeland of the Three Fires Confederacy. These sovereign lands were granted by the Ojibwe, Odawa, Potawatomi, and Wyandot Nations, in 1807, through the Treaty of Detroit. Wayne State University Press affirms Indigenous sovereignty and honors all tribes with a connection to Detroit. With our Native neighbors, the press works to advance educational equity and promote a better future for the earth and all people.

Wayne State University Press
Leonard N. Simons Building
4809 Woodward Avenue
Detroit, Michigan 48201-1309

Visit us online at wsupress.wayne.edu

CONTENTS

IV: Studio Labor and Operations

V: Rereading Race

VI: Women at Work

ACKNOWLEDGMENTS

We would like to thank David Cuff, Richard Nemesvari, Robin Waugh, and all of the participants of the "Classical Hollywood Studies in the 21st Century" conference held at Wilfrid Laurier University in May 2018. It has been a privilege to collaborate with the conference participants who subsequently developed their work and made such excellent contributions to this anthology. We also wish to thank Marie Sweetman, our editor at Wayne State University Press, whose keen guidance and boundless patience have made this book possible. We are grateful for the permission to reproduce selections from the following copyrighted material:

- The chapter "Another Hollywood Picture? *A Star Is Born* (1937) and the Self-Reflexivity of the Backstudio Picture" by Steven Cohan includes sections from the author's book *Hollywood by Hollywood: The Backstudio Picture and the Mystique of Making Movies* (2018) and is used with kind permission of Oxford University Press.
- The chapter "Disney, DuPont, and Faber Birren: Hollywood and the Color Revolution" by Kirsten Moana Thompson is a revised version of sections of "The Colour Revolution: Disney, DuPont and Faber Birren," which appeared in *Cinéma&Cie International Film Studies Journal*, ed. Elena Gipponi and Joshua Yumibe, 19, no. 32 (2019): 39–52, and is used with kind permission of Mimesis Press.
- The chapter "Censoring Racism: The Production Code and Hollywood's Chinese Americans" by Philippa Gates includes sections from the author's book *Criminalization/Assimilation: Chinese/Americans and Chinatowns in Classical Hollywood Film* (2019) and is used with kind permission of Rutgers University Press.
- The chapter "MGM: Landmarks in the Decline of a Major Hollywood Studio" by Tino Balio includes sections from the author's book *MGM* (2018), the inaugural volume of the Routledge Hollywood Centenary Series, and is used with kind permission of Routledge.

We dedicate this book to film archivists and preservationists who work to ensure that the documents, films, and other materials on which books like this one depend continue to be discovered, maintained, and made accessible to future researchers.

I

SETTING THE SCENE

INTRODUCTION

Katherine Spring

Classical Hollywood cinema has been a central preoccupation of Euro-American film studies since the discipline's crystallization some fifty years ago. At that time, as the academic study of cinema shed its affiliation with university departments of social science and aligned increasingly with humanistic pursuits, the discipline coalesced and flourished by way of the establishment of professional societies, the institution of degree and diploma programs, and the publication of scholarly monographs and journals.[1] While it would be erroneous to claim that scholars prioritized the study of classical cinema at the expense of other national cinemas and modes of filmmaking, it is hard to deny the critical import of studio-era films in early academic film studies. As a brief example, consider the autumn 1975 issue of *Screen*. The issue is celebrated for its inclusion of one of the discipline's most influential and widely circulated articles, Laura Mulvey's "Visual Pleasure and Narrative Cinema." But of the six articles that appeared in that issue, Mulvey's was one of four that centered on studio-era films; the others were Jacqueline Rose's article on Paramount's *Peter Pan* (Brenon 1924), Edward Branigan's article on point-of-view shots favored by the "traditional Hollywood film," and Edward Buscombe's "Notes on Columbia Pictures Corporation 1926–41." Eric Smoodin has explained how Mulvey's and Buscombe's work advanced different theoretical and methodological priorities—feminist psychoanalytic film theory and industrial history, respectively—and in so doing heralded different paths for film studies.[2] But equally remarkable to this methodological diversity is the issue's concentration of studio-era films and filmmakers.

The usual explanation for the emphasis by 1970s film studies on classical cinema points to dominant theories in the field of the time—authorship, genre, and ideology, including early feminist film studies—which championed the study of filmmakers who, despite their setting within formulaic institutions, managed to produce distinctive works of art. Hollywood's studio system was the quintessential exemplar of such an institution, and both its industrial organization and its products availed themselves to be "read" as inscriptions of dominant capitalist and patriarchal ideology.[3] A subsidiary explanation, intimated by Matthew Croombs, may have been the eagerness on the part of American and British critics to approach Hollywood cinema with the same fervor as did their French counterparts, the critics of *Cahiers du cinéma*, in the 1950s.[4] Whatever the reason, the significance of Hollywood cinema to the discipline was apparent early on. When one of the first British film journals, *Movie*, reappeared in 1974 after a three-year hiatus, Steve Neale observed that in the newest issue, "1940's and 1950's Hollywood films are re-affirmed as the evaluative yardstick and auteurism is reaffirmed as a prime mode of analysis."[5] This statement, if expanded to include 1920s and 1930s Hollywood cinema, could apply readily both to scholarly efforts within university departments and to critical ones outside of the academy.[6]

Its predominance notwithstanding, "traditional Hollywood film" did not have a precise definition in early writings. As John Belton has recounted, scholars writing prior to the mid-1980s "repeatedly referred to a phenomenon called 'classical Hollywood cinema.' But the exact nature of this 'dominant cinema,' which they somewhat vaguely characterized as 'illusionistic,' 'transparent-invisible,' and/or 'patriarchal,' was never clearly defined."[7] *The Classical Hollywood Cinema: Film Style and Mode of Production to 1960*, a 506-page volume coauthored by David Bordwell, Janet Staiger, and Kristin Thompson and published jointly by Columbia University Press and Routledge & Kegan Paul in 1985, provided that definition. The book, now considered a landmark text in the discipline of film studies, staked three broad claims.[8] First, rather than offer sweeping theoretical interpretations, it advanced middle-level arguments that were deduced from studio memoranda, trade industry papers and journals, engineer and technician reports, and screenwriting manuals, as well as from systematic, shot-by-shot analyses of a near-randomized sample of films instead of a canonized one. Second, it explained how a set of technological, institutional, economic, and discursive practices could give rise to, sustain, and be reinforced by a stylistic paradigm "whose principles remain[ed] quite constant across decades, genres, studios, and personnel" and yet resisted monolithic status, thus offering filmmakers a range of stylistic choice within that paradigm.[9] Third, the book connected classical Hollywood style to a theory of spectatorship that assumes an active spectator whose attention is guided by spatial and temporal cues and whose primary drive in film viewing is to "form hypotheses, make inferences, erect expectations, and draw conclusions about the film's characters and actions."[10] This model of spectatorship, developed more fully in Bordwell's book *Narration in the Fiction Film* (also 1985), introduced a critical intervention into prevailing theories of Lacanian psychoanalysis, Althusserian Marxism, and Barthesian semiotics, and cleared a path for the cognitive-psychological study of film.[11] In these ways, *The Classical Hollywood Cinema* established standards for methodologically rigorous archival research and laid the foundation for a research program—historical poetics—that continues to flourish.

Classical Hollywood remains a thriving topic of scholarly discourse in spite of the proliferation, and even fragmentation, of the subject in recent decades.[12] As evidence of such fragmentation, one need look no further than the 2019 conference program of the Society for Cinema and Media Studies, in which President Pamela Robertson Wojcik reflected on the growth of the organization since its formation sixty years prior as the Society of Cinematologists. Not only had membership grown from thirty-seven constituents to nearly three thousand, but also, as Wojcik wrote, the conference showed "the range and breadth of what is now considered 'cinematology,' with panels and awards on diverse topics that encompass game studies, podcasts, animation, reality TV, sports media, contemporary film, and early cinema; and approaches that include affect studies, ecocriticism, archival research, critical race studies, and queer theory, among others."[13] One might quarrel with the classification of all those media and approaches under the category "cinematology," but that is the point: film, be it celluloid or digital, no longer occupies a privileged position as an object of analysis in the discipline's largest professional organization.

Yet, in the face of cinema's diffusion into other fields and approaches, scholarship on classical Hollywood cinema in recent years has undergone expansive growth and reassessment. The increasing availability of research materials, for example, has spurred tremendous productivity. In addition to the appearance of online archives, such as the Media History Digital Library, and the development of new means for watching movies, such as subscription streaming services, brick-and-mortar archives are ever more accessible to scholars. The emergence of these resources, alongside the inauguration of the Society for Cinema and Media Studies' Classical Hollywood Scholarly

Interest Group in 2015, suggests that scholars of classical cinema are now better equipped than ever to answer research questions about studio-era filmmaking. But what types of questions are they asking, and what methods are they employing to answer them? Thirty-five years after the publication of *The Classical Hollywood Cinema*, whither classical Hollywood in the multifaceted future of film studies?

It was upon reflection of these questions that Philippa Gates and I secured a grant from the Social Sciences and Humanities Research Council of Canada to host a conference in May 2018 at Wilfrid Laurier University in Waterloo, Canada. Somewhat ambitiously titled "Classical Hollywood Studies in the 21st Century," the three-day event was organized as a forum for scholars to reconsider established positions in the field, share new archival discoveries, and discuss innovative approaches to "doing" film history. Thirty-eight participants from Canada, the United States, the United Kingdom, Europe, and Australia presented papers and participated in a tour of the TIFF Film Reference Library in Toronto, film screenings, and a panel devoted to the discussion of strategies for sustaining academic and popular audiences of the classical cinema.

In the absence of a focused conference theme, our call for papers cast a relatively wide net, but three days of conference presentations exposed above all the legacy of historical poetics on contemporary scholarship. By and large, the conference's papers tended to situate particular aspects of classical Hollywood cinema—be they institutional, like labor operations or self-regulatory practices, or aesthetic, like genre conventions or narrative form—in proximate, sometimes interlocking historical contexts, whether economic, legal, industrial, artistic, cultural, social, political, or technological in nature. Furthermore, while efforts to theorize classicism and classical cinema in terms of broader conceptual frameworks were by no means absent, what came to the fore was a synthesis of familiar territory with new areas: that is, scholars were pursuing middle-level research questions about stylistic and industrial phenomena but were at several junctures positioning these explanations within more recent inquiries into gender theory, race theory, media archaeology, media industry studies, and historiography writ large.[14] Some papers leveraged the analysis of primary documents into self-conscious accounts of the nature of archives, for instance, while others questioned earlier narratives of film history in light of recent scholarship on media industries. In these ways, many papers both retained principles of revisionist historiography and brought them into the light of more recent developments in the field. In sum, the conference revealed the formative and sustained value of classical Hollywood cinema to projects of contemporary film studies.

This volume, *Resetting the Scene: Classical Hollywood Revisited*, aims to advance the conference objectives by presenting a volume of papers in substantively revised and expanded form and featuring some of today's most significant and innovative scholarship on classical cinema. Some chapters offer critical analyses of films and extratextual materials within social and industrial contexts, such as censorship regulations or representational norms of gender. Some focus on studio-era economies and structures of labor that influenced filmmaking practices and visual style. Others employ new archival research and tools as a means of reevaluating older methods and offering new historiographies. The relative brevity of each chapter reflects our commitment to providing readers with a wide variety of insightful, accessible, and original scholarship. This assembly of numerous concise studies, rather than fewer, lengthier ones, has allowed us to showcase the diverse nature of scholarship in the field.

This is not to say that *Resetting the Scene: Classical Hollywood Revisited* is exhaustive. Of course, a single volume cannot encompass all of the critical shifts and debates in the field today. Indeed, one of the upshots of the proliferation of film studies has been the intersection of classical Hollywood studies with an array of other fields of inquiry in addition to the above-mentioned ones, including affect and embodiment theory, queer theory, critical race theory, ecocriticism, star studies, screenwriting studies, and media industry studies. A critical consideration of each of these subjects in relation to classical Hollywood could occupy at least an anthology unto itself. But the chapters that follow often do more than just touch upon these fields. For instance, the field of star studies frames the work of Bradley Schauer and Will Scheibel, each of whom sheds light on how films, advertising, or other press coverage shaped the construction of Hollywood star identities. The questions evoked by Eric Hoyt and Patrick Keating resonate within the domain of media archaeology, especially with regards to how new digital tools mediate our discoveries of classical cinema's industrial origins and stylistic traits, respectively. Media industry studies, including analyses of industrial self-promotion and self-regulation, are evoked in chapters by Kyle Edwards, Paul Monticone, and Kirsten Moana Thompson. Critical race theory informs the work of Ryan Jay Friedman, Philippa Gates,

Barry Keith Grant, and Charlene Regester. These are just a few examples of the ways in which *Resetting the Scene: Classical Hollywood Revisited* expands the parameters of earlier studies of classical cinema.

The book also builds upon related anthologies and monographs that have appeared in the past few years and are evidence of continued interest in the field. Two such anthologies, *The Classical Hollywood Reader* (2012), edited by Steve Neale, and *The American Film History Reader* (2015), coedited by Jon Lewis and Eric Smoodin, assemble previously published work to represent a range of approaches to the study of American film history.[15] In so doing, both collections imply a shared understanding among scholars of the critical value of studying the history and historiography of classical Hollywood cinema.[16] Also important in this respect is *American Film History: Selected Readings, Origins to 1960* (2015), which, although designed primarily as a textbook for undergraduate students rather than as a showcase of current scholarship, offers key descriptive accounts of important facets of American film history, including the representation of women in silent cinema, silent film comedy, the star system, the transition to sound, avant-garde cinema of the 1920s, Hollywood animation, and authorship.[17] These three collections have appeared alongside the publication of American film histories that dedicate many pages to studio-era filmmaking as well as numerous monographs that address the work of particular filmmakers, studios, genres, and representational strategies of classical cinema.[18]

With chapters that highlight both specific historical case studies and broader methodological approaches, *Resetting the Scene: Classical Hollywood Revisited* expands upon an already rich body of scholarship and inspires future work. This collection affirms classical Hollywood cinema as an object of scholarly and pedagogical interest, and one whose definition as a distinct institutional and aesthetic system continues to renew scholarly interest well into the twenty-first century.

SUMMARY OF CHAPTERS

The book's sections are organized to highlight key intellectual trends and areas of research. For instance, while Patrick Keating's chapter on videographic criticism, which features a fine-grained analysis of film lighting, would find a welcome home in the section "Film Style and Practice," we have placed it in the section "New Approaches" to signal the value of videographic criticism as a method of analysis for twenty-first-century scholars. Helen Hanson's chapter on the work of Metro-Goldwyn-Mayer (MGM) technician Lela Simone could readily complement the book's sections on either studio labor or classical genres, but we chose to include it in the section on gender to highlight the creative contributions of previously undervalued women to classical cinema.

The crux of section I, "Setting the Scene," is David Bordwell's reflection on *The Classical Hollywood Cinema* and his address of three questions that arose in the book's wake: "What happened after 1960? What were early alternatives to the continuity style? And what did filmmaking of the 1940s contribute to Hollywood's narrative traditions?" The answers to these questions coalesce around a research program, historical poetics, that has defined Bordwell's scholarship over nearly four decades and has inspired an abundance of research by others, including many of the chapters that follow. The heart of historical poetics, and a cornerstone of classical Hollywood studies, is the close analysis of film style. Section II, "Film Style and Practice," offers three case studies in stylistic analysis. First, Scott Higgins explains the concept of virtuosity within the classical mode of production, which privileged "invisible" technique. Analyzing films from across the work of director Vincente Minnelli, Higgins identifies a consistency in the auteur's approach to staging, framing, and décor. The so-called Minnelli swirl functioned both to serve narrative concerns and to encourage aesthetic appreciation, the dual features of artworks that are defined as virtuosic. Shifting focus to sonic style, Kathryn Kalinak brings to light the practice of musical recycling, through which composers used the same musical passages in multiple films and built up references through a process of "aural intertexuality." Given the frequency with which this practice occurred, musical recycling is a welcome addition to the taxonomy of practices that we use to describe the norms of Hollywood film music. Last, inspired by the question "How classical was classical cinema?" Chris Cagle brings attention to peculiar stylistic strategies in late studio-era films, including *Daisy Kenyon* (Preminger 1947) and *Seconds* (Frankenheimer 1966). Rather than explain these peculiarities by subsuming them to the broad scope of classicism, Cagle appeals to two analogies from art history, mannerism and baroque, and in turn offers a rich alternative to our understanding of the periodization of American film style.

Section III, "Classical Genres," does not so much restate the importance of genre to the classical mode of production as it exemplifies some of the "bounds of difference" made possible by classicism (which, it should be noted, is addressed by several other chapters across the volume and, in turn, signals the import of an ongoing debate in the field).[19] My chapter centers on how entertainment trade papers of the late 1920s defined the film musical in a variety of ways during the genre's nascent years, when the conventions that came to define the musical were in the process of coalescing. Trade papers not only hinted at the pronounced experimentation of the genre but also shaped their readers' expectations of the musical's conventions. Steven Cohan's chapter, which derives from his newest monograph, focuses on one of the key characteristics, self-reflexivity, of a genre of cinema with which we are all familiar—the "movie within a movie"—but that until now has lacked a coherent definition. Using as illustration the 1937 production of *A Star Is Born* (Wellman) and its marketing campaign, Cohan outlines one of the genre's key qualities: its use of self-reflexivity as a branding strategy. As he writes, "The genre endures because it brands filmmaking with the Hollywood mystique." Rounding out the section, Blair Davis's chapter highlights the flexibility of genre categorization. His examination of the vital role played by B-films of the 1930s and 1940s in the formation of the classical science fiction film indicates both the consistency of genre norms across Hollywood studios and the extent to which science fiction cinema encouraged the exploration of classical boundaries.

Section IV, "Studio Labor and Operations," draws back the curtain on the professional practices of the workers and executives of studios and related industries. In so doing, the section underlines the vitality of archival research as a means of dismantling myths about studio authorship and replacing them with richer understandings of labor practices that evolved among a range of constitutive agents—from managerial executives to contracted stars. The opening chapter by Charlie Keil and Denise McKenna advances a much-needed history of the industrial and aesthetic foundations upon which the classical studio system was built. While that system engendered and depended upon a famously hierarchical distribution of labor, its earliest practices, as the authors explicate through three case studies, were predicated on creative collaboration. Discourses of collaboration, community, and cohesiveness became central features of Hollywood's emergent identity. Another kind of collaboration—cross-promotion among different industries—is illustrated by Kirsten Moana Thompson's carefully plotted history showing how negotiations among the Disney studio, the color consultant Faber Birren, and the DuPont chemical company engendered the synthetic color palette that came to define the distinctive look of Disney's cel animation in the 1930s. From this perspective, Thompson concludes that "animated color was a material product of industrial modernity" and thereby highlights the interwoven nature of industrial and aesthetic practices of the studio era.

Another key feature of industrial modernity, product efficiency, is the focus of Kyle Edwards's study of B-film production at Warner Bros. Although previous scholars have discussed the major studios' efforts to maximize efficiency, Edwards shows that while the corporate mandate to maximize efficiency helped producers to refine strategies for story development, scheduling, and staffing, it also was not without risk: the law of diminishing returns was a significant force in the dissolution of the studio's B-unit. Bradley Schauer draws attention to the labor of stars in the postwar era, when the studios by and large relinquished the standard seven-year star contract. One studio, Universal-International (U-I), distinguished itself not only by retaining the contract but also by exploiting it to transform inexperienced talent into a roster of contract players by way of an acting school. Schauer explains some of the reasons why U-I embraced the contract during such a precarious period of filmmaking and exhibition and why the talent development program ultimately failed while at the same time bolstered U-I's reputation into the post-studio era.

The subsequent two sections consider representations of marginalized racial and gendered identities. Section V, "Rereading Race," opens with Philippa Gates's examination of the influence of industry self-regulation on racial representation, investigating specifically how the Production Code Administration affected the depiction of Chinese characters in studio-era cinema. Based on findings published in her most recent monograph, including correspondence between the studios and the Chinese consul of Los Angeles, Gates shows how studio producers attempted to balance the demands of the Chinese government with the guidelines set forth by the Production Code Administration. Ryan Jay Friedman also considers the regulation of racialized bodies on-screen, focusing on the specialty numbers performed by African Americans in Hollywood musicals. The lack of narrative motivation that typifies specialty numbers can be explained, in part, by the genre's reliance on formal excess and, in part, by industrial and social factors, since numbers were inserted in such a way that racist censors could excise them with ease in southern states. Friedman argues, however, that specialty numbers may be best fathomed as signifiers of competing forces: on the one hand, as Hollywood's projection of America's "cultural melting pot" discourse to mask racial difference and segregationist policies, and, on the other hand, as spaces where black performers could not only compete with white performers but also, through their performances, comment on the "racial motivation" that legitimized their appearances in the first place.

The remaining two chapters attend to the subject of black bodies in nonmusical genres, wherein appearances of black characters cannot be explained by generic motivation and instead are integrated more or less into narrative demands. Charlene Regester analyzes the narrative functions of Sam McDaniel's characters in *Double Indemnity* (Wilder 1944) and *The Ice Palace* (Sherman 1960), both of which capitalize on McDaniel's racialized presence to suit narrative ends. Representative of different genres—film noir and historical adventure, respectively—and released sixteen years apart, both films render McDaniel's racialized body as a signifier of moral dubiousness, one that precipitates a metaphorical "darkening" of the white characters against whom McDaniel is cast. Barry Keith Grant expands present scholarship on science fiction cinema by considering examples that challenge the genre's normative white ideology. The "overdetermined whiteness" of science fiction is curious given the genre's reliance upon alternative and otherworldly social and material realities, and it is this commitment to whiteness that makes two norm-defying examples, *The World, the Flesh, and the Devil* (MacDougall 1959) and *The Meteor Man* (Townsend 1993), all the more significant as social critique both during and after the studio era.

Section VI, "Women at Work," contributes to the essential efforts of contemporary scholars to challenge male-dominated histories of the studio era and its genres. The latter is addressed by Liz Clarke, who brings new critical attention to the representation of women in the genre of the war film during the 1910s. Clarke weaves a thread from the serial queen melodramas produced during the first half of the decade to production in the latter half that depicted heroic women serving on the World War I battlefront rather than on the home front. Shedding new light on the "most masculine of genres," Clarke's account provides a vital revisionist history of the American silent war film. Off-screen, women's labor remains disproportionately represented by Hollywood historiography, and Helen Hanson's account of Lela Simone, the little-known music supervisor for some of the most acclaimed musical numbers produced for Arthur Freed's MGM Unit, is an outstanding example of recent scholarship that recovers the role of women in studio operations. As Hanson shows, Simone's career highlights the ways in which genre, as an institutional category of studio-era filmmaking, informed labor practices, production routines, and discourses of aesthetic value. Finally, Will Scheibel examines contradictory conceptions of work in relation to star image—specifically, that of Gene Tierney in the early 1950s, a period marked by Tierney's mental illness. Tierney's frankness about her condition generated press coverage that, on the one hand, implied marriage and motherhood as the source of her illness and, on the other hand, legitimated her return to work as proof of her mental fitness. As Scheibel argues, these discourses reflected changes in social attitudes about working women in the domestic sphere.

The next section ushers us into the post-studio era. As is amply documented, the demise of the studio system altered every mode of industry practice—production, distribution, exhibition, reception—even while many norms associated with classical narrative form and style endured. Section VII, "Classicism after the Studio Era," opens with a chapter by Tino Balio about the demise of MGM, a major studio that had established industry standards for both the central-producer and the unit-producer modes of production during Hollywood's heyday. Balio maintains that the conservatism of the company, as evidenced by its delayed response to synchronized sound, widescreen cinema, and other industry transformations, was a harbinger of the studio's all-too-late entry into independent production of the 1960s, which in turn precipitated its demise. The two subsequent chapters, respectively by Lisa Dombrowski and Janet Staiger, also evoke questions about the periodization of Hollywood cinema, particularly around the extent to which post-studio independent filmmaking marked (and continues to mark) ruptures from studio-era classical form. As Dombrowski points out, the films directed by Robert Altman are often celebrated as exemplars of New Hollywood cinema, and their frustration of classical norms of narrative and style is read as the flaunting of an authorial presence. Dombrowski's analysis of archival documents from the Robert Altman Collection, however, shows how the transformation from script to screen of *Gingerbread Man* (1998) and *Gosford Park* (2001) may be seen both to refract classical norms and to question the potency of authorial expressivity that is typically associated with independent, package-unit filmmaking. The role of authorship in the context of contemporary modes of production is also the subject of Janet Staiger's chapter, which sheds light on recent practices of screenwriting and how they are analyzed by contemporary scholars. Since the 1970s, screenwriters have been granted independent contracts, but they labor under implicit, and seemingly contradictory, guidelines: scripts both adhere to formulaic (and arguably classical) forms of narrative but foreground authorship by violating scripting protocols. In different ways, then, Dombrowski's and Staiger's chapters each uphold a central thesis of *The Classical Hollywood Cinema*: film form and style are inexorably affected by modes of production.

Finally, to project future avenues for the field, section VIII, titled "New Approaches," highlights novel methods and strategies for studying Hollywood cinema. The chapter by Eric Hoyt shines a spotlight on some of the lesser-known resources at the Media History Digital Library. Whereas scholars have mined its collection of fan magazines and major trade papers to show what "Hollywood" in the 1920s meant to the rest of the world, Hoyt turns to the pages of less familiar Los Angeles trade papers that circulated among local movie workers and assesses these residents' understanding of their place in the Hollywood community. Patrick Keating reflects on the scholarly and pedagogical merits of videographic criticism, a twenty-first-century method for close analysis made possible by the widespread availability of films in digital formats and accessible software for audiovisual editing. For Keating, who presented his own video essay at the 2018 conference, the video essay's inclination toward two modes—the explanatory and the poetic—has special relevance to the study of classical Hollywood cinema, a mode of filmmaking whose "excessive obviousness" can be enhanced and even redeemed by the video essayist's poetic approach. "The essay is a cine-poem just as much as it is a powerful piece of pedagogy," Keating writes, hopefully presaging the use of video essays in future studies of classical cinema.

Another trend in the discipline, the fragmentation of film studies, has inspired Paul Monticone's chapter on the potential lessons to be gained from the more recently emergent field of media industry studies, which accounts explicitly for the institutions that mediate between commercial entities and culture industries. Perhaps, as Monticone suggests in his work on the Motion Picture Producers and Distributors of America, those lessons will provide fresh perspectives on classical Hollywood cinema. Rounding off the collection is a chapter by Richard Maltby, who seeks middle ground between the premises of *The Classical Hollywood Cinema* and "new cinema history": whereas one makes central the film (as a text) and its relationship to its mode of production, the other prioritizes the study of the social and cultural functions of cinema. Ambitious in scope, and explicitly evocative of the past and future of classical Hollywood studies, Maltby's chapter is an eminently fitting conclusion to a collection that aspires to showcase the lively state of the field and the range of subjects and methods embraced by current scholars.

NOTES

1 Histories of the discipline are found in Dana Polan, *Scenes of Instruction: The Beginnings of the U.S. Study of Film* (Berkeley: University of California Press, 2007); Eric Smoodin, "Introduction," in *Looking Past the Screen: Case Studies in American Film History and Method*, ed. Jon Lewis and Eric Smoodin (Durham, NC: Duke University Press, 2007), 5–7; and Lee Grieveson and Haidee Wasson, eds., *Inventing Film Studies* (Durham, NC: Duke University Press, 2008). See especially Stephen Groening, "Appendix: Timeline for a History of Anglophone Film Culture and Film Studies," in Grieveson and Wasson, *Inventing Film Studies*, 399–418.

2 Smoodin, "Introduction," 8–9.

3 Accounts of dominant trends in 1970s film theory are found in Robert Stam, *Film Theory: An Introduction* (Malden, MA: Blackwell, 2000); Richard Rushton and Gary Bettinson, *What Is Film Theory? An Introduction to Contemporary Debates* (Maidenhead, UK: Open University Press, 2010); and Ruth Doughty and Christine Etherington-Wright, *Understanding Film Theory*, 2nd ed. (London: Palgrave, 2018).

4 Matthew Croombs, "Pasts and Futures of 1970s Film Theory," *Scope: An Online Journal of Film and Television Studies* 20 (June 2011), https://www.nottingham.ac.uk/scope/documents/2011/june-2011/croombs.pdf.

5 Steve Neale, "The Re-Appearance of *Movie*," *Screen* 16, no. 3 (1975): 112.

6 On the latter, see the erudite redress of history in Polan, *Scenes of Instruction*, 20.

7 John Belton, "American Cinema and Film History," in *The Oxford Guide to Film Studies*, ed. John Hill and Pamela Church Gibson (Oxford: Oxford University Press, 1998), 231.

8 David Bordwell, Janet Staiger, and Kristin Thompson, *The Classical Hollywood Cinema: Film Style and Mode of Production to 1960* (New York: Columbia University Press, 1985). José Arroyo has recounted the accolades and critiques that followed the book's publication. Choice quotes representing the former include the following: "It is going to change the way American film history is studied" (Tom Gunning); "No work in the field will, or should be, every quite the same" (D. J. Wenden); "Destined to become itself a classic film studies" (Thomas Elsaesser); and "A landmark in the history of academic film studies in the United States" (Richard Allen). José Arroyo, "Bordwell Considered: Cognitivism, Colonialism and Canadian Cinematic Culture," *CineAction* 28 (Spring 1992): 74–88. An exchange about the book's objectives and scope took place in the late 1980s. See Barry King, "The Classical Hollywood Cinema: A Review," *Screen* 27, no. 6 (1986): 74–89; and Andrew Britton, "The Philosophy of the Pigeonhole: Wisconsin Formalism and 'Classical Style,' " *CineAction* 15 (Winter 1988–89): 47–63. Two of the book's authors responded respectively to King; see Kristin Thompson, "Wisconsin Project or King's Projection," *Screen* 29, no. 1 (1988): 48–53; and Janet Staiger, "Reading King's Reading," *Screen* 29, no. 1 (1988): 54–70.

9 Bordwell, Staiger, and Thompson, *Classical Hollywood Cinema*, 2.

10 Bordwell, Staiger, and Thompson, *Classical Hollywood Cinema*, 7.

11 See Carl Plantinga, "Cognitive Film Theory: An Insider's Appraisal," *Cinémas: Revue d'études cinématographiques* 12, no. 2 (2002): 15–37.

12 Lee Grieveson and Haidee Wasson, "The Academy and Motion Pictures," in *Inventing Film Studies*, xviii–xxix.

13 Pamela Robertson Wojcik, "Letter from the President," *SCMS 2019 Conference Program*, March 2019, 3, http://www.cmstudies.org/resource/resmgr/2019_conference/SCMS2019INTFP-webversion.pdf.

14 David Bordwell, "Contemporary Film Studies and the Vicissitudes of Grand Theory," in *Post-Theory: Reconstructing Film Studies*, ed. David Bordwell and Noël Carroll (Madison: University of Wisconsin Press, 1996), 26–27. The consideration of film history in the context of media history answers a call issued by Janet Staiger in "The Future of the Past," *Cinema Journal* 44, no. 1 (2004), 27.

15 Steve Neale, ed., *Classical Hollywood Reader* (Abingdon, UK: Routledge, 2012); Jon Lewis and Eric Smoodin, eds., *The American Film History Reader* (Abingdon, UK: Routledge, 2015).

16 Historiography is also the focus of *Looking Past the Screen: Case Studies in American Film History and Method*, ed. Jon Lewis and Eric Smoodin (Durham, NC: Duke University Press, 2007).

17   Cynthia Lucia, Roy Grundmann, and Art Simone, eds., *American Film History: Selected Readings, Origins to 1960* (Malden, MA: Wiley-Blackwell, 2015).

18   Comprehensive histories of studio-era American cinema can be found in John Belton, *American Cinema/American Culture*, 5th ed. (New York: McGraw-Hill, 2017); Douglas Gomery, *The Hollywood Studio System: A History* (London: BFI, 2006); Jon Lewis, *American Film: A History*, 2nd ed. (New York: Norton, 2018); and Richard Maltby, *Hollywood Cinema*, 2nd ed. (Malden, MA: Wiley-Blackwell, 2003). What follows is not an exhaustive list but rather a collection of scholarly monographs whose range of subjects points up the broad scope of classical Hollywood studies that have been published in just the past five years: David Blanke, *Cecil B. DeMille, Classical Hollywood, and Modern American Mass Culture: 1910–1960* (London: Palgrave MacMillan, 2019); Hye Seung Chung, *Hollywood Diplomacy: Film Regulation, Foreign Relations, and East Asian Representations* (New Brunswick, NJ: Rutgers University Press, 2020); Philippa Gates, *Criminalization/Assimilation: Chinese/Americans and Chinatowns in Classical Hollywood Film* (New Brunswick, NJ: Rutgers University Press, 2019); Patrick Keating, *The Dynamic Frame: Camera Movement in Classical Hollywood* (New York: Columbia University Press, 2019); Steve Neale, *Screening the Stage: Case Studies of Film Adaptations of Stage Plays and Musicals in the Classical Hollywood Era, 1914–1956* (New Barnet, UK: John Libbey, 2017); Miriam J. Petty, *Stealing the Show: African American Performers and Audiences in 1930s Hollywood* (Berkeley: University of California Press, 2016); Veronica Pravadelli, *Classic Hollywood: Lifestyles and Film Styles of American Cinema, 1930–1960*, trans. Michael Theodore Meadows (Urbana: University of Illinois Press, 2015); Steven Rybin, *Gestures of Love: Romancing Performance in Classical Hollywood Cinema* (Albany: SUNY Press, 2018); Ellen Scott, *Cinema Civil Rights: Regulation, Repression, and Race in the Classical Hollywood Era* (New Brunswick, NJ: Rutgers University Press, 2015); and Zoë Wallin, *Classical Hollywood Film Cycles* (New York: Routledge, 2019).

19   David Bordwell, "The Bounds of Difference," in Bordwell, Staiger, and Thompson, *Classical Hollywood Cinema*, 72–87.

1

REINVENTING *THE CLASSICAL HOLLYWOOD CINEMA,* OVER AND OVER

David Bordwell

One important research initiative of the 1960s and 1970s was a consideration of norms of filmic construction. The move had been prefigured by French critics of the 1940s who had remarked on the standardization of style evident in the American studios. André Bazin took this idea further, particularly in his account of "the evolution of film language." Later Noël Burch, echoing Roland Barthes's remarks on literature, proposed that a "zero-degree" style had dominated the West. At about the same time, Raymond Durgnat reflected on the conditions of what he called the "Old Wave."[1] Using the tools of continental semiology, Christian Metz laid out the "Grand Syntagmatique," an ambitious dissection of the relations between cutting patterns and the articulation of time and space in mainstream cinema.[2]

The Classical Hollywood Cinema: Film Style and Mode of Production to 1960 joined this trend.[3] My collaborators on this book, Janet Staiger and Kristin Thompson, and I tackled two questions: *What are dominant principles and practices of form and style in Hollywood feature filmmaking between 1917 and 1960? How may we explain some of the changes in those principles and practices across that period?*

Our inquiry was film centered. Some research projects—say, pursuing questions of moviegoing habits—could proceed if all the films in the world were to disappear. That's not a criticism of those projects; it's just to say that the form and style of the films are of little or no consequence for the mechanisms the researchers are trying to illuminate.

To say that our inquiry was film-centric isn't to say that it's "formalist" in the sense that it stays "within the text." Granted, our questions weren't aimed at scrutinizing financing, audiences, advertising, theater siting, technology, and a host of other areas worth investigating. But some of these factors informed our analyses and explanations. We needed to invoke pertinent, proximate institutional and technological factors that helped shape the way films looked and sounded.

We thought that three concepts were necessary to answer our questions. First was the concept of norms as large-scale, generalizable standards for practices and forms and styles. A norm wasn't a mandate but more of a menu that favored some options over others, depending on the task at hand.

A second concept was that of institutions, organizations of rules and roles, providing individual agents with constraints and opportunities. There were the studios, supply firms, and ancillary stakeholders such as the American Society of Cinematographers. More abstractly, Janet traced institutional forces involving a hierarchy of control and a division of labor, both coordinated in large part by the continuity script.

Finally, there was a tacit concept of problem and solution, which explained the emergence of practices within norms and institutions. Part of Kristin's effort in the book was to show how the decision to make feature-length films in the early 1910s created a cascade of problems bearing on narrative form. Similarly, the problems of sound filming led to adjustments in shooting styles in the early 1930s.

In general, I think the book revealed important ties between craft conditions and production processes, on the one hand, and the resulting films, on the other. We argued that studio division of labor allowed not only reliable output but a standard menu of artistic options. Going beyond the individual filmmaker, we traced how adjacent institutions—not just the studio but also professional associations, supply firms, trade papers, and the like—worked to define and maintain the style. We also suggested reading the professional literature rhetorically, seeing industry discourse as a way for individuals and organizations to set agendas and to crystallize preferred solutions to problems. We tried to show how technological innovations like color and widescreen cinema took particular turns within this matrix of activities. In sum, the book treated Hollywood filmmaking as a flexible but bounded set of norms of style and story, sustained by a stable mode of production.

The effort certainly wasn't beyond criticism, and it has received its share. I responded to some of the most common, and to my mind misleading, ones in a blog entry online.[4] Still, there's scarcely a paragraph I wrote that I wouldn't tinker with now. (I think that Janet Staiger's and Kristin Thompson's contributions have survived better.) Much of my research since the book has been an effort to expand, clarify, nuance, and correct ideas I set forth in 1985.

More positively, writing my portions of *The Classical Hollywood Cinema* and then going on to write *Narration in the Fiction Film* led me to think that we could mount something like a poetics of cinema.[5] It would be a systematic study of principles and practices at the level of single films, groups of films, trends, or traditions. It would rely on a comparative method that favored proximate explanations involving norms, agents, and institutions in particular times and places.

I tried out this poetics-oriented framework in studying Hong Kong film, Japanese cinema, widescreen film, contemporary trends in international narrative, and other areas.[6] In what follows, I sketch three other research projects that revisit, and I hope refine, questions about Hollywood that we raised in our 1985 book. *What happened after 1960? What were early alternatives to the continuity style? And what did filmmaking of the 1940s contribute to Hollywood's narrative traditions?*

AFTER 1960: CONTINUITY AND CHANGE

Some readers suggested that we treated classical Hollywood storytelling and style as a "monolith" that exhibited an implausible stability. But a great many artistic systems have persisted for a long time by adhering to some basic principles. Artists still paint perspective pictures, musicians compose sonatas and symphonies, dramatists write well-made plays on the Ibsen model, and writers produce psychological novels. If other domains of cultural production rely on firm traditions, why couldn't Hollywood movies?

Of course, we weren't really measuring a monolith. We tracked many changes in the look and feel of the films, such as the shift to a "soft style" of cinematography, the emergence of sound cinema, the development of deep-focus cinematography, the standardization of widescreen film, and others. We also proposed ways of understanding phases in the mode of production, from the cameraman system in the earliest years up through the package-unit system that emerged in the 1940s. But we also claimed that such changes fitted into the broader needs defined by the system from 1917 onward. The changes were "retoolings" but not radical alterations in the system.

To say that *Psycho* (Hitchcock 1960) wouldn't be possible in, say, 1920 makes sense, just as saying that Sibelius's and Shostakovich's symphonies differ from those of Mozart. But that's just to acknowledge that we need to track both continuity and change in various properties of the artwork. In *The Classical Hollywood Cinema*, I floated the possibility of conceiving change at the levels of devices, systems, and large-scale principles of causality, time, and space. Since then, I've suggested that we can think of stability another way, using the triumvirate concepts of story world, plot structure, and narration. Along these lines, a great many changes across the history of Hollywood bear on story worlds. Innovation most often consists of finding new settings, periods, characters, and situations that will entice viewers. For example, *Get Out* (Peele 2017) is constructed as a classical film (including a last-minute rescue), but its story world, in which modern bourgeois life reinstitutes slave ownership, is strikingly original.

Principles of construction—plot structure and narrational options, including stylistic texture—change more slowly. And they change within limits, however unpredictable those may be. In the book, I suggested we follow the hint proposed by Leonard Meyer, who itemizes various configurations of stylistic change. We don't have to accept certain models of change, such as the birth/maturity/death of a style, if others are more appropriate. The one that fits Hollywood cinema best still seems to be what Meyer calls "*trended change*," which

> takes place within a limiting set of preconditions, but the potential inherent in the established relationships may be realized in a number of different ways and the order of the realization may be variable. Change is successive and gradual, but not necessarily sequential; and its rate and extent are variable, depending more upon external circumstances than upon internal [i.e., purely stylistic] preconditions.[7]

Those external circumstances range, in the case of Hollywood, among various causal inputs: the intentions of individual agents, changes in technology, new sources of narrative material from other media, altered institutional arrangements, and similar contextual factors. The presence of trended change is one reason why an account of changes in the Hollywood style can't be limited to the films themselves. The preconditions of the classical approach—those principles we've tried to spell out—get instantiated "in a number of different ways."

One more explanatory tool has become increasingly important in my later work: E. H. Gombrich's idea of schemas. These are inherited artistic patterns that serve as points of departure for ongoing creative work. A schema may simply be replicated, as in shot/reverse shot cutting or the use of a track-in for emphasis. A schema may be revised, too. You can revise a schema by finding a functional equivalent, as when zoom lenses replaced track-ins. (There's probably no pure functional equivalent, since there's always a gain and a loss, sometimes at a fine-grained level, in the revision.) Or you can revise a schema by finding a new function for it, as when cross-cutting is used to present nonsimultaneous action (Griffith in *Intolerance* [1916]; Nolan in *Dunkirk* [2017]; and Gerwig in *Little Women* [2019]). And you, the filmmaker, can reject a schema altogether, as when long-take shooting replaces analytical editing. But then very often the rejection relies on other schemas (such as planimetric staging, as in Wes Anderson's films).

These conceptual tools allow us to be fairly specific about continuity and change in the Hollywood narrative system. At the level of style, there is a robust continuity of many basic practices. It's now established beyond doubt that the 180-degree system of staging, shooting, and cutting scenes was consolidated around 1917. It remains normative today, along with other traditional schemas of lighting, sound mixing, camera movement, and scoring. At the level of narrative, the core principle remains goal-oriented plotting around one or two protagonists operating in two lines of action (romance and another sphere) and resolving a series of conflicts through a crisis and climax and sustained by appointments and deadlines. This template remains central to mainstream movies. Narration is still reliant on the interplay of curiosity, suspense, and surprise, effects created by manipulation in the range and depth of our knowledge, an alternation between restricted and unrestricted access.

Since *The Classical Hollywood Cinema* was published, Kristin Thompson and I have tried to elaborate these premises in more detail. For example, Kristin proposed that the "three-act screenplay," an idea that came to prominence as we were writing the book, was better understood in another way. Prototypically, the ordinary feature film has four parts: a setup, a complicating action, a development, and a climax, with an epilogue or tag at the very end. Crucial to her argument is conceiving each of these as involved with the protagonists' goals, which develop in the course of the action.[8]

Another line of inquiry tries to answer the suggestion that some films are organized more loosely, particularly those in "spectacle"-driven genres like action films and musicals. Elsewhere I've argued that a close look at particular films in those genres reveals an extensive degree of classical unity. In action films, for instance, fights, chases, and explosions don't function as pure spectacle. They create obstacles, change goals, develop motifs, and perform other classically defined roles.[9]

Still, that's not to say the system is uniform. *The Classical Hollywood Cinema* tried to spell out the formal and stylistic properties that nearly all studio pictures share. But it didn't devote enough attention to minority narrative schemas within the studio era—network narratives like *Grand Hotel* (Goulding 1932), more episodic family sagas like *Life with Father* (Curtiz 1947), and portmanteau or anthology films like *If I Had a Million* (Cruze et al. 1932). These still obey classical precepts of causality, time, and space, but they represent possibilities that deserve more analysis. This I've tried to give them in various publications.[10]

Many readers assumed that our decision to end the book's inquiry in 1960 meant that films since then belong to a "postclassical" cinema. In our final chapter, we argued that the classical system of storytelling persisted beyond that point but underwent changes—notably, the selective absorption of techniques from European "art cinema." This is a line of thinking that has been fruitfully followed by several scholars. For my part, I wanted to track other post-1960 changes in the Hollywood system. In *The Way Hollywood Tells It* and subsequent work, I suggested that, again, we find the familiar strategies of trended change and schema revision.[11]

Accordingly, continuity editing persists, but in a form I call "intensified continuity," in which the filmmakers rely on tighter framings, faster cutting, longer lenses, and more frequent camera movements, often handheld. Similarly, there emerged new forms of narrative complexity, with multiple protagonists, the juggling of time (often motivated by science fiction premises), enhanced subjectivity, principles of network narrative, and an inclination toward novelty through "worldmaking" on the model of *Star Wars* (Lucas et al. 1977–2019). All of these can be seen as revisions of schemas from earlier periods, particularly the 1940s.

As we'd expect, we could investigate the "external circumstances" encouraging these trended changes. Among those I proposed were the influence of television, models of narrative in other media, and the need for young filmmakers, sensing their "belatedness" in relation to the studio tradition, to reinvent that tradition for a new audience. Not least, the ability to re-view a film on VHS and later DVD encouraged filmmakers to load their work with Easter eggs and citations that fans could enjoy at leisure.

From a problem/solution perspective, filmmakers from the 1960s through the 2000s faced the task of achieving novelty in competition with their peers. They solved it in various ways, some traditional (adding new wrinkles to established genres) and some more modern (establishing an authorial signature, as Wes Anderson and Oliver Stone did). One of the most interesting options, I think, is what we might call the "hyper-classical film," the film so densely constructed along classical principles that it presents a kind of virtuoso traditionalism. Examples I'd pick are *Jerry Maguire* (Crowe 1996), *Die Hard* (McTiernan 1988), *Magnolia* (Anderson 1999), *L.A. Confidential* (Hanson 1997), and *The Prestige* (Nolan 2006), but there are doubtless others. Instead, then, of a postclassical cinema, we have a kind of mannerist version of classicism, heightening and exaggerating some of its characteristics but not going beyond them. Trended change keeps innovations within limits.

1917 AND ALL THAT: TABLEAU STAGING

As *The Classical Hollywood Cinema* was being written, exciting progress was being made in the study of early cinema. A new generation of scholars was reinterpreting the emergence of "film language." In our book, Kristin took on the task of tracing how the so-called primitive cinema of distant, single-shot scenes gave way to the editing strategies characteristic of classical film.

She argued that filmmakers responded to the need to tell lengthy, fairly complicated stories driven by psychological pressures. As filmmakers mounted more complex scenes, editing was considered a solution to the basic problem of guiding attention within a shot. On a parallel track, Janet showed that the continuity script, with its breakdown of scenes into shots that could be planned in advance, encouraged a fine-grain division of labor and solved the problem of the demand for rapid and efficient output. The arrival of editing was promoted by a shift to what Janet called the producer-unit system around 1914.

Kristin's and Janet's work joined the broader impulse to rethink common claims about D. W. Griffith as "the father of film language." Like other researchers, they showed that the standardization of continuity schemas, whatever some owed to Griffith, went far beyond his work rather rapidly. It became evident that his handling of staging and editing was fairly idiosyncratic from the first, and certainly by 1917.

I think it's fair to say that most scholars of early film style concentrated on the emergence of editing. This had the tacit effect of granting the standard story that, before the arrival of cutting, filmic storytelling was "theatrical." But in the 1990s researchers began to propose, in effect, that this "theatrical" style was itself another bundle of norms, no less forceful and expressive than editing. Yuri Tsivian traced the emergence of "precision staging" in directors' use of mirrors, while Lea Jacobs and Ben Brewster produced a sweeping study of early film's debts to theater, focusing on dramaturgy and performance.[12] For my part, reseeing *Ingeborg Holm* (Sjöström 1913) at the Pordenone Silent Film Festival in 1993 drove home to me that depth staging enabled the sort of flow of attention traditionally attributed to editing.

Accordingly, I began to study "tableau cinema" as a style reliant on staging and a fixed camera. It was operative in Europe as well as in the United States between 1908 and 1920, and it became elaborated and refined even as editing tactics were being sharpened and nuanced as well. From this standpoint, as far as the playing space was concerned, cinematic scenes didn't seem theatrical at all. A theater stage, at least in the proscenium tradition, is wide and shallow; the field of a camera lens is narrow and deep. The camera captures a visual pyramid, with the apex at the lens. This allows a flow of visibility, of characters masking one another or items of the set from moment to moment. Practitioners seem to have been perfectly aware of the demands of the "cinematic stage."[13]

For film scholars, the prototypes of depth staging were famous shots in films by Orson Welles and William Wyler, with large figures in the foreground. During the 1910s, though, the tableau tradition yielded more distant foregrounds, figures captured in long shots or knees-up framings. In *The Man from Home* (DeMille 1914), for instance, attention is shaped by lighting, movement, centrality in the frame, advance toward the camera, frontally placed figures, and other compositional factors. The result is a smooth, complex choreography. (See figs. 1.1–1.4.)

A more intimate form of this process can be seen in Lois Weber and Phillips Smalley's 1914 film *False Colours* (see figs. 1.5–1.9). Here, slight shifts of foreground and background figures are coordinated with minimal editing.

1.1. *The Man from Home* (1914): Confronting the scheming aristocrats, Daniel Pike opens the salon door. A burst of light and Pike's movement draw our eye to the middle ground left.

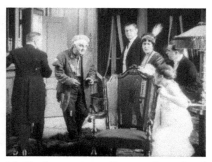

1.2. The fugitive Ivanoff enters, frontal and moving toward frame center. He recognizes the wife who has betrayed him, and she fearfully crouches in the foreground.

1.3. Ivanoff has now recognized the Earl of Hawcastle as the man who ran off with his wife. The Earl is in the background, but we can't see him. Mrs. Simpson pivots. . . .

1.4. . . . to reveal the Earl reaching to open the curtains in the far distance. This sort of blocking-and-revealing technique is impossible on the orthodox stage, because sight lines in an auditorium reveal different views of the playing space. Here, for additional emphasis, a spotlight picks out the Earl's face. Our shift of attention is facilitated by the fact that no one else is moving and most of the figures look to the area we are driven to notice.

1.5. *False Colours* (1914): Dixie comes to Flo with Flo's mother. At this point Flo recognizes Dixie as the woman she's been impersonating and is deeply ashamed. The reunion is filmed to keep Flo frontal and centered.

1.6. As Dixie is about to close the door, the theater manager arrives. What Dixie doesn't know is that her father is standing in the corridor as well.

1.7. After a moment of suspense, the father steps into the doorway, and Dixie sees him for the first time in seventeen years. His back blots out everything in the background but her reaction . . .

1.8. . . . until Flo's face appears in the distance. She's terrified to be confronting the man she has deceived. The valet who follows stands unmoving on the left, not distracting us from the drama in the distance.

1.9. A cut into the room takes us to another phase of the drama, with father and daughter in the foreground and Flo the impostor watching from the rear. Thanks to staging in depth, we get action and reaction in the same shot, whereas the editing techniques soon to dominate American cinema would spread them across several shots.

By 1917, extended tableau scenes virtually vanished from American movies. Editing won. In Europe, the tableau style persisted through the 1910s, with some filmmakers switching to American-style editing. By 1920, it seems to me, only German directors clung to it, and some, such as Robert Reinert, embraced quite striking variants.

In production, the tableau technique, with its sustained shots, put all the responsibilities on the director, the actors, and the moment of shooting. Producers could not plan the process efficiently, and without a breakdown into shots, scenes couldn't be altered in postproduction. The tableau favored directors, while editing played to producers.

But it would be wrong to think that directors didn't welcome cutting. Throughout the 1910s we find a palpable excitement in the revelation of editing's powers. Apart from guiding attention, editing could summon up stronger pictorial impact. Short shots and abrupt axial cuts had no real equivalent in the tableau approach. Editing had a visceral punch that enhanced the emotional stories Hollywood had to tell. And I would argue that a younger generation—that of Frank Borzage, John Ford, Raoul Walsh, William Desmond Taylor, and others who came along in the mid- to late 1910s—saw editing as the sharp edge of innovation.

Still, the tableau style did not wholly die out. Its schemas survived in classical cinema's establishing shots. As a more pervasive approach, it was revived at various points in history—during the early years of CinemaScope and other widescreen processes, as well as by filmmakers like Theo Angelopoulos and Hou Hsiao-hsien. Although intensified continuity editing still dominates American studio cinema and television, the tableau options remain available to filmmakers who see their expressive possibilities.

THE 1940S: COLLECTIVE PROBLEMS

In *The Way Hollywood Tells It*, I speculated that many formal and stylistic developments since the 1960s owed debts to the experiments of the 1940s. Several years and blog posts later, I published *Reinventing Hollywood: How 1940s Filmmakers Changed Movie Storytelling*.[14] This was an effort to examine, at a finer-grained level, narrative innovations in a single period. The analogy was, I suppose, to genre criticism. Just as a genre critic traces out a branching system of conventions that are subject to recasting, so I tried to map the storytelling conventions and inventions of the time and to suggest some causes. In other words, another exercise in historical poetics.

In some chapters of *The Classical Hollywood Cinema*, we had evidence that the filmmaking community could respond collectively to common problems. My study of the conversion to sound and the Mazda lighting tests turned up considerable cooperation. In the 1930s, some common tasks were the mastering of new genres (e.g., the gangster film, the musical) and the conquest of sound technology. In the 1940s, ambitious filmmakers could try to push new subjects and themes (e.g., sex, social criticism) and try to refresh traditional storytelling.

The huge success of the industry in the 1940s, when movie attendance skyrocketed and profits surged, was one enabling condition for innovation. Not that no movie lost money, but most didn't. Similarly, an influx of new talent—young directors and writers, as well as émigrés—fostered fresh approaches. New genres, such as the hard-boiled detective film and the psychological suspense thriller, fostered more complex plotting. Alongside mysteries, middlebrow bestsellers like *How Green Was My Valley* (Ford 1941), *H. M. Pulham, Esq.* (Vidor 1941), and *The Human Comedy* (Brown 1943) encouraged more daring narratives, and even minor literary efforts could become major films (*The Best Years of Our Lives*, Wyler 1946; *Letter to Three Wives*, Mankiewicz 1949). Radio also furnished models of complex storytelling, as in the adaptation of *Sorry, Wrong Number* (Litvak 1948).

Filmmakers of the period were well aware of the pressures toward innovation. In story conference transcripts, David O. Selznick toyed with many alternative ways to narrate the fantasy romance *Portrait of Jennie* (Dieterle 1948). Darryl F. Zanuck laid out the conditions: "It is not enough just to tell an interesting story. Half the battle depends on *how* you tell the story. As a matter of fact, the most important half depends on how you tell the story."[15] Zanuck's suggestion is echoed in the comments of a screenwriter who noted that "the selection of information can make the story more interesting than it actually is."[16]

The result, I think, was a startling proliferation of narrative options, a vast expansion of the menu. Nearly all had predecessors in earlier eras of Hollywood, but the 1940s saw them converge, crystallize, and become more refined. For instance, flashbacks were a mainstay of silent cinema, but they largely dropped out of use in the 1930s. They came back en masse during the boom years. Remakes, such as *Waterloo Bridge* (LeRoy 1940), included flashbacks not in the original, while literary adaptations, such as *Madame Bovary* (Minnelli 1949) and *The Big Clock* (Farrow 1948), added flashbacks to their literary sources. Screenwriters and directors seemed to compete intensely for ever more unusual formats. Some were framed within investigations or inquiries (*Citizen Kane* [Welles 1941], *A Woman's Face* [Cukor 1941]). Some appeared as recollections or reminiscences (*Lydia* [Duvivier 1941], *Double Indemnity* [Wilder 1944]). There were wildly scrambled flashbacks (*Beyond Glory* [Farrow 1948], *Backfire* [Sherman 1950]), as well as lying ones (*Thru Different Eyes* [Loring 1942], *Stage Fright* [Hitchcock 1950]).

Other long-standing techniques were updated: subjective viewpoint, voice-over, and images from memory or dreams came to a new prominence. They allowed films to achieve a "novelistic" density somewhat different from the more objective, detached treatment of action found in most 1930s films. These devices are sometimes identified narrowly with film noir or women's melodrama, but they spread to romantic comedies, family sagas, and even the occasional Western. *Our Town* (Wood 1940) relies heavily on such techniques, as does the romantic comedy *The Affairs of Susan* (Seiter 1945) and the social comedy *Unfaithfully Yours* (Sturges 1948). In addition, 1940s filmmakers pushed further with ensemble films (sometimes plotted as "network narratives"), multiple-protagonist plots (particularly in combat pictures), and block construction.

These stylized techniques were sometimes attributed to the influence of literary and theatrical modernism, but one result of my research was the prospect that Hollywood owed more to a more general mainstreaming of modernist techniques across the arts, aimed at broad audiences. Theater, popular fiction, and radio had selectively assimilated modernist techniques like time shuffling and stream of consciousness. The results, more accessible to broad audiences, pushed Hollywood along similar paths. At the same time, I learned not to overlook unusual narrative strategies that emerged spontaneously in popular culture, chiefly in mystery and suspense fiction. Mystery novels, Ben Hecht pointed out, "are ingenious because they have to be."[17]

One innovation of *The Classical Hollywood Cinema*, I think, was an enhanced appreciation of filmmakers as part of a community that could cooperate as well as compete. That sense intensified when I started to study Hong Kong cinema, a very tight world in which the members openly collaborated with and stole from each other at a rapid rate. Another such enclave was 1940s Hollywood, and the churn of narrative innovations there brought home to me the accuracy of a remark by Jean-Claude Carrière:

> The makers of films, who are themselves viewers of films made by others, have a rough idea of whether or not they will be understood by their contemporaries. The latter, for their part, adapt (unwittingly, often unconsciously) to forms of expression which briefly seem daring but quickly become commonplace. . . . It was through the repetition of forms, through daily contact with all kinds of audiences, that the language took shape and branched out.[18]

Filmmakers make films for audiences, but they also make films for each other. In 1940s Hollywood, I'm convinced, the creators felt a need to outpace one another at the same time they were willing to learn from each other's efforts.

I hardly need to add that these innovations remained firmly classical. They still operate with goal-oriented protagonists, double plotlines, appointments and deadlines, and all the rest. They simply show that the system is capable of constant renewal, expansion, and elaboration. As ever, trended change brought forth a wide variety of creative options.

Like *On the History of Film Style*, *The Way Hollywood Tells It*, and later essays and web entries, *Reinventing Hollywood* reinvented my thinking about classical form and style. That project forced me to consider films, arguments, and ideas I hadn't fully developed, and it allowed me to research, in a depth not available in the pre-internet 1980s, the dynamics at work in the creative community. How could I not feel more keenly the weaknesses in my stretches of the earliest book? Now I know more (a lot, I hope). This is the nature of research: we try to cast out error, refine our questions and concepts, acquire more data, nuance the evidence—and make progress.

All of which is to say that the research project of *The Classical Hollywood Cinema* became for me a research program. Something similar happened, I think, for both Janet and Kristin.[19] Further, it seems, that project helped stimulate others. In the last thirty years a great number of scholars have studied form and style in studio films, not just as the expression of a singular creator but as the result of a cluster of causes, with institutional ones playing crucial roles.[20] Individual research programs have coalesced into a research tradition, one that I find exciting and not a little gratifying.

NOTES

1 I summarize the views of the 1940s *nouvelle critique*, Bazin, Burch, and Durgnat, in *On the History of Film Style*, 2nd ed. (Madison, WI: Irvington Way Institute Press, 2018), chapters 3 and 4.

2 Christian Metz, "Problems of Denotation in the Fiction Film," in *Film Language: A Semiotics of the Cinema*, trans. Michael Taylor (New York: Oxford University Press, 1974), 108–46.

3 David Bordwell, Janet Staiger, and Kristin Thompson, *The Classical Hollywood Cinema: Film Style and Mode of Production to 1960* (New York: Columbia University Press, 1985).

4 See "The Classical Hollywood Whatzis," *Observations on Film Art* (blog), www.davidbordwell.net/blog. All subsequent blog references are to this website, where the entry title may be searched.

5 David Bordwell, *Narration in the Fiction Film* (Madison: University of Wisconsin Press, 1985).

6 See David Bordwell, *Planet Hong Kong: Popular Cinema and the Art of Entertainment*, 2nd ed. (Madison, WI: Irvington Way Institute Press, 2011), and the essays in David Bordwell, *Poetics of Cinema* (New York: Routledge, 2008).

7 Leonard B. Meyer, *Music, the Arts, and Ideas* (Chicago: University of Chicago Press, 1967), 99. See also Meyer, *Style and Music: Theory, History, and Ideology* (Philadelphia: University of Pennsylvania Press, 1989), 102–3.

8 Kristin Thompson, *Storytelling in the New Hollywood: Analyzing Classical Narrative Structure* (Cambridge, MA: Harvard University Press, 1999), and the blog entries "Time Goes by Turns" and "Caught in the Acts."

9 See "Anatomy of the Action Picture," David Bordwell's Website on Cinema, http://www.davidbordwell.net/essays/anatomy.php.

10 See the blog entry "1932: MGM Invents the Future," and David Bordwell, *Reinventing Hollywood: How 1940s Filmmakers Changed Movie Storytelling* (Chicago: University of Chicago Press, 2017), chapter 4.

11 David Bordwell, *The Way Hollywood Tells It: Story and Style in Modern Movies* (Berkeley: University of California Press, 2006).

12 Yuri Tsivian, "Two 'Stylists' of the Teens: Franz Hofer and Yevgenii Bauer," in *A Second Life: German Cinema's First Decades*, ed. Thomas Elsaesser (Amsterdam: Amsterdam University Press, 1996), 264–76; Ben Brewster and Lea Jacobs, *Theatre to Cinema: Stage Pictorialism and the Early Feature Film* (New York: Oxford University Press, 2003).

13 See Bordwell, *On the History of Film Style*; *Figures Traced in Light: On Cinematic Staging* (Berkeley: University of California Press, 2005); essays in *Poetics of Cinema*; and blog entries under the category of "Tableau staging" and "Directors: Capellani."

14 Bordwell, *Reinventing Hollywood*.

15 Quoted in *Memo from Darryl F. Zanuck: The Golden Years at Twentieth Century-Fox*, ed. Rudy Behlmer (New York: Grove, 1993), 123.

16 Eugene Vale, *The Technique of Screenplay Writing* (New York: DeVorss, 1944), 75.

17 Quoted in Philip K. Scheuer, "A Town Called Hollywood," *Los Angeles Times*, June 30, 1940, C3.

18 Jean-Claude Carrière, *The Secret Language of Film*, trans. Jeremy Leggatt (New York: Pantheon, 1994), 15.

19 For Janet Staiger, see, for example: *Bad Women: Regulating Sexuality in Early American Cinema, 1907–1915* (Minneapolis: University of Minnesota Press, 1995), "Authorship Approaches," in *Authorship and Film*, ed. David A. Gerstner and Janet Staiger (New York: Routledge, 2002), 27–57, and *Interpreting Films: Studies in the Historical Reception of American Cinema* (Princeton, NJ: Princeton University Press, 1992); for Kristin Thompson, see, for example: *Storytelling in the New Hollywood: Understanding Classical Narrative Technique* (Cambridge, MA: Harvard University Press, 1999), and *The Frodo Franchise: The Lord of the Rings and Modern Hollywood* (Berkeley: University of California Press, 2007).

20 There are too many to single out here, but I'd mention at least John Caldwell, *Production Culture: Industrial Reflexivity and Critical Practice in Film and Television* (Berkeley: University of California Press, 2008); Lisa Dombrowski, *The Films of Samuel Fuller: If You Die, I'll Kill You* (Middletown, CT: Wesleyan University Press, 2008); Scott Higgins, *Harnessing the Technicolor Rainbow* (Austin: University of Texas Press, 2007); Henry Jenkins, *What Made Pistachio Nuts? Early Sound Comedy and the Vaudeville Aesthetic* (New York: Columbia University Press, 1992); Patrick Keating, *Hollywood Lighting from the Silent Era to Film Noir* (New York: Columbia University Press, 2010); Charlie Keil, *Early American Cinema in Transition: Story, Style, and Filmmaking 1907–1913* (Madison: University of Wisconsin Press, 2002); Jason Mittell, *Complex TV: The Poetics of Contemporary Television Storytelling* (New York: New York University Press, 2015); Bradley Schauer, *Escape Velocity: American Science Fiction Film, 1950–1982* (Middletown, CT: Wesleyan University Press,

2017); Jeff Smith, *The Sounds of Commerce* (New York: Columbia University Press, 1998); Katherine Spring, *Saying It With Songs: Popular Music and the Coming of Sound to Hollywood* (New York: Oxford University Press, 2013); and Maureen Turim, *Flashbacks in Film: Memory and History* (New York: Routledge, 1991). Comparable work on other national cinemas includes Donald Kirihara, *Patterns of Time: Mizoguchi and the 1930s* (Madison: University of Wisconsin Press, 1992); Maria Belodubrovskaya, *Not According to Plan: Filmmaking under Stalin* (Ithaca, NY: Cornell University Press, 2017); and Richard Neupert, *A History of the French New Wave*, 2nd ed. (Madison: University of Wisconsin Press, 2007).

II

FILM STYLE
AND PRACTICE

2

THE CENTER AND THE SWIRL

Vincente Minnelli's Decorative Virtuosity

Scott Higgins

David Bordwell, Janet Staiger, and Kristin Thompson describe formal virtuosity as a matter of fulfilling classical goals with finesse, economy, and
ingenuity.[1] The concept encourages us to seek artistry in films that embody,
rather than resist, studio-era standards of "invisible" technique. An auteur
who excelled within the bounds of a single production unit, Vincente Minnelli crafted meticulous images and brought all the resources of his studio
to bear on the seamless coordination of production design, cinematography,
and performance. Formal analysis of Minnelli's compositional techniques
(staging, framing, décor) reveals a decorative style that is at once exceedingly
intricate and easily grasped. Ever the window decorator, Minnelli arrays
color, shape, movement, and detail to serve the story while also engaging
visual perception in a rigorous, playful, and sometimes challenging manner.
Specifically, he often arranges actors and objects in a fashion that drives
attention around the frame and toward the center. The "Minnelli swirl"
exemplifies the way classicism enabled artists to achieve virtuosity by revis-
ing schemata and finding novel solutions to practical storytelling problems.

A brief sequence shot near the start of *The Bad and the Beautiful* (1952)
exemplifies Minnelli's finely tuned melding of staging, composition, sound,
and camera movement. The studio era's vaunted "invisible style" was, of
course, a spectrum running from practical proficiencies to outright flam-
boyance, and different parts of a film were accorded different places on that
scale. Establishing shots and montage sequences, for instance, could exhibit
stylization that matched their potentially overt narration. This sequence,
which is part of a synoptic flashback, can afford some flare. Embedded in the

recollections of Fred Amiel (Barry Sullivan), the scene arrives on a wave of compressed narrative that takes us from a day that he and Jonathan Shields (Kirk Douglas) spent shooting a B-Western to an evening on which they crashed producer Harry Pebbel's (Walter Pidgeon) swank Hollywood party. Minnelli presents the party in a long take that travels among the guests as Shields, Amiel, Syd (Paul Stewart), and Kay (Vanessa Brown) worm their way into the festivities from a balcony. The sequence shot establishes both this particular party and the Hollywood milieu as a whole, moving from the rantings of a German director (Kurt Kasznar) to a hard-selling "gabby" agent (Frank Gerstle), past a lounge singer (Peggy King), and finally landing on a screen diva (Dee Turnell) noisily bloviating about the travails of stardom.

The shot's virtuosity is in the fluid precision with which Minnelli accomplishes basic goals. One could easily suppose a hypothetical zero-point version of this scene that begins with a master and cuts to each of the party tableaux, perhaps connecting them through the interlopers' eyeline matches. Minnelli's choice to handle the scene in a single take adds some complexity in staging and timing the actors, but this does not necessarily distinguish it; establishing shots and camera movements go together like coffee and cigarettes in the studio era. The scene's classical grace, its effortless elegance, lies in the way character and camera movement channel attention through cascading compositions. Minnelli organizes his frame around rising and falling centers of attention with symmetrical stabilities challenged by figure movement and sound. The compositional flow mirrors and expresses the dissonance of grandstanding egos at this Hollywood party. Film form neither subverts nor overwhelms the fundamental narrative tasks; it achieves them with uncommon complexity and perceptual force.

We might understand this virtuosity in terms of schema and revision. Minnelli innovates by drawing on and developing compositional techniques he had been exploring since his earliest musicals. For Lena Horne's rendition of "Just One of Those Things" in *Panama Hattie* (McLeod 1942), Minnelli, who staged the musical numbers for the film, centers her standing among a ring of spectators and gently pushes in from long to medium shot. The compositional technique is nothing new—we can find the same schema in countless other musicals. Minnelli's version, though, is more precise and varied. Light and height grant Horne the power of the center, but Minnelli orbits her with movement and activity. Her surroundings respond to shot scale and camera movement. In long shot, the bodies and faces of the men near her are held steady, but puffs of smoke billow and drift upward and leftward. As we approach the medium shot, larger movements in the unfocused background begin to appear. Patrons mill at the bar, and then a pair of passersby (Minnelli commonly doubles extras) provide highlights that sweep from left to right as they glance toward the singer and exit the bar.

Once the camera halts its journey, kinetic energy is picked up by the closer ring of listeners, men who drag on their stogies and lean slightly in and out of shadow. All of this reinforces Horne's performance (see fig. 2.1). If our eye should drift to another area, chances are we will meet a glance or movement that nudges us back to the center. The frame around the star is alive and scintillating, not a backdrop but a dynamic setting.

The following year, Minnelli elaborates on this compositional pattern in *Cabin in the Sky* (1943). For Horne's "Honey in the Honeycomb" he adds a mirror behind her that reflects what appears to be a small army of extras moving about to the music. He gives us a more substantial development of compositional centering in Ethel Waters and Eddie "Rochester" Robinson's duet of "Cabin in the Sky." Here the camera begins close to the figures and drifts back to accommodate the community chorus that gathers around

2.1. Four frames from one shot in *Panama Hattie* (1942). Minnelli stages identically dressed extras in the far background near the start of the shot. Later, the men seated behind Lena Horne alternate between leaning in and out of shadow.

them. The group includes another Minnelli pair, two identically clothed young men who anchor the left of the frame as we pull back. The camera pauses on a pastoral extreme long shot and then glides forward for Waters's crescendo as cast members rearrange themselves to rebalance the picture. For example, a washerwoman who fills in the right side of the frame in extreme long shot walks behind the crowd to reappear in an opening on the left side of the frame as the camera closes in (see fig. 2.2). In coordinating his crane movement with an adjustment of figure position to create the final image, Minnelli exhibits formal virtuosity. In the single take, he gives us an evolving composition that settles on two pictorial moments, each adjusted for unity and balance by the movement of and within the frame.

Variations on this compositional theme abound in Minnelli's work. I first noticed this pattern in *Meet Me in St. Louis* (1944), where he draws Technicolor into the game. The famous climactic image of "The Trolley Song" gives Esther (Judy Garland) the dynamic swirl, and for the "Skip to My Lou" number at the going-away party for Lon (Henry H. Daniels Jr.), the camera cranes in through an open window, progressively revealing space

2.2. Four frames from a single shot in *Cabin in the Sky* (1943). Minnelli introduces two identically dressed young men to balance the frame as the camera pulls out. Then, he directs one of his extras to cross sides of the composition as the camera moves back in.

and rewarding the eye with a circuit of cues around the central figure. Tootie (Margaret O'Brien) receives the same treatment when she joins the party later in the scene (see fig. 2.3).

In each case, a performer is ringed by observers who help direct us inward while guiding our attention around and into the depth of the image. The tactic is on display in *The Pirate* (1948), *The Band Wagon* (1953), and *Gigi* (1958) as well (see fig. 2.4). Flamboyant compositions like these are suited to musicals, where they embellish star performance and accent glamour. Minnelli's version elaborates unusually complex relationships between the center and the swirl.

In Minnelli's hands, this flowing, choreographed style was not limited to musicals. He acknowledged as much in a lecture he presented in 1954 entitled "The Tradition of the Musical" (now held by the Margaret Herrick Library), which he illustrated with scenes from the nonmusicals *The Clock* (1945), *Madame Bovary* (1949), *Father of the Bride* (1950), and *The Bad and the Beautiful*.[2] For example, Minnelli gives the scheme a new context in *Madame Bovary*, most notably when the title character (Jennifer Jones) attends the Marquis D'Andervilliers's ball. She collects admirers in her orbit around a divan and then glances at her reflection, itself encircled by an impossibly intricate wreath of cherubs and fronds (and cherubic fronds). Decorative composition becomes an arresting melodramatic frieze that encapsulates the heroine's delusionary obsession with storybook beauty (see

2.3. Three Minnelli swirls from *Meet Me in St. Louis* (1944).

2.4. Minnelli swirls in *The Pirate* (1948), *The Band Wagon* (1953), and *Gigi* (1958).

fig. 2.5). The swirling compositions are a prelude to Bovary's neurotic waltz, which quickly escalates to frenzied stylization worthy of any production number.

Minnelli gives the technique a decidedly masculine twist when Robert Mitchum's character, Wade Hunnicutt, serves the meat at his pig roast in *Home from the Hill* (1960). With Wade encircled by guests, Minnelli adjusts and balances accents to signal the character's potency and to highlight an interaction with his soon-to-be mistress in a red dress (see fig. 2.6). The Minnelli swirl arrays detail to achieve a kind of pictorial gestalt while also amplifying the main players. What began as a means of proving his mettle in filming musical performance provided a foundation for dramatic pictorial virtuosity.

In *The Bad and the Beautiful*, Minnelli combines and revises schemata to address dramatic goals in a fresh manner. He brings the swirl into contact with the sequence shot, a combination that he employed to spectacular effect in *Panama Hattie*'s exquisite song and dance number "The Spring." In contrast to Lena Horne's and the Berry Brothers' acrobatic tour de force, *The Bad and the Beautiful* party sequence does not present a particularly challenging problem; it could be handled with pedestrian coverage. But Minnelli takes the occasion to flex his aesthetic muscle and explore the possibilities of an evolving composition. The scene opens on a semi-swirl, with a bouquet in the center, a Hollywood Bovary on the divan, and our arrogant director holding forth. The composition splits into two centers of attention—the director on the right and the Bovary on the left. Just as our heroes enter the background, highlighted through aperture framing, the ranting director helps balance things. He turns toward the divan, allowing us to more fully attend to the interlopers craning to see through the window (see fig. 2.7). The party is chaotic, pulling us in different directions, but Minnelli, nonetheless, channels our view, briefly unifying the foreground when he wants us to notice the background.

Next Minnelli uses character movement to adjust the composition. The director's exasperated conversation with a party guest pushes the camera backward through the set, opening room for the reentry of our main characters through another window. Our previous center of interest slides off left as the entourage slides in right. The director's complaint "Montage Montage Montage, but where's the story?" nicely counterpoints Minnelli's continuous attentional shell game.

Almost immediately a new point of interest emerges on the right, first signaled by the sound of the gabby agent's patter and then visually anchored by the revelation of a static, portly, and ravenous guest. The camera continues

2.5. Minnelli uses the swirl to express Madame Bovary's obsession with artifice in *Madame Bovary* (1949).

2.6. Two frames of a single shot from *Home from the Hill* (1960). As Wade Hunnicutt serves the roast pig, his mistress moves to the foreground right, where she draws attention and balances the compositional accent carried by the boy's red shirt on the left.

2.7. Minnelli splits the composition around competing centers and then opens room for his main characters in the background in *The Bad and the Beautiful* (1952).

2.8. In these four frames from the sequence shot, the ranting director forces the camera back, and as he crosses to the left, our main characters enter from the right. Minnelli flags a new point of interest as the camera moves past the man eating and then splits interest with the appearance of the singer on the right.

to pull back and pan right, and Minnelli organizes the room by giving us a new target, a landing spot we can anticipate. Again, though, he splits attention. The song rises in the mix as our characters move into a conspicuous gap between the agent and the singer. Kay's white jacket framed between her companions' dark tuxedos provides a sharp contrast toward which the camera now advances (see fig. 2.8).

Along the way, Minnelli teases the singer as an attentional node via both the sound mix and the camera's slight rightward drift. But when Jonathan and Amiel turn toward the background, they leave Kay and Syd symmetrically flanked by seated guests. Again we find a compositional center, and again it dances away from us (see fig. 2.9).

The shot reveals its final destination as the diva's voice takes precedence and a trio of guests (including another of Minnelli's passing pairs) enter from the left to take seats at the right. Minnelli uses these lateral movements to convey the party's energy and, more practically, to highlight parts of the frame that they briefly occlude. We strain to see more. And as the hubbub clears out of the foreground, we find the diva in a full swirl, with Jonathan and Amiel momentarily drawn into her orbit.

The arrangement flirts with compositional stability, but the movie star's command is fleeting and off-center. Minnelli leaves an aisle exploited by a waiter who clears the way to a door at the rear right, carrying Jonathan and Amiel with him. Meanwhile, our newly seated guest on the right directs her attention toward the rear—reinforcing our interest in that next room. The

2.9. Four frames from the sequence shot in *The Bad and the Beautiful*. Kay and Syd briefly hold the center of a balanced shot before dancing off right. Two identically clad party guests cross the frame and help draw attention toward the Hollywood diva holding forth in the background where Jonathan and Amiel pause.

2.10. Minnelli redirects attention at the end of the shot. The waiter's path highlights a door at the rear right, and Jonathan and Ameil follow.

shot ends with attention split once again, the diva working hard to hold her audience but the main characters and that doorway tugging us away (see fig. 2.10). We cut into the poker room with a ring of gamblers at the center, and Minnelli starts the game again.

Few things suit Minnelli's art better than a party scene. To my eye, the closest analogues to *The Bad and the Beautiful*'s Hollywood soiree are the "Skip to My Lou" dance in the Smith family living room and the "Drop That Name" number in *Bells Are Ringing* (1960). But while the compositional flow of those musical parties invites us to luxuriate in plenitude and ease, *The Bad and the Beautiful* delivers an uneasy cacophony of just-missed unities and distracted attention. This, of course, befits a film that rips at the seams of Hollywood illusion. The scene is something of an anti-musical. It is also the work of an artist achieving distinction by staging actors as though he were choreographing a dance and by framing actions as though he were displaying a performer. Virtuosity, here, is a matter of rich perceptual engagement, directing and redirecting attention toward ever more elusive centers and swirls.

NOTES

1   David Bordwell, Janet Staiger, and Kristin Thompson, *The Classical Hollywood Cinema: Film Style and Mode of Production to 1960* (New York: Columbia University Press, 1985). See especially parts 1, 3, and 7.

2   Vincent Minnelli, "Tradition of the Musical," San Francisco Museum of Art Lecture (May 7, 1954), Minnelli Vincente—writings 1954, undated. 12.f-209. Margaret Herrick Library, Academy of Motion Picture Arts and Sciences, Los Angeles, CA.

3

RESETTLING THE SCORE

Musical Recycling in the Hollywood Studio System

Kathryn Kalinak

The appropriation of preexisting music in film has begun to engage film music scholars, and a rich and lively body of scholarship has developed around the topic in the twenty-first century. Journals in film studies and musicology have devoted special issues to the subject, such as *Beethoven Forum* on the appropriation of Beethoven in film and *The Soundtrack* on popular song.[1] Anthologies, including Phil Powrie and Robynn Stilwell's *Changing Tunes: The Use of Pre-existing Music in Film* and Jonathan Godsall's *Reeled In: The Use of Pre-existing Music in Narrative Film*, have mapped out the field.[2] Case studies on music in specific genres or in the work of specific directors now include attention to the use of preexisting music: Daniel Goldmark's *Tunes for Toons*, Kate McQuiston's *"We'll Meet Again": Music in the Films of Stanley Kubrick*, Christine Lee Gengaro's *Listening to Stanley Kubrick: The Music in His Films*, and Gayle Magee's *Robert Altman's Soundtracks*.[3] Three foundational studies loom large in this accounting: Jeff Smith's *The Sounds of Commerce: Marketing Popular Film Music*, Anahid Kassabian's *Hearing Film: Tracking Identification in Contemporary Hollywood Film Music*, and Dean Duncan's *Charms That Soothe: Classical Music and the Narrative Film*.[4] This list is hardly exhaustive and is restricted to book-length studies.

On the cutting edge of this subfield, scholars in classical Hollywood studies have turned to the appropriation of preexisting music from other film scores. As Estella Tincknell wrote in an editorial in *The Soundtrack* in 2014, "The relative critical neglect of this . . . common process of remediation and reinvention within musical and film scholarship [is] . . . ripe for reversal." [5] That reversal has begun, and the appropriation of preexisting film scores has now come under scrutiny, such as in Michael Slowik's "Diegetic Withdrawals and Other Worlds: Film Music Strategies before *Kong*," Nathan Platte's "Before *Kong* Was King: Competing Methods in Hollywood Underscore," and Jeff Smith's "The Fine Art of Repurposing: A Look at Scores for Hollywood B Films in the 1930s." Most recently, Platte, in *Making Music in Selznick's Hollywood*, has analyzed the appropriation of preexisting scores in David O. Selznick's films, uncovering nine examples in *Rebecca* (Hitchcock 1940) alone. [6]

I am interested in examples where Hollywood film composers appropriate from a unique preexisting source: themselves. [7] In classical Hollywood, appropriation from one score to another was a common practice. Music editors, to save time and money, pulled cues from preexisting scores. Producers, who deemed themselves knowledgeable about music, put their hand in and did the same (or directed music department personnel to do so). The temp track had a considerable impact in this regard. A collection of cues largely drawn from preexisting music, including other film scores, designed to accompany a film during production, the temp track provided a ready source for appropriation. Cues from the temp track often wound up in a final release version especially when time was short. [8] And composers appropriated from themselves, borrowing cues from their own film scores. I refer to this phenomenon of reusing preexisting music as "recycling." I like this term because it suggests not only reuse but also repurposing, a concept I would like to explore.

Composers did not recycle capriciously. In the examples I have uncovered, I have found what Platte has found: "a governing rationale." [9] Sometimes, largely in the interest of time, composers recycled by simply quoting from themselves—lifting previously composed cues and reusing them more or less without revision. Richard Hageman recycled a thrilling cue originally composed for the climactic escape sequence in John Ford's seafaring adventure *The Long Voyage Home* (1940)—almost note for note—into the main title music of the John Wayne Western *Angel and the Badman* (Grant 1947). Why not? The cue encodes dynamism in its tempo, rhythmic structure, and melodic contour, and it works for both.

Other times when composers recycled, they repurposed, adapting the original cue for a related but new use. Max Steiner, for instance, in *Mildred Pierce* (Curtiz 1945) recycles the love theme of Charlotte (Bette Davis) and

Jerry (Paul Henreid) from *Now, Voyager* (Rapper 1942) as an underscore to the first romantic encounter of Monte (Zachary Scott) and Mildred (Joan Crawford). Steiner may have seized an opportunity to promote (and financially benefit from) an earlier composition of his that had been turned into a song and marketed as "It Can't Be Wrong." The song was recorded by Dick Haymes, Vera Lynn, and the Vagabonds, among others. The melody is recycled instrumentally in *Mildred Pierce* as a love theme of sorts for Mildred and Monte, most memorably in the beach house, when Monte puts a record on the player and, in a cheeky self-reference, Steiner recycles an instrumental version of "It Can't Be Wrong." Steiner adapted the cue for the new situation, however, recasting the lushly romantic symphonic version of *Now, Voyager* into a syncopated and jazzy rendition with a bass clarinet introducing the tune. In so doing, Steiner underscored, literally, the tawdriness of Monte and Mildred's affair in comparison to the self-sacrificing and noble passion of Charlotte and Jerry. To emphasize the point, the recording begins to skip as Mildred surrenders to Monte and whispers into his ear the passionate words: "Monte, the record."

It is not hard to see how recycling happens. The score could not be started until the film was edited, and the final sound mix could not be finished until the score was recorded. Thus, the music department was under tremendous pressure to pass the recorded score along to the sound department quickly. A typical time frame for composition would be four to six weeks, with many films on even more abbreviated schedules. Dimitri Tiomkin remembers working on *Alice in Wonderland* (McLeod 1933) "20 hours a day for 10 days."[10] There were, however, other strategies to ensure that scores could be turned out quickly: the team approach, where several composers worked on the score simultaneously but only one got the credit; the last-minute rescue, where additional composers would be assigned at the end, again uncredited, to help the credited composer finish on time; and musical recycling from the temp track, other film scores, or stock music in studio music libraries.

None of those options sat well with most composers, and many could be prickly about authorship: Bernard Herrmann demanded that his name be taken off the credits of *The Magnificent Ambersons* (Welles 1942) when he heard cues by another composer at the premiere; Miklós Rózsa refused to work for Selznick again after Selznick pulled a cue from Rózsa's score for *Spellbound* (Hitchcock 1945) and substituted one from Franz Waxman's

3.1. The song version of the love theme from *Now, Voyager* (1942). Composers often took the opportunity to market music from their film scores as sheet music, which provided extra publicity and revenue for them. In an early example of synchrony, the sheet music promoted the film while the film promoted the song. Harms Music was Warner Bros.'s publishing arm. Author's collection.

Rebecca; Max Steiner, in an exceptional act of defiance, wrote to Selznick himself to object to the use of a recycled cue from a preexisting Waxman score, a "botched up job," in *Gone with the Wind* (Fleming 1939);[11] and Erich Wolfgang Korngold insisted that his credit be changed from "musical composition" to "musical arrangements" because he appropriated some Franz Liszt in order to finish *Captain Blood* (Curtiz 1935) on time. Korngold would learn to mine his own concert music. For *The Adventures of Robin Hood* (Keighley and Curtiz 1938), he recycled from himself: a concert overture and an operetta.

I would like to unpack an interesting example from Tiomkin's score for the Western *The Big Sky* (Hawks 1952). Hawks, famously, would describe the master plot of his film as "a love story between two men."[12] Whether Tiomkin took his cue from Hawks, was inspired by undercurrents in the film itself, or was oblivious to both, he created a score that is strangely compatible with the film's homoerotic subtext. Musical recycling is part of this framework. For an intimate scene between the two male protagonists in *The Big Sky*—one is near-mortally wounded, the other rescues him from death with the help of an Indian princess—Tiomkin turned to another film he had scored featuring a highly charged relationship between two men and recycled a motif from it: *Strangers on a Train* (Hitchcock 1951), which Tiomkin had scored the year before.

On the face of it, it is an odd appropriation. Tiomkin was becoming the go-to composer for Westerns; he had previously scored *Duel in the Sun* (Vidor 1947) and *Red River* (Hawks 1948) and had just finished *High Noon* (Zinnemann 1952). And he had an unused score for *The Westerner* (Wyler 1940) lying around.[13] Yet with so much Western music at hand, Tiomkin turned to a thriller—and from a different studio at that. *Strangers on a Train* features two men who meet, accidentally, on a train. They each have someone they would like dead. One of them, Bruno (Robert Walker), devises a plan to swap murders: "You do my murder. I do yours. . . . Criss-cross." Guy (Farley Granger) responds sarcastically, but it is all the go-ahead Bruno needs to put the plan in motion and murder Guy's wife.

Hollywood's strict Production Code prohibited the explicit presentation of homosexuality. So Bruno's is coded through the stereotypical conventions that developed to represent it: Bruno has no wife or girlfriend; he hates his father and has an unnaturally close relationship to his mother; he detests children; he is fastidious about his appearance and is a flashy dresser; and he is not interested in sports. He tries to pick up Guy on the train and later tries to lure him into the park at night. The scene in Bruno's private train compartment where Bruno has invited Guy for lunch was so provocative that Hollywood censors mandated cuts.[14] Bruno murders the wife of the man he is attracted to. It is, by this point, a commonplace critical insight that Guy's sexuality is as conflicted as Bruno's. His sarcastic reply on the train—"Sure Bruno. I like all your theories"—is not only a tacit approval of the crisscross murder scheme but also a subconscious acknowledgment of his attraction to Bruno and his flirtation with homosexuality.

That Tiomkin understood this subtext is demonstrated in his score. In the first sequence, he composed a musical cue to accompany the introduction of Bruno and Guy, with each man shown from the waist down exiting a cab at Union Station. Differences in costume, body language, and gesture telegraph their personalities, professions, and social class. Tiomkin intriguingly juxtaposes musical conventions for gender: a "masculine" motif played in the low brasses followed by its reiterative echo in a lighter or "feminine" variation played higher in the strings (and, for Guy, on the harp as well). These are followed by a jazzy horn rejoinder.

Tiomkin taps into musical signifiers for homosexuality as well—a musical vocabulary, if you will, for the representation of homosexuality in Hollywood film, a set of conventions to connote, allude, suggest, and imply. This included the privileging of woodwinds and, in general, odd and unconventional instrumentations, non-melodic leitmotifs, chromaticism, dissonance, and especially jazzy harmonies and performance practices. Think of Joel Cairo's entrance in *The Maltese Falcon* (Huston 1941), an upward glissando-like figure first in the strings with a harp featured prominently and then in the woodwinds. Or Waldo Lydecker's leitmotif from *Laura* (Preminger 1944), a chromatic, non-melodic downward figure introduced by a solo piccolo. Bruno's leitmotif shares features with these musical moments: chromaticism, a reliance on woodwinds and odd instrumentations (the vibraphone and, in one case, a solo tuba), and a non-melodic motif with a downward melodic contour. In the Jefferson Memorial cue, Bruno's leitmotif is preceded by a "slow atonal gliss[ando]."[15] Jack Sullivan, who wrote an entire book on Hitchcock's music, is hearing the same things that I am: he describes Bruno's leitmotif as "queasy" and its harmonics "creepy." Further, he argues that Guy's leitmotif "carries mocking irony"; the opening cue is "Gershwin-esque"; and the love theme for Ann and Guy,

3.2. Bruno's leitmotif.

whose romance is "spoiled" first by Miriam, Guy's wife, and then by Bruno, is "elaborate" and "swooning."[16] But the implications of these descriptions remain unexplored in his text.

Tiomkin would recycle Bruno's "queasy" and "creepy" leitmotif one year later in *The Big Sky*, a Western adventure set on a riverboat along the Missouri River with two male protagonists, Jim (Kirk Douglas) and Boone (Dewey Martin), at the helm. *The Big Sky* is one of Tiomkin's lushest, most melodic, and most Romantically inflected film scores, and while Tiomkin composed several leitmotifs for the film, he did not compose one for the male protagonists. As a result, many scenes between the two men, including their crucial first meeting, are left unscored. This creates an odd effect: lush, Romantic melodies underscore most of *The Big Sky*, but most scenes between the two men transpire without any musical accompaniment whatsoever. As Scott Paulin astutely points out, "The absence of music can be as telling . . . as its presence."[17] And so it is here. Film music often acts as a "gateway to intense emotional experience" and plays a key role in the construction of desire and the projection of fantasy.[18] Thus, in classical Hollywood film, it is typically absent in scenes, especially intimate scenes, between two men in order to defuse the potential of a homosexual reading—hence, Tiomkin's avoidance of underscoring in scenes between the two men, which eliminates the need for a leitmotif altogether.

Yet, in one of the most climactic scenes in the film (and also its most intimate), where one man, near-mortally wounded, is tended and comforted by the other, Tiomkin entered the breach. And without a ready theme at hand for the two men, Tiomkin turned to another score about two men with a charged relationship and recycled a leitmotif from it. Tiomkin reuses the opening phrase of Bruno's leitmotif as Boone searches for his fallen friend, and the rest of the leitmotif, a series of descending chromatic phrases, when Boone finds him. Bruno's leitmotif is toned down in *The Big Sky* from some of the weirder instrumentations in *Strangers on a Train* (English horns and violas, clarinets and cellos, flutes and bassoons, and a solo tuba), and it is tucked away in a busy musical cue. But it changes the tenor of the scene. The instrumentation is different here from the rest of the score, a more transparent style of orchestration with a reliance on the woodwinds instead of the strings that Tiomkin typically defaults to; the harmonics are "queasier" (less conventionally tonal and more chromatic); and melody, which dominates the rest of the score, is noticeably missing. The effect of the music is to destabilize the sequence. That Tiomkin chooses to accompany the most intimate scene in the film between the two men with music is interesting in itself, and music's presence, coupled with the recycling of Bruno's leitmotif, moves the homosexual dimension of *The Big Sky* closer to the surface, highlighting Hawks's "love story between two men" and calling attention to an aspect of the film that Hawks had least under control: its homoeroticism.

Musical appropriation of preexisting music in film is a kind of intertext, an interplay of reference from one text to another. One might argue that in a film score all meaning is intertextual, because of its connection to other texts, filmic, musical, and otherwise. Some connections will be so commonly understood by audiences that they constitute conventions virtually everyone will recognize—tremolo strings for suspense, for instance. Other connections will be less universally apprehended, and only a small portion of the audience may recognize them. An even smaller portion would be aware of recycling. K. J. Donnelly, in writing about Bernard Herrmann, has suggested that Herrmann's recycling is the musical equivalent of one of Hitchcock's cameo appearances.[19] I like to think of recycling as part of how Hollywood composers signed their work, part of an authorial signature that drew attention to the immense contribution their scores made to a film.

NOTES

1   *Beethoven Forum* 10, no. 2 (2003); *The Soundtrack* 7, no. 2 (2014).

2   Phil Powrie and Robynn Stilwell, eds., *Changing Tunes: The Use of Pre-existing Music in Film* (Aldershot, UK: Ashgate, 2006); Jonathan Godsall, *Reeled In: The Use of Pre-existing Music in Narrative Film* (Aldershot, UK: Ashgate, 2019).

3   Daniel Goldmark, *Tunes for 'Toons: Music and the Hollywood Cartoon* (Berkeley: University of California Press, 2007); Kate McQuiston, *We'll Meet Again: Musical Design in the Films of Stanley Kubrick* (New York: Oxford University Press, 2013); Christine Lee Gengaro, *Listening to Stanley Kubrick: The Music*

in His Films (Lanham, MD: Scarecrow Press, 2012); Sherwood Magee, *Robert Altman's Soundtracks* (New York: Oxford University Press, 2014).

4   Jeff Smith, *The Sounds of Commerce: Marketing Popular Film Music* (New York: Columbia University Press, 1998); Anahid Kassabian, *Hearing Film: Tracking Identification in Contemporary Hollywood Film Music* (London: Routledge, 2000); Dean Duncan, *Charms That Soothe: Classical Music and the Narrative Film* (New York: Fordham University Press, 2003).

5   Estella Tincknell, "Editorial," *The Soundtrack* 7, no. 2 (2014): 63.

6   Michael Slowik, "Diegetic Withdrawals and Other Worlds: Film Music Strategies before *Kong*," *Cinema Journal* 53, no. 1 (2013): 1–15, and "Experiments in Early Sound Film Music: Strategies and Recordings, 1928–1930," *American Music* 31, no. 4 (2013): 450–74; Nathan Platte, "Before *Kong* Was King: Competing Methods in Hollywood Underscore," *Journal for the Society for American Music* 8, no. 3 (2014): 311–37; Jeff Smith, "The Fine Art of Repurposing: A Look at Scores for Hollywood B Films in the 1930s," in *The Routledge Companion to Screen Music and Sound*, ed. Miguel Mera, Ronald Sadoff, and Ben Winters (New York: Routledge, 2017), 228–39; Nathan Platte, *Making Music in Selznick's Hollywood* (New York: Oxford University Press, 2018), 197–212.

7   Important work has also been done on the related practice of film composers recycling their non-film work (concert, opera, radio) into their film scores and vice versa. See William Wrobel, "Self-Borrowing in the Music of Bernard Herrmann," *Journal of Film Music* 1, no. 2–3 (2003): 249–71; and Ben Winters, *The Adventures of Robin Hood: A Film Score Guide* (Lanham, MD: Scarecrow Press, 2007), 43–49. Recycling his concert and operatic work in film and vice versa became such a distinctive feature of Korngold's oeuvre that Winters argues, "Musical borrowing must be . . . considered a major facet of his compositional style" (41).

8   Important work on the role of the music editor and the power of the temp track has been inaugurated by Ronald H. Sadoff, "The Role of the Music Editor and the 'Temp Track,' a Blueprint for the Score, Source Music, and Source Music of Films," *Popular Music* 25, no. 2 (2006): 163–83; and Jack Curtis Dubowsky, "The Evolving 'Temp Score' in Animation," *Music, Sound, and the Moving Image* 5, no. 1 (2011): 1–24.

9   Nathan Platte, " 'Regeneration' in *Rebecca*: Confronting Compilation in Franz Waxman's Score," *Journal of Film Music* 5, no. 1–2 (2012): 175.

10   Dimitri Tiomkin, quoted in Dave Epstein, Studio Publicity, "Biography," 5.

11 Platte, *Making Music*, 192.

12 Howard Hawks quoted in Peter Bogdanovich, "Interview with Howard Hawks (1962)," in *Howard Hawks Interviews*, ed. Scott Breivold (Jackson: University Press of Mississippi, 2006), 17.

13 Tiomkin's score for *The Westerner* was discarded by William Wyler and replaced with one by Alfred Newman.

14 British censors had no such squeamishness; the entire sequence survives in British prints.

15 Dimitri Tiomkin, *Strangers on a Train*, Conductor Copy, Dimitri Tiomkin Collection, USC, Los Angeles, CA.

16 Jack Sullivan, *Hitchcock's Music* (New Haven, CT: Yale University Press, 2006), 157–58.

17 Scott Paulin, "Unheard Sexualities: Queer Theory and the Soundtrack," *Spectator* 17, no. 2 (1997): 38.

18 Paulin, "Unheard Sexualities," 40, 38.

19 K. J. Donnelly, "Musical Romanticism v. the Sexual Aberrations of the Criminal Female: *Marnie* (1964)," in *Partners in Suspense: Critical Essays on Bernard Herrmann and Alfred Hitchcock*, ed. Steven Rawle and K. J. Donnelly (Manchester, UK: Manchester University Press, 2017), 142.

4

HOLLYWOOD MANNERISM

Chris Cagle

Across prestige films, dramas, and even other genre films, a prevalent trend of the 1940s was a type of stylistic excess. Consider the example of *Humoresque* (Negulesco 1946), a melodrama distinctive in some ways, ordinary in others. The party scene in which a concert violinist (John Garfield) and a socialite (Joan Crawford) meet shows the kind of fluid camerawork that characterizes other films of its genre and production category in the mid-1940s. A shot tilts up from a medium shot of a piano player's hands to a woman smoking a cigarette. The camera tracks back to hold on a medium long shot (the woman accepts a drink), then tracks back and pans left to hold briefly on Crawford, center frame, and then pans past the party guests to show an empty entrance to the room. After a second, Garfield enters.

At first glance this scene merely represents the stylistic tendencies of classical Hollywood. The lighting is what might broadly be considered glamour lighting. The camerawork is controlled and emphatic. The editing pace is slow, reserving faster editing for brief shots of key information. Most of all, the first shot performs a narrational function by using visual means to convey story information. In tracking between three static compositions, the first shot of the scene introduces three key sets of characters. In the last, the camera even anticipates the action, namely, John Garfield's entry into the scene. These are all the hallmarks of classical Hollywood style.

All the same, something is unusual about the scene, something a little belabored. Gone is a simple scene analysis. A 1930s film, even a prestige film, tended to have its space chopped up into bits to highlight key narrative information. It could use expressive camera movement, but usually this was done as a flourish to establish a scene or to provide emotional emphasis rather than to serve as an outright alternative to analytical editing.

In *Humoresque*, a complex camera movement serves as such an alternative, breaking down the scene into narratively significant compositions ("shots," so to speak) without cutting. The camera in effect gains agency, not simply because it, rather than the editing, tells the narrative but because it too must maneuver in and out of the paths of the party guests, much like the server with the tray of drinks. The roving camera, moreover, leads to a more complex lighting scheme and use of set space. In sum, compared to the more common and straightforward way to shoot and edit its scenes, *Humoresque* is stylized.

Hollywood's stylization has not gone completely unnoticed. Bazin's discussion of the changes in 1940s film style, Mary Ann Doane's reading of *Humoresque* as a melodrama, and David Bordwell's notion of the "bounds of difference" within classical Hollywood all remark on stylistic surplus.[1] However, starting in the late 1930s but especially into the 1940s and peaking in the late 1940s, A-films and prestige-oriented dramas exhibited a consistent stylistic surplus best thought of as a cinematic mannerism. Specifically, the films' use of space and lighting recalls mannerist painting in its distortion and elongation of space and flatness of surface. More generally, these Hollywood films are mannerist in a broader sense of presenting an alternative to strictly classical style that nonetheless maintains a restraint and formality.

STRATEGIES OF FORMAL EXAGGERATION

Mannerism is an aesthetic usually articulated in relation to late Renaissance painting, and in this sense, we can speak of a Mannerism with a capital *M*: namely, a distinct art movement. Italian Mannerism as a style thwarts the expectation of properly rendered Quattrocento space. Liana de Girolami Cheney remarks on the "disjointed relationship between the space of the canvas and the space of the painting."[2] Similarly, Craig Hugh Smyth notes the flat light, partial foreshortening, and angularity of poses. Bodies become either excessively foreshortened or elongated, with limbs out of proportion to heads. Multiple compositional planes do not share space and fight for the viewer's attention.[3] These specific attributes speak to painting in which style refuses to subsume itself completely to content. In a reaction against the classical ideals of the Renaissance, Mannerism did not entirely discard classical restraint, as baroque painting would do, but it dismantled it from within, by formal exaggeration.

Alternately, mannerism with a lowercase *m* suggests an exaggeration of style. In the context of the European heritage film, Belén Vidal outlines this broader version of mannerism. In mannerism, she argues, "the narrative priorities of the cinematic image shift to the visual emphasis and affective meanings of figuration . . . as attention to the 'surface' visual qualities of a motif that is afforded special weight and duration."[4] Mannerism suggests an emphasis on style as a surface trait. Patrick Keating's work on classical Hollywood cinematography has usefully identified two broad aesthetic approaches among studio-era cinematographers. The first are the classicists who sought to balance aesthetic aims in lighting, whereas the second emphasized one aim at the expense of others. These more stylized cinematographers Keating labels "mannerists."[5] This broader notion of mannerism departs from classical norms of harmony, order, and balance, without outright being anticlassical in form.

Hollywood cinema of the 1940s exhibited both Mannerism and mannerism. Some of its formal exaggerations are merely stylized, whereas others share formal similarities with Mannerist painting. The most proximate quality to Mannerism would be the disarticulation of space. Cinematic classicism famously preserves spatial relations on-screen despite and because of its disjunctive approach to shooting. Analytical editing breaks down the space, and continuity rules smooth over the ruptures. Together, the classical film spectator inhabits and creates a space that is whole, unbroken. Much of the project of 1970s film theory was to describe the classical cinema's constant regulation of space for the spectator.[6]

Films like Alfred Hitchcock's *The Paradine Case* (1947), meanwhile, partially disorient the spectator (but not outright) with a roving camera and disjunctive editing. Most famous is the trick shot in the courtroom scene, in which the camera's track around Mrs. Paradine (Alida Valli) neatly matches a rear projection shot pan of her valet (Louis Jordan) walking into the courtroom; the effect is to separate foreground and background in an uncanny fashion.[7] The use of the crab dolly allowed other scenes to adopt a complex yet fluid movement, breaking out of a linear path.[8] When the police arrest Mrs. Paradine, for instance, some unusual cutting (the axis of action is unclear throughout) gives way to a circular track around Mrs. Paradine, while foreground and background revolve in a close relationship (see fig. 4.1). *The Paradine Case* suggests the grip of mannerism on the scene analysis of a director known for a precise montage aesthetic.

4.1. Intricate blocking and grayscale cinematography in *Daisy Kenyon* (1947).

The Paradine Case was part of a larger trend toward complex scene analysis and intricate blocking. This change came against the backdrop of an increased preference for the long take over scene analysis and a turn to deep focus cinematography.[9] As Keating argues, this long-take cinema fueled an elaboration of camera movement: "Building on the long takes of the early 1940s, many films of the late 1940s pushed the aesthetic of fluidity even further, as if directors were engaged in a competition to see who could craft the most elaborate shot."[10] The example of *Humoresque* above illustrates the possibility of using long takes and cinematic depth with multiple shot distances and compositions. The opening of *Ride the Pink Horse* (Montgomery 1947) is another good example, with its complex interplay between camera, set, and actor. A three-minute and twenty-second long take follows its main character (Robert Montgomery) around a bus station, framing him in eight distinctive narratively meaningful compositions, from extreme long shot to medium shot, then to tight close-up, and then back to medium long shot. While unique in its particular approach, *Ride the Pink Horse* reveals that the mobile camera was actually a more common variant on classical decoupage than the statically composed sequence shot.

The mannerist films are distinctive in using camera movement to go beyond mere emotional and narrative emphasis. The camera not only moves more but also moves in a more intricate relationship to actors. Classical filmmaking in general relies on highly planned blocking, accounting for its rehearsed aesthetic as opposed to the generally improvised and reactive aesthetic of postclassical filmmaking. What is unusual about mannerism is the extent to which blocking becomes elaborate and noticeable. At times, films develop an interplay between actor and camera, sometimes drawing nearer, sometimes growing apart. The party scene in *The Magnificent Ambersons* (Welles 1942), which stages an elaborate following shot through multiple rooms of the Ambersons' mansion, has narrational implications, and, as Robin Wood argues, the camera in *Letter from an Unknown Woman* (Ophüls 1948) distances the narrative from the character at critical moments.[11] The mannerist approach can use elaborate figure-camera relations in ways not clearly tied to form-content unity. Otto Preminger's work is a good case in point, as in the opening scene of *Daisy Kenyon* (1947), in which the camera engages a constant interplay with the three moving actors. The scene's second shot, for instance, pans left to follow Mary (Martha Stewart), a model and friend of commercial artist Daisy, before tracking in on Dan (Dana Andrews) as he appears and enters the next room. The camera pauses on a triangular framing, with Dan in the foreground and the women in the background. The shot pauses on this composition and then tracks to follow Dan as he enters the kitchen for coffee. Typically a classical film would either simplify the set and its space or cut the scene into more shots. Another shot in the scene shows Dan standing in and out of the way of the camera's view of Mary, creating an intricate blocking in which the composition is constantly recomposed (see fig. 4.2). Moreover, each actor is in a distinct lighting plane to create different grayscale tones.

Mannerism disarticulates expected or verisimilar spatial relations. Often, cinematographers separate compositions into separate planes of space. The increased capability and preference for depth of image gave cinematographers the challenge of separating foreground and background. Their strategies varied, but, especially for serious dramas adopting a mannerist style, many lit their figures and chose apertures that reduced depth into distinct planes of action. This stylistic trait is the one most directly tied to mannerist painting, whose illusionistic cues often belie a spatial exaggeration.

4.2. Abstracted foreground-background planes in *The Paradine Case* (1947).

The use of mirrors in 1940s films reflects a broader mannerist turn. Mannerist films stage action in front of mirrors self-consciously, as in *I Remember Mama* (Stevens 1948), which opens with an unusual track into Katrin (Barbara Bel Geddes) as she directly addresses the spectator. Mirror reflections can give a fuller rendering of volumetric space, but when combined with restricted editing, they can also suggest a space without revealing it. One unusual example is a café scene in *The Razor's Edge* (Goulding 1946) in which characters Larry Darrell (Tyrone Power) and W. Somerset Maugham (Herbert Marshall) encounter Elliott Templeton (Clifton Webb) in a café. One shot shows Darrell and Maugham, backs to the camera, with Templeton in the background walking toward the bar; as the two walk off frame right, the camera pans and tracks left to follow Templeton. The next shot seems to show a deep focus composition with the bar in the background, Darrell and Maugham in the mid-foreground (facing away and looking at the background), and a wooden rail in the foreground. However, as Darrell turns his head right, the camera pans left to reveal the composition to be a mirror reflection from the vantage of the men's dining booth. The spatial effect is disorienting. Certain films use mirrors thematically, but here it serves little narrative purpose and merely provides a filmmaking flourish that seamlessly (though unnecessarily) combines a reestablishing shot with a closer two-shot.

Mannerist Hollywood also has a distinct pictorial look. Classical filmmaking tended to default to higher-key lighting: well lit, with enough contrast to render figures and give visual interest to the image, but not enough to threaten legibility. Low-key, or high-contrast, lighting could be justified generically or used in certain scenes with a pictorial quality. What is striking about 1940s cinematography is the fondness for medium key, a sometimes muddled, sometimes gradated exploration of gray. Faces get washed out (*The Razor's Edge*), figures get obscured (*Daisy Kenyon*), or figures get lit in precise tones of gray (*Manhunt* [Lang 1941]). Each might be thought of as a response to a specific aesthetic challenge of faster film stocks and lenses. The general classical response was toward realist cinematography maintaining sufficient tonal contrast to separate foreground and background. Another possibility was in noir lighting, which played with extreme contrast and practicals. Both approaches involved downplaying middle tones of gray. Mannerism adopted an in-between approach by looking for experimentation with new lighting and film stock possibilities without losing the nuance of the image. The cinematographers' ability to work in the middle of the gray range showed a degree of difficulty, but the result generally did not read as self-consciously artistic as either the pictorialist or modernist practice did.

MANNERISM AND THE BAROQUE

Mannerism's other is not only classicism but also the baroque. André Bazin influentially posited that studio-era Hollywood embodied a classical aesthetic, but he also frequently turned to the analogy with the baroque, considering Welles, Antonioni, and other filmmakers to be baroque in their style.[12] In an essay on the Hollywood Western, he writes, "The perfection, or the classic stage, which the genre had reached implied that it had to justify its survival by introducing new elements. . . . Take the new films of John Ford. *My Darling Clementine* and *Fort Apache* could well be examples of baroque embellishment of the classicism of *Stagecoach*."[13] Bazin's argument here is complex, since he is arguing both for and against a model of baroque Hollywood, but notable in his essay is the idea of the baroque as an evolution from classicism.

Where mannerism relies on formal exaggeration, the baroque trips into outright tonal excess. Gone in the baroque is mannerism's formal detachment, tossed aside in favor of over-the-top treatment of the subject matter, whether through overly emphatic camera movement, rapid editing, or a jarring sound-image relationship. John Frankenheimer's *Seconds* (1966) is a good example. The thriller follows the trajectory of a disaffected bank executive, Arthur Hamilton (John Randolph), as he takes advantage of a secretive company's service to provide an entirely new identity for him, complete with plastic surgery, new legal documents, and a new home and career. Particularly in the film's opening sequences (before the identity change), Frankenheimer and cinematographer James Wong Howe use a number of techniques that destabilize the spatial relationships on-screen. Wide-angle lenses combine with handheld cinematography or alternate with normal lens reverse shots. In two instances, the actor will be in close-up while on a moving cart that carries him, almost floating, through the scenic space. Later, extreme wide-angle lenses distort some shots, including Arthur's drug-induced hallucination. *Seconds*, in general, alternates style for style's sake and a highly psychologized use of editing and cinematography to suggest character subjectivity.

Many of the stylistic choices in *Seconds* are idiosyncratic, but Frankenheimer and Howe were not alone in their baroque tendencies. Several postwar auteurs worked in a baroque vein for either most or part of their careers: these include Orson Welles, Samuel Fuller, Robert Aldrich, and Robert Wise. These directors have a preference for spatial distortion, including wide-angle, low-angle, and edge-framed shots. They use editing for kinetic or psychological reasons, giving rise to the shock cut or rapid montage. The cinematography tends toward high-contrast or nonnaturalistic color. Taken as a whole, too, the genre of the 1950s family melodrama shows baroque aesthetics in use of color or music choices that go against classical restraint. The ending scene of *Some Came Running* (Minnelli 1958), with flashing colored spotlights on the characters, shows this baroque tone. A director like Douglas Sirk could engage in baroque moments, such as the samba scene in *Written on the Wind* (1956), or in mannerist moments of fluid camerawork and direction, such as the interior shots in *The Tarnished Angels* (1957).[14]

A few tendencies differentiate cinematic mannerism from baroque Hollywood. Mannerism involves stylistic flourish more than blatant exaggeration. Moreover, mannerist filmmaking comes across as a more robust version of classical storytelling. It takes classicism's emphatic devices (camera movement and blocking) and amplifies them, generally without calling attention to them. Baroque approaches, on the other hand, push stylization into outright exaggeration and tonal excess. While not modernist in its aesthetic, baroque Hollywood makes more obvious assertions of style. Both mannerism and baroque approaches can be formalist, but their approaches to formalism are different.

These analogies with art history are imperfect. In the realm of art history and literature, there is a tension between mannerism as a clear periodizing concept and mannerism as a general aesthetic.[15] Just as classicism is not a perfect descriptor of a twentieth-century popular art form, the analogy of mannerism and baroque collapse a century of art history into a mere decade of cinematic history. Moreover, baroque particularly may overlay with other aesthetic categories, like modernism or expressionism. The evolutionary model is at odds with another, equally useful, model in which mannerism and baroque are just two stylistic options open to filmmakers across time periods. Patrick Keating points out that mannerism is an analogy that is both instructive and perhaps not too literal. In distinction to Bazin's model, he argues for a coexistence of mannerism and classicism and a shared set of aesthetic practices: "The High Renaissance artist, the Mannerist artist, and the Baroque artist all value order and fidelity; they just prioritize them differently."[16] For all its problems, the art history analogy *is* useful, since variations from classicism help describe what scholars call "late classicism" with more specificity. And both mannerism and baroque capture part of the complicated relationship between the stylistic experimentations of the 1940s and 1950s and the stable (if evolving and innovating) storytelling formulas of the studio era.

CONCLUSION: HOW CLASSICAL WAS CLASSICAL HOLLYWOOD?

In his revisionist account of Hollywood's relationship to the nineteenth-century novel and the well-made play, Rick Altman asks, half rhetorically, "How classical was classical narrative?"[17] His question could just as easily be in service of another implicit question: How classical was classical Hollywood? Altman suggests that classical Hollywood was classical in some respects but not in others, and he argues against separating out "excess" from the textual forms of classicism. Altman was one of a number of prominent theoretical voices challenging the classical narration model articulated by the foundational study of David Bordwell, Kristin Thompson, and Janet Staiger.[18] Whereas historians subscribing to the centrality of classicism see an ability of classical norms to recuperate challenges, others subscribing to what one might call the "yes, but" approach look for countercurrents in classicism. Notably, these countercurrents are often part of the classical canon, not at the margins of the studios' output: for example, *Casablanca* (Curtiz 1942) for Rick Altman or slapstick comedy for Miriam Hansen. Hansen argues that studio-era films demonstrate classical patterns but that these alone do not account for their affective pull or their ideological meaning. Her formulation perhaps best captures this broader theoretical focus on countercurrents of classicism.[19]

For the most part, Hollywood mannerism occurred neither in the canonical heart of the studio era nor at its margins. The concept can help describe some canonical works like *The Magnificent Ambersons* and give a new light to half-forgotten genre films. However, mannerism grew out of the prestige picture of the 1940s, especially in the second half of the decade. As such, mannerism was the counterpart to the narrative innovation and experimentation that David Bordwell has identified in the decade and for which he has provided the main causes: the financial success of the studios and a culture of "cooperative competition."[20] As I have argued, mannerism meant more than stylistic assertion, though it did involve such assertion. Hollywood mannerism was a stylistic sensibility that exaggerated as much as possible within the rules of classicism and without breaking either its spectatorial immersion or its formal elegance. These formal qualities—disarticulation of space, camera mobility as an alternative to analytical editing, complex and even fussy blocking, and intricate gray scale in cinematography—do not exhaust the possible constraints of a mannerist style. Some mannerist qualities are not unique to the 1940s, but it is worth pointing out how many of the examples of assertive narrational voice come from the 1940s. The stylization was part of a larger experimentation among filmmakers to incorporate European filmmaking trends and to see how cinema could carry more complex tonal attitudes. Art history analogies can carry us only so far, but the repetitions of stylistic traits suggest that these 1940s films had a distinct sensibility and belonged to an unacknowledged movement within Hollywood.

NOTES

1 André Bazin, "The Evolution of the Language of Cinema," in *What Is Cinema?* vol. 1, trans. and ed. Hugh Gray (Berkeley: University of California Press, 1967), 23–40; Mary Ann Doane, *Desire to Desire: The Woman's Film of the 1940s* (Bloomington: Indiana University Press, 1987); and David Bordwell, "The Bounds of Difference," in David Bordwell, Janet Staiger, and Kristin Thompson, *Classical Hollywood Cinema: Film Style and Mode of Production to 1960* (New York: Columbia University Press, 1985), 72–86.

2 Liana de Girolami Cheney, *Readings in Italian Mannerism* (New York: Peter Lang, 2004), 7.

3 Craig Hugh Smyth, *Mannerism and Maniera* (Locust Valley, NY: J. J. Augustin, 1963).

4 Belén Vidal, *Figuring the Past: Period Film and the Mannerist Aesthetic* (Amsterdam: Amsterdam University Press, 2012), 11.

5 Patrick Keating, *Hollywood Lighting from the Silent Era to Film Noir* (New York: Columbia University, 2009), 191.

6 See Stephen Heath, "Narrative Space," in *Questions of Cinema* (Bloomington: Indiana University Press, 1981), 19–75.

7 Hitchcock describes this process shot in François Truffaut, with Helen G. Scott, *Hitchcock*, rev. ed. (New York: Simon and Schuster, 1984), 175–76.

8 For more on the role of the crab dolly in the overall trend toward long take cinema in the 1940s, see Steve Neale, "Introduction 2: The Long Take—Concepts, Practices, Technologies, and Histories," in *The Long Take: Critical Approaches*, ed. John Gibbs and Douglas Pye (London: Palgrave Macmillan, 2017), 27–41; see also Patrick Keating, *The Dynamic Frame: Camera Movement in Classical Hollywood* (New York: Columbia University Press, 2019), 251.

9 Bazin, "Evolution of the Language of Cinema"; David Bordwell, "Deep Focus Photography," in Bordwell, Staiger, and Thompson, *Classical Hollywood Cinema*, 590–92; more recently, see also Bordwell's analysis of *Panic in the Streets* (Kazan 1950) in "Modest Virtuosity: A Plea to Filmmakers, Old and Young," *Observations on Film Art* (blog), December 13, 2015, http://www.davidbordwell.net/blog/2015/12/13/modest-virtuosity-a-plea-to-filmmakers-old-and-young/.

10 Keating, *Dynamic Frame*, 248.

11 Robin Wood, "*Letter from an Unknown Woman*," in *Personal Views: Explorations in Film* (Detroit, MI: Wayne State University Press, 2006), 115–34.

12 Bazin, "Evolution of the Language of Cinema," 34; Bazin, "De Sica: Metteur en Scene," in *What Is Cinema?*, vol. 2, trans. and ed. Hugh Gray (Berkeley: University of California Press, 1971), 61–78.

13 André Bazin, "The Evolution of the Western," in *What Is Cinema?*, 2:150.

14 For a reading of Sirk's earlier *To New Shores* (1937) as baroque, see Lutz Koepnik, "Sirk and the Culture Industry: 'Zu neuen Ufern' and 'The First Legion,'" *Film Criticism* 23, no. 2–3 (1999): 104.

15 John M. Steadman, *Redefining a Period Style: "Renaissance," "Mannerist," and "Baroque" in Literature* (Pittsburgh, PA: Duquesne University Press, 1990).

16 Keating, *Hollywood Lighting*, 191.

17 Rick Altman, "Dickens, Griffith, and Film Theory Today," in *Classical Hollywood Narrative: The Paradigm Wars*, ed. Jane Gaines (Durham, NC: Duke University Press, 1992), 14.

18 Bordwell, Staiger, and Thompson, *Classical Hollywood Cinema*.

19 Miriam Bratu Hansen, "The Mass Production of the Senses: Classical Cinema as Vernacular Modernism," *Modernism/Modernity* 6, no. 2 (1999): 59–77.

20 David Bordwell, *Reinventing Hollywood: How 1940s Filmmakers Changed Movie Storytelling* (Chicago: University of Chicago Press, 2017), 18–29.

III

CLASSICAL GENRES

5

TRADING ON SONGS

The Emergence of the Film Musical as a Genre Label

Katherine Spring

Popular histories of the American film musical tend to posit the genre's origin in one of two sources, each of which is bound to Hollywood's transition to sound: *The Jazz Singer*, released in October 1927, or *The Broadway Melody*, released twenty months later. As John Kobal writes in *A History of the Movie Musical*, *The Jazz Singer* heralded "not only sound, but also a whole new genre—the musical," and Richard Barrios asserts that *The Broadway Melody* "marks the true beginning of the musical. . . . Everything that would go into making a film musical [could] be found in *The Broadway Melody* in one form or another."[1] From one of these two progenitors, the history of the studio-era musical springs forth and proceeds through the Busby Berkeley musicals at Warner Bros. to the Fred Astaire and Ginger Rogers vehicles at RKO to the works of the Arthur Freed Unit at MGM, the latter of which remain paragons of the genre.[2]

As Rick Altman has pointed out, this standard history "leaves much to be desired," not least because its teleological drive toward the integrated musical of the 1950s obscures the degree of heterogeneity that characterized the musical, or more specifically the relationship between narrative and song in feature-length films, in the first few years of synchronized-sound filmmaking by Hollywood's studios.[3] If the musical is defined according to a paradigm constituted by the products of the Freed Unit, then it is tempting to impose a priori that definition onto the earliest examples of films that incorporate songs in narratively significant ways. Doing so, however, is a historical misstep that overlooks how such films were understood and promoted at the time of their production and release. Donald Crafton has written that "around 1929–1930, it was the rare movie that was *not* a musical in some sense of the term," and elsewhere I have shown that at that time popular songs appeared in more than half of American feature-length films, wherein they served a variety of dramatic functions.[4] As well, in his study of terminology that appeared in the film fan magazine *Photoplay*, Altman has noted that until late 1930 the term "musical" appeared not as a noun but rather as an adjective to modify "such diverse nouns as comedy, romance, melodrama, entertainment, attraction, dialog, and revue."[5] Many of Hollywood's earliest sound films were labeled as musicals only ex post facto. As we now know, *The Jazz Singer* upon its release was referred to not as a musical but rather as a "heart interest story" and a "comedy drama" despite that the titular protagonist sings a half-dozen numbers over the course of the plot.[6]

Contemporary scholarship has begun to account for the film musical's heterogeneous roots in theatrical traditions, but it remains to be understood how the term "musical" was deployed as a genre label by film reviewers in entertainment trade papers during the genre's nascent years.[7] This chapter aims to provide some clarification and, in so doing, to position film reviews as sites of discursive production apposite for analysis. Reviews, after all, both reflect industry norms and shape readers' expectations; as such, they may be considered "crucial artefacts" in what Matthew Freeman has called the "discursive context of study."[8] And while this study is more modest in scope than Steve Neale's systematic analysis of how the term "melodrama" circulated in American trade papers of the classical period,[9] it likewise aims to improve our understanding of how the term "musical" was used in trade papers to describe and categorize early sound films that shared at least one semantic element: on-screen song performances.

My sample consists of film reviews published in two trade papers, *Variety* and *Film Daily*, for 193 studio-produced films that were released over the span of two years, from January 1929 to December 1930, arguably the peak years in the industry's conversion from silent to sound filmmaking.[10] The films were selected through the use of information supplied by the AFI Catalog of Feature Films as well as keyword searches in the Media History Digital Library.[11] *Variety* and *Film Daily* were chosen for their divergent readership. Whereas *Variety*'s readership included members of a number of entertainment industries, including vaudeville, music, and the theatrical stage in addition to cinema, *Film Daily* focused on stakeholders in the film industry, especially motion picture exhibitors. Using Altman's concept of "crisis historiography" as a launching point, this chapter presents three findings from the study, each of which in turn clarifies or revises previous assumptions about the history of the musical genre. Taken together, the findings reveal how the term "musical" circulated alongside references to the genre's new and requisite technological partner, synchronized sound.

In *Silent Film Sound*, Altman defines "crisis historiography" as an approach to writing history that accounts for the multiple, related technologies necessarily involved in the formation of a single, representational technology.[12] For example, scholars considering the American film industry's conversion to sound inevitably confront the multiple "jurisdictions" occupied by electrical sound technology in the fields of telephony, phonography, and radio.[13] History written from this approach emphasizes not the fully formed technology with which we are now familiar but rather the technology's contemporaneous social uses and functions among a range of users. As Altman puts it, crisis historiography assumes that "the definition of a representational technology is *both historically and socially contingent.* That is, the media are not fully and self-evidently defined by their components and configurations. They also depend on the way users develop and understand them."[14] In addition, technologies emerge in an "identity crisis"; they are "always born nameless . . . with multiple monikers rather than a single stable name."[15] Crisis historiography is an apt approach for understanding what at first glance seems to be generic confusion that characterized the early musical's status in trade paper reviews.

Before considering the reviews from this perspective, however, it is important to note that reviewers were quick to conventionalize and standardize their acknowledgment of the technology that made the musical possible: synchronous sound. At the outset of 1929, the studios' increase of synch-sound production yielded new terminology for reviews. In *Variety*, the descriptors "Silent," "Dialog," or "Sound"—the latter referring to a film with a synchronized score but no synchronous dialogue—appeared in boldface under the title of each film. By the middle of that year, as sound filmmaking took hold and the future of silent film looked doubtful, these labels were replaced by two others: "All Dialog" or "All Dialog, With Songs."[16] The key date is July 2, 1930, when labels began to be used to signify three types of films: foreign productions ("All Dialog"), films with sequences shot in Technicolor (e.g., "All Technicolor"), and films with songs ("With Songs").

Film Daily used the descriptors "Silent," "All-Talker," "Part-Talker," or "Synchronized," until April 6, 1930, when the paper restructured its reviews to remove prominent sound keywords for all but exceptions to what was by then the all-talker industry norm.[17]

Nonetheless, the label "with songs" seems to have been applied inconsistently. For instance, both *Lucky Boy* (Taurog and Wilson 1929) and *Syncopation* (Glennon 1929), released six weeks apart in early 1929, motivate song performances through the protagonists' vocations as vaudeville performers rather than the hallmark "breaking into song and dance" that characterized later musicals. But whereas *Variety* gave the descriptor "Dialog and Songs" to *Lucky Boy*, it labeled *Syncopation* merely "Dialog," despite the paper's ensuing description of the film as being "typical of today's musical comedies." *Film Daily*, meanwhile, described *Lucky Boy* as a "Do-Re-Mi Picture" and *Syncopation* as a "comedy drama." *The Time, the Place, and the Girl* (Bretherton 1929), based on a 1907 stage musical, was categorized by *Variety* as "All Dialog" rather than "Dialog with Songs" but according to *Film Daily* was a "musical comedy."[18] *Smiling Irish Eyes* (Seiter 1929), released in the same month, was for *Variety* "All Dialog, With Songs" yet for *Film Daily* a "comedy drama."[19] These are brief but representative examples of the haphazard nature by which films with songs were described even while the monikers for sound technology, like "dialog" and "all-talker," were swiftly formalized.

Unlike sound technology, the film musical was not "born nameless." The prevalence of musical theater as a form of popular entertainment in the 1920s furnished film reviewers with nomenclature associated with the stage musical's major genres: musical comedy, revue, and operetta. However, while a film's association with the theatrical stage all but guaranteed its designation as a musical in the trade papers, the boundaries between stage genres themselves were fluid. Operetta ("opera lite") and musical comedy, for example, shared conventions for integrating songs, music, and dialogue into a narrative form. Thus, as with the "with songs" attachment described above, labels indicative of musical genres were applied variously to early sound films. For instance, Warner Bros.'s *The Desert Song* (Del Ruth 1929), based on a stage operetta that played in New York three years prior to the film's release in April 1929, was described as "light opera" in *Variety* and named an "operetta" by *Film Daily*, bespeaking slippage between the terms.[20] *Film Daily* also noted that *The Desert Song* was "made in musical comedy, not motion picture mold," intimating but not elaborating upon an argument for medium specificity that might distinguish musical theater from cinema. *The Broadway Melody* (Beaumont 1929), which attained general release in June 1929, was described by a *Film Daily* reviewer as a "comedy drama of Broadway show life" but was endorsed by *Variety* as "the first screen musical," a phrase that seems as much a response to MGM's heavy promotion of the film as the "first musical comedy brought to the screen" as it does an explanation of the film's later identification by scholars as the first bona fide example of the genre.[21] In light of these examples that emphasize the cinema's relationship to theater, bearing out Don Crafton's observation that the earliest sound films constituted "canned Broadway," it is worth noting that the first review in *Film Daily* to employ a label from musical theater was, in fact, for *The Rainbow Man* (Neumeyer 1929), a film that had *no* precedent on the stage. Released on May 18, 1929, the film was deemed a "musical comedy," appropriately so for its integration of multiple songs into its plot about a minstrel performer.[22]

Through the summer and fall of 1929, a number of releases continued to be labeled as musical comedy *or* comedy drama, including *On With the Show!* (Crosland), *Marianne* (Leonard), and *Sweetie* (Tuttle). A surprising omission is *Gold Diggers of Broadway* (Del Ruth), cataloged by the AFI as a musical comedy but named a "comedy" in *Film Daily* and noted in *Variety* as a stage adaptation but without a generic descriptor.[23] These disparities seem to have evaporated over the course of late 1929 and early 1930, when reviews in *Variety* and *Film Daily* tended to manifest similar descriptors; for example, *Show of Shows* (Adolfi) was a revue; *The Vagabond King*, an operetta (Berger); and *Animal Crackers* (Heerman), a musical comedy.[24] By mid-1930, genre labels, in addition to references to synchronous sound technology, were standardized.

It would be wrong to claim, though, that prior to this standardization the descriptors affiliated with musical genres (musical comedy, revue, operetta) were used haphazardly. A second finding revealed by the reviews is that these descriptors were reserved for films in which characters were cast as singers and dancers and whose musical performances were therefore motivated by verisimilar circumstances rather than generic ones. Films exhibiting the formal disruptiveness that would come to define the integrated screen musical were seldom referred to as musicals at the time of their release. To illustrate this point, it is helpful to compare the use of songs in *Sally* (Dillon

1929), a First National/Warner Bros. production, with MGM's *Devil-May-Care* (Franklin 1929). Released just four days apart in late December, both films include approximately the same number of songs, most of which are performed in their entirety. As well, both films were branded "All Dialog, With Songs," and their reviews appeared alongside one another in *Variety* and *Film Daily*. Yet, whereas *Sally* was called a musical or musical comedy, *Devil-May-Care*, though advertised by MGM as a "musical romance," was described as a comedy drama with songs (*Variety*), a romantic drama with music (*Film Daily*), and a costume drama with music (*Motion Picture News*).[25]

The discrepancy owes to the role of songs in each film. The rags-to-riches plot of *Sally* features the illustrious musical comedy star Marilyn Miller in the nominal role of an aspiring dancer who is admired by aristocrat Blair Farrell (Alexander Gray). Sally works as a server, occasionally finding dancing work, until she is hired to impersonate a famous Russian dancer at an engagement party. From there she is cast in a follies revue show, where on opening night she is reunited with Blair, whom she marries. Over the course of this plot there appear eight songs, five of which are performed in their entirety and are motivated by Sally's would-be career on Broadway. At the Elmtree tavern where she waits on tables, Sally sings "All I Want to Do Do Do Is Dance" to impress a booking agent. Later, in her role as the impersonator, she sings "Just a Wild Rose." Two additional songs, "If I'm Dreaming (Don't Wake Me Too Soon)" and "Look for the Silver Lining," are motivated by the blossoming romance between Sally and Blair. In these cases, the songs provide a conduit for Sally's emotional expression, and the proficiency with which she sings is convincing given her character's aspirations.

Devil-May-Care, in which nary a showbiz personality appears, motivates its songs by different means. The plot centers on Armand de Treville, a nineteenth-century Bonapartist played by silent film star Roman Novarro in his first talking film. In the Hundred Days War between Napoleon's exile to Elba and his return to Paris, Armand escapes death and heads to the south of France, where he meets and falls in love with Léonie (Dorothy Jordan). Throughout, Armand's performance of song numbers is triggered either by his romantic longings, which finds expression, for instance, in "The Shepherd's Serenade" (performed once in its entirety and twice as partial cues), or by his wit, as when he lambasts the king through the song "Bon Jour, Louie." Given that Armand is not an aspiring entertainer but rather a

Bonapartist fugitive, it is hard to conceive of his singing as being motivated by narrative or realistic means. Armand sings when the feeling strikes, just as do characters in integrated musicals that postdate the transition to sound.

In form and musical style, *Devil-May-Care* resembles a stage operetta, and although it was called as much by advertisements taken out by Warner Bros.,[26] the term "operetta" remains absent from reviews. Perhaps this discrepancy owes to the film's source, which was not an operetta but rather a French play, *La Bataille des Dames*, or *When Ladies Battle*, written by Eugène Scribe and Ernest Legouve in the mid-nineteenth century.[27] *Sally*, on the other hand, was adapted from and bore all the markings of a Ziegfeld musical production that premiered on Broadway nearly ten years prior to the film's release. Warner Bros. spared little expense in replicating the production value of the Broadway extravaganza, not only by engaging Marilyn Miller but also by shooting it in two-strip Technicolor. The stage progenitor of *Sally*, as well as the plot's emphasis on a show business hopeful, warranted the use of a label affiliated with an established musical genre.

A third finding of this survey of film reviews is that backstage stories were rarely described in relation to their constitutive, even essential, musical performances. For example, *Footlights and Fools* (Seiter 1929) includes five songs and serves as a vehicle for a musical comedy star (played by Colleen Moore) but was named a "backstage story," a melodrama, and "a backstage story but [with] plenty of songs and music," the qualifier "but" serving to suggest that songs and music have the capacity to redeem a backstage plot.[28] *Nix on Dames* (Gallaher 1929) was a "backstage comedy," and *The Song of Love* (Kenton 1929) was a "backstage narrative" and "drama of the backstage" with scarcely a mention of music in reviews despite Belle Baker's six song performances.[29] *Applause* (Mamoulian 1929) was described by *Film Daily* as a "drab drama of backstage burlesque life, with only a sprinkling of comedy." That same film was indicated in *Variety* by the phrase "All Dialog" instead of the more accurate "All Dialog, With Songs."[30] All of these examples bespeak the reviewers' relative uncertainty about the relationship between notions of musicality and backstage plots.

In sum, trade reviews indicate that films containing songs in 1929 and 1930 were understood either in terms of their theatrical predecessors or as silent-era genres with songs. The musical itself was not a new concept, and its prior existence on Broadway and the theatrical stage is amply represented in the number of contemporaneous films identified as musical comedies, revues, and operettas. Since genre keywords like "musical comedy" or "operetta" did not need to be invented, their absence from reviews of films with prominent musical content during this transitional period is especially conspicuous but ultimately indicative of the uncertainty among the trade reviewers of how to leave room for music as a feature to be distinguished from the novelty of sound technology. Any uncertainty on the part of reviewers about how to categorize and promote films according to genre found an improbable antidote in the diminishment of songs and musicals toward the end of 1931. When a new cycle of musicals emerged in 1933, around the same time that "shooting a sound film came to mean shooting a silent film with sound," the genre presented itself as one that was unified by formal conventions and extratextual discourse—features that were absent during the transitional years and yet remain essential to our account of the genre's history.[31]

NOTES

Thanks to M. L. Clark for research assistance.

1   John Kobal, *A History of the Movie Musical: Gotta Sing, Gotta Dance*, rev. ed. (New York: Exeter Books, 1983), 22; Richard Barrios, *A Song in the Dark: The Birth of the Musical Film*, 2nd ed. (Oxford: Oxford University Press, 2010), 59. *The Jazz Singer* is also referred to as a musical in Corey K. Creekmur and Linda Y. Mokdad, "Introduction," in *The International Film Musical*, ed. Creekmur and Mokdad (Edinburgh: Edinburgh University Press, 2013); and Thomas S. Hischak, *Musicals in Film: A Guide to the Genre* (Santa Barbara, CA: Greenwood, 2017), xiv.

2   Amanda McQueen challenges the rise-and-fall narrative of the musical's history in "After 'The Golden Age': An Industrial History of the Hollywood Musical, 1955–1975," PhD diss., University of Wisconsin–Madison, 2016.

3   Rick Altman, *The American Film Musical* (Bloomington: Indiana University Press, 1987), 112. See also Rick Altman, *Film/Genre* (London: BFI, 1999).

4   Donald Crafton, *The Talkies: American Cinema's Transition to Sound, 1926–1931* (Berkeley: University of California Press, 1997), 315, original emphasis; Katherine Spring, *Saying It With Songs: Popular Music and the Coming of Sound to Hollywood Cinema* (New York: Oxford University Press, 2013).

5   Altman, *Film/Genre*, 32.

6   *Variety*, October 12, 1927, 16; *Film Daily*, October 23, 1927, 6. A study of the provenances and uses of songs in *The Jazz Singer* is found in Daniel Goldmark, "Adapting *The Jazz Singer* from Short Story to Screen: A Musical Profile," *Journal of the American Musicological Society* 70, no. 3 (2017): 767–817.

7   Michael Slowik, "Interlude: The Hollywood Musical," in *After the Silents: Hollywood Film Music in the Early Sound Era, 1926–1934* (New York: Columbia University Press, 2004), 136–79.

8   Matthew Freeman, *Industrial Approaches to Media: A Methodological Gateway to Industry Studies* (London: Palgrave, 2016), 135–38.

9   Steve Neale, "Melo Talk: On the Meaning and Use of the Term 'Melodrama' in the American Trade Press," *Velvet Light Trap* 32 (Fall 1993): 66–89.

10 Of the two hundred films released in the final quarter of the 1928–29 season, eighty-six were "100 percent talking." By 1929, most cinemas in the largest cities of the United States were wired for sound, and in 1930 Hollywood's studios ceased production of silent films altogether. See Crafton, *The Talkies*, 171; and Andrew Hanssen, "Revenue Sharing and the Coming of Sound," in *An Economic History of Film*, ed. Michael Pokorny and John Sedgwick (Oxon, UK: Routledge, 2005), 91.

11 The AFI Catalog distinguishes between musicals and other genre films with the subgenre description "with songs," for example, "comedy, with songs." This distinction led me to speculate about AFI's criteria for genre categorization. Correspondence with Sarah Clothier, manager of the AFI Catalog, confirmed that catalogers consult contemporaneous primary sources and "replicated (as best [they] can) the language, terms, taxonomies, criteria, etc. that were consistent with the time of production." The definitions of the genre categories used by the catalog are the following: "*Musical:* Used for fictional films in which musical numbers advance or are integral to the plot or in which the action concerns the presentation of a musical show. *Musical comedy:* Used for fictional films that have a high degree of comedy in the story. Not used as a genre for comedies that may have an incidental song (those would be Comedy, with Songs). *With Songs:* Used only as a second occurrence with any standalone genre . . . for a film that contains songs. (This label is used only) if there are two or more songs performed within a film; (it is) not used for films that may have a title song and one song within the film." Email correspondence with Sarah Clothier, May 4, 2018.

12 Rick Altman, *Silent Film Sound* (New York: Columbia University Press, 2004), 15–23.

13 Steve J. Wurtzler, *Electrical Sounds: Technological Change and the Rise of Corporate Mass Media* (New York: Columbia University Press, 2008), especially 10–15.

14 Altman, Rick, *Silent Film Sound*, 16.

15 Altman, *Silent Film Sound*, 19. For instance, what we call a television is "in one sense just a radio with images" (16); a more recent example is the cell phone, which for most users is a composite camera, video streamer, social media device, and telephonic device—even while the phrase "dial a number" retains wide currency.

16 On the doubtful future of silent filmmaking, see *Variety*, June 5, 1929, 7. One of the few exceptions to the categories of "All Dialog" or "All Dialog, With Songs" was the designation of *The Desert Song*, released by Warner Bros. in April 1929 as "Musical-Dialog," with the subheading "Light Opera." *Variety*, April 10, 1929, 16.

17 The sole exception I found is *The Desert Song*, labeled "Operetta."

18 *Variety*, July 10, 1931, 13; *Film Daily*, October 6, 1929, 8.

19 *Variety*, July 31, 1929, 17; *Film Daily*, July 28, 1929, 8.

20 *Variety*, April 10, 1929, 16; *Film Daily*, May 5, 1929, 9.

21 *Variety*, February 13, 1929, 13. *Motion Picture News* did not provide a genre label for *The Broadway Melody* but described the film as one that included "real drama, musical comedy, and comedy." *Motion Picture News*, February 16, 1929, 500.

22 *Film Daily*, April 14, 1929, 13. The AFI Catalog entry for *The Rainbow Man* lists May 18, 1929, as the release date with this note: "According to a production directory in the 9 Mar 1929 *Exhibitors Herald-World*, the starting date for *The Rainbow Man* was 1 Feb 1929." AFI Catalog, https://search-proquest-com.libproxy.wlu.ca/docview/1746584786?accountid=15090.

23 *Film Daily*, September 8, 1929, 9; *Variety*, September 4, 1929, 13.

24 *Variety*, November 27, 1929, 21; *Film Daily*, November 24, 1929, 8; *Variety*, February 26, 1930, 24; *Film Daily*, February 23, 1930, 10; *Variety* September 3, 1930, 19; *Film Daily*, August 3, 1930, 11.

25 *Variety*, December 25, 1929, 20, 26; *Film Daily*, December 29, 1929, 8; *Motion Picture News*, December 28, 1929, 25.

26 *Film Daily*, December 26, 1929, 3.

27 *Devil-May-Care* was adapted into an operetta by Jules Barbier in 1886. I have been unable to find evidence of performances in the United States, and references in the trades to the film's source are invariably to the French play.

28 *Variety*, November 13, 1929, 12; *Motion Picture News*, March 15, 1930, 79; *Talking Screen*, January 1930, 57.

29 *Film Daily*, November 24, 1929, 9; *Variety*, November 20, 1929, 30; *Film Daily*, November 17, 1929, 8.

30 *Film Daily*, October 13, 1929, 8; *Variety*, October 9, 1929, 31.

31 David Bordwell, "The Introduction of Sound," in David Bordwell, Janet Staiger, and Kristin Thompson, *The Classical Hollywood Cinema: Film Style and Mode of Production to 1960* (New York: Columbia University Press), 306.

6

ANOTHER HOLLYWOOD PICTURE?

A Star Is Born (1937) and the Self-Reflexivity of the Backstudio Picture

Steven Cohan

In 1937, *New York Times* critic Frank Nugent wrote a column about "the surprising number of back-studio pictures which have been dashing down the Times Square pike in the last few months." Although Nugent noted that the cycle did have antecedents, he believed that *A Star Is Born* (Wellman 1937), still considered the quintessential backstudio picture, "is commonly supposed to have started things. . . . Where the process will end, for the cycle apparently is just beginning, no one—this round-eyed corner least of all—can predict with any assurance."[1]

Today, the end point of backstudio pictures is as unpredictable as it was in 1937. For that matter, since it begins in the silent era and extends to recent Academy Award competitions one hundred years later, the film purporting to take viewers inside Hollywood's dream factory coincides with the history of American movies. But while the film about making movies has persisted, it has rarely been treated as a genre, and, what is more, no name describing this type of motion picture has stuck. Whereas Nugent called it a "back-studio picture," David O. Selznick referred to *A Star Is Born* as his "Hollywood picture."[2] Film scholars have most often called pictures of this sort "movies about the movies"[3] or "movies on movies,"[4] while also coining various alternatives such as "the Hollywood-on-Hollywood film"[5] or "Hollywood-focused films."[6] As for the movies themselves, the advertising for *Sunset Boulevard* (Wilder 1950) subtitled Billy Wilder's insider's view "A Hollywood Story," while a character in William Castle's *Hollywood Story* (1951) puts down "back*camera* pictures." Because of its comparability with the backstage musical, I prefer Nugent's "back-studio" designation, even though the name has not caught on with scholars or filmmakers.

Both the backstage musical and the backstudio picture go behind the scenes to demystify production as a condition for remystifying it. What gives the backstudio picture coherence and heft as its own genre, albeit one not, like the musical, readily identifiable through reiterated formal conventions, is a fascination with commercial filmmaking—which is also to say that this genre endures because it brands filmmaking with the Hollywood mystique. As a backstudio picture depicts it, Hollywood is simultaneously (1) an actual locale in the Los Angeles metropolitan area, (2) a business dedicated to the standardized production of motion pictures, and (3) an enduring cultural fantasy about fame, leisure, consumption, sexuality, artistry, and modernity. This overlapping of the literal (the locale) onto the material (the business) and the symbolic (the fantasy) has registered the impact of the film industry's transformations as an institution even when the genre mystifies these changes in story terms. It is also the means by which the genre authenticates while glamourizing the industry's representation of labor. The backstudio picture, in short, is most concerned with controlling perceptions of how the industry works, with masking how its product depends on industrial labor (including stardom), and with determining how that work's value accrues from the Hollywood brand stamped onto the product. No matter if success in Hollywood is valorized or damned in a particular film—either way, the genre's branding function remains intact and appealing.

Even the most memorable and complex of backstudios contextualize their depictions of filmmaking in their own production as Hollywood artifacts. Such self-reflexivity was and still is a primary means of their generic identity. For detailed illustration, I shall follow Nugent's lead and look closely at the 1937 *A Star Is Born* through its marketing campaign and trailer: despite its claims of going truly behind the scenes—"Now, for the first time, you can see *the truth*," one poster declares—Selznick's Hollywood picture codifies, even celebrates, the self-reflexivity that earlier backstudios like *Show People* (Vidor 1928) introduced and that later ones like *Singin' in the Rain* (Kelly and Donen 1952), *The Player* (Altman 1992), *Tropic Thunder* (Stiller 2008), and *La La Land* (Chazelle 2016) draw upon. In the final section of the chapter, I consider what "truths" about Hollywood and stardom *A Star Is Born* endorses.

AUTHENTICATING *A STAR IS BORN*

In 1936, as Selznick struggled to come up with a title for his new Hollywood picture, he wrote to his New York story editor, Katherine Brown: "Our feeling is that Hollywood has become identified with cheap titles of cheap pictures, and this more true today than ever because of 'Hollywood Boulevard,' which has been outstanding failure as Paramount Quickie, and also because of Hollywood Hotel, which Warners are making as musical, and which will probably be released before our picture."[7] The pressbook and trailer for *A Star Is Born* consequently take pains to document its greater authenticity in contrast with those competing "cheap pictures," which, in the producer's eyes, had diminished the appeal of movies about Hollywood.

The pressbook from United Artists for *A Star Is Born* outlines several promotions that are obvious ballyhoo, such as arranging for a contest in the newspapers asking readers to identify Hollywood landmarks like Grauman's Chinese theater that are featured in the film or to solicit letters from young women explaining "Why I'd like to be a Movie Star." Other recommendations for exploitation are more elaborate. Exhibitors are advised to recreate a soundstage movie set in the theater lobby, perhaps even to invite a local drama group to perform a scene there. The pressbook also recommends playing up "Hollywood's own language: This is the kind of inside stuff that gives every picture fan a thrill." For use as either a newspaper plant or a giveaway, "A glossary of Technical Movie Terms" lists definitions of Hollywood argot such as "gaffer" and "grip."[8]

Additionally, articles to be fed to local newspapers suggest how, in its representation of a "real" Hollywood, *A Star Is Born* is like a hall of mirrors. One piece parallels Janet Gaynor's "rise from extra ranks" with that of her character, and a photo still from the film of her character accepting the Academy Award recalls Gaynor's own Oscar win, with the caption stating, "History repeats itself." Another ersatz newspaper article exclaims, "Film within Film on Set within Set on Lot within Lot." "A motion picture within a motion picture," this article begins, "was made on a soundstage within a soundstage on a film lot within a film lot at Selznick International Studio recently."[9]

The most elaborate and fascinating self-reflexive element of the publicity campaign opens the pressbook with a full page describing "eight 22″ by 30″ pictorial displays lithographed on heavy stock paper in brown color." These

6.1. An advertisement from the pressbook for *A Star Is Born* (1937). Author's collection.

displays, which an exhibitor can purchase singly or as a full set of eight, illustrate with photos or drawings "and descriptive captions" behind-the-scenes perspectives of the Selznick production, foregrounding the manufacturing of *A Star Is Born* in much the same way that DVD supplements now claim transparency for contemporary pictures. Indeed, the eight titles that make up this *A Star Is Born* promotion anticipate the typical slate of background material on DVDs almost down to the letter: "Famous Movieland Scenes, Background of the Picture," "Details in Preparation," "Preparing the Story," "Building the Sets," "Style Creations for Miss Gaynor," "Technical and Tonal Accuracy," "Behind the Scenes," and "Advertising and Publicity." These topics are pretty interchangeable with what can be found on today's DVD menus.

The displays use *A Star Is Born*, itself a movie about the movies, to document the making of a movie from its various stages of preparation through to its eventual promotion. Even more striking is how these displays treat *A Star Is Born* as the referent for their documentation. We are assured that the set of exhibits "was prepared by the MPPDA [the Motion Picture Producers and Distributors of America, a forerunner of the Motion Picture Association of America] as part of its education campaign on films and film-making. These exhibits will be displayed simultaneously in 2000 Public Libraries, Schools, Clubs and Photoplay Study Groups in towns throughout the country."[10] According to the MPPDA, *A Star Is Born* accurately represents how movies are made, taking viewers behind the scenes to provide the full back-studio view; at the same time, the eight displays themselves substantiate the film's authenticity. The promotional discourse is so circular that there no longer seems to be an outside to the insider's perspective.

Not surprisingly, given the marketing campaign designed for the press-book, an equally self-reflexive discourse structures the trailer for *A Star Is Born*. It begins with an introduction to Hollywood, California, "the most glamourous city on earth," via landmarks that were by 1937 already stock markers of "a city where men and women skyrocket to fame or plunge to oblivion. What happens amid such glamorous places as the Ambassador pool? The Trocadero on the Gold Coast of the film city? At the Brown Derby where famous stars meet? Or in the gay setting of Santa Anita Park? It's all part of the fantastic Hollywood at playtime." The trailer then juxtaposes such frivolous play with the seriousness of the film industry's labor: "Here behind the walls of Selznick International Studio we see Hollywood at work."

In depicting "Hollywood at work," the trailer identifies what that work means to signify. Using footage of her character being made up for a screen test, the trailer proudly announces that "a new Janet Gaynor is in the making, a Janet Gaynor never before seen on the screen." Following equal time for costar Fredric March, "more swashbuckling than ever before," the trailer moves further behind the scenes, showing William Wellman directing his two stars. He gives instruction to "Freddy" on how to act in a love scene with Gaynor and shouts, "Roll 'em." We then immediately see a clip from the finished film but one now recontextualized by the trailer to make it seem as if we were watching this scene as it was being filmed by Wellman in the Selznick studio.

Reflecting Selznick's worry that previous backstudio cheapies had caused audience backlash, this trailer promises "Hollywood's first true story." It therefore warns audiences: "But don't come to see *A Star Is Born* expecting to find a Cinderella story or a glorification of motion pictures. Instead, you will be shocked by the price that must be paid in heartbreak and tears for every moment of triumph in Hollywood." Elaborating upon this theme, the announcer refers to this film's "bold revelations of how screen careers are ruined," all the while casting these revelations as a "rich human interest story," one showing how "Hollywood is filled with happiness and despair, joy and tragedy, a crazy quilt of madness, sanity, laughter, and tears." Ultimately, the announcer promises that "Janet Gaynor and Fredric March in *A Star Is Born* give you a Hollywood the world has not known. They answer for the first time the question, What is the cold fear clutching the hearts of the famous?"

Much like the plans for exploitation laid out by its pressbook, then, the trailer for *A Star Is Born* crystallizes how a backstudio picture self-reflexively authenticates both its industrial revelations and its branding of "Hollywood." According to the logic of a backstudio picture, the extrafictive guarantee of truthfulness lies in the film product itself, which is then viewed doubly as a diegetic representation (the fictional story referring in one way or another to real-life practices, people, and histories) and as an objective correlative of both the industry (the product perpetuating the mystique of the movies) and its location (that "glamorous city" in California). Thus, scenes from *A Star Is Born* (such as Gaynor in a makeup chair or, later on, of her accepting an Oscar and of March interrupting the ceremony to plead for a job) illustrate what the announcer says about the "new" Gaynor or about the eventual payment "in heartbreak and tears for every moment of triumph in Hollywood." With these claims so illustrated by the Selznick production, the trailer wants us to see how *A Star Is Born* is capable of merging fiction and reality. Similarly, it is not the Selznick studio's refusal to offer "a Cinderella story" but its manufacturing of *A Star Is Born* that contrasts with both the frivolity of Hollywood "playtime" and the make-believe that "a glorification of motion pictures" perpetuates.

All the same, the *A Star Is Born* trailer *is* glorifying motion pictures through its self-reflexivity. This strategy performs the symbolic condensation that gives "Hollywood" its currency as a place (the initial display of Southern California landmarks) that in turn is understood to be equivalent with the film industry (the Selznick studio at work, shown making this film) while also being synonymous with the fantasy that glorifies the work, enabling it to signify as an institution (the "rich human interest story of Hollywood," which turns out to comprise the triumphs and tragedies of stardom for characters and actors alike). The process of recounting what happens behind the scenes secures the import of Hollywood through its product. This trailer, in sum, fully recognizes that the ultimate referent of *A Star Is Born* is its own material existence as a backstudio picture.

SELF-REFLEXIVE HOLLYWOOD

Aside from the speeches about the price of stardom in heartbreak or the odds against breaking into the movies, *A Star Is Born* is itself less openly defensive about its authenticity in going behind the scenes to recount the opposite of a "Cinderella story." Even so, *A Star Is Born* opens and closes with pages from its final shooting script, and this trope discursively frames the film's own authenticity as a self-knowing Hollywood product.[11] The script not only originates but also transcribes the final speech we have just seen Janet Gaynor deliver on film: "This is Mrs. Norman Maine." Presented intact as an artifact of filmmaking, the script nonetheless gets the first *and* last word on Hollywood.

As much to the point, *A Star Is Born* follows earlier backstudio films with its treatment of Esther Blodgett's (Janet Gaynor's) arrival in Los Angeles. It prepares for this moment with a title card that echoes the openings of *Show People* and subsequent backstudio pictures from the 1930s. As Esther departs from a dark, snow-covered train depot in North Dakota, an intertitle identifies her destination, visualizing it as a utopian landscape of sun-drenched leisure and recreation: "HOLLYWOOD! . . . the beckoning El Dorado . . . Metropolis of Make Believe in the California Hills." A shot of those hills cuts to a man diving into a hotel swimming pool as a couple watches from under a sun umbrella and others look on from the shade of their cabana awnings.

With Hollywood visualized as such a utopian space, a montage reveals how all modes of transportation travel in the same direction: a bus, a train, and a propeller plane all bear signs with "City of Los Angeles" identified as their journey's end. Noticeably, though, Hollywood, not Los Angeles, is named "the beckoning El Dorado," the new goal of the frontier myth propounded by Esther's grandmother (May Robson) when she sends Esther off to California with a speech that translates nineteenth-century manifest destiny into twentieth-century movie stardom. Likewise, the sequence omits Esther's arrival at the city's train station and instead suggests that the real termination of her journey is Grauman's Chinese theater. With suitcase still in hand, apparently the first thing Esther does upon reaching Los Angeles is to head for that theater's forecourt. Only after she gazes at the celebrated footprints immortalized in cement does she then look for lodgings nearby.

The point made by the particularities of Esther's arrival in Southern California is twofold. First, this sequence reiterates what by this time—in prior films such as *Show People, Show Girl in Hollywood* (LeRoy 1930), *Make Me a Star* (Beaudine 1932), *Hollywood Boulevard* (Florey 1936), and *Hollywood Hotel* (Berkeley 1937)—had become the backstudio film's convention of showing the boulevard as the gateway to a spatially unified Hollywood, which, in turn, serves as a portal to the restricted studio factories. Second, as the underside of this convention, the trope visualizes the gulf between the boulevard and the studios. Upon registering at Oleander Arms "nr. Hollywood Blvd.," Esther asks the clerk, "Are all the studios really near here?" He replies sarcastically, "All except Gaumont British."

In somewhat the same way, and still following the example of other backstudio pictures of this era such as Selznick's earlier *What Price Hollywood?* (Cukor 1932), *A Star Is Born* uses Hollywood's own industrial discourses to establish the authenticity of Esther's and Norman Maine's stardom. Throughout, inserts of industrial texts document her rise, their marriage, and his fall through billboards (when signage with Vicki Lester's name effaces Norman Maine's from original advertising for *The Enchanted Hour*); tabloid newspaper headlines ("VICKI LOVES IN TRAILER!"); gossip columns ("What famous male star has stopped gargling the grog and is now taking a non-alcoholic honeymoon?"); and a seasonal program for exhibitors ("Mr. Exhibitor, Here's a message of vital importance to you: Get Rich with Oliver Niles Productions!") and the trades ("Norman Maine Contract With Niles Cancelled"). Moreover, the opening imagery establishing Hollywood as the beckoning El Dorado slyly reveals this film's self-reflexive texture: as the camera pans across the swimming pool of the Ambassador Hotel, we come to see that it is the location for a film shoot.

As its means of earning its authority as "Hollywood's first true story," *A Star Is Born* filmically and extrafilmically relies upon an assortment of self-authenticating discourses that underpin and crystallize its generic identity as a backstudio picture. Furthermore, Esther Blodgett in *A Star Is Born* (1937) is introduced as a movie fan, linking her figure to that of the studio girl or movie-struck girl of the 1910s and 1920s. Returning home after seeing a Norman Maine film, Esther ignores her aunt's complaint that all she thinks about is going to Hollywood when she picks up a movie magazine to read. "You'd better think about getting a good husband and stop mooning about Hollywood," the aunt advises. Esther's granny, however, supports those dreams, calling Hollywood her granddaughter's "wilderness" and comparing it to the Dakota frontier that the older woman had helped to settle in the previous century. The grandmother sends Esther off to Hollywood, now imagined as the modern-day American frontier, with the pioneering spirit of conquering the movies. As Esther later states in the Central Casting office, she believes in herself and has faith that she may be

6.2. Filmmaking at the Ambassador Hotel. *A Star Is Born* (1937).

"the one" to reach stardom, alone among the thousands who fail. Despite the explicit discouragement, it turns out Esther does have what it takes to be singled out—native talent, screen charisma, and good luck, but most of all, the mediation of someone powerful and already inside the industry, namely, Norman Maine, her future husband.

The trailer for *A Star Is Born* promises that it will not be another "Cinderella story or a glorification of motion pictures," but that assurance is a bit misleading, for once fairy godfather Norman takes Esther in hand, the newly named Vicki Lester has a relatively easy time attaining stardom. Norman arranges for the screen test at Oliver Niles's (Adolphe Menjou) studio, acts with Esther in it, and then talks Niles into casting her in his film. But crucial to this film's tracing of her birth as a new type of star and despite her fierce determination to succeed in Hollywood against all odds, Esther has an uncomplicated sweetness that her predecessors lack, in part due to Gaynor's performance and star persona and in part due to the script. Niles sees Esther's star potential because "tastes are going back to the natural." Given her naturalness, the antithesis of the glamorous film stars like Marlene Dietrich and Joan Crawford who were already if temporarily going out of fashion,[12] Esther just has "to be," which is the lesson the makeup department learns when trying to redo her face. Drawing for inspiration on Crawford's smear of a mouth and Dietrich's contoured cheeks, the makeup artists commit the same error Esther had made at the industry party with her bid to get the attention of producers by doing impressions of female stars like Greta Garbo and Mae West: they only need to let her be "herself" as she was with Norman when they met face-to-face.

Paradoxically, though, in order to sell her naturalness the Niles studio still has to make Esther Blodgett into a Hollywood artifact, giving her instruction in diction and posture and inventing a new name and biography for her so that "Esther Victoria Blodgett" becomes reversed and shortened to "Vicki Lester." This name change is important for how *A Star Is Born* depicts female stardom in its industrial context—and successfully tames it. "Vicki Lester" is more docile, more manageable than the quietly but still fiercely determined Esther Blodgett of the film's opening sequences. Stardom tames her pioneering spirit, which may be why, unlike Norman, Oliver Niles calls her "Vicki" rather than "Esther." "Vicki Lester" is a more tractable personality. The symmetry of her rise to stardom as set against Norman's fall is thus more than simply a formal structuring device. This double trajectory reveals how the errant male star absorbs the disruptive energy of his female counterpart, which is to say that *he* functions as the means through which *she* can, in turn, personify a "sweeter" expression of stardom as carefully nurtured and protected by Hollywood.

The more docile Esther becomes as Vicki Lester, the more Norman resists studio authority over his private life, so his outbursts do more than offer evidence of an unpredictable and ungovernable temperament. Rather, the drunken outbursts appear to be his means of fighting back, causing momentary ruptures in the studio's authorship of and authority over Norman Maine's identity. His relationship with Esther, in fact, tracks the studio's inability to manage him. Their meeting face-to-face occurs in the kitchen of that industry party; not only do Norman and then Esther break the dishware she is supposed to be washing and putting away, but he also entices her to walk away from her first paying job in Hollywood. Similarly, after the sneak preview of her debut in their film, Norman leads Esther toward a rear exit to avoid Niles and his entourage, who are awaiting the new star to congratulate her publicly in the theater lobby. The couple's elopement foils public relations director Matt Libby's (Lionel Stander) plan for a big, publicized event that could give Norman some good press for a change, and the private ceremony itself occurs in an out-of-the-way town without their Hollywood names. Finally, after their marriage, Norman wants their estate to offer a refuge from work. Once cut by the studio, Norman becomes a loose cannon and threat to his wife's career, as when he makes that humiliating spectacle of himself at the Oscars. How fitting, then, that his funeral turns out to be the big Hollywood event that he had prevented his wedding from becoming with their elopement.

Esther's self-identification as "Mrs. Norman Maine" in the finale *is* a well-earned moment of grand pathos, to be sure, worthy of its legendary status in crystalizing the price one pays—namely, heartbreak—for Hollywood stardom. But that moment also concludes the institutional containment of Norman Maine, effacing his presence as an unruly male movie star by turning him into a tearful memory and transferring his name to her new identity as his grieving widow; the show must go on, the star must keep her commitments despite her grief. As Vicki Lester's new alter ego, moreover, "Mrs. Norman Maine" is a willing stand-in for the studio system at large: the institution that gives birth to, nurtures, and protects its obedient female progeny.

Before and after *A Star Is Born*, and in one way or another, nearly every movie about filmmaking declares that it is tearing the veil from the face of Hollywood's mysteries; nearly every one of those movies then removes one veil only to disclose several more underneath. In his *New York Times* column about backstudios, Nugent referred to this tactic as "the Hollywood striptease," since for all the apparent behind-the-scene revelations, the goal is still "to preserve the glamorous illusion" and to protect "the greatest of its mysteries."[13] True enough. But one has to ask if an "authentic" backstudio look behind the scenes ever was, let alone still is, the genre's point. After all, backstudio pictures in all periods of the industry's history give an impression of transparency, but that may really be to recognize the genre's perpetuation of its various strategies of self-reflexive authentication in every era of its production. In the twenty-first century, the aspirations directed toward Hollywood—namely, to achieve the social and economic empowerment represented by the lifestyles that reward the industry's stars, creatives, and other assorted players for their passionate love of the movies—continue to make Los Angeles the magnet for ambitious young wannabe stars or filmmakers who head to the West Coast directly after their college graduation. Already inspiring that ambition in the early twentieth century by giving it narrative form, the backstudio picture has given emotional heft to filmmaking as the quintessential and mostly white American success story: anyone with a creative hunger and single-minded drive, the genre shows, can make it in the movies.

NOTES

1 Frank S. Nugent, "Another Dance of the Seven Veils: The Screen Reveals Its Mysteries to the Public, Yet Manages to Hide Behind the Cloak of Illusion," *New York Times*, October 10, 1937, X5.

2 Rudy Behlmer, ed., *Memo from: David O. Selznick* (New York: Avon Books, 1973), 143.

3 John Davis, "Inside Hollywood," in *Movies about Movies/Chicago '77*, ed. Sharon Kern (Chicago: The Film Center, School of the Art Institute of Chicago, 1977), 4–7; Christopher Ames, *Movies about the Movies: Hollywood Reflected* (Lexington: University Press of Kentucky, 1997); Mark Shiel, *Hollywood Cinema and the Real Los Angeles* (London: Reaktion Books, 2012).

4 Richard Meyers, *Movies on Movies: How Hollywood Sees Itself* (New York: Drake, 1978).

5 Ames, *Movies About the Movies.*

6 Leo Braudy, *The Hollywood Sign: Fantasy and Reality of an American Icon* (New Haven, CT: Yale University Press, 2011).

7 Behlmer, *Memo from: David O. Selznick*, 143.

8 Press book for *A Star Is Born* (1937), 11–12 (author's collection).

9 Press book for *A Star Is Born* (1937), 19–21.

10 Press book for *A Star Is Born* (1937), 3.

11 J. E. Smyth, *Reconstructing American Historical Cinema: From Cimarron to Citizen Kane* (Lexington: University Press of Kentucky, 2006), 269.

12 Catherine Jurca, *Hollywood 1938: Motion Pictures' Greatest Year* (Berkeley: University of California Press, 2012), 125.

13 Nugent, "Another Dance of the Seven Veils."

7

SCIENCE FICTION, GENRE HYBRIDITY, AND CANONIZATION IN CLASSICAL HOLLYWOOD

Blair Davis

The history of science fiction's evolution in Hollywood is thoroughly complex but still underexamined—a symptom of how not all genres are considered equal within film history. Sci-fi's emergence as a dominant genre in the early 1950s was preceded by numerous fits and starts (mostly at the level of the B-film and the serial) and marked by extensive cross-genre mingling. For two decades, science fiction remained an ever-emerging genre in the United States with no set parameters, usually integrated into existing genres rather than charting its own path in full. But the fact that relatively little scholarly work has been done on the origins of what has by now become one of Hollywood's most profitable genres signals the need to revisit how genre films as a whole have been handled via the processes of canonization that occur within popular and academic institutions.[1]

While some scholarship has focused on films like *Just Imagine* (Butler 1930)[2] and well-known serials like *Flash Gordon* (Stephani 1936) and *Buck Rogers* (Beebe and Goodkind 1939),[3] American sci-fi is marked more so by a slew of forgotten films that combine science fiction with such genres as horror, the Western, jungle films, and adventure movies. In the 1930s, this included serials like *The Lost City* (Revier 1935), *The Phantom Empire* (Brower and Eason 1935), *Undersea Kingdom* (Eason and Kane 1936), and *The Phantom Creeps* (Beebe and Goodkind 1939). In the 1940s, horror films like Universal's *Man-Made Monster* (Waggner 1941) and Columbia's *The Devil Commands* (Dmytryk 1941) offered scientific thrills early in the decade, while cliff-hangers like Republic's *The Purple Monster Strikes* (Bennet and Brannon 1945) and *King of the Rocket Men* (Brannon 1949) presented a new vision of science fiction later in the decade, one that offered alien threats from beyond the stars and not just peril born of our own planet's mad scientists.

As J. P. Telotte examines in his 1999 book *A Distant Technology: Science Fiction Film and the Machine Age*, sci-fi cinema was at first a predominantly European conception. The majority of the book focuses on the genre's development in Soviet, German, French, and British film history up to the end of the 1930s.[4] Science fiction did not evolve into a genre whose dominant tropes, themes, and visual patterns could be traced with any consistency in America until the early 1950s. Prior to that, it was often embedded in or combined with other genres in Hollywood: there was extensive cross-pollination, but no dominant strain emerged until the tail end of the studio system era. Most of the scholarly work done on sci-fi films spends little time (if any) looking at Hollywood's output in the 1930s and 1940s; Vivian Sobchack's influential study *Screening Space: The American Science Fiction Film* does not mention a single sci-fi film from either decade, not even better-known serials like *Flash Gordon* and *Buck Rogers*.[5] We know so little about the multi-decade processes of experimentation and evolution leading up to films like *Destination Moon* (Pichel 1950) and *The Day the Earth Stood Still* (Wise 1951). More work remains to be done not only in retracing the origins of the sci-fi genre but also in how we conceptualize the origins of film genres overall—as territories whose borders were not willfully and suddenly erected but, instead, formed through longer periods of testing and negotiation.

Much of this dilemma stems from the overall neglect of B-filmmaking and Poverty Row cinema in the classical era. Chapterplay serials were a major forum for scientific concerns, but, because their reputation remains that of films largely intended for children, they have rarely been taken seriously. In contrast, European sci-fi is widely considered to be sophisticated, adult fare—often made by directors who now rank among the top auteurs in film history, like Fritz Lang (*Metropolis* [1927], *Frau im Mond* [1929]) and René Clair (*Paris Qui Dort* [1924]). But the *Cahiers du Cinéma* crowd regularly praised Hollywood's B-films, from Godard's infamous dedication to Monogram Pictures, to Francois Truffaut's 1953 piece on *Dr. Cyclops* (Schoedsack 1940) praising what he called "grade-Z films" for the ways in which they advocated "the worthlessness of science without a conscience" as well as "respect for women."[6] Such factors, he says, allow certain "grade-Z films [to] link up with the great adult cinema of Hitchcock, Renoir and Rossellini."[7] Such sentiments have rarely been echoed since.

In 1946, Allied Artists Productions was formed as a unit of Monogram Pictures to concentrate on relatively larger budget and somewhat more prestigious efforts (at least compared to ongoing series like the Charlie Chan and Bowery Boys films). The term "B-plus pictures" was used to designate the higher-class tone of Allied Artists' films. Republic Pictures followed suit, with Orson Welles's *Macbeth* (1948) and the John Wayne films *Sands of Iwo Jima* (Dwan 1949) and *The Quiet Man* (Ford 1952) blurring the lines between A-films and Poverty Row in the late 1940s and early 1950s.

What we now point to as the real start of science fiction cinema in America was born out of this period and the risks taken by small studios to make big films. As I outlined in *The Battle for the Bs*, the films that often get chronicled as the start of the science fiction genre in Hollywood as the 1950s began were a distinct product of B-filmmaking traditions and Poverty Row precursors.[8] Before *Destination Moon* was released in August 1950, Lippert Pictures enjoyed tremendous success with *Rocketship X-M* (1950). That film was directed by Kurt Neumann, who helmed three low-budget Tarzan movies and several B-Westerns and crime capers in the five years beforehand. Not all cinematic innovations are at the hands of auteurs. Some come from the trenches of smaller B-movie studios.

It was B-films that moved science out of the laboratory and into the stratosphere in the 1940s. In his 1972 book *Focus on the Science Fiction Film*, one of the earliest studies of the genre, William Johnson discusses how sci-fi films shifted away from mad scientists by the end of the 1940s to focus on larger-scale representations of science and technology: "The new, post-World War II crop of realistic fantasies was unmistakably American in tone and setting, and most of them featured technology as something more pervasive than a single invention or a private laboratory."[9]

Without the steps taken by Poverty Row films in this decade to chart a new direction for how science could be conceptualized on-screen—from the ways in which *Man-Made Monster* and *The Devil Commands* (Dmytryk 1941) explored the perils and potentials of electricity in 1941, to the mid-decade alien invasions and lunar battles of *The Purple Monster Strikes* and *Brick Bradford* (Bennet and Carr 1947), to the atomic action and flying saucers of *King of the Rocket Men* and *Bruce Gentry* (Bennet and Carr 1949) at the end of the decade—the interstellar efforts of 1950s sci-fi films may not have emerged until much later. What horror and sci-fi films lacked in expensive effects used to create on-screen technological spectacle in the 1940s, they often made up for with the scope of their ideas. Not every such film was focused solely on a creature on the loose. Some were about bold ideas surrounding the dangers and potentials of science, albeit with limits in place in terms of the production methods used to express those concepts. This is even truer at the level of Poverty Row cinema and the chapterplay serials, where, if anything, the ideas were wilder even though they were so cheaply and quickly made.

The study of B-films offers a challenge to film scholarship regarding how we understand the roles that genres played for studios and audiences alike. The hybridity at work in how these 1930s and 1940s films handle sci-fi tropes and imagery complicates the canonical understanding of the genre's Hollywood origins. It also points toward larger patterns in classical Hollywood regarding how studios of all sizes regularly treated film genres in fluid rather than fixed ways and as constant sites of experimentation where the boundaries between genres were tested, bent, and occasionally broken.

7.1. Lobby card for chapter 4 of the 1945 Republic sci-fi serial *The Purple Monster Strikes*, starring Roy Barcroft as a Martian invader.

In *The Ideology of Genre*, Thomas O. Beebee notes that "generic instability is so prevalent a feature of the postmodern" that we should question whether postmodern genres even exist.[10] But instability was a regular presence in classical Hollywood, too—we must delve deeper into the borders between genres in this era, because they are less entrenched than believed.

Fredric Jameson said that "genres are *institutions*, or social contracts" between creator and audience. The function of a genre, he argues, "is to specify the proper use of a particular cultural artifact."[11] Colin McArthur told us in 1972 that genres are like "an agreed code between film maker and audience."[12] This rhetoric surrounding the idea of a contract or code has stuck. Outside of film studies, we use the word "code" to refer to important abstract concepts, like a code of honor, codes of behavior, a code of ethics. Even the term "dress code" has been used for processes of race-based and class-based discrimination. Clearly the stakes are high in terms of how the word "code" implies certain standards of acceptability, or as Jameson phrases it, "proper use," in discussing film genres.

In film studies, discrimination is seen in terms of which films are excluded from institutional canonization, from pedagogic practice, and from critical elevation and reevaluation. Some genre films have enjoyed more prestige than others, such as the many 1940s crime films that were later elevated by critics in the name of film noir. I have argued elsewhere for how horror films were a training ground for numerous film noir directors and cinematographers.[13]

Films like *Stranger on the Third Floor* (Ingster 1940) were actively marketed as horror films even while serving for many critics in retrospect as pioneers for the themes and images of film noir. Others such as *Black Friday* (Lubin 1940) and *The Monster and the Girl* (Heisler 1941) remain unheralded despite their overtly noir visual, narrative, and thematic elements. The boundaries between film noir and horror were fuzzy at the start of the 1940s, as were distinctions between horror and science fiction in films like *Dr. Cyclops* (1940), *The Ape* (Nigh 1940), *Before I Hang* (Grinde 1940), *The Man with Nine Lives* (Grinde 1940), *The Devil Commands* (1941), and *Man-Made Monster* (1941).

While film genre theorists like Rick Altman and Steve Neale have chronicled the ways in which studio marketing teams played up different genre elements within the same film in their trailers and pressbooks, this phenomenon usually refers to more subtle elements rather than blatant

7.2. Lobby card for the 1941 Universal horror/sci-fi film *Man-Made Monster,* starring Lionel Atwell as a scientist who turns Lon Chaney Jr. into an electrically charged monster.

ones. The seductive power of Bela Lugosi's eyes in *Dracula* (Browning 1931) as he lured his female victims allowed the film to be sold as both horror and romance, tying into the film's release on Valentine's Day. We would be hard-pressed now to call the film a horror romance, but this strategy was effective in drawing a wider range of viewers than it might otherwise have had it been labeled strictly a horror film.

The ways in which such supporting genre elements are on display in A-films are much subtler than the overt juxtapositions of different genres at work in many B-films and serials of the classical Hollywood era. When Chicago gangsters pull into town in a shiny sedan, wearing tailored suits as they enter the local saloon in the 1936 Gene Autry Western *The Old Corral* (Kane) from Republic Pictures, traditional theories about audience expectations and genre are pushed near their breaking point. Same with Autry's *Round Up Time in Texas* (Kane 1937), in which he and his trusty sidekick Smiley Burnette travel to the jungles of South Africa. There, they deliver horses to Gene's diamond-miner brother, surviving an attack by a native tribe and bloodthirsty lions in the process. Roy Rogers got in on the cross-genre action, too, when he was recruited as a government agent to stop a gang of fedora-clad saboteurs who drive black sedans in Republic's *King of the Cowboys* (Kane 1943).

But you won't see those films—or *The Devil Commands*, *The Monster and the Girl*, or *The Purple Monster Strikes*—pop up in Academy Award show montages, on American Film Institute lists, or on the syllabi of film history courses. From the anti-cinema bias of cultural critics like F. R. Leavis in the 1930s to modern academic grant-making bodies, film scholars have often needed to defend the legitimacy of film studies. This has framed much of the writing about cinema over the years, even as far back as Hugo Münsterberg's *The Photoplay: A Psychological Study* in 1916, a time when the theater was considered a more worthy pursuit.

There has long been conflict in film theory between the emotional and the intellectual enjoyment of movies, which has led to inconsistencies in the evaluation of genre films.[14] The reasons why certain films become elevated from their "generic" status into the auteurist realm often have less to do with the films themselves than it does with the aesthetic frames of references—or personal tastes, in other words—of the critics watching them. Traditional considerations of genre films have been influenced by the need to establish film theory as a viable scholarly discipline. A major example of this was the critical elevation of film noir in the 1970s, which was the result of a new generation of film critics who used the emerging popularity of auteur criticism to reclaim from obscurity certain favorite films from their youth. These films had a definitive influence in establishing the critical frames of reference that would later be brought to their work in film theory, and it is largely for this reason that film noir has played such an important role in auteur criticism. Comparatively, the horror films of the 1930s and 1940s that served as a stylistic influence on film noir have not enjoyed the same critical reevaluation via the auteur theory. Nor have the hybrids of horror and science fiction throughout the classical Hollywood era been properly assessed for their contributions to sci-fi's entrenchment as a genre by the early 1950s. While science fiction became a forum for using alien invaders and interstellar expeditions as metaphors for modern social concerns, the genre's origins saw it explore a much wider range of visual and narrative options concerning the representation of science and technology on-screen.

Film criticism regularly singles out so-called bad films to justify the critical study of those films deemed superior. This aesthetic distinction can then be held up to the outsider as proof that not all films are created equal. The specific B-films, serials, horror films, sci-fi, singing cowboy movies, and other forums for cross-genre experimentation during the classical Hollywood era have been steadily ignored, dismissed, or mocked by all but a handful of scholars. One reason is their low budgets, since B-filmmaking in general is still viewed by many fans and scholars as a dubious endeavor. The other reason is that their stories involve things like jetpacks, brain transplants, underground dwellers, and various atomic-powered contraptions, all of which apparently seem far less elegant than the tropes of other genres.

B-films and serials were a key testing ground for science fiction in the 1940s. In addition to smaller, nonintegrated studios like Columbia and Universal, low-budget companies like Republic, Lippert Pictures, and Eagle Lion drove the rise of sci-fi in the 1950s by responding to market trends at the B-filmmaking level that the major studios were unaware of. Hollywood is not a canvas awaiting artists who are moved by their muse to pluck inspiration from past eras and cultural movements in aid of creating innovative works that will transform moviemaking. Hollywood is a machine oiled by the black ink of studio ledgers. Its cogs and gears churn steadily. Innovations rarely emerge without prior warning. New directions arise by testing which paths will bear the most traffic. American science fiction cinema was born out of the steps taken by B-filmmakers in the 1940s, a decade in which sci-fi may not have resembled what the genre would soon become in Hollywood but that was vital to the genre's origins.

NOTES

1   In addition to the academic work done in film history, institutions like the American Film Institute and the Academy of Motion Picture Arts and Sciences play a large role in constructing the mental models of cinema (which include values of aesthetic judgment and cultural importance, for a start) for many filmgoers.

2   See J. P. Telotte, *Science Fiction Film* (Cambridge: Cambridge University Press, 2001).

3   Mark Bould, "Adapting Flash Gordon," *Film International* 5, no. 2 (2007): 18–26.

4   J. P. Telotte, *A Distant Technology: Science Fiction Film and the Machine Age* (Hanover, NH: Wesleyan University Press, 1999).

5   Vivian Sobchack, *Screening Space: The American Science Fiction Film* (New Brunswick, NJ: Rutgers University Press, 1987).

6   François Truffaut, "Dr. Cyclops," in *Focus on the Science Fiction Film*, ed. William Johnson (Englewood Cliffs, NJ: Prentice-Hall, 1972), 48.

7   Truffaut, "Dr. Cyclops," 48.

8   Blair Davis, *The Battle for the Bs: 1950s Hollywood and the Rebirth of Low-Budget Cinema* (New Brunswick, NJ: Rutgers University Press, 2012).

9   William Johnson, "Introduction," in *Focus on the Science Fiction Film*, 7.

10 Thomas O. Beebee, *The Ideology of Genre: A Comparative Study of Generic Instability* (University Park: Pennsylvania State University Press, 1994), 11.

11 Fredric Jameson, *The Political Unconscious: Narrative as a Socially Symbolic Act* (Ithaca, NY: Cornell University Press, 1982), 106.

12 Colin MacArthur, *Underworld USA* (London: Harvill Secker, 1972), 20.

13 Blair Davis, "Horror Meets Noir: The Evolution of Cinematic Style, 1931–1958," in *Horror Film: Creating and Marketing Fear*, ed. Steffen Hantke (Jackson: University Press of Mississippi, 2004), 191–212.

14 This distinction between emotion and intellect might also be framed in terms of the potential for films to be mere commercial products versus works of art capable of inciting change. Judith Hess Wright (echoing the Marxist critique of popular culture in works like Theodor Adorno and Max Horkheimer's *Dialectic of Enlightenment*) notes how genre films often serve as pleasant, cathartic distractions from real-world problems: "These films came into being and were financially successful because they temporarily relieved the fears aroused by the recognition of social and political conflicts; they helped to discourage any action that might otherwise follow upon the pressure generated by living with these conflicts. Genre films produce satisfaction rather than action, pity and fear rather than revolt. They serve the interests of the ruling class by assisting in the maintenance of the status quo." Hess Wright, "Genre Films and the Status Quo," in *Film Genre Reader III*, ed. Barry Keith Grant (Austin: University of Texas Press, 2003), 42.

IV

STUDIO LABOR
AND OPERATIONS

8

HOLLYWOOD

Promoting Collaboration

Charlie Keil and Denise McKenna

In the preface to *The Classical Hollywood Cinema*, David Bordwell, Janet Staiger, and Kristin Thompson launch their study with a series of definitions of Hollywood, the source of American classicism. They do so to demonstrate the breadth of meanings that Hollywood has accrued as a cultural phenomenon, ideological force, and economic dynamo. The authors also effectively differentiate *their* invocation of Hollywood from prevailing narratives in American film history: for Bordwell, Staiger, and Thompson, the term "Hollywood" primarily stands in for a mode of production that shaped the formal norms of the emerging classical filmic text. Yoking Hollywood to classicism underscores the historical specificity of this mode of cinematic practice.

We would like to break apart that dyad temporarily to focus on the gradual construction of "Hollywood" as a meaning-laden place-name during the same period as classicism's inception. Unlike classicism, the term "Hollywood" possessed no aesthetic pedigree, no previously established connotations. Instead, the meanings attached to Hollywood were fashioned as the American film industry came of age and acquired a position of prominence within the cultural landscape. The selection of "Hollywood" as the site and synonym for a mature, if distinctive, industry gained impetus from a series of discourses, all aiming to invest the manufacture of motion pictures with industrial, managerial, and cultural credibility. Rooting the practices of the film industry in a specific place made sense from a promotional standpoint and allowed specific attributes, including cohesiveness, stability, and predictability, to be tied to the very workplaces that were instituting departmentalized production methods eventually labeled the "studio system."

Yet as much as that system depended on a hierarchical and stratified division of labor, it also required various types of intradepartmental and inter-studio collaboration. The idea of creative collaboration, then, was central not only to the studio system but also to the image of "Hollywood" promulgated by the film industry. Additionally, the ongoing conflict between *artistry* (or, at the very least, a form of imaginative labor) and *industry* remained an animating tension that pervaded depictions and definitions of Hollywood. A photo illustration from a 1925 book called *Mirrors of Hollywood* literalizes such contradictions: here, Frank Borzage's command over the camera substantiates his authority to explain the requirements for screen fame. The representation of his casual directorial control is reinforced by a cut-out image beneath him of women extras in scanty costumes (from the set of a Lubitsch film) being painted for a scene. At once charming and persuasive, the fanciful collage suggests that this combination of director and technology has the power to manage both the anarchic energy of its talent and the gendered chaos that lurks just below the surface of any Hollywood production.

Hollywood's unique manufacturing conditions necessitated a particular form of collective labor whose very instability and volatility required constant readjustment, especially during the industry's early years on the West Coast. Successfully promoting filmmaking as a positive force required the industry to align its immediate economic goals (the efficient production of motion pictures and their wide distribution) with the firmly established values of the community where it had made its home. Accordingly, collaboration became a key element in Hollywood's self-definition, permeating the discourse that defined studio labor but also informing the cooperative strategies adopted in the industry's relations with external agents.

In what follows, we will examine how diverse types of collaborative labor functioned across three distinct yet overlapping areas, all central to the production of Hollywood's emergent identity. That identity ultimately helped knit together the industrial and aesthetic foundations of the classical studio system. Moving from the national to the municipal, we will examine the early studio system's bicoastal management structure, the organization of protective professional bodies as a form of proto-cluster collectivity, and the promotion of Hollywood as an idealized space for living and working, primarily in the pages of the local journal *Holly Leaves.*[1]

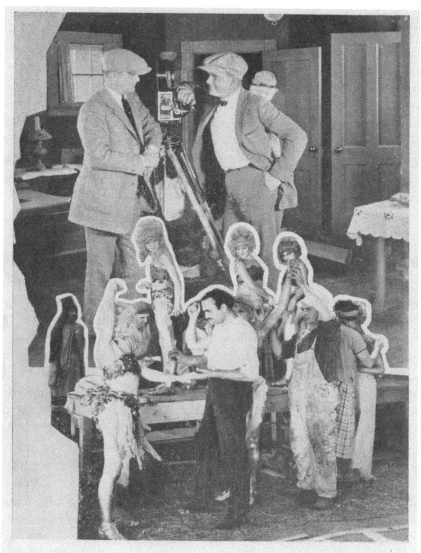

FRANK BORZAGE, NOTED DIRECTOR, EXPLAINS TO CHARLES
DONALD FOX WHAT IS REQUIRED OF THOSE WHO SEEK
SCREEN FAME.
PAINTING EXTRAS FOR SCENES IN "SO THIS IS MARRIAGE."

8.1. Photo collage from Charles Donald Fox's *Mirrors of Hollywood* (1925).

Across each of these case studies, we trace how obstacles to settling in Los Angeles—physical distance from the East, a paucity of local resources, and cultural conservatism—were resolved by the alliances forged among filmmakers, industry executives, city boosters, and real estate developers. These foundational collaborations were essential to Los Angeles becoming a filmmaking center, although they were later obscured and superseded by the broader project of producing "Hollywood" as an idealized representation of the American film industry. Critically, the project of creating "Hollywood" brought together community and industry to fashion a site that could be profitably promoted. For this reason, collaboration strikes us as a key feature of industrial self-definition and ultimately an important if often overlooked factor in connecting the meanings of "Hollywood" to the sustenance of classicism.

BICOASTAL MANAGEMENT AND THE SCENARIO PROBLEM

Learning how to collaborate effectively was put to the test when filmmaking companies found themselves split between two sides of the continent. The shift to the West Coast as the primary home for film production was already well underway in 1915, when trade journals estimated that close to three-quarters of all films produced were being made in the Los Angeles region: such a shift occasioned a concomitant adjustment in the film industry's management model. This transition to California-based production, particularly for companies previously operating out of only one Eastern city, required an adaptive approach to the newly bifurcated structure. And the demands of new management approaches were exacerbated by the burgeoning rate of production hastened by West Coast expansion, requiring procedures that would offset increased production expenses and infrastructure investment. Ideally, companies would learn to devise consistent approaches to style and narrative as a functional solution to mass-producing compelling stories.

To see how this played out in practical terms, we can examine the case of Famous Players-Lasky, the forerunner of Paramount. During the pivotal 1916–19 period, Cecil B. DeMille managed West Coast operations, while Jesse Lasky took charge of production in the East. Famous Players-Lasky, headed by Adolph Zukor, was at the forefront of a newly devised distribution system that saw production companies selling blocks of feature films to exhibitors, using rising stars as the incentive for the purchases. The success of Famous Players-Lasky's approach called for accelerated production schedules that were dependent on the constant supply of filmable scenarios. But perusal of the archival record of memos generated within the company during the late 1910s reveals how scenario creation remained a vexing problem for Famous Players-Lasky. Procuring appropriate source materials and converting those materials into useable continuity scripts put a premium on consistent creativity and posed significant challenges to cost containment and management efficiency, thereby highlighting bicoastal tensions.

As Charles Eyton, an executive at the Lasky Hollywood studio, pointed out in a letter from December 12, 1917, improperly prepared scenarios were a function of inadequate oversight, and they guaranteed economic uncertainty; as he put it, "Time is still the essential thing in this business, and time unnecessarily lost in story preparation is the foundation on which all other losses build, as everybody and everything stands by—waiting for the scenario." [2] It is clear that the scenario becomes contested terrain in correspondence between Lasky and DeMille, which is rife with frustration over insufficient script preparation: Lasky is desperate to maintain an adequate supply and exercise quality control through a centralized scenario department based in the East, while DeMille chafes at the directives coming from New York that threaten his managerial autonomy. As early as 1916, DeMille was demanding that the matter of script preparation be taken up "immediately with the Board [to] discuss the establishment of a department out here [i.e., in Hollywood], with Billy [i.e., William, Cecil's brother] to head same and have five writers. [Otherwise] the present scenario method will undo all that I have done in past three years and I do not propose to see the structure here that I have built destroyed." [3] By 1917, DeMille does concede that establishing a parallel West Coast–based committee system for vetting script material (as recommended by Lasky and probably including New York–based personnel) would be advisable but still resists any implication that East Coast staffers are somehow better equipped to assess script quality:

> I note in your report that the scenario department frequently uses this phrase, "the Home Office." While there is no question in anybody's mind that the New York office is the seat of government, there is considerable doubt in our minds that it is the seat of great literary and dramatic discernment. . . . I do not believe that we should be considered as a branch office and our ideas and suggestions treated as those of a "country cousin." [4]

Ultimately, the claims of management teams on each coast would be reconciled, with a clearer division of duties established. However, one could say that if DeMille lost his battle, Hollywood eventually won the war: although large-scale financial planning continued to occur on the East Coast, matters germane to the studios were largely the province of the vice president in charge of production, stationed on the West Coast. Tellingly, as the center of creative decision-making shifted to Hollywood, control of the studios became the province of producer-manager figures such as Lasky, elevated to the role of mogul, rather than director hybrids such as DeMille. Hollywood's future model of creative collaboration would firmly position filmmakers within a hierarchical structure that circumscribed the director's power to a substantial degree, in a system that ensured the maintenance of the predictable aesthetic standards upon which classicism depended.

CLUSTERS AND COMMUNITY

As the Lasky-DeMille correspondence indicates, the film industry's establishment on the West Coast during a ten-year period encompassed numerous jurisdictional skirmishes. But the embattled industry also endured incessant reputational crises. Chastened legally for exploitative content, lambasted in the press for predatory hiring practices and star scandals, and subject to restrictive zoning practices by the Los Angeles City Council, the film industry often found itself on the defensive. These crises point to how external pressures forced individual and otherwise competitive studios to consolidate their position as a collective in order to negotiate with the city and to refine the leadership roles of producers and directors as industry spokesmen. In fast order, various protective organizations, such as the Motion Picture Directors Association, the Motion Picture Conservation Association, the Motion Picture Protective Organization, and the Motion Picture Producers Association, were formed, in the years 1915–16, as the industry was challenged to account for itself institutionally and aesthetically. But if the formation of earlier bodies such as the Motion Picture Patents Company was largely driven by market forces, the establishment of associations in the midteens bespoke a desire for reputational enhancement seeking cultural influence and not just profit. These newly created professional organizations mimicked local power structures and helped craft an "official" voice that could speak for the industry in meetings involving the city, women's groups, and business organizations.

Perhaps more critically, protective bodies aided in the construction of the social networks necessary for effective collaboration across competitive interests, a key feature in Hollywood's emergence. We can understand this process in relation to the concept of the industrial cluster, wherein "entrepreneurs may act collectively to shape local environments by building institutions that further the interests of the emerging industry. . . . [These] systems of innovation are not due to predictable linear processes, but rely on the adaptive, self-organizing behavior of entrepreneurs, who in turn rely on support from their local environment." [5] The cooperative spirit that led individual companies to cohere around the formation of numerous associations was further extended to include city boosters and media outlets. This expanding collaborative network incorporating film personnel, Los Angeles's broader business community, and the municipal government aligned all of these entities behind the collective effort to ensure healthy regional commerce that was grounded in the film industry's success.

Enlisting "Hollywood" as the preferred name for filmmaking activity functioned as a form of economic speculation fused with discursive calculation. The name emerged as the by-product of often contestatory efforts to integrate the objectives of a wide range of forces whose only common goal was establishing motion picture production in an identifiable, circumscribed, West Coast locale. The productive fusion of small-town values and enterprising business expertise permeates such discourse, an approach typified by efforts of the Hollywood Business Men's Club to attract the industry's distribution arm (including the print manufacturing sector) to Hollywood. The club's rhetoric acknowledged not only the economic benefits but also community building and real estate sales: as the club argued in *Holly Leaves*, "[Such expansion] would bring to Hollywood a larger population of business men, skilled craftsmen, scientific men and experts in photography, who would come with their families to make their homes here and to become integral parts of the community." [6]

The star scandals of the early 1920s and the public relations challenge that the scandals posed pushed *small-town* Hollywood to enlist its own status as a normal and representative community to help shore up the suspect reputation of *filmdom* Hollywood. Ironically, this entailed acknowledging the numerous fault lines that had defined the relationship between the two

Hollywoods. As a *Holly Leaves* article titled "Bridging the Chasm" put it: "What Hollywood needs above all is unity and comm-unity, and the coming into our population of a large element, bound to the motion picture industry on the one side and incorporated into the community life on the other, might result in successfully bridging the chasm that has so long split Hollywood in two." Dependent on the industry for its economic livelihood and cognizant of how cinema's tarnished image could damage its prospects as a growing community, Hollywood could no longer extricate itself from "Hollywood." It could, however, become its better half, functioning as an affirmation of civic normalcy and small-town values. Further downplaying areas of conflict, locally generated discourse foregrounded the more pedestrian industrial dimension of moviemaking: citing gainful employment, minimal pollution, and low noise levels, commentators celebrated the film industry as a model of nonintrusive manufacture even as it sustained the economic monoculture of the community. Reflecting filmmaking's growing centrality to Hollywood as a municipality, *Holly Leaves* increased its coverage of the motion picture industry, reporting not only on social comings and goings but also on productions and guild meetings and introducing a special "Film Feature Section."

This context of enhanced collaboration led to numerous local promotional efforts, including a proliferation of books and pamphlets enumerating the benefits of living in Hollywood. Such publications originated with municipal bodies such as the Hollywood Board of Trade (which became the more substantial Hollywood Chamber of Commerce in 1921) as well as local banks and were typical of the region's long history of booster literature. By encompassing the film industry, these tracts reassured prospective homeowners and tourists, who might have found themselves taken aback by the recent wave of negative press generated by the star scandals, of the region's continuing virtues as a site for play and investment. So while putting the city's best face forward is clearly an act of self-preservation, it is also a defensive strategy that links the two Hollywoods.

These collaborative efforts and attitudes speak, sometimes overtly, to the dual identity—the fusion of community and industry—that "Hollywood" had acquired by this time. And they further speak to the unique quality of the film industry, whose détente with its surrounding community not only allowed for the ascendancy of "Hollywood" but also invested the industry's image with a veneer of stability that imposed order on the disorderly process of being creative. Little wonder, then, that "classical" and "Hollywood" would find themselves twinned qualifiers for a type of cinema that depended upon a bounded form of collaborative creation.

NOTES

1 According to Gregory Paul Williams, *Holly Leaves* began its publication run in 1911 and retained its name until 1925, when its original publisher was bought out by Fawcett Publications and the magazine's name changed to *Hollywood*. See Williams, *The Story of Hollywood: An Illustrated History* (Los Angeles: BL Press), 60, 185.

2 Cecil B. DeMille Papers, L. Tom Perry Special Collections Library, Harold B. Lee Library, Brigham Young University, UT, Box 238, Folder 16.

3 Telegram dated September 13, 1916, Cecil B. DeMille Papers, Box 238, Folder 13.

4 Cecil B. DeMille Papers, Box 240, Folder 1.

5 Maryann P. Feldman, Johanna Francis, and Janet Bercovitz, "Creating a Cluster while Building a Firm: Entrepreneurs and the Formation of Industrial Clusters," *Regional Studies* 39, no. 1 (2005): 130.

6 "Editorial: Bridging the Chasm," *Holly Leaves*, March 26, 1921, 22.

7 "Editorial: Bridging the Chasm," 22.

9

DISNEY, DUPONT, AND FABER BIRREN

HOLLYWOOD AND THE COLOR REVOLUTION

Kirsten Moana Thompson

Color cinematography and the Ink and Paint department were key attractions in Disney films, while also playing a spectacular narrative role in features like *Snow White and the Seven Dwarfs* (Hand 1937) and *The Reluctant Dragon* (Luske and Werker 1941). Celebrating its new color range in Technicolor, Disney's promotional rhetoric emphasized its material color production as novel, exotic, and luxurious.[1] The aesthetic quality of its color was emphasized in a 1930s Disney press release—"In seeking perfection in color reproduction Disney technicians have . . . developed paints which in beauty and reliability excel all watercolors of the past"[2]—and celebrated on-screen in *The Reluctant Dragon*'s "Rainbow Room," in a montage sequence showcasing the Disney Ink and Paint department's transformation of prodiegetic pigments and paints into the final color image. From its first Silly Symphony in color, *Flowers and Trees* (Gillett 1932), color was a value that marked Disney's product as qualitatively different from earlier two-strip subtractive color processes in animation like Technicolor III, Multicolor, or the later Cinecolor.[3] With an exclusive contract for Technicolor IV between 1932 and 1934, Disney produced cartoons with a new color palette that no other cartoon studio could match.[4] With complementary (red and green) and triadic (red, blue, and yellow) color schemes in narratives where toys, candy, and Christmas were frequent devices for expressive display in its Silly Symphony series, like *The Night Before Christmas* (Jackson 1933) or *The Cookie Carnival* (Sharpsteen 1935), Disney also offered a more nuanced pastel palette in the feature film *Snow White*, with light browns, blues, and greens.[5] In its animated stories, the studio imagined color's material production process as magical, even transgressive, with off-screen gender ideologies and labor practices sometimes shaping on-screen representational practices.[6] For example, in *Snow White*, the Wicked Queen uses colored liquids to transform her beautiful surface into an ugly hag, musing to herself:

> Now, a formula to transform my beauty into ugliness, change my queenly raiment to a peddler's cloak. Mummy dust to make me old; to shroud my clothes, the black of night; to age my voice, an old hag's cackle; to whiten my hair, a scream of fright; a blast of wind to fan my hate; a thunderbolt to mix it well; now begin thy magic spell!

The Wicked Queen's spell showcases color's materiality as a transformative agent, while it also alerts us to the connection between cosmetic surface and normative ideas of femininity and beauty. As the Wicked Queen bathes a red apple in a poisonous cauldron of sickly green color, advising us, "Look on the skin! The symbol of what lies within!," her transformation also exposes her literal and metaphorical ugliness. This diabolical corruption

9.1. Animated color on display in the Wicked Queen's laboratory in *Snow White and the Seven Dwarfs* (1937). © Disney Studios.

by means of color links the scene to a long philosophical tradition (*disegno* vs. *colore*) in which color was considered inferior to classical form and in which the line was privileged over hue. Here the supernatural story line is a narrative pretext to foreground color *as color*, as transparent as the laboratory glassware. From the Wicked Queen's magical potions to her bright red apple in its bubbling cauldron, color was in constant transformational change: it was *animated*.

In pioneering the early adoption of Technicolor IV well before most major studios took up the new color process, the Disney studio was a key site in the color revolution for the increasing dissemination of color in popular culture and everyday life, while DuPont's own production of plastics, synthetic chemicals, and other materials for industrial and consumer mass production also shaped interior and exterior color design in the late nineteenth and early twentieth centuries.[7] Beginning in the early 1920s, and as part of its strategic targeting of Hollywood as an important market, DuPont provided two key materials to Disney as the studio produced its cel animation and later expanded into color in 1932: first, the transparent nitrate (and later acetate and plastic) cels under the name of Pyralin, and second, Monastral pigments used by Disney to manufacture its in-house paint for the final artwork produced on these cels. Influenced by color consultants like Faber Birren, whose philosophical and psychological understandings of color informed the range and palette of its product line, as well as its marketing to consumers, business, and government, DuPont in turn helped transform twentieth-century color, from paint to plastics, textiles, lighting, and architecture. As two leading corporations in American manufacturing and entertainment, DuPont and Disney offer a useful case study for understanding the complex intersections of material history and aesthetic design that shaped visual culture in the color revolution.

DUPONT AND DISNEY'S MATERIAL RELATIONSHIPS

Founded on the gunpowder mills on the Brandywine River by E. I. du Pont de Nemours in Wilmington, Delaware, in 1802, the DuPont corporation would become a huge conglomerate by the twentieth century, developing or buying the patents for Nylon, Kevlar, Teflon, Lycra, and hundreds of other chemicals and establishing major industrial and consumer lines in explosives, insecticides, fungicides, rubber, dyestuffs, paints, and pigments.[8] Many

DuPont products stemmed from similar roots, beginning with a twentieth-century expansion shaped by the huge range of products derived from one key raw material, cellulose, or the fiber from the cell walls of plants. Different treatment methods of cellulose with nitric (and, later, acetic) acid led to a huge range of diverse products, encapsulated by its slogan "Better Things for Better Living—Through Chemistry," including Cellophane, celluloid film, Rayon, and Pyralin. In 1912, DuPont's monopoly on the explosives industry ended with an antitrust decision that forced the company to diversify, and the company turned to new markets and users, in particular, the film industry.[9]

DuPont's transparent Pyralin or Pyroxylin plastic film, marketed in 1920 as the "material of a thousand uses,"[10] was a new synthetic plastic that could mimic dozens of natural products from ivory to tortoiseshell and leather, a distinctive feature of what Jeffrey Miekle calls "celluloid's powers of mimicry."[11] Manufactured in tubes, rods, and sheets, it could be bonded to metal, wood, plastic, and glass, and providing insulation against heat, cold, and sound, it had a high structural strength. Pyralin and the later acetate plastic, or "Plastacele," were nonflammable and widely used in consumer devices from fountain pens to combs, piano keys, poker chips, eyeglasses, and toiletry products. In the form of thin sheets called cels, Pyralin was lightweight and abrasion resistant, offering a temporary surface on which artwork could be painted and then photographed frame by frame to create the illusion of movement in animation. Colorlessness and transparency were essential properties ensuring maximal legibility of the vibrancy of colors painted on the palimpsest of cels and background paintings, while the additional benefits of flexibility and durability afforded by plasticizers ensured that the cels could withstand the manipulations of Disney's inkers, painters, and camera operators.[12]

Hollywood was not only a market for DuPont products like Pyralin but also a means by which DuPont promoted the value of its products to other potential customers. In February 1923, "Pyralin's Unique Use in the Movies" appeared in the *DuPont Magazine*, featuring Bud Fisher's popular animated characters Mutt and Jeff from the Raoul Barré studio, along with illustrations provided by *Scientific American* editor and *Cinema Handbook* author A. C. Lescaboura.[13] Although Disney is not mentioned at this early stage, Laugh-o-Gram Studio bankruptcy records show that at least as early as November 30, 1923, DuPont was already a supplier, with Disney invoiced for an unpaid bill for two hundred 20" x 50" sheets of Pyralin.[14]

In the December 1934 issue of the *DuPont Magazine*, Hazel Sewell, head of Disney's Ink and Paint department, appeared in a photo promoting a Pyralin cel of Mickey Mouse, and in the very next issue, DuPont used Disney's popular new character to advertise Pyralin's suitability for animation. On September 6, 1938, in another trade magazine, DuPont advertised Pyralin through its use on the recently released feature *Snow White*, with the company also offering customer service teams to "cooperate with you in determining how Pyralin may be used practically and usefully applied in solving problems pertaining to your business." [15] Meanwhile, correspondence in the 1930s between Disney and DuPont shows the studio's increasing production demands of *Snow White*, with DuPont accommodating them by decreasing the size and width of the Pyralin plastic cels at Disney's request. [16]

DuPont also promoted its other nitrocellulose products to the film industry, from nitrate and replacement safety film to explosives for clearing land for movie production and lacquer paint for set design and movie props. [17] In "Lacquer's Screen Career," DuPont's trade literature suggested that its color paint signified quality and luxury on the sets of Cecil B. DeMille's 1934 production *Cleopatra* and, by extension, that DuPont color was part of the glamour of Cleopatra's court *and* of Hollywood. [18] Even though *Cleopatra* was shot in black and white, the high sheen of DuPont's expensive color paint offered high production values and, as its advertising suggested, transformed cheap props and sets into expensive objects. DuPont trade ads repeatedly emphasized the quality of their Pyralin and Duco paint lines to justify their expensive price tag: "Best—because they have no settling in the can, the pigment being permanently suspended in the solution," said one 1920s ad for Pyralin Enamels. [19]

DuPont and Disney's material relationship extended from Pyralin plastics and paints into black-and-white and color pigments. Disney established an Ink and Paint department in its first studio in Kingswell in 1923. A problem encountered by all animation studios was that off-the-shelf Grumbacher paints failed to adhere to the slippery surface of the nitrate cels, and eventually specialized manufacturers like the Catalina Color Co. (later Cartoon Colour Co.) would emerge to supply the animation industry with specialty paints that would adhere to these surfaces. However, unlike Warner Bros. and MGM, the Disney studio shifted to manufacturing its own paint, as it was cheaper to buy the pigments from suppliers like DuPont and produce paints in bulk on the studio lot.

The luminosity, hue, and saturation of animated colors on-screen were shaped by the use of specific prodiegetic materials, from the pencils, pastels, chalks, and watercolor or oil paints to the lighting conditions employed and the type of platen glass under which the cels were photographed. Similarly, the cinematographic processes in which these cels were then photographed and printed, and the conditions under which the films were projected, from ambient illumination to the light bulbs, lens, and focus of the projector, also affected the sharpness and brilliance of the colors exhibited, as Disney was all too aware.[20]

Made by the women of the Ink and Paint department with the assistance of a specialized laboratory, paint was manufactured following color formula index cards, together with their specific "letdowns," the lighter or darker tints that compensated for the multiple cel layers that made up the composite artwork of cel animation. Having acquired the Krebs Company in 1929, which focused on lithopone and titanium dioxide, DuPont specialized in the bulk of Disney's most vibrant colors.[21] Comparisons between the paint product codes on Disney's color formula cards based on the Munsell color system and the 1941 catalog *Du Pont Standard Pigment Colors* reveal these pigment preferences.[22] The brilliancy of DuPont pigments included chrome yellows, chrome greens, iron blues, and organic lakes and toners, particularly Pthalocyanine blue (BT-297 D, which was sold under the trade name Monastral blue) and Platinum Violet (BP-273-D), which were used for rich detailing like the Wicked Queen's and Snow White's purple and blue costumes in *Snow White*.[23] By 1953 DuPont also offered new pastel hues derived from titanium dioxide, such as blue-green, copper, pink, and rose, that cut across product lines, from automobiles to telephone handsets, printing inks, floor coverings, and textile fibers.[24]

After the shift in 1939 to the new Burbank studio, the Color Paint Lab headed by Mary Weiser and the Production Process Lab headed by Emilio Bianchi were established. Disney employee Herman Schultheis described the color production process in this way:

> The paints are mixed in the paint lab at the studio from formulas by trained chemists. Pigments (animal, vegetable and mineral) are ground and mixed. Several hundred hues with 7 values each (from dark to light) are kept here. Inharmonious colors are avoided and

pastel shades are used mostly. Color schemes have to be changed when character moves from sun into shadow, etc.[25]

Disney's opaque paint had a much higher quotient of gum arabic in comparison to Warner Bros's unstable casein-based paint. Its textural thickness made the paint adhere to the cel and gave it a jewel-like quality because the pigments would sink to the bottom, with the paint above it, adhering to the cel and enhancing its intensity.[26] As my previous research has shown, the color formulas confirm that there was a qualitative difference in Disney paint: its colors were more brilliant because of its vibrant DuPont pigments, while its technical application was easier because of its greater viscosity and elasticity.[27]

Thus far, we have seen that Disney's use of DuPont Pyralin, pigments, and paints demonstrated the studio's insistence on quality and vibrancy in its prodiegetic materials, enriching the artwork photographed by its Technicolor cameras that would in turn position Disney as an innovative technological leader in the use of color in Hollywood and animated film markets. Manufacturing its paints in bulk from DuPont pigments not only saved Disney money but also afforded it creative control to broaden and nuance its rich color palette for its feature films, while also using color as an important brand signifier of aesthetic value and spectacle. Similarly, DuPont's targeting of the Hollywood film industry was an important part of the company's diversification of its products, from celluloid to lacquer paint, in which DuPont marketed its goods as indices of aesthetic luxury and value, while also using the glamour of its association with stars like Mickey Mouse to cross-promote itself to other business. For both Disney and DuPont, color played a central role in their promotional strategies to differentiate themselves in the marketplace. DuPont was a leading producer of the synthetic raw materials for the consumer goods and services that would feed the color revolution, while Disney's early adoption of synthetic pigments marked the company out as an innovative producer of the entertainment industry in color. Each company would also come to use the services of a leading color engineer, designer, and philosopher named Faber Birren (1900–1988).

FABER BIRREN AND COLOR AT WORK

In early 1939, as part of Walt Disney Studio's newly established internal training program, in which notable scholars, artists, and teachers offered lectures for its animation workers, leading color consultant Faber Birren delivered ten talks at the studio over two weeks, discussing "the history, science, psychology and modern applications of color."[28] Birren authored forty books and 254 articles on color, and his consultancy American Color Trends pioneered industrial color design for factories, hospitals, schools, and companies, including DuPont, Monsanto, Allied Chemical, and General Electric. To enhance productivity and safety in factories, Birren developed a color-coded system (orange for alerts, green for safety equipment, yellow for hazards, blue for caution, and so on) and also produced similar color protocols for the US Navy, Army, and Coastguard. His influential work understood that functionalist color design minimized eye fatigue, maximized visibility, and directed visual attention, producing an unconscious form of automatic response in the worker: "The trick is to establish a seeing condition that automatically, in and of itself, makes the task easier."[29] Birren also specialized in the psychological effects of color design, advising how changing hues could help advertising and businesses through talks, trade articles, and journalism.[30] Designing a Color Conditioning program for DuPont that examined the psychological effects of color in industrial and consumer spaces like factories and offices,[31] Birren made specific recommendations for changes in hue in order to enhance consumer appetite and increase spending; in his words, "color has become a valuable *worker* on the plant pay roll."[32]

Trained at the Art Institute of Chicago, Birren developed color preferences that were strongly influenced by Ewald Hering and Wilhelm Ostwald, and his consulting for both Disney and DuPont emphasized the ways in which color perception played an active role in color preferences that was rooted in human physiology.[33] Birren is an important figure who links the corporate world of industrial and consumer mass production to art, through his close focus on psychology and the cultural and historical understandings of color aesthetics. His lecture "Color Preferences," delivered on April 20, 1939, at Disney, drew from Birren's newly published *Monument to Color* (1938)[34] and was supplemented by demonstrations to the Disney artists of "paints, lights, and other materials, making his teachings visible, memorable, and most importantly, true to color."[35] Birren's color theories built from his art history training, discussing, for example, how the chiaroscuro work of da Vinci or Rembrandt revealed their intuitive understanding of hue, light, and shadow. From these Birren developed his own theories of color harmonies that were built around tints, tones, and shades. Influenced by Hering's triangular chart of color, as well as theories by Ostwald, Birren developed a color chart that mapped these principles in a triangle made up of seven forms (hue, white, black, tint, shade, tone, and gray), for his ultimate goal was the systematization of color harmonies that could be deployed in mass culture: "Good color in industry, in products and commodities of everyday consumption, is high art. It is art spread everywhere among people and applied to the things they need and the things that answer their human wants." [36]

In his lecture to the Disney artists, Birren pointed out the role of color preferences in consumer attention in retail, describing research by "a manufacturer of toilet articles" that "found that people like red and blue; next is purple, then green, with orange and yellow last." [37] Birren's observations around color preferences drew upon certain chromophobic and gendered cultural assumptions, asserting that "the negro ranks red and blue highest," along with "children, Indians and primitive peoples," and "even in insane asylums the greatest response will be to red and blue—they are the two big thrills." [38] Yet regardless of what people claimed ("What people say they like isn't always the thing they will respond to"), Birren argued that "in most everything we studied so far there is a consistent reminder that it is the simple things that people respond to—red, blue and green." [39] Birren's approach to color understood it as sensation, but one that could be scientifically studied: in *Monument to Color*, he said, "Argue all you want that color is emotional and therefore beyond rule and law—the fact remains that even emotion can be sensibly analyzed." [40] Birren emphasized that the important thing was to think in terms of the mass: "You're not concerned with 'functional' color schemes" but with "the mass of people with the absolute type of color preferences," and elsewhere he noted that "it is always the mass reaction that counts." [41] He concluded that "I have tried to play with color freely . . . hoping that out of this will grow an attitude on your part that will make you think of *all* people, of *audiences* rather than *individuals*." [42] Faber considered the Disney artists to be critical shapers of color preferences, as he urged them, "I think it is your problem not to ask people what they like, but to *know* what they like." [43]

Birren's philosophies of color shaped the industrial palette through his functional color design for DuPont's textiles, paints, and plastics divisions, while his focus on blue, red, and green and contrasting color schemes in his lectures for the Disney company emphasized mass appeal in color preferences. Like his work in industrial color design as the *automatization* of the attention and energy of the worker by minimizing eyestrain and directing visual atten-tion, Birren's approach to the cultural aesthetics of color returns repeatedly to a focus on mass preferences, whereby the artist's role should be to mediate these mass preferences. In this focus on the mass, the midcentury color consultants, or color "engineers" as they were called, exemplify the design principles of the corporations for whom they worked, in which color could be scientifically measured, understood, and reverse engineered.

Animated color was a material product of industrial modernity. From DuPont's corporate research that produced new synthetic pigments and plastics to the aesthetic manifestos of color consultants like Birren, Disney's use of DuPont plastics and pigments as production materials enabled a rich color range and a scintillating jewel-like quality in the studio's prodiegetic artwork. The contractual relationships of supply and demand were also mutually beneficial, enabling each company to cross-promote their products as endowed with values of luxurious quality. Disney and DuPont's business relationship helped underscore a color revolution that was manufactured, designed, and consumed to order: in the words of Faber Birren, "Color is a modern art, built upon modern progress." [44]

NOTES

1   For more on Disney's Ink and Paint Department's color paints and pigments, see Kirsten Moana Thompson, "'Quick—Like a Bunny!' The Ink and Paint Machine, Female Labour and Color Production," *Animation Studies* 9 (Febru-ary 2014), https://journal.animationstudies.org/kirsten-thompson-quick-like -a-bunny/, accessed February 6, 2019.

2   "Premium" (Walt Disney Studios Press Release, [n.d]). Walt Disney Clippings, 1938–1946, Publicity Ephemera, UCLA Performing Arts.

3   James Layton and David Pierce, *The Dawn of Technicolor, 1915–1935* (Roch-ester, NY: George Eastman, 2015), 268–77.

4   However, Ted Eshbaugh made an important early Technicolor IV test cartoon, *Wizard of Oz* (1932–33), that was never theatrically released. John McElwee, "A Cartoon Pioneer We've Forgotten," *Greenbriar Picture Shows* (blog), Octo-ber 21, 2014, http://greenbriarpictureshows.blogspot.com/2014/10/a-cartoon -master-weve-forgotten.html, accessed February 6, 2019.

5   Robert Herring described it this way: "The new Technicolour [*sic*] gives clear full yellow, pale blue that is clean. Light browns as well as dark browns; rich

ivy green besides emerald and olive. The lightest of colors are possible, shell pinks, the strange greens of layers of water, lily white." Herring, "The Cartoon Color-Film," *Close Up*, March 10, 1933, 86.

6   See Kirsten Moana Thompson, "Colorful Material Histories: The Disney Paint Formulae, the Paint Laboratory and the Ink and Paint Department," *Animation Practice, Process and Production* 4, no. 1 (2014): 45–66. Contemporary artist Sarah Maple's photographic installation *Snow White the Scientist* (2011) underscores the transgressive connection between femininity and color production in her *Princess Series*, which reimagines Disney heroines in modern workplaces. See https://www.sarahmaple.com/portraits, accessed February 6, 2019.

7   Regina Lee Blaszczyk, *The Color Revolution* (Cambridge, MA: MIT Press, 2012). Key texts on Disney color include Richard Neupert, "Painting a Plausible World: Disney's Color Prototypes," in *Disney Discourse: Producing the Magic Kingdom*, ed. Eric Smoodin (New York: Routledge, 1994), 106–17; J. P. Telotte, *The Mouse Machine: Disney and Technology* (Urbana: University of Illinois Press, 2008); and Esther Leslie, *Hollywood Flatlands: Animation, Critical Theory and the Avant-Garde* (London: Verso, 2002).

8   E. I. du Pont de Nemours & Company, *DuPont: The Autobiography of an American Enterprise: The Story of E. I. Du Pont de Nemours & Company* (New York: Scribner/Simon and Schuster, 1952); and Alfred Du Pont Chandler and Stephen Salisbury, *Pierre S. Du Pont and the Making of the Modern Corporation* (New York: Harper, 1971).

9   Luci Marzola, "'Better Pictures Through Chemistry': DuPont and the Fight for the Hollywood Film Stock Market," *Velvet Light Trap* 76 (Fall 2015): 7.

10 "Collection of 9 Folders Illustrating the Advertisements of Pyralin," *DuPont Advertisements* (Wilmington, DE: E. I. du Pont de Nemours & Co.), 6, DuPont Collection, Manuscripts and Archives Department, Hagley Museum and Library, Wilmington, DE.

11 Cited in Nicole Shukin, *Animal Capital: Rendering Life in Biopolitical Times* (Minneapolis: University of Minnesota Press, 2009), 108.

12 Because of these plasticizers, the surface of the artwork eventually became an unstable chemical compound subject to cracking, chipping, and degassing. Kristen McCormick and Michael R. Schilling, "Animation Cels: Preserving a Portion of Cinematic History," *Conservation of Plastics* (Spring 2014): 1–7.

13 "Pyralin's Unique Use in the Movies," *DuPont Magazine*, February 1923, 5.

14 Michael Barrier, *The Animated Man: A Life of Walt Disney* (Los Angeles: University of California Press, 2007), 335n91; Timothy Susanin, *Walt Before*

Disney: Disney's Early Years, 1919–1928 (Jackson: University Press of Mississippi, 2011), 242n57.

15 Photo in the *DuPont Magazine*, December 1934, 10; R. T. Ellis, "Behind the Scenes with Mickey Mouse," *DuPont Magazine*, February 1935, 5; advertisement for *Snow White*, September 6, 1938, courtesy Russell Merritt, 2015.

16 "Animation's Volatile Relationship with Plastic," June 1, 2015, https://d23 .com/getty-animation-research-library/, accessed February 6, 2019.

17 "How Mighty Is Dynamite?," *DuPont Magazine*, November 1934, 1, 16.

18 N. Laing, "Lacquer's Screen Career," *DuPont Magazine*, February 1935, 8–9, 24; D. V. Gregory and A. V. Wetlaufer, "How Glossy Is Glossy?," *DuPont Magazine*, April 1930, 18.

19 "DuPont Pyralin Enamels: Best for Non Breakables," *DuPont Advertisements*, Group A, Papers 4 and 5 (n.p.), DuPont Collection.

20 For Disney's efforts to educate projectionists, see Paul R. Cramer, "Cooperative Job Ahead," *International Photographer* 10, no. 2 (1938): 22–26.

21 The formula cards also indicate other suppliers: Hoover (browns, blacks); SCM (yellows, cadmium reds); Harcros/Pfizer (oxide reds, yellows and greens); and Mobay/ Harmon and Imperial/Harshaw (reds/MV6606 or Red 88; MX686 or Red 83).

22 *Du Pont Standard Pigment Colors* (Wilmington, DE: E. I. du Pont de Nemours & Co., ca. 1941), DuPont Collection.

23 Disney Color Laboratory/Ink and Paint Department records; Lew Stude, interview by author, Burbank, CA, May 1, 2014, and August 1–3, 2015.

24 Emily Heine, "Color Sells Itself," *DuPont Magazine*, April–May 1957, 2–5.

25 John Canemaker, *The Last Notebook: Herman Schultheis and the Secrets of Walt Disney's Movie Magic* (Los Angeles: Walt Disney Family Foundation Press, 2014), 251. All paint consists of three major ingredients: the pigment (or hue); the vehicle or base in which the pigment is suspended (oil or water); and the binder, which can offer gloss, elasticity, or strength, together with softeners for pliability and humectants to attenuate drying.

26 Stephen Worth, interview and correspondence with author, Pacoima, CA, April 30, 2014, and August 13, 2015.

27 Thompson, "Colorful Material Histories," 55.

28 Birren, "Color Preferences" (Lecture, April 20, 1939), in *Before Ever After: The Lost Lectures of Walt Disney's Animation Studio*, ed. Don Hahn and Tracy Miller-Zarnecke (Los Angeles: Disney Editions, 2016), 286.

29 Birren, "Color in the Plant," *DuPont Magazine*, October 1945, 10–16.

30   Birren, "Color and You," *DuPont Magazine*, June 1948, 16–17.

31   Birren, "Color and You," 17.

32   Birren, "Color in the Plant," 16; italics added.

33   Walter Sargent, *The Enjoyment and Use of Color* (New York: Scribner, 1924); Faber Birren, *Monument to Color* (New York: McFarland, 1938), 34–35.

34   Birren, *Monument*, 34.

35   Birren, "Color Preferences," 286.

36   Birren, *Monument*, 50.

37   Birren, "Color Preferences," 289–90. Although Birren doesn't state who the manufacturer is, I believe it's likely to be DuPont, given his prior relationship with the company.

38   Birren, "Color Preferences," 291–92.

39   Birren, "Color Preferences," 289.

40   Birren, *Monument*, 11, 27.

41   Birren, "Color Preferences," 289, 291.

42   Birren, "Color Preferences," 292; italics added.

43   Birren, "Color Preferences," 292.

44   Birren, *Monument*, 27.

10

B-FILM PRODUCTION AND RISK MANAGEMENT AT WARNER BROS. IN THE LATE 1930s

Kyle Edwards

Even as they showcased spectacle and excess on-screen, much to the delight of audiences, and often celebrated such practices in the promotional campaigns for their films, major studios of the classical Hollywood era developed management structures and production practices that sought to minimize the risk inherent in their industry, one in which each of their products carried significant financial uncertainty. As Chris Bilton notes in his analysis of risk and strategy in the creative industries, media producers struggle with the inherent problem of creating "symbolic goods" for which they must project the "future value" of each product in setting production and marketing budgets.¹ Media companies seek a variety of ways to limit that uncertainty, most notably the utilization and promotion of actors (or stars), as well as preexisting film genres, with built-in audience awareness and, therefore, reliable commercial appeal. During the classical Hollywood studio era, vertical integration offered another opportunity for some firms to exert more control over their products and, as a result, to minimize risk.

I will explore here some of the ways in which companies sought to offset uncertainty internally, by increasing efficiency through the careful planning of production schedules, the systematic deployment of contract labor to accommodate those schedules, the precise budgeting and monitoring of each production, and the repurposing of sets, costumes, and other property, all in an effort to limit unnecessary spending and to prevent the loss of unused or underutilized resources. These measures, when implemented successfully, can offer significant benefits, while paradoxically presenting additional challenges to the organization and the commercial potential of its products.[2]

To demonstrate how efficiency found its way into the Hollywood film industry, we need to go back to the first decade of the twentieth century, when Frederick Winslow Taylor, a mechanical engineer by trade, published a series of papers that outlined his theory of scientific management. Taylor maintained that the solution to diminishing natural resources and competition in international markets could be found in the careful measurement and mathematical analysis of existing industrial practices and the subsequent design of systems to maximize production capacity. "The best management is a true science, and the fundamental principles of scientific management are applicable to all kinds of human activities," wrote Taylor in *The Principles of Scientific Management* (1911).[3]

Further support was offered in Harrington Emerson's *The Twelve Principles of Efficiency* (1911), which described how wasteful practices had led to the demise of businesses and nation-states throughout history and then outlined a series of steps by which attentive readers, by increasing productivity, could achieve a "new morality," where "ideas, . . . not labor, not capital, not land [create] wealth."[4] Books and articles advocating efficiency in such areas as housekeeping, religious observance, and academic study soon appeared, while an "Institute of Efficiency," led by Emerson, was formed and promised prospective students the opportunity to learn "the art of getting more results with less work . . . [and] get the most out of your brain and your body."[5]

By the 1920s, large corporations and government agencies had absorbed the ethos of scientific management, and business leaders in various industries touted their success stories, with US Secretary of Commerce Herbert Hoover spearheading the effort to "maximize worker, managerial and industrial productivity" and instituting a "war on waste"—or "Hooverizing," as it was called—that led to the landmark study *Waste in Industry* (1921).[6] Throughout the 1920s, Hoover's efforts led to the institution of standardized systems of weights and measures, as well as uniform packaging for canned goods, loaves of bread, and other consumer products.

Efficiency became a central tenet in the industrial organization and operations of the American film industry, which experienced rapid growth and consolidation throughout the 1920s.[7] The largest filmmaking corporations, now vertically integrated and with vast corporate umbrellas, enormous employee pools, and intricate chains of communication, assiduously planned the production, distribution, and exhibition of each film and carefully accounted for all costs and revenues. To ensure the continuous use of personnel, property, assets, and exhibition outlets, most of the major studios established A-units and B-units for production and then subdivided their A-units further according to production and marketing budgets.[8]

Perhaps no major filmmaking corporation embodied the tenets of efficiency like Warner Bros., where the concept permeated nearly all areas of long-term planning and day-to-day operations. Efficiency represented a strategy—a "system" indoctrinated in nearly all levels and branches of the corporation, informing decisions that extended from production scheduling, to employee management, to set design, to story development and enabling the studio to maximize the productivity of present resources, whether those "materials" represented props, production equipment, or employees.[9] As production chief Jack Warner explained, "[With] an entire cast and crew standing around and doing nothing and collecting salary, we have to get things moving!"[10]

In a December 1937 profile of Warner Bros. in *Fortune*, company treasurer Abe Warner compared his company with another paragon of industrial efficiency, Ford Motor Company: "The Ford of the Movies is how Major Abe Warner likes to think of Warner Bros. . . . [T]hey lead the low-price field and the profit to Warner is in the volume rather than in an occasional smash hit." *Fortune* elaborates, "By never buying unnecessary stories, rarely making retakes, and always knocking temperament on the head where they can, the Warners probably get more production money onto the screen than any other studio."[11] Here the *Fortune* article identifies a series of decisions at Warner Bros. that eliminate waste and, in their cumulative power, yield "maximum productivity," as Frederick Winslow Taylor once described the goal of scientific management. For Taylor, such an approach could create "maximum prosperity"; for Warner Bros., the results are not only financial but also behavioral, serving to codify employee conduct—that is, "knocking temperament on the head"—and to inform story selection and development—enabling the distinction between necessary and "unnecessary" stories.

Perhaps no individual was more important to Warner Bros.'s administration of efficiency than Darryl Zanuck, the associate executive in charge of production between 1925 and 1933. The young executive not only oversaw production on the lot but also formulated an incredible number of stories for Warner Bros. films. Allegedly, Zanuck was responsible for the scenarios and parts of the scripts for up to twenty films per year, wrote under four names, and possessed the ability to generate story ideas and compose script drafts in the span of twenty-four hours. The young producer's working methods—turning out story ideas and scripts quickly and thus condensing the story development process—clearly matched the predilections of his employer, who was devoted to minimizing story costs by reducing the need for writers. As Jack Warner once commented, "[Zanuck] could write ten times faster than any ordinary man." [12]

Warner Bros. and the rest of the film industry began to feel the effects of the Depression in 1931. Fiscal restraint was placed at a premium. But this practice was nothing new to the company, where Jack Warner had gained a reputation for his constant attention to wasteful practices and unnecessary expenses. According to legend, he checked lights before leaving the studio each night, made sure that all props and costumes were returned to the appropriate departments, and kept workers in plain view so as to quell "loafing." While informal and generally unaccountable in the ledgers, these methods had an important effect on decisions made throughout the organization: they indoctrinated a culture of efficiency at the studio, where all employees were under the view of the studio chief and expected to conform to his standards of behavior and operations. For example, until the mid-1930s, Warner Bros. producers generally did not receive screen credit for pictures they oversaw; among their various tasks in managing production, the most important according to Warner was to identify, report, and eliminate wasteful practices on the set.

In business organizations, such methods have the advantage of simplifying complex chains of communication and clarifying corporate strategy to ensure all employees understand, internalize, and dutifully execute a company's objectives. At Warner Bros., the continuous presence of Jack Warner at the studio, his direct communication with top management (Albert Warner and Harry Warner) and executive producers (Zanuck and later Hal Wallis), and the limitation of employee empowerment and reward led to the desired "temperament" among personnel and, in turn, to a company-wide devotion to efficiency. [13]

The establishment of a B-unit at Warner Bros, which was formalized with the appointment of studio producer-director Bryan Foy as head of B-films, and an emphasis upon series filmmaking in the mid-1930s enabled Warner Bros. to wring additional value out of company-controlled resources.

As John Sedgwick and Michael Pokorny observe in their essay "The Risk Environment of Film Making," this production category also allowed the company to balance its "portfolio of products," which in turn offset some of the risk associated with the company's mid- and high-budget film releases.[14]

The miniscule budgets and condensed shooting schedules associated with B-films coincided with Warner Bros.'s ethos of efficiency. So too did series filmmaking. As Tino Balio has observed, "By keeping production costs in line with this ready-made demand, series pictures [were] almost guaranteed a profit."[15] The very nature of the series film carried the promise of a subsequent installment, thus building audience awareness and offering a dependable product for exhibitors. In addition, each entry in a film series allowed for an increasing level of production efficiency.[16] By the late 1930s, Warner Bros. had instituted a production emphasis in the film series, with B-film releases based around original and adapted characters such as the Dead End Kids, Nancy Drew, and the female reporter-detective Torchy Blane.

The *Torchy Blane* series, which included nine B-films released between 1937 and 1939, demonstrates the relationship between Warner Bros.'s principles and its practices with respect to film production.[17] Warner Bros. instituted the *Torchy* series through the acquisition of a short story, titled "No Hard Feelings," by short story writer Frederick Nebel.[18] Sensing the potential for multiple films around the fast-talking, whip-smart reporter Torchy Blane, the company paid Nebel and pulp detective magazine *Black Mask* for the rights to the twenty-five Torchy Blane stories and the characters appearing therein.[19]

Although the deal included the promise of screen credit to Nebel, the author's name did not appear on the title credits for *The Adventurous Blonde* (McDonald 1937) and *Blondes at Work* (McDonald 1938). As one studio employee wrote: "Very possibly this is because the Torchy Blane pictures which we are making are virtually 100% original. . . . On the other hand, the pictures on which his credit was neglected, being B pictures, may simply have been released without his seeing them."[20] As this memo indicates, Warner Bros. prioritized the use and reuse of the title character, whom studio staff writers had been placing in original scenarios for their weekly wage and then assigning the rights to the studio for the grand sum of one dollar.[21]

The *Torchy Blane* films were budgeted modestly, with production costs running between $116,000 and $156,000, and produced quickly, with shoots lasting from nineteen to twenty-one days. Unit managers kept constant tabs on the production schedule, cast, and crew, communicating with production manager T. C. Wright, who in turn reported to Foy and Warner through a series of daily reports. One such instance occurred during the production of *Smart Blonde* (McDonald 1937), when Carrol Sax wrote to Wright that the shoot had fallen behind by a day due to the amount of work required of Glenda Farrell and to the inexperienced director and crew.[22] A memo (dated June 17, 1937) from Sax to Wright during the production of *The Adventurous Blonde* expressed continuing concerns about director McDonald: "McDonald made 12 takes in one setup and 8 in another. Had a long talk with him today and suggested that he watch excessive takes and pickups. I advised him that in a case like this Mr. Warner might object very seriously. McDonald understands and in the future will govern himself accordingly."[23] Despite his tendency to request additional takes and pickups, McDonald kept the four *Torchy* films he directed under budget, as did the cast and crew, who became increasingly efficient as the series continued into 1938 and 1939. The expiration of McDonald's contract led Foy to rotate through several directors for subsequent installments of the series.

Not until William Beaudine was assigned to direct *Torchy Gets Her Man* (1938) did Warner, Wright, and Foy find a director who could maximize productivity and efficiency during production. "One-Shot Beaudine," as he later became known, brought in each of his two *Torchy* films well under budget and ahead of schedule.[24] Initially, Beaudine's tendency to avoid retakes and integrate stock footage excited unit manager Lee Hugunin, who reported to Wright in August 1938: "This director has averaged approximately 21 setups per day for every day since the picture started. He is constantly saving money by working with us and shooting out of continuity whenever it is to our advantage from a cost standpoint."[25] The following day, Hugunin praised Beaudine's resourcefulness: "Beaudine looked at stock shots of the Garden Party shot by Berkeley for one of the *Goldigger* [*sic*] productions and he found several excellent shots that he can use. He also looked at scenes from the Submarine sequence in MURDER WILL OUT and [found] several good cuts he can use."[26] Later, though, that pattern began to cause concern. Hugunin writes:

> Picture finished with sixty-one minutes of time and the Supervisor is beginning to worry about the possibility of being short on footage. . . .
> As of AUGUST 31, the day before the picture closed, we accrued charges of $114,576 as against the budget of $156,000, which leaves a balance of $41,000. This exceptionally large overage on a FOY picture

10.1. A page from the original pressbook for *Smart Blonde* (1937), which introduces the Warner Bros. series to exhibitors. *Cinema Pressbooks of the Major Hollywood Studios*, Oakland University.

is due principally to its having been budgeted for 21 days, whereas the director brought it in in 16 days, and throughout the picture continuously cooperated in the matter of using our stock and saving expense along every other line possible. . . . This picture is a shining example of what can be accomplished when the director is pulling with the Production Office 100 per cent.[27]

Although this report seems to mark the culmination of Jack Warner's edict to "keep things moving" and, by so doing, to maximize efficiency, Beaudine was not assigned to any more *Torchy Blane* films and soon left Warner Bros. to direct for B-film producers Monogram Pictures, Producers Releasing Corporation, and others.

In the *Torchy* series and, more generally, in the production policies and management culture it instituted in the 1930s, Warner Bros. demonstrates the degree to which the structured integration of efficiency into commercial film production could increase productivity and limit waste and thereby offset the risk associated with each film release. However, these practices could also threaten the morale of its employees, the perception of originality associated with each film, and therefore the commercial potential (or "future value") of its products.[28]

Just as important at Warner Bros., an efficiently run production unit—or, in this case, a hyperefficient unit—might carry the unexpected consequence of mitigating managerial control, in a sense ceding control to the system itself. As one might expect, this did not sit well with Jack Warner. By 1940, Warner Bros. had abandoned most of its film series, ending the *Nancy Drew* and *Torchy Blane* series and loaning out the *Dead End Kids* ensemble to Universal for a spate of features and serialized shorts under the *Little Tough Guys* moniker. Ironically, this assumption of increased financial exposure through a prioritization upon A-films was motivated in part (and in a cyclical feature of risk taking described by Sedgwick and Pokorny) by the confidence the company gained through its successful efforts to increase productivity and decrease risk through B-film production in the 1930s.

NOTES

1   Chris Bilton, *The New Adhocracy: Strategy, Risk and the Small Creative Firm* (Warwick: Centre for Cultural Policy Studies, 1999).

2   For examinations of risk in the context of the film industry, see Michael Pokorny and John Sedgwick, "The Financial and Economic Risks of Film Production," in *Film and Risk*, ed. Mette Hjort (Detroit, MI: Wayne State University Press, 2012), 181–96; M. B von Rimscha, "Managing Risk in Motion Picture Project Development," *Journal of Media Business Studies* 6, no. 4 (2009): 75–101; Anna Dempster, "Managing Uncertainty in Creative

Industries: Lessons from Jerry Springer the Opera," *Creativity and Innovation Management* 15, no. 3 (2006): 224–33; Robert G. Picard, "Unique Characteristics and Business Dynamics of Media Products," *Journal of Media Business Studies* 2, no. 2 (2005): 61–69; Vincent T. Covello and Jeryl Mumpower, "Risk Analysis and Risk Management: An Historical Perspective," *Risk Analysis* 5, no. 2 (1985): 103–20.

3   Frederick Winslow Taylor, *Principles of Scientific Management* (New York: Harper & Brothers, 1911), 7. Taylor's additional papers on scientific management include "Shop Management," "The Art of Cutting Metals," "A Piece Rate System," and "Notes on Belting."

4   Harrington Emerson, *The Twelve Principles of Efficiency* (New York: The Engineering Magazine, 1911), x, 27–35. By 1917, *The Twelve Principles of Efficiency* was already in its fifth edition. Also instrumental in validating scientific management was Henry L. Gantt, whose Gantt chart enabled companies to time and record each shop floor operation from beginning to end and, by so doing, identify inefficiencies in current practices. See Gantt, *Work, Wages, and Profit* (New York: The Engineering Magazine, 1910).

5   "Advertisement: Institute of Efficiency," *Literary Digest*, 1917, reprinted in Cecelia Tichi, *Shifting Gears: Technology, Literature, Culture in Modernist America* (Chapel Hill: University of North Carolina Press, 1987), 80. Tichi reprints several advertisements heralding efficiency and offers a valuable summary of the efficiency movement in popular culture and its influence on literary culture and form (75–96).

6   Hoover, "Industrial Standardization," reprinted in *Scientific Management Since Taylor*, ed. Edward Eyre Hunt (New York: McGraw-Hill, 1924), 189–96. Hoover also wrote the foreword to *Waste in Industry* (New York: McGraw-Hill, 1921), which was based on extensive surveys of production practices in various American industries and sponsored by the Committee on Elimination of Waste in Industry of the Federated American Engineering Societies. While waste has numerous meanings, here I use the term as the "unrealized value" resulting from the misuse or inactivity of company-controlled resources. This sense of waste is based on the expositions of the concept offered in David Rockefeller's *Unused Resources and Economic Waste* (Chicago: University of Chicago Press, 1941) and W. H. Hutt's *The Theory of Idle Resources* (London: J. Cape, 1939), both of which were contemporary to the period under scrutiny in this chapter.

7   For a longer description of this arrangement and its rationale, see Tino Balio, *Grand Design: Hollywood as a Modern Business Enterprise, 1930–1939* (Berkeley: University of California Press, 1993), 73–76, 98–107.

8   In *The Classical Hollywood Cinema*, Janet Staiger examines the transition to a producer-controlled management organization, which enabled companies to assume tighter control over rising costs and the increasingly complex sets of tasks demanded in motion picture production. Staiger argues that the central-producer system descended directly from scientific management, the need for which became especially vital with the standardization of "classical Hollywood film technique," and the emergence of the feature-length film as the dominant product of film exhibition. According to Staiger, "Both of these factors required production planning," as well as active oversight by managers during and after production. David Bordwell, Janet Staiger, and Kristin Thompson, *The Classical Hollywood Cinema: Film Style and Mode of Production to 1960* (New York: Columbia University Press, 1985), 128–38.

9   There are several excellent accounts of the history of Warner Bros. during this period, including Nick Roddick, *A New Deal in Entertainment: Warner Brothers in the 1930s* (London: BFI, 1983); Douglas Gomery, *The Hollywood Studio System: A History* (London: BFI, 2005); Thomas Schatz, *The Genius of the System: Hollywood Filmmaking in the Studio Era* (New York: Holt, 2015); Cass Warner Sperling and Cork Millner, *Hollywood Be Thy Name: The Warner Brothers Story* (Rocklin, CA: Prima, 1994); and David Thomson, *Warner Bros: The Making of an American Movie Studio* (New Haven, CT: Yale University Press, 2017).

10   "Memo: Jack L. Warner to Walter MacEwan," December 12, 1937, quoted in Robert Gustafson, "The Buying of Ideas: Source Acquisition at Warner Bros., 1930–1949," PhD diss., University of Wisconsin–Madison, 1993, 179.

11   "Warner Brothers," *Fortune*, December 1937, 110–13, 206–20.

12   Quoted in Schatz, *Genius of the System*, 62.

13   As Schatz observes, "Warners directors, in particular, were attuned to a factory-based assembly-line production system." In this system, directors and writers were valued for their productivity. Those individuals exhibiting this trait, like director Mervyn LeRoy, were granted a higher level of authority and creative control. Schatz, *Genius of the System*, 139–40.

14   John Sedgwick and Michael Pokorny, "The Risk Environment of Film Making: Warner Bros in the Inter-War Years," *Explorations in Economic History*

35, no. 2 (1998): 196–220. The author's analysis of Warner Bros.'s strategy during this period is based on Mark Glancy's invaluable examination of the company's box office performance in "Warner Bros. Film Grosses, 1921–1951: The William Schaefer Ledger," *Historical Journal of Film, Radio and Television* 15, no. 1 (1995): 55–74.

15   Balio, *Grand Design*, 101.

16   For further discussion of the logic of series filmmaking, see Kyle Edwards, "'Monogram Means Business': B-film Marketing and Series Filmmaking at Monogram Pictures," *Film History* 23, no. 4 (2011): 386–400.

17   Warner Bros. produced nine *Torchy Blane* films: *Smart Blonde* (McDonald 1937), *Fly-Away Baby* (McDonald 1937), *The Adventurous Blonde* (McDonald 1937), *Blondes at Work* (McDonald 1938), *Torchy Blane in Panama* (Clemens 1938), *Torchy Gets Her Man* (Beaudine 1938), *Torchy Blane in Chinatown* (Beaudine 1939), *Torchy Runs for Mayor* (McCarey 1939), and *Torchy Blane: Playing with Dynamite* (Smith 1939).

18   Frederick Nebel, "No Hard Feelings," *Black Mask* (February 1936).

19   "Agreement: Warner Bros. Pictures and Frederick Nebel," *TORCHY BLANE* SERIES (1937–1939), Box: 2881, File: *Torchy Blane* Series, Warner Bros. Collection, University of Southern California Special Collections (hereafter referred to as Warner Bros. Collection).

20   "Memo: MacEwan to Obringer," January 27, 1938, *TORCHY BLANE* SERIES (1937–1939), Box: 2881, File: *Torchy Blane* Series, Warner Bros. Collection.

21   See, for example, the agreement for *Torchy Finds Out*: "Agreement: Warner Bros. Pictures and Albert Demond," August 19, 1938, *TORCHY BLANE* SERIES (1937–1939), Box: 2881, File: *Torchy Blane* Series. Warner Bros. Collection.

22   "Memo: Sax to Wright," n.d., *TORCHY BLANE* SERIES (1937–1939), Box 1494A, File: *Smart Blonde* 115, Warner Bros. Collection.

23   "Memo: Sax to Wright," June 17, 1937, *TORCHY BLANE* SERIES (1937–1939), Box: 1494A, File: *Adventurous Blonde* Production Reports, Warner Bros. Collection.

24   For further information about Beaudine, see Wendy L. Marshall, *William Beaudine: From Silents to Television* (Lanham, MD: Scarecrow Press, 2005).

25   "Memo: Hugunin to Wright," August 23, 1938, *TORCHY BLANE* SERIES (1937–1939), Box 2161, File: *Torchy Blane in Chinatown*, Warner Bros. Collection.

26 "Memo: Hugunin to Wright," August 24, 1938, *TORCHY BLANE* SERIES (1937–1939), Box 2161, File: *Torchy Blane in Chinatown*, Warner Bros. Collection.

27 "Memo: Wright to Hugunin," September 2, 1938, *TORCHY BLANE* SERIES (1937–1939), Box 2161, File: *Torchy Blane in Chinatown*, Warner Bros. Collection.

28 The studio correspondence reprinted in Rudy Behlmer's *Inside Warner Bros. (1935–1951)* (New York: Fireside Books, 1985) offers a vivid depiction of the conflict between the company and several actors, including (but by no means limited to) James Cagney, Humphrey Bogart, and Bette Davis.

11

STOCKING THE STABLES

Universal-International's Talent Development Program, 1949-56

Bradley Schauer

One of the most significant changes in the postwar American film industry was the transition away from long-term studio labor contracts, as part of what Janet Staiger has described as the shift to a "package-unit" system driven by fewer, more expensive independent productions rather than the mass production across budget categories that characterized the classical studio era.[1] The postwar box office recession and the Supreme Court–ordered divorcement and divestiture of the vertically integrated studios' theater chains contributed to the general decline in feature film production that had begun during the war. With fewer films in production it was no longer cost-effective to keep hundreds of workers under contract; therefore, beginning in 1948 and continuing through the 1950s, the number of contract personnel across Hollywood fell sharply.[2] Actors were no exception: by 1953 the number of actors under contract had plunged from approximately 750 in 1947 to only about 300.[3] The most famous stars went into business for themselves, using their newfound independence to demand higher salaries and creative control. But the average studio player was simply laid off and left to scrounge for work. At the beginning of 1953, the *Hollywood Reporter* predicted that "there will be no more than a handful of long-term contracts at any of the major studios" by year's end.[4]

One beacon of hope for the aspiring actor was Universal-International (U-I), which not only kept a sizable stable of contract players through the mid-1950s but also committed to training young actors through its talent development program, the most elaborate of its kind in postwar Hollywood.

The uniqueness of U-I's approach to star development in the early 1950s was a function of its unusual industrial status at the time; as a studio with relatively limited resources but great ambition, it hoped to avoid high-priced stars by developing homegrown talent that it could control with low-cost, long-term contracts. Described by fan magazine *Picturegoer* in 1954 as Universal's "most important single contribution to the cinema," the talent school was attended by actors such as Rock Hudson, Clint Eastwood, and Piper Laurie.[5] In the end, however, the school failed to generate sufficient star power to justify its costs (at its peak, Universal boasted that it was spending $1 million a year on the program).[6] Ironically, some of the school's students, most notably Tony Curtis, went on to become major stars, but for other studios. The talent program was created in part to provide cheap talent for U-I's inexpensive Westerns and action films, but the low industrial status of these films effectively prevented actors like Curtis from reaching their star potential at the studio that trained them. The failure of its talent school was an important indication that U-I's position in the marketplace had to change if it were to survive. By the end of the 1950s, U-I had mostly replaced its young talent and mass-produced genre films with fewer, more expensive films led by top stars. This enabled the studio to transcend its status as a "major minor" and become one of the most successful film companies of the postclassical era. Yet the influence of U-I's acting program would continue well into the 1960s as the major studios turned to fresh talent to act in their television programs, as well as to gain leverage against the contractual demands of established stars.

Like most of the major film studios, Universal had a talent program for several years in the mid-1930s.[7] The idea resurfaced in 1949 when Universal-International (Universal had merged with independent studio International Pictures three years earlier) hired Sophie Rosenstein, who had been the drama coach at Warner Bros. since 1938 and had authored the 1936 book *Modern Acting: A Manual*. Rosenstein brought the same rigorous training program from Warner Bros. to U-I; she was well known for her script analysis classes in which actors-in-training would study characters' motivations and goals. Additionally, Rosenstein led her classes in the close analysis of a new film each week, often slowing down the footage, stopping it, or muting the audio track so students could focus on body movement and gestures.[8] When Rosenstein died of cancer in 1952 at the age of forty-five, she was replaced by Estelle Harman, who had taught and directed at the University of Southern California and the University of California, Los Angeles. In 1954 Broadway director Jess Kimmel took over as head of the school for its remaining two years.[9]

Aside from film and script analysis, the curriculum at the talent program included diction, dance and rhythmic movement, horseback riding (essential for credibility in U-I's Westerns), swimming, fencing, and gymnasium, with each class having its own dedicated instructor.[10] Students attended lectures from the heads of different departments at U-I; directors and writers offered seminars focused on the relationship between narrative and performance;[11] and stars from other studios, such as Marlon Brando and Rod Steiger, visited and met with the aspiring actors.[12] When they weren't appearing in films, the students would work on the studio lot, performing basic dialogue looping duties or helping with screen tests.[13] Off the lot, they would be sent to premieres or on national publicity tours to polish their public relations skills and introduce themselves to exhibitors.[14]

U-I's revival of its talent program in 1949 was linked to an important shift in the studio's production strategies. For the previous three years, the studio, newly under the management of International's Leo Spitz and William Goetz and looking to establish itself as a major distributor, had dropped nearly all B-films and emphasized big-budget releases, often produced independently and featuring well-known talent. This proved financially disastrous: the expensive films attracted good reviews but limited interest at the box office, and there were no profits from B-films to compensate for the losses. Chastened, the studio developed a new, split production model: the first category involved A-films with top independent stars, who were paid a percentage of the gross rather than a salary. The profit participation deals allowed the studio to produce A-films at relatively low budgets, because the star's salary was back-loaded. The first and best-known example of this arrangement was James Stewart's deal for *Winchester '73* (Mann 1950): unable to meet Stewart's usual salary of $250,000, U-I agreed to pay the actor half of the studio's earnings, after production and distribution costs were subtracted.[15] Both Stewart and U-I profited from the deal: *Winchester '73* earned over $2 million at the box office while costing only $850,000, and Stewart earned more than twice his typical asking price. U-I continued this practice with a number of other male stars, including Errol Flynn, Tyrone Power, and Alan Ladd.[16]

The other category of films produced by U-I in the early 1950s were programmers, mid-budget films (about $700,000) that were aspirational

A-films or B-films upgraded with Technicolor, location shooting, or narrative gimmicks (like Francis the Talking Mule, who starred in a wildly popular series of films from 1950 to 1956). The intention was to convince first-run exhibitors to book the films on a percentage basis at the top of the bill, despite their limited budgets. This proved a successful strategy for U-I, which earned a profit from approximately three-quarters of the twenty to thirty programmers it released each year. The small but relatively reliable profits from programmers kept the studio in the black through the mid-1950s.[17]

U-I's return to the high-volume production strategy of the 1930s and 1940s necessitated cheap and versatile in-house talent who could perform in several films a year. The new acting school was the ideal way to cultivate this talent. Each actor was signed to the usual seven-year contract, with starting weekly salaries ranging from $75 to $150 and renewal options (with raises) every six months.[18] According to Patrick McGilligan, as many as sixty actors were interviewed for the talent program each month, with approximately ten receiving a formal audition, two or three a screen test, and perhaps only one accepted into the program itself.[19] Once he or she had gained entry to the talent program, a student's progress was monitored by production executives, who read monthly reports penned by instructors. Each year the school's actors presented a talent show at the four-hundred-seat Phantom Theater on the Universal lot to an audience consisting of critics, agents, and, most important, casting directors from other studios. If an actor made an impression, U-I would gladly loan them out to a competing studio; not only would U-I pocket the loan-out fee, but if the actor went on to star in a high-profile film for another studio, it would only increase his or her value to U-I upon the actor's return. U-I casting director Robert Palmer declared that the costly talent show "returns its value to the studio many times in loanout terms alone."[20]

Aside from the earnings generated from loan-outs, U-I's talent development program of the 1950s also helped to legitimate the studio, which, having been known for low-budget films for so long, was eager to bolster its status in the new postwar marketplace. The publicity around the program emphasized the high cost, rigor, and thoroughness of the school's training: for example, a 1955 feature article in the Long Beach *Independent Press-Telegram* declared that in the studio's "million dollar 'college of movie knowledge,'" the "young players work harder in class than they do in pictures."[21]

This kind of publicity also worked to feed the talent program, as U-I built a reputation as a studio that would support young actors. For instance, when arriving in Hollywood, Tony Curtis sought out Universal because he knew it, among all of the majors, was looking for industry newcomers.[22]

However, enhancements to the studio's public reputation aside, if one were to judge U-I's talent program based solely on its ability to create stars, it was surely a failure. In 1954, Robert Palmer claimed that the studio would be happy if one actor per year broke out as a top box office attraction.[23] Even by this modest standard, the school did not yield strong results. Over the school's initial seven-year run, Rock Hudson was the only student who became a major star for Universal.[24] War hero Audie Murphy starred in over twenty Westerns for U-I from 1950 to 1966, but with the exception of the autobiographical hit *To Hell and Back* (Hibbs 1955), these were programmers (or cheaper) that were only modestly successful at the box office. Other actors, like George Nader and Julie Adams, starred primarily in programmers with the occasional costarring role in a higher-profile A-film. More common was the fate of actors like Ruth Hampton and Bradford Jackson, who appeared in a few bit parts before being released from their contracts.

One impediment to the success of U-I's talent program was the reluctance of exhibitors to book films starring new talent, unless they were in a supporting role accompanying a headlining star.[25] In addition, anecdotal evidence suggests that the opportunities given to talent school actors were limited due to systemic problems within the studio itself. In his book on Clint Eastwood, Richard Schickel writes that U-I's casting department saw the talent program as a threat and was reluctant to cast actors from the school. According to former contract player Brett Halsey, producers considered the acting students nonprofessional and felt as though it was beneath them to cast them. In Eastwood's retrospective view, the acting students were "untouchables."[26] This lack of synergy between the talent school, which represented a considerable investment for U-I, and the personnel responsible for placing the students in features represents a significant breakdown in the studio's management structure.

But the most important factor behind the failure of the talent program was U-I's heavy reliance on programmers, which were not effective talent showcases. Intended to appeal to "action houses," or neighborhood theaters that specialized in Westerns, war films, and other male-oriented genres, programmers were designed to employ a fast narrative pace; however, this left little room for characterization that extended beyond broad archetypes.[27] Limited by generic roles, actors were unable to distinguish themselves. For male stars, U-I's programmers called for a traditional rugged masculinity that was becoming somewhat outmoded in feature films as the 1950s progressed. Steven Cohan has argued that U-I's two top male stars of the period, Rock Hudson and Tony Curtis, performed masculinity in a complex fashion that blurred conventional boundaries between male and female, heterosexual and homosexual, with Hudson as a sensitive and wholesome "pureboy" and Curtis as the male equivalent of a "glamour girl."[28] These were precisely not the actors best suited for he-man roles as gunfighters and swashbucklers, with Hudson starring in *The Golden Blade* (Juran 1953) and *Gun Fury* (Walsh 1953) and Curtis in *The Prince Who Was a Thief* (Maté 1951) and *Son of Ali Baba* (Neumann 1952). It was only when Hudson and Curtis moved away from action programmers that they achieved real stardom. Likewise, after leaving U-I, actresses like Piper Laurie and Shelley Winters found their calling as character actors rather than as the romantic leads in various Westerns and adventure films.

Culturally and industrially, programmers were also considered an inferior product—financially successful relative to their budgets but lacking the marketing push or distribution to deluxe theaters that an A-film would receive. By casting promising talent in films like *Smuggler's Island* (Ludwig 1951) and *Taza, Son of Cochise* (Sirk 1954), U-I was not only limiting its visibility in the marketplace but also running the risk that it would become associated exclusively with second-class material. Ironically, as U-I was not yet directly involved in television production, experience in programmers was most useful as training not for A-level features but for television, where action genres proliferated. Many actors, from Hugh O'Brien (*The Life and Legend of Wyatt Earp* [1955–61]) to Jack Kelly (*Maverick* [1957–62]) and Clint Eastwood (*Rawhide* [1959–66]), went on to find success in television for other studios after being dropped from U-I's talent program.

Finally, U-I's liberal loan-out policy, while it may have generated easy money for the studio, ultimately worked against the talent program. Tony Curtis is a case in point: signing with U-I in 1948, Curtis was cast in a number of bit parts and quickly became popular with teenagers due to his striking good looks. As press agent Frank McFadden noted in 1961, "In six months the fan magazines were giving him star-type treatment, even though he was still only a bit player."[29] In November 1950, Curtis was the subject of a lengthy feature article in *Modern Screen*, though he did not receive his first starring role until 1951.[30] By 1957 Curtis was a legitimate star, but it was due not to the steady stream of routine programmers in which he starred for U-I but rather to the projects for which he was loaned to other studios. Curtis's agent, Lew Wasserman, endeavored to cast him in supporting roles in A-films; the actor's first breakthrough was in *Trapeze* (Reed 1956), a smash hit released by United Artists and starring Burt Lancaster. This led to supporting roles in *Sweet Smell of Success* (Mackendrick 1957), for which Curtis received critical acclaim, as well as United Artists' blockbuster *The Vikings* (Fleischer 1958) and *The Defiant Ones* (Kramer 1958), for which the actor received an Oscar nomination.

In theory, by starring in hit films for other studios, Curtis was only increasing his value to his home studio. But U-I was not equipped to take advantage of their contract player's new fame. After *Trapeze*, Curtis starred in two crime programmers at U-I that barely cracked $1 million at the box office. Wasserman then negotiated a new contract for Curtis in which he could alternate between U-I and other studios.[31] Not only did U-I not get full access to its star, but because Curtis was receiving a percentage of the gross by this point in his career, his salary costs to U-I were no different than those of an independent star.[32] Curtis should have been the ideal success story for U-I's talent program, but instead his career trajectory highlighted its limitations. Upon achieving stardom, Curtis distanced himself from U-I's training: in a 1961 *Life* magazine profile, the actor insisted that he regularly cut classes, and a year later in *Variety*, he "ridiculed the idea that he had learned anything from the talent program itself," arguing that the school only served to foster homogeneity among the studio's actors.[33]

In August 1956, U-I overhauled the talent program, focusing not on untrained talent but on those who had already attended drama school.[34] The studio could no longer afford to wait several years to see if raw talent could be shaped into something special; it was investing several years of training and salary in actors who either never became stars or, like Curtis, took too long to become stars. Television was also beginning to serve as an effective training ground for young actors, rendering the talent program largely superfluous. Jess Kimmel resigned at the end of 1956, and the school was closed.[35] Universal continued to sign young actors, with the intention of putting them in higher-profile films rather than programmers. In September 1957, U-I executive Alfred E. Daff argued, "There is no sense in talking about developing young talent if you cast them in mediocre pictures. You must take the initiative and make the investment." [36]

With programmers struggling in the face of competition from television, the studio closed for nearly six months at the end of 1957. U-I reemerged as a lean, modern studio with a limited production slate focused almost exclusively on A-films like *Pillow Talk* (Gordon 1959) and *Imitation of Life* (Sirk 1959). Ironically, other studios were moving in the opposite direction, signing young talent to long-term contracts in the hope of securing leverage against stars who demanded profit participation. For instance, Twentieth Century-Fox, increasing its in-house production output in the late 1950s, opened a talent school in the Universal mold that ran from 1957 to 1962. [37] Other studio talent schools emerged intermittently over the course of the 1960s, providing low-cost contract players for both film and television. After its merger with MCA in 1962, Universal reintroduced its talent development program, now run by talent agents Monique James and Eleanor Kilgallen. The company initially signed sixty-seven actors, forty-five of whom were assigned to television programs produced by MCA's Revue Studios. [38] By the end of the 1960s most of the studio-based talent schools had closed, with studios realizing that production levels were simply too low and talent programs too expensive and inefficient to be useful. The one holdout, appropriately enough, was Universal, which did not close its program until 1980. [39] Decades after the talent school founded by Sophie Rosenstein closed, Universal had remained committed to the dream of the homegrown superstar.

NOTES

1   David Bordwell, Janet Staiger, and Kristin Thompson, *The Classical Hollywood Cinema: Film Style and Mode of Production to 1960*. (New York: Columbia University Press, 1985), 330–38.

2   Thomas M. Pryor, "Axing in Hollywood," *New York Times*, July 18, 1948, X3.

3   Bosley Crowther, "Picture of Hollywood in the Depths," *New York Times*, June 14, 1953, SM17.

4   "Long-Term Deals on Way Out," *Hollywood Reporter*, January 20, 1953, 1.

5   Donovan Pedalty, "How Hollywood Makes Its Stars Shine," *Picturegoer*, September 25, 1954, 18.

6   Pedalty, "How Hollywood Makes Its Stars Shine," 18.

7   "U's New Face Coast School," *Variety*, May 9, 1933, 2.

8   Cynthia Baron, *Modern Acting: The Lost Chapter of American Film and The-ater* (London: Palgrave MacMillan, 2016), 178–81.

9   Baron, *Modern Acting*, 244.

10 "Stock Player System Returns to Hollywood," *Los Angeles Times*, October 1, 1950, 9.

11 Philip K. Scheuer, "U-I School for Stars Profits Handsomely in Talent and Money," *Los Angeles Times*, May 31, 1953, D1, 4.

12 Peter McGilligan, *Clint: The Life and Legend* (New York: St. Martin's Press, 2002), 74.

13 Richard Schickel, *Clint Eastwood: A Biography* (New York: Vintage Books, 1996), 67.

14 Scheuer, "U-I School for Stars"; "Exhib Hypo for New Pix Faces," *Variety*, December 12, 1951, 16.

15 Marc Eliot, *Jimmy Stewart: A Biography* (New York: Harmony Books, 2006), 245–46.

16 Philip K. Scheuer, "Top Stars Now Share in Profits of Motion Pictures," *Los Angeles Times*, July 24, 1955, D2.

17 See Bradley Schauer, "First-Run and Cut-Rate: Universal-International and the Postwar Programmer," *Quarterly Review of Film & Video* 35, no. 4 (2018): 349–71.

18 "Stock Player System"; Tony Curtis with Peter Golenbock, *American Prince: A Memoir* (New York: Three Rivers Press, 2009), 6.

19 McGilligan, *Clint*, 59.

20 Scheuer, "U-I School for Stars," 16.

21 "The Three R's in Hollywood," *Independent Press-Telegram*, September 25, 1955, 159.

22 Curtis with Golenbock, *American Prince*, 3.

23 "U-I Talent Program Costs $1,000,000," *Motion Picture Daily*, October 27, 1954, 1, 12.

24 Jeff Chandler was also technically a student in the program in the early 1950s but had already been cast in his Oscar-nominated role as Cochise in Fox's *Broken Arrow* (Daves 1950) before U-I's program began.

25 "Exhib Hypo for New Pix Faces," *Variety*, December 12, 1951, 1, 16.

26 Schickel, *Clint Eastwood*, 73–74.

27 Schauer, "First-Run and Cut-Rate."

28 Steven Cohan, *Masked Men: Masculinity and the Movies in the Fifties* (Bloomington: Indiana University Press, 1997), 297–99, 308–9.

29 Shana Alexander, "Bee-yoody-ful Life of a Movie Caliph," *Life*, November 17, 1961, 169.

30 Jane Wilkie, "Nobody's Pretty Boy Now," *Modern Screen*, November 1950, 31–32, 103–6.

31 Curtis with Golenbock, *American Prince*, 179.

32 "'Sorehead Producers Bum-Rap Stars But Not to Their Faces'—Tony Curtis," *Variety*, May 1, 1963, 5, 21.

33 Alexander, "Bee-yoody-ful Life"; "Tony Curtis Sans Agent," *Variety*, October 3, 1962, 4.

34 "U Tightens Up on Entry Rules for Tyro Players," *Variety*, August 22, 1956, 4.

35 "Jess Kimmel Resigns," *New York Times*, December 15, 1956, 20.

36 "Daff's 'Formula U' on Star-Building: Spot 'em Where It Counts—Big Pix," *Variety*, September 11, 1957, 7, 12.

37 Philip K. Scheuer, "Giant Talent Hunt Started by Twentieth Century-Fox," *Los Angeles Times*, May 5, 1957, E1; "Fox Talent School Ends," *Boxoffice*, June 11, 1962, W-5.

38 "U-MCA's Longrange 'New Faces' Program," *Variety*, December 5, 1962, 2.

39 "TV, Pic Co. Formed by Kilgallen, James," *Variety*, November 5, 1980, 6.

V

REREADING RACE

12

CENSORING RACISM

THE PRODUCTION CODE AND HOLLYWOOD'S CHINESE AMERICANS

Philippa Gates

While scholars have analyzed the impact of the Production Code in terms of the on-screen representation of sex and violence, its regulation of race has not been explored to the same extent. And, while Susan Courtney, Thomas Doherty, Francis Couvares, and Ellen C. Scott have explored the Code in relation to the representation of African Americans,[1] the discussion of the representation of the Chinese and Chinese Americans has been limited to only a couple of scholars focusing on a couple of films: Doherty and Eric Smoodin on *The Bitter Tea of General Yen* (Capra 1932), Hye Seung Chung on *Shanghai Express* (von Sternberg 1932), and Ruth Vasey on *West of Shanghai* (Farrow 1937).[2] On the topic of race, the Code did not offer extensive guidance, only that "the history, institutions, prominent people and citizenry of all nations shall be represented fairly."[3] What exactly "fairly" meant seemed to be open to interpretation by both producers and the Production Code Administration (PCA); however, certainly the Chinese government and its international representatives felt that Hollywood required guidance on the matter.

The debate continues over whether being present on the screen is positive in and of itself—even if as a stereotype. Richard Rushton and Gary Bettinson confirm that "distinguishing between positive and negative images remains an important, if overemphasized area of debate."[4] This chapter is intended to contribute to current scholarship on the representation of race with its focus on not *whether* images are positive or negative but instead *why* they are. There is an assumption that Hollywood's images of the Chinese and Chinese Americans were solely the product of a screenwriter's imagination, a film producer's race bias, or the industry's reflection of broader social hierarchies and inequities. In this chapter, however, I will show through specific film examples how decisions about raced representations were vetted by regulatory bodies and intentionally allowed, altered, or eliminated. In other words, the representation of race on the screen was the product of a complex negotiation of censorship issues, political interests, and shifting social attitudes. From the dissatisfaction of Chinese American groups and the Chinese government with American representations of the Chinese to the attempt by the Office of War Information (OWI) to improve diplomatic relations with China during World War II, there were many individuals and organizations with a vested interest in Hollywood's representation of Chinese people. Through an examination of the correspondence between the PCA, the OWI, and film producers, I will demonstrate that the PCA's motivation for avoiding racist representations on-screen was not social progressivism but predominantly commercial protectionism.

YELLOW PERIL

Race relations in the United States since World War II have been defined mainly through the comparison of white and black experiences; however, from the mid-nineteenth century to the mid-twentieth, white American fears about racial and cultural purity focused on the Chinese. As John Kuo Wei Tchen argues, "The use of Chinese things, ideas, and people in the United States, in various imagined and real forms, has been instrumental in forming this nation's cultural identity"—first, as "an advanced civilization" to emulate and then as a place to conquer as part of America's Manifest Destiny to expand ever westward.[5] The wave of Chinese immigration to North America in the mid-nineteenth century to build the transcontinental railroads sparked "yellow peril" fears of an alien invasion. As Gina Marchetti argues, the idea of the yellow peril has its roots in medieval Europe's fears that Genghis Khan and his Mongol tribes would invade and overpower Europe.[6] In America, the fear was that Chinese sojourners might not return to China and, instead, settle and, through sheer numbers, replace America's Anglo-European culture with their own. Gary Okihiro argues that we should not regard the yellow peril fears of white America as "irrational" but as "constructed with a purpose in mind and function to sustain social order."[7] And Sucheng Chan details the variety of methods used to sustain the existing social order: economic discrimination, political disenfranchisement, prejudice, violence, exclusion, segregation, and incarceration.[8] The most effective legal measures were the passing of the Chinese Exclusion Act in 1882, which halted the influx of Chinese laborers and denying those born in China citizenship in America, and the 1924 Immigration Act, which prevented all immigration from China.[9] These laws not only prevented immigration from China but also determined how white Americans regarded Chinese immigrants, influencing the work of prominent authors, journalists, and also Hollywood's moviemakers.

CHINESE AMERICAN PROTEST

In a reflection of the perceived yellow peril, American films depicted Chinatowns as riddled not only with disease—with opium dens, slave girls, and rat eating—but also crime—with tong wars, hatchet men, and Fu Manchu–type "Oriental" villains. The negative portrayal of Chinese characters did not go unnoticed or unopposed, however, and was protested by Chinese American communities from the first days of feature-length film. For example, in a 1916 article, the president of the Chinese Students' Club of Iowa University wrote,

> So far as known, what they display about the Chinese may be fairly summed up in a few words—smoking opium, gambling, fighting, robbery, murder, arson, rape, or any combination thereof. . . . But, unfortunately, more than this, their very frequency and monotony profoundly mislead the American public to think that such are all the Chinese.[10]

In 1919, Chinese American audiences also objected to *The Tong-Man* (Worthington 1919), which featured Japanese American star Sessue Hayakawa as a Chinese American hero—but also an opium dealer and tong assassin. The Chinese Presbyterian Mission and the Chinese Students Christian Association penned a letter of protest that stated, "We cannot help but feel that the film will do more harm than good towards the friendly relations between us and our American friends. We feel that we are badly misrepresented by Mr. Hayakawa in this film and it was certainly not of an educational benefit."[11] Relatedly, the Pacific Film Archive program for a 1988 screening of the film explains,

> The questionable depiction of their culture caused an uproar in the Chinese community and an injunction was sought against the film's

exhibition. The presiding judge in the case denied the injunction, claiming, "This is a picture that shows action in real life. There is nothing misleading about it. It is entertaining, gripping and instructive." [12]

The judge's decision in the case of *The Tong-Man* reflected the racial bias of mainstream society at the time, which Hollywood practices evidently echoed.

Up until 1927, such protest could only be made to exhibitors, producers, or newspapers; with the creation of the Studio Relations Committee dedicated to overseeing content in Hollywood films, there was a new recourse for protest. The concern of domestic social groups over the representation of Chinese people in film, however, seemed to hold little sway over decisions made by the Studio Relations Committee and its successor, the PCA. Instead, it was the loss of potential overseas revenues in China that impacted PCA decisions, especially as China became a growing market in the 1930s and then a wartime ally in the 1940s.

CHINA'S PROTEST

As Dorothy Jones details, the dissatisfaction of the Chinese government with American film content could have serious ramifications: the government could demand substantial editing of a film, deny a film distribution altogether, or close the Chinese offices of an American studio. [13] It was for those reasons that the PCA showed concern that the stereotyped representations of the Chinese might be offensive to Chinese audiences. Producers, on the other hand, seemed—at least for the most part—ignorant of those concerns and continued to submit problematic scripts to the PCA. For example, in a letter to Henry Henigson at Universal about the 1930 film *East Is West* (Bell), John Wilson at the PCA explained,

> The portrayal of the traffic in women and the attitude of the Chinese [villain] toward his women, we believe will be very offensive to modern China—and we are certain that the portrayal of life in the Chinese colonies in America, with their Tong wars as it is done in the story, will create such resentment that the Chinese government will take action that will not only be quite dangerous to your company but a reflection on the industry as a whole. [14]

The fear for Hollywood, it seemed, was that the actions of one studio over one film could impact access to the Chinese market of all studios and all films.

Wilson was right to be apprehensive about the film. *East Is West* was initially rejected by the censor board in British Columbia because it depicted the trafficking of Chinese women, offered an interracial romance, and presented an Amerasian villain with multiple mistresses.[15] The film eventually

12.1. *East Is West* (1930) featured Mexican-born Lupe Vélez in "yellowface" as the film's Chinese heroine. From *Cine-Mundial* (January 1931), courtesy of Media History Digital Library.

passed on appeal, but it was rejected in France, and the Chinese consul protested the government of Cuba to ban the film.[16] Even in the United States, some censors took issue with the film: for example, in Chicago the film received a "pink ticket," an "adults only" classification.[17]

Wilson also informed Universal that the film had been protested by both Chinese Americans and the Chinese:

> The Chinese students and citizens of our country are offended at the portrayal of such films dealing with this Yellow Slavery. It has been brought to our attention that such films as *East is West* and similar stories have been strongly objected to in China, and from business and political reasons should not be shown.[18]

In 1935, Joseph Breen, then chief at the PCA, received a request to remake the film; however, he reminded Universal that the film was "a very dangerous one from half a dozen angles" and had met with "considerable protest" from the Chinese government.[19] In 1937, Universal took another shot at capitalizing on the story and applied to reissue the 1930 film; Breen again reiterated that the film was problematic for its suggestions of miscegenation and illicit sex.[20] In the end, no remake or reissue happened.

CHINESE ADVISERS

To improve their films' chances to be exhibited in China, Hollywood producers used a few different narrative and production strategies. An example of a narrative strategy is *East Is West*, as Vasey explains, for which "the studio promised to write in a Chinese hero for every Chinese 'heavy' " to try to balance the film's representation; however, the success of this strategy is questionable since the film was banned in several countries.[21] Another narrative strategy was to change a Chinese villain to one that was "half-caste," as the industry labeled mixed-race characters at the time. Films that offered Eurasian or Amerasian villains included *Chinatown after Dark* (Paton 1931), *Shadow of Chinatown* (Hill 1936), and *Daughter of the Tong* (Ray 1939). The Eurasian villain was considered less offensive to the Chinese than a Chinese villain, because their villainy stems not from their blood (i.e., being "other," as in the case of the "Oriental" villain) but from the *pollution* of their blood as the product of miscegenation, which was illegal at the time. Whether the Chinese government approved of the depiction of the Eurasian or Amerasian villain is not evident; certainly, the PCA documents do not evince any concerns.

A production strategy many producers explored was to work closely with T. K. Chang, the Chinese consul in Los Angeles, and/or Chinese technical advisers to garner expert advice throughout the production process. As Breen explained to Colonel Herron in the Foreign Department of the Motion Picture Producers and Distributors of America, "I think you know that the Chinese consul is quite active among the studios at the present time."[22] The film *The Good Earth* (Franklin 1937) was both critically acclaimed and popular at the box office but, by today's standards, is problematic in terms of race with two non-Asian actors in the leading roles. The film, however, was made in direct consultation with a Chinese technical adviser, as a publicity still reveals, with the caption "Chinese interpreter, microphone in hand, . . . relaying his directions in sibilant Cantonese to the Oriental crowds."[23]

Harold Lloyd had run into trouble in China over *Welcome Danger* (Bruckman 1929), with 350 students protesting a screening of the film in Shanghai "for having offended the dignity of the Chinese people."[24] To avoid a similar outbreak of rioting for *The Cat's Paw* (Taylor 1934), Lloyd worked with a Chinese adviser.[25] As the studio press sheet for the film detailed, Lloyd worked with Dr. Lew Chee, a physician and technical expert, who directed the several hundred Chinese extras and also taught Lloyd Mandarin and Cantonese. After meeting with the Chinese vice consul, Yi-seng S. Kiang, Lloyd agreed to speak Mandarin in the scenes set in China to please the Chinese government and speak Cantonese in the scenes set in the United States to please Chinese American audiences. Despite Lloyd's efforts, the film was protested by the Chinese Diplomatic Service in Italy, as reported by Frank Harris, general manager of the Harold Lloyd Corporation.[26] Harris reported that with some "slight changes" the film was approved in Italy but concluded his memo with the comment, "Truly, 'the ways of the Chinese are a mystery'"—unfortunately demonstrating the exact attitude that the Chinese consul and government were struggling with in Hollywood.[27]

CONTINUED TROUBLE

Despite Hollywood's seeming desire to appease the Chinese government, the PCA still reported issues and had to write to studios, both major studios and Poverty Row, reminding them that the terms "Chink" and "Chinaman" were

Harold Lloyd Returns to Hollywood Via China

A CHINATOWN with authentic atmosphere moves in on Hollywood for Harold Lloyd's first picture in two years, "The Cat's-Paw," by Clarence Budington Kelland.

"The Cat's-Paw" is the first published story Lloyd ever purchased for production, and represents a new policy for him. He gets away from gag comedy, relying upon story situations.

Lloyd plays a young man who has grown up in China, where his father is a missionary. He returns to America, becomes involved in a political ring, and is elected mayor of a good-sized city. Members of the ring frame him to protect their interests. Harold, imbued with Oriental philosophy, attempts to meet his problem as a Chinese gentleman would. This leads to amusing situations.

36

12.2. Harold Lloyd worked with Chinese advisers on *The Cat's Paw* (1934) to avoid a negative reception in China. From *Photoplay* (September 1934), courtesy of Media History Digital Library.

offensive, including for *I Cover the Waterfront* (Cruze 1933) and *Border Phantom* (Luby 1937).[28] A film that proved particularly problematic was *Outlaws of the Orient* (Schoedsack 1937). Breen informed the film's producer, Larry Darmour, that the Chinese laborers in the film should not be referred to "in a derogatory manner [or as] Chinks [and] yellow dogs."[29] Breen reported to Herron that T. K. Chang had approached Darmour some months previous "to protest against the making of the picture" and then later made some recommendations for the script.[30] In his opinion, Breen felt that "Darmour had done more than he should have done, in his efforts to placate the Chinese viewpoint"; however, Chang was adamant that "the picture would never do [and] would give great offense to his people."[31] Exasperated, Breen left his meeting with Chang with the impression that Hollywood would "not be able, at any time, to use a Chinese in any characterization" and meet with China's approval. In the end, Chang "unofficially advised Darmour not to present the film to the Chinese censors" or to try to exhibit it in China, and Breen thought that Hollywood should respect the Chinese consul's various concerns. Breen wrote to Herron,

> As I view it—we can be "free, sovereign, and independent" and tell everybody to go to hell, and make all the pictures we want, with Chinese, German, French (or anybody else) characterized in every way possible. On the other hand, if we want to continue to maintain our very lucrative foreign fields, we shall have to be, possibly, less "free, and sovereign—and less independent."[32]

Whether or not Breen or the producers appreciated the impact of the characterizations of the Chinese on audiences, they did appreciate the impact on their bottom line. The experience with *Welcome Danger* and *East Is West* had convinced the PCA "that it is not economically sound to make a picture of this kind without first securing official Chinese approval."[33]

OFFICE OF WAR INFORMATION

During World War II, in addition to feeling the pressure applied by the PCA, studios faced pushback also from the OWI, which vetted productions for wartime messages. As Ellen C. Scott explains, while the PCA's actions were driven by fear of protest, the OWI's were driven by progressive politics, including eradicating misinformation about different racial groups.[34] Indeed, as Hye

Seung Chung confirms, the OWI's "national and political agendas often super-seded the religious and moral mandates of the Production Code." [35] For the most part, the PCA adopted the OWI's stance in its recommendations. For example, for *Rubber Racketeers* (Young 1942), the PCA warned its producers,

> The words "dirty yellow" and "yellow," referring to the Chinese valet, Tom, (a sympathetic character) should be changed, inasmuch as they may give offence to the nationals of one of our allies in the present war. This also applies to the expression "heathen Chinee," even though spoken by Tom. [36]

With *Nob Hill* (Hathaway 1945), Breen wrote to Colonel Jason Joy at Twenti-eth Century-Fox, "We urgently recommend that you drop this business of the pigtailed Chinese, occasionally seen, since this characterization seems highly offensive to our allied Chinese, in that it symbolizes their servitude." [37] Breen then recommended that Joy obtain a Chinese technical adviser for the film.

The irony is that Joy was the person who had done Breen's job at the Stu-dio Relations Committee, the predecessor to the PCA. That Joy did not con-sider the representations as offensive to Chinese audiences suggests that the PCA had become increasingly sensitive to its foreign market in its decade of existence—even if Hollywood producers had not. In 1946, in an article in the *Hollywood Reporter*, director Arthur Lubin wrote, "Hollywood's sole mission is to produce pictures which gross huge sums of money and of course this can-not be accomplished if you go around sticking out your tongue at people and calling them nasty names." [38] However, "nasty names" are exactly what some producers continued to use right up into the 1950s. The scripts for both *Bos-ton Blackie's Chinese Venture* (Friedman 1949) and *The Breaking Point* (Curtiz 1950) contained the term "Chink," despite that in 1939 the Code had specifi-cally listed the term as one to be avoided as "obviously offensive to the patrons of motion pictures in the United States and more particularly to the patrons of motion pictures in foreign countries and, therefore, should be omitted." [39]

CONCLUSION

With the rise of the civil rights movement and along with films that explored African American race relations, some mainstream films began to revise the place of Asian immigrants in American history and society, for example,

The Crimson Kimono (Fuller 1959), *Walk Like a Dragon* (Clavell 1960), and *Flower Drum Song* (Koster 1961). Other films, however, continued to offer representations of Chinese immigrants that harkened back to the nineteenth century, including *Confessions of an Opium Eater* (Zugsmith 1962). The mounting impact of the civil rights movement meant that domestic groups now, unlike in the 1910s, had a more effective and respected voice. In the case of *Confessions of an Opium Eater*, *Variety* reported that the Los Angeles Chinese Committee against Defamation protested the film.[40] After a two-hour meeting with the group, director Albert Zugsmith reported, "One or two points that they brought up were valid and I'm going to go along with them. The other points were without validity."[41] The committee's official response, in contrast, was "no comment." A review of the film confirms that the committee was in the right: "This crude piece of claptrap has to be seen to be believed: it is a hotchpotch of Chinatown melodrama (circa 1920 vintage) with rival tongs, starved girls captive in cages, secret panels, sliding doors, sewer escape routes, opium dens and nightmares."[42]

There was motivation in the classical Hollywood era to avoid negative representations of Chinese people and culture: for the PCA, it was an increased international market; for the OWI, it was diplomatic relations. After World War II, however, producers continued to present scripts and films with Chinese stereotypes, and without the regulatory actions of the PCA, those representations would have continued with only a few producers seemingly desirous of updating Hollywood's image of the Chinese. While film history has focused on how the Production Code regulated sex, nudity, and violence, the PCA's impact on Hollywood's representation of foreign nationals and ethnic Americans is equally important. Without the PCA's regulatory actions, classical Hollywood's representation of Chinese people—while problematic by today's standards—would have been so much worse.

NOTES

The author gratefully acknowledges the financial support for this chapter's research from a grant funded partly by Wilfrid Laurier University operating funds and partly by the Social Sciences and Humanities Research Council of Canada Institutional Grant awarded to Wilfrid Laurier University.

1   Susan Courtney, *Hollywood Fantasies of Miscegenation: Spectacular Narratives of Gender and Race, 1903–1967* (Princeton, NJ: Princeton University Press,

2005); Thomas Doherty, *Hollywood's Censor: Joseph I. Breen & the Production Code Administration* (New York: Columbia University Press, 2007); Francis Couvares, "So This Is Censorship: Race, Sex, and Censorship in Movies of the 1920s and 1930s," *Journal of American Studies* 24, no. 3 (2011): 581–97; Ellen C. Scott, *Cinema Civil Rights: Regulation, Repression, and Race in the Classical Hollywood Era* (New Brunswick, NJ: Rutgers University Press, 2015).

2   Ruth Vasey, *The World According to Hollywood, 1918–1939* (Exeter, UK: University of Exeter Press, 1997), 175–79; Thomas Doherty, *Pre-Code Hollywood: Sex, Immorality, and Insurrection in American Cinema, 1930–1934* (New York: Columbia University Press, 1999), 272–73; Eric Smoodin, "Going Hollywood Sooner or Later: Chinese Censorship and *The Bitter Tea of General Yen*," in *Looking Past the Screen: Case Studies in American Film History and Method*, ed. Jon Lewis and Eric Smoodin (Durham, NC: Duke University Press, 2007), 169–200; and Hye Seung Chung, "Hollywood Diplomacy and *The Purple Heart* (1944): Preserving Wartime Alliances through Film Regulation," *Historical Journal of Film, Radio and Television* 38, no. 3 (2017): 3–4.

3   Motion Picture Producers and Distributors of America, *A Code to Govern the Making of Motion and Talking Pictures*, June 13, 1934, 9, Margaret Herrick Library Digital Collections, Academy of Motion Pictures Arts and Sciences.

4   Richard Rushton and Gary Bettinson, *What Is Film Theory? An Introduction to Contemporary Debates* (New York: McGraw-Hill, 2010), 92.

5   John Kuo Wei Tchen, *New York before Chinatown: Orientalism and the Shaping of American Culture, 1776–1882* (Baltimore, MD: Johns Hopkins University Press, 1999), xv.

6   Gina Marchetti, *Romance and the "Yellow Peril": Race, Sex, and Discursive Strategies in Hollywood Fiction* (Berkeley: University of California Press, 1993), 2.

7   Gary Y. Okihiro, *Margins and Mainstreams: Asians in American History and Culture* (Seattle: University of Washington Press, 1994), 137–38.

8   Sucheng Chan, *Asian Americans: An Interpretive History* (Boston, MA: Twayne, 1991), 45.

9   The 1882 act permitted "desirable" classes, including merchants, teachers, and diplomats.

10 T. L. Li, "A Plea for Truthful Portrayal," *Moving Picture World*, October 14, 1916, 240.

11 "Chinese Protest 'Tong Man' Rim," *Marin Journal*, February 12, 1920, 5.

12 Quoted in program for *The Tong-Man*, 1988, Pacific Film Archive, Berkeley, CA.

13 Dorothy B. Jones, *The Portrayal of China and India on the American Screen, 1896–1955: The Evolution of Chinese and Indian Themes, Locales, and Characters as Portrayed on the American Screen* (Cambridge, MA: Massachusetts Institute of Technology, 1955), 38.

14 John V. Wilson to Henry Henigson, Universal, May 23, 1930, file for *East Is West* (1930), Motion Picture Association of America (MPAA)— Production Code Administration (PCA) Records, Margaret Herrick Library, Los Angeles, CA.

15 T. B. Fithian to John Wilson, Association of Motion Picture Producers (AMPP), December 4, 1930, file for *East Is West* (1930), MPAA—PCA Records.

16 Frederick L. Herron to Col. Jason Joy, AMPP, January 15, 1931, and Jason Joy, AMPP Memo, May 6, 1931, file for *East Is West* (1930), MPAA—PCA Records.

17 "'East Is West' Is Pinked; Race, Not Sex, Angle," *Variety*, October 29, 1930, 5.

18 T. B. Fithian to John Wilson, AMPP, December 4, 1930, file for *East Is West* (1930), MPAA—PCA Records.

19 Joseph Breen to Col. Frederick Herron, MPPDA, August 29, 1935, and Joseph Breen to Harry Zehner, Universal, August 30, 1935, file for *East Is West* (1930), MPAA—PCA.

20 Joseph Breen to Harry Zehner, Universal, May 13, 1937, file for *East Is West* (1930), MPAA—PCA Records.

21 Vasey, *The World according to Hollywood*, 142.

22 Joseph Breen to Col. F. L. Herron, MPPDA, September 13, 1937, file for *Daughter of Shanghai* (1937), MPAA—PCA Records.

23 Publicity still, file for *The Good Earth* (1937), Core Collection Files—Production Files, Margaret Herrick Library, Los Angeles, CA.

24 Paul K. Whang, "Boycotting American Movies," *World Tomorrow* 13, no. 8 (1930): 339.

25 "Purely Chinese: Harold Lloyd's Careful of Dialects in his 'Cat's Paw,'" *Variety*, April 3, 1934, 3.

26 Frank Harris to William R. Fraser, Harold Lloyd Corp., December 4, 1934, file for *The Cat's Paw* (1934), Harold Lloyd Papers, Margaret Herrick Library, Los Angeles, CA.

27 Frank Harris to William R. Fraser, Harold Lloyd Corp., December 6, 1934, file for *The Cat's Paw* (1934), Harold Lloyd Papers. The film was banned in Nanking in 1936.

28 James Wingate to Edwin Small, February 15, 1933, file for *I Cover the Water-front* (1933) MPAA—PCA Records; Joseph Breen to William Berke, December 14, 1935, and Joseph Breen to A. W. Hackel, November 9, 1936, file for *Border Phantom* (1937), MPAA—PCA Records.

29 Joseph Breen to Larry Darmour, Larry Darmour Productions, February 2, 1937, and February 3, 1937, file for *Outlaws of the Orient* (1937), MPAA—PCA Records.

30 Joseph Breen to Col. F. L. Herron, MPPDA, June 4, 1937, file for *Outlaws of the Orient* (1937), MPAA—PCA Records.

31 Joseph Breen to Col. F. L. Herron, MPPDA, June 11, 1937, file for *Outlaws of the Orient* (1937), MPAA—PCA Records.

32 Joseph Breen to Col. F. L. Herron, MPPDA, June 11, 1937, file for *Outlaws of the Orient* (1937), MPAA—PCA Records.

33 Fred W. Beetson to Daryl Zanuck, Warner Bros., October 28, 1931, file for *The Hatchet Man* (1932), MPAA—PCA Records.

34 Scott, *Cinema Civil Rights*, 42.

35 Chung, "Hollywood Diplomacy and *The Purple Heart* (1944)," 5.

36 PCA to Franklin King, May 8, 1942. File for *Rubber Racketeers* (1942), MPAA—PCA Records.

37 Joseph Breen to Colonel Jason S. Joy, Twentieth Century Fox, March 14, 1944, file for *Nob Hill* (1945), MPAA—PCA Records.

38 Arthur Lubin, "Life among the Censors," *Hollywood Reporter*, September 23, 1946, n.p.

39 Joseph Breen to J. L. Warner, Warner Bros., March 17, 1950, file for *Boston Blackie's Chinese Venture* (1949), MPAA—PCA Records; Stephen S. Jackson to Harry Cohn, March 15, 1948, file for *The Breaking Point* (1950) MPAA—PCA Records. The Code amendment was instituted November 1, 1939.

40 "L.A. Chinese Group Protests Zugsmith Filming 'Opium,'" *Variety*, January 26, 1961, n.p.

41 Quoted in review from unidentified trade paper, January 27, 1961, file for *Confessions of an Opium Eater* (1962), Core Collection Files—Production Files, Margaret Herrick Library.

42 Review of *Confessions of an Opium Eater*, *Monthly Film Bulletin* (1963), 145.

13

SIGNIFYING EXCESS

THE AFRICAN AMERICAN SPECIALTY NUMBER AND THE CLASSICAL MUSICAL

Ryan Jay Friedman

About forty-five minutes into the MGM musical *Broadway Rhythm* (Del Ruth 1944), three of the white main characters visit a cabaret called the Jungle Club. The film uses a shot of the Jungle Club's exterior showcase as a bridge between the previous scene and the one that takes place inside: the camera tracks toward the plate glass, conveying the feeling of physically entering this new space. The showcase contains a cardboard cutout of a performer in costume, recognizable immediately as Lena Horne, and stenciled on the window beneath the name of the club are the words "appearing nightly/Fernway de la Fer." The ensuing scene consists mainly of Horne/de la Fer's performance of "Brazilian Boogie," which is prefaced and motivated—albeit minimally—by the meeting between the protagonist, Johnnie Demming (George Murphy), a leading theatrical producer, and a Hollywood star, Helen Hoyt (Ginny Simms). Accompanied at first by his comic sidekick Felix (Ben Blue), Johnnie has arranged a meeting with Helen to convince her to appear in his next show and to woo her. They converse briefly before the lights dim and "Brazilian Boogie" begins; they resume as soon as the song ends. Along with the composition of the cast, the manner in which the number is incorporated into the film identifies this scene as an instance of a particular convention of 1930s and 1940s film musicals: the African American specialty number.

"Brazilian Boogie" has no role in advancing the narrative; in fact, it pauses and provides a diversion from the plot at hand. Set off by a pair of abrupt transitions, which seem to unmoor the space where the performance

13.1. "Brazilian Boogie" from *Broadway Rhythm* (1944).

happens from the space where white main characters exist, the number is a part of the film but not, as it were, fully integrated into its structure. It provides a cameo for Horne, who has no lines and appears again only once in another specialty number. Fernway de la Fer is a character of sorts but only to the extent that she has a name other than that of the actor herself and that a bit of dialogue establishes her as a professional entertainer within the fictional world of the film. Note that *Broadway Rhythm* also features a specialty by the African American virtuoso jazz pianist and vocalist Hazel Scott: the opening credits list her name in the column of character names and then, next to it, "By Herself" in the column of actor names. Horne herself was given this unusual billing in the other MGM film in which both she and Scott appeared, *I Dood It* (Minnelli 1943).[1]

In every conceivable way, specialties like the ones in *Broadway Rhythm* exemplify what the theoretical discourse of classical Hollywood narrative terms "excess." Included by virtue of their exclusion, these scenes devote screen time to actors who are not psychologically individuated or motivated and, therefore, do not perform "actions," which, in the classical paradigm, act as the primary structure of meaning. It is precisely this register of meaning making from which African Americans are barred in classical films, musicals perhaps especially.[2] In David Bordwell, Kristin Thompson, and Janet Staiger's groundbreaking theorizations, whatever has no narrative motivation within classical cinema occupies the category of "excess," which is always aligned, implicitly or explicitly, with "style"—the merely aesthetic, that which, by definition, has no function.[3]

Perhaps surprisingly, the standard line in African American film criticism, dating back to the flourishing of the so-called black images approach in the early 1970s, does not offer much help in excavating the significance of numbers like "Brazilian Boogie." For earlier critics like Donald Bogle, such scenes exemplify the restricted set of roles available to black performers, reinforcing "the myth that Negroes were naturally rhythmic and natural-born entertainers."[4] The African American specialty, like other "bits and pieces of black action" in 1940s Hollywood films, is merely symptomatic of what Bogle calls the "Negro Entertainment Syndrome."[5] He treats the musical specialty as a "platform for displaying the [African American] entertainer to his [or her] best advantage," which "evolved" as a containment strategy—a "built-in cutting procedure."[6] "Because musical numbers were not integrated into the script," Bogle writes, "the scenes featuring blacks could be cut from the films without spoiling them should local (or Southern) theater owners feel their audiences would object to seeing a Negro."[7]

Although Bogle's approach begins with ideology, rather than form, it leads us to the same conclusion: that the African American musical specialty is a kind of radical excess, with no motivation or meaning other than a categorical one. For Bogle, as for many subsequent scholars of the African American screen image, the specialty is a literal excrescence, a part of the film that is always already under erasure.[8] The practice of cutting these scenes was, indeed, common in at least one southern jurisdiction, Memphis, Tennessee, whose censor, Lloyd Binford, was a self-appointed guardian of Jim Crow with an outspoken enmity for black performers like Horne, who refused to play menial roles.[9] Although such practices are crucial to understanding the reception history of film musicals during this period, using them as the primary means of characterizing African American specialties risks exaggerating these scenes' marginal status. In the most interesting examples from this period—*I Dood It*, MGM's *Lady Be Good* (McLeod 1941), Twentieth Century-Fox's *Orchestra Wives* (Mayo 1942), and, indeed, *Broadway*

Rhythm, to pick just a few—the length, number, placement, and embedded-
ness in the diegesis of black specialties belie the assumption that they could
be excised without disrupting the continuity of the film or leaving behind any
noticeable traces. Even when *Broadway Rhythm* was exhibited in Memphis,
Binford reportedly cut Horne's scenes but left in Scott's.[10] More importantly
still, reducing the African American specialty numbers to a "built-in cutting
procedure" reinforces the notion that they are essentially insignificant.

Two concurrent moves are needed to get out of this critical impasse.
The first is to provide an alternative account of what the formal "dominant"
is in these films—classical-era musicals, but especially those made during
World War II. Instead of "narrative causality," the dominant in these films is
what might be called, transvaluing a trope that Bogle uses and drawing on
a key image in *Broadway Rhythm*, "the showcase."[11] The second is to insist
on the nontotality of this, or any, dominant. As Rick Altman argues, a static
concept of "excess" as beginning where the dominant leaves off reduces the
former to "the outlaw by which the law reaffirms itself."[12] In their complex
relation to social laws, norms and conventions of form reflect the "multiple
logics" at work in any system of power.[13] Altman uses a provocative and, in
this context, especially apt analogy from the history of the desegregation
struggle to illustrate his point: "They all know the law, but they refuse to
leave the Greensboro lunchroom."[14] The social laws encoded in what unifies
and gives form in the films are subject to internal challenges, and it is in and
through these challenges, I would argue, that meaning is made.

As Altman has shown, *The Classical Hollywood Cinema*'s discussion
of "motivation" highlights the extent to which the musical genre is an out-
lier within the theoretical account of classical narrative.[15] The genre's heavy
reliance on what Bordwell calls "generic" and "artistic" motivation, its foregrounding of spectacle, and its relative lack of concern with individual character action as a driver of plot all serve to associate the genre with excess.[16]
But within the history of the genre, these "excessive" formal features seem to
be the norm rather than the exception. Especially during the studios' turn
to "revue"-style musicals during World War II—and especially within the
camp-aesthetic universe of MGM's Freed Unit, from which a disproportion-
ate number of the films featuring African American specialties come—it is
difficult to maintain the premise that unity is the primary formal rule.[17]

The "focusing component" of a film like *Broadway Rhythm* is the
showcase: the display window in which a range of musical styles, valued

according to extracinematic trends or fashion cycles, can be exhibited seri-
ally.[18] By bringing to the fore the logic of the consumer marketplace, the
idea of the showcase is useful in breaking down the rigid substance-versus-
style binary, which, as Altman has shown, the classical theory inherits from
Russian Formalism. In *Broadway Rhythm*, as in the larger body of World
War II–era musicals, style is, in crucial ways, substance—the place where
value, and therefore meaning, is created. Consider the regionally and culturally heterogenous mise-en-scène of "Brazilian Boogie." The decor inside the
Jungle Club is vaguely Polynesian, while the performers' costumes—lots of
bold colors, candy stripes, and exposed skin—evoke everything from Car-
men Miranda, to blackface minstrelsy, to Hollywood's stock ways of dressing
characters from the Caribbean. Likewise, the song being performed is about
a dance, which is described as a new hybrid style. It is "a half-breed," the
child of North American (really African American) "swing" and Brazilian
"samba." These qualities are said to make this dance "the perfect propaganda" for the times, a period when Hollywood films were broadcasting
political messages both about the United States as a cultural melting pot and
about the nation's relationship to its Latin American allies.

13.2. The Jungle Club showcase in *Broadway Rhythm* (1944).

Although "Brazilian Boogie" stands out from the film in its self-reflexivity, it echoes the main, backstage plot in how it works through a range of paradigmatic oppositions: North America versus South America, normative versus "exotic" femininity, and "pure entertainment" versus engaged art. These are the very things that preoccupy the *Broadway Rhythm*'s protagonist Johnnie; as he explains in the film, he is tired of just giving "the public what it wants" and longs to produce a show that "has scope, vision, and carries a message." Struggling to find a compelling female lead for this new concept, he becomes interested in Helen only when she masquerades as "La Polita," a singer reputed to be from Brazil.[19]

The terms making up these paradigmatic oppositions act as the primary carriers of meaning across the film's narrative, thin as it may be; in as much as *Broadway Rhythm* is "about" anything, it is about reflecting on these values as means of differentiating show business commodities. And it is not by coincidence that these oppositions reflect, albeit in a highly simplified form, the dilemmas facing film producers during the war as they responded to new cultural pressures: the swing craze and the studios' concomitant efforts to tap into youth-cultural fads around specific songs, orchestras, and social dance styles; Hollywood's embrace of the Good Neighbor Policy; the NAACP's efforts to improve roles for African American actors; the challenges to the presumed class orientation of black culture being mounted by popular performers like Horne and Scott, who were associated with New York City's Café Society; and so on. All of these pressures are themselves products of the crisis of American consciousness provoked by the contradiction between an idealizing official narrative of the United States as an egalitarian, multiethnic society and the realities of Jim Crow and other segregationist practices. Therefore, when the film talks about swing, about Brazil, about cultural mixing, and so on, it is really talking about race, the crucial institutional determinant or "motivation" that classical cinema otherwise seeks to conceal under a facade of normalized whiteness.

In this respect, scholarship like Bogle's is indispensable, as it attempts to locate the articulations of segregationist social law in American cinema. Whereas the status of active/motivated character is foreclosed to black performers like Horne and Scott, the musical showcase affords an opportunity to appear and demonstrate technical virtuosity that is, at least, ostensibly, the same one afforded to non–African American performers. This opportunity engenders within the films a sense of competition—typically virtual or imaginary—between black and white performers. In turn, it opens up a space to challenge what I would call the "racial motivation" of classical Hollywood cinema, the formal dominance of the idea of racial difference.

In her oddly liminal role in *Broadway Rhythm* as Fernway de la Fer, who auditions for a show that Helen Hoyt decides to coproduce, Lena Horne is asking why she is not the star whom Johnnie Demming was seeking for his new show. Horne's de la Fer is no more or less "Brazilian" than is Ginny Simms's Hoyt, but Horne does have a personal connection to the history of the Black Atlantic, which allows her to articulate a different kind of relationship to the popular-cultural materials on exhibit in the film. At the moment where we can begin to observe the points of overlap and comparison between the main themes of a musical and the seemingly disconnected narrative threads that emerge in its specialties, the "second voice" that Altman locates in the classical film-text becomes audible. The African American musical specialty is allowed to *signify* in the sense of the black rhetorical practice of interpretation and commentary through imitation and parody.[20] As highly self-reflexive showcases of contemporary entertainment styles—most of them having African American roots—World War II–era musicals abound in these overlaps and comparisons, and it is the work of black musical specialty performers that brings them to light.

NOTES

1   On these naming conventions, see my "By Herself: Intersectionality, African American Specialty Performers, and Eleanor Powell," in *Hollywood at the Intersection of Race and Identity*, ed. Delia Malia Konzett (New Brunswick, NJ: Rutgers University Press, 2020). Apart from Horne, Scott, and the musicians and dancers who perform with them (all uncredited), the only other African American actor in the cast is Eddie Anderson. Anderson also "plays himself" but in an inverted fashion: his character, also named Eddie, is Johnnie's father's valet, a version of the Rochester van Jones persona that he had developed on *The Jack Benny Program*, beginning in the late 1930s. His off-screen persona had been so completely defined by this radio role that he was usually billed as "Eddie 'Rochester' Anderson."

2   Recall Stanley Cavell's observation that "types of black human beings were not created in [classical-era] film: black people were stereotypes—mammies, shiftless servants, loyal retainers, entertainers. We were not given, and were

not in a position to be given, individualities that projected particular ways of inhabiting a social life; we recognized only the role." Cavell, *The World Viewed: Reflections on the Ontology of Film* (New York: Viking, 1971), 33. Cavell's definition of character—an "individuality" that embodies a universal human "type"—crucially partakes of the Aristotelean conception that defines classical Hollywood narrative theory. Although Cavell is correct that classical Hollywood cinema denies African Americans "ordinary" humanity, he fails to acknowledge that, because whiteness is a prerequisite for the kind of Aristotlean (false) universality that he associates with the great film stars, attaining the status of individual type is neither a conceivable nor necessarily a desirable goal for African American cinematic roles or the performers playing them.

3   See David Bordwell, Janet Staiger, and Kristin Thompson, *The Classical Hollywood Cinema: Film Style and Mode of Production* (New York: Columbia University Press, 1985), 11; David Bordwell, *Narration in the Fiction Film* (Madison: University of Wisconsin Press, 1985), 50, 53; and Kristin Thompson, "The Concept of Cinematic Excess," in *Narrative, Apparatus, Ideology: A Film Theory Reader*, ed. Philip Rosen (New York: Columbia University Press, 1986), 132.

4   Donald Bogle, *Toms, Coons, Mulattoes, Mammies, and Bucks: An Interpretive History of Blacks in American Films* (New York: Continuum, 1989), 118.

5   Bogle, *Toms, Coons, Mulattoes, Mammies, and Bucks*, 118, 132.

6   Bogle, *Toms, Coons, Mulattoes, Mammies, and Bucks*, 119, 121.

7   Bogle, *Toms, Coons, Mulattoes, Mammies, and Bucks*, 121.

8   An important exception to the generalization I am making here is Arthur Knight's *Disintegrating the Musical: Black Performance and American Musical Film* (Durham, NC: Duke University Press, 2002), which, though not a "comprehensive study of specialty numbers," is preoccupied with the ways in which "fragmentary" moments of African American musical performance serve as sites of struggle for and over meaning (17, 19).

9   Lester Velie, "You Can't See That Movie: Censorship in Action," *Collier's*, May 6, 1950, 11–12, 66.

10   "More Negro Scenes Cut Out in Dixie Set New Problems For Pix Producers," *Variety*, July 12, 1944, 1, 32. See also Laurie B. Green, *Battling the Plantation Mentality: Memphis and the Black Freedom Struggle* (Chapel Hill: University of North Carolina Press, 2007), 154.

11   Bordwell, Staiger, and Thompson, *Classical Hollywood Cinema*, 12. Their formative work of the early to mid-1980s draws this concept from Russian

Formalist poetics, especially the work of Roman Jakobson, who defines the dominant "as the focusing component of a work of art: it rules, determines, and transforms the remaining components. . . . The dominant specifies the work." Jakobson, "The Dominant," in *Readings in Russian Poetics: Formalist and Structuralist Views*, ed. Ladislav Matejka and Krystyna Pomorska (Ann Arbor: Michigan Slavic Publications, 1978), 82. According to Bordwell, Staiger, and Thompson, the "specific sort of narrative causality" that "operates as the dominant" is motivated individual character action (*Classical Hollywood Cinema*, 12).

12   Rick Altman, "Dickens, Griffith, and Film Theory Today," in *Classical Hollywood Narrative: The Paradigm Wars*, ed. Jane Gaines (Durham, NC: Duke University Press, 1992), 33–34.

13   Altman, "Dickens, Griffith, and Film Theory Today," 34.

14   Altman, "Dickens, Griffith, and Film Theory Today," 34.

15   Altman, "Dickens, Griffith, and Film Theory Today," 33.

16   Bordwell, Staiger, and Thompson, *Classical Hollywood Cinema*, 19–22.

17   See Thomas Schatz, *Boom and Bust: American Cinema in the 1940s* (Berkeley: University of California Press, 1999), 223–24; and Steven Cohan, *Incongruous Entertainment: Camp, Cultural Value, and the MGM Musical* (Durham, NC: Duke University Press, 2005), 41.

18   Jakobson, "The Dominant," 82.

19   Oddly, but not surprisingly for this film, Helen's audition as the Brazilian La Polita consists of her singing a song in Spanish in a setting that evokes Andalusia: she wears a black silk dress and mantilla, while her male backup dancers wield matador's capes.

20   I mean here to pick up on the secondary meaning of "signifying" as an African American rhetorical practice of interpretation and commentary through imitation and parody. See Henry Louis Gates Jr., *The Signifying Monkey: A Theory of African-American Literary Criticism* (Oxford: Oxford University Press, 1988).

14

DARK DESIRES AND WHITE OBSESSIONS

Sam McDaniel as a Marker of Blackness in *Double Indemnity* (1944) and *Ice Palace* (1960)

Charlene Regester

THE RACIALIZATION OF NOIR

Numerous scholars have acknowledged that film noir is replete with references to race. Attesting to how race infiltrates noir dramas, Manthia Diawara argues, "In *film noir* the opposition between dark and light, underworld and 'above board,' good and evil, is blurred and it is the collapse of these boundaries that causes characters to partake of the attributes of blackness."[1] It is not just the black presence that marks a film as being connected to blackness, however; Diawara continues, "*Film noir* is black because the characters have lost the privilege of whiteness by pursuing lifestyles that are misogynistic, cowardly, duplicitous, that exhibit themselves in an eroticization of violence."[2] For example, in *Double Indemnity* (Wilder 1944), the white characters become associated with the underworld and immoral behavior, marking them as "dark" characters. Both the femme fatale, Phyllis Dietrichson (Barbara Stanwyck), and the "good guy gone bad," Walter Neff (Fred MacMurray), are automatically linked to blackness because of their disposition to criminality and immorality. Elaborating on the racialization/ Otherness that these noir characters embody, Eric Lott contends that the film introduces racialized characters who participate in marking the film as a "dark drama," including the black garage attendant who helps to establish Walter's whereabouts, the black janitor who fingerprints Walter, the "Westwood Jew, Lou Schwartz, whose name . . . derives from the Yiddish word for 'black,'" and Lola's Italian boyfriend, Nino Zachetti, who are "the film's resident Others."[3] According to Lott, these characters help "secure [Walter's] uncriminal whiteness while suggesting [his] moral fall."[4] The film includes other racialized references and marginalized characters that together affirm the film's association with blackness—for example, Phyllis's anklet, which can be read as a "slave bracelet,"[5] the Dietrichson's Spanish-style house, the game of Chinese checkers that Lola and Phyllis play, the Mexican restaurant Walter and Lola visit, the Greek man who deliberately torches his truck for insurance benefits, and the Italian man who becomes involved with both Phyllis and her stepdaughter. Collectively, these racial references or racialized characters demonstrate how *Double Indemnity* crosses racial borders and, through their appropriation of Otherness, marks the white characters as dark. Lott insists, "Film noir is in this sense, a sort of whiteface dreamwork of social anxieties with explicitly racial sources, condensed on film into the criminal undertakings of abjected whites."[6]

This chapter explores how African American actor Sam McDaniel's presence in the noir film *Double Indemnity* and the adventure film *Ice Palace* (Sherman 1960) contributes to the metaphorical "darkening" of the white protagonists. While McDaniel's characters themselves are not immoral, the films' equation of blackness with evilness, immorality, and criminality in American culture entails an association between black characters' presence and such negative attributes. McDaniel, brother to actresses Etta McDaniel and Hattie McDaniel (the latter, an Academy Award winner), appeared in an extensive number of films over the course of his career but primarily as an extra or atmosphere player. Though he garnered only small parts and remains obscure in film history, his contributions to the screen are significant in that his black presence significantly impacted the construction of the protagonists' whiteness. This chapter proposes that McDaniel's blackness influenced the development, evolution, and construction of whiteness associated with the white characters who, in *Double Indemnity*, descend into immorality related to murder and deception, and who, in *Ice Palace*, become embodiments of Otherness, allowing spectators to experience Otherness vicariously.

A MARKER OF MORAL BLACKNESS: *DOUBLE INDEMNITY*

When *Double Indemnity* was released, it was considered controversial, in part because of the immorality of its protagonist, Walter Neff, played by Fred

MacMurray, who to that point was known for playing mainly likeable good guys. The film, however, was also recognized for its racially incendiary subtext, which exposed America's rigid racial divide in the segregated United States in the 1940s, when the film was released. Seldom did whites actually cross the "real" or "imagined" boundaries to engage in blackness—but they did so on-screen, aligning themselves with blacks and blackness and, as a result, demarcating their sameness or difference. Although McDaniel's on-screen presence is minimal in the film, it serves to encourage the white characters to become increasingly immoral and entice them toward criminality. This, of course, is not to suggest that the white characters could not have been criminal on their own without the black presence; however, in the absence of the black presence, these white characters would otherwise lead normal "white lives"; through the presence of the racial Other, their "normal" white lives are disrupted. In the transition from normality to abnormality, the black Other destabilizes the normality of whiteness, which becomes apparent when the white characters develop an affinity for immoral behavior.

In *Double Indemnity*, Walter, an insurance agent, falls in love with his client's wife, Phyllis, and the two conspire to murder her husband for insurance money. Walter succeeds in killing Mr. Dietrichson and making his death appear a suicide until Walter's supervisor, Keyes (Edward G. Robinson), becomes suspicious. The film ends with Phyllis shooting Walter, leaving him to slowly bleed to death. Walter's comments on his lack of visible scars until wounded by Phyllis suggest, as Lott argues, a man "so scarred by his own deceit, violence, and cunning and so fully immersed in blackened cinematic compositions that his darkness threatens to manifest itself on his very skin."[7] In this instance, Lott describes Walter's descent into blackness as related to the visible signifier of skin, a marker of racial identity; therefore, Walter's racialization is implied, and even though his skin is not physically darkened (except by blood), his physical injury signifies how his darkness has become visibly represented on the body. Collectively, the visible marking on Walter's body and the murderous behavior of the white characters demonstrate how blackness infuses the film as whites descend into immorality. Affirming the role that race plays in *Double Indemnity*, E. Ann Kaplan argues, "Race is film noir's repressed unconscious Signifier."[8]

McDaniel plays Charlie, the black attendant for Walter's apartment garage who, although only present in a couple of scenes, fulfills an important narrative function by providing Walter with an alibi for Dietrichson's murder. As Walter articulates in voice-over, "I wanted my time all accounted for—for the rest of the afternoon and up to the last possible moment in the evening. . . . I got home around seven and drove right into the garage." He encounters Charlie, who encourages Walter to have his vehicle washed. Before he departs the garage on foot, Walter explains to Charlie that he intends to remain inside his apartment for the night. To bolster his false alibi, Walter calls his coworker Lou Schwartz on a work-related matter. Both Charlie and Lou, then, are able to verify Walter's apparent time and location, giving him the illusion of a solid alibi, yet Walter's association to Charlie represents the dependence of the Self on the Other as he gives in to his darkest desires. Following Dietrichson's murder, Walter seeks Charlie's confirmation of his alibi. As Walter explains in the voice-over, "There was one last thing to do. I wanted the garage man to see me again." Entering the garage from the apartment building, Walter finds Charlie waxing the hood of his car. Since Charlie has not finished his job yet, Walter says that he will walk to the drugstore for something to eat. Initially, Walter feels somewhat self-assured and comments, "That was all there was to it. Nothing had slipped, nothing had been overlooked, there was nothing to give us away." Shortly thereafter,

14.1. Sam McDaniel's presence in *Double Indemnity* (1944) signifies the white hero's descent into blackness.

however, Walter's self-confidence dissipates and is replaced by doubt. It is noteworthy that a black presence appears both before and after the murder. Charlie's second appearance in the film seems at first to reassure Walter that he might get away with murder, but, subsequently, it reaffirms Walter's internal darkening.

In addition to Charlie, other black characters appear in the film, representing moments when the immorality of the two white protagonists is linked to the presence of a black person— most notably, several black porters (Oscar Smith, Frank Billy Mitchell, Floyd Shackelford, James Adamson, et al.) at the train station and on the train, which Walter will use to stage Dietrichson's suicide to cover up his murder. I argue that these black characters are strategically introduced to "darken" the white characters who embrace their immorality. By the end of the film, Walter's self-assurance disintegrates: he and Phyllis turn on each other, and Walter ultimately confesses his crimes to Keyes. Speaking into his Dictaphone, Walter explains, "Look, Keyes, I am not trying to whitewash myself [an admission of his 'darkness']. I fought it, only maybe I didn't fight it hard enough." This admission affirms Walter's disposition to blackness, darkness, and immorality—a disposition that the presence of McDaniel (and other black actors) validates.

ALIGNED WITH OTHERNESS: *ICE PALACE*

Double Indemnity and *Ice Palace* both feature McDaniel as the black racial Other to juxtapose the white protagonists and to construct them as embodiments of Otherness. *Ice Palace* was adapted from Edna Ferber's 1958 novel, which explored Alaskan statehood and its two protagonists' diametrically opposed moral convictions and divergent racial beliefs regarding race mixing. Ferber was inspired to chronicle the history of Alaska "both [for] its frontier spirit and the U.S. government's colonization and economic exploitation of the territory."[9] Of specific interest to Ferber was the settlement of veterans in Alaska and the region's diverse population, the result of trappers and fishermen intermarrying with Native women, "the descendants of Russian-Eskimo Creoles," and children born to "white air force pilots and Eskimo women."[10] Fabricating this history, Ferber's work coincided with a new era of liberalism regarding race mixing that attracted the attention of film producers. The film's director, Vincent Sherman, however, had reservations regarding the project's viability and believed the novel was inappropriate for screen adaptation. After renowned actor Richard Burton was recruited for the film's lead, Sherman committed to the project.[11] The film version of *Ice Palace* focuses on Zeb "Czar" Kennedy (Burton) and Thor Storm (Robert Ryan), whose friendship is disrupted because of ideological differences. Their divide is exacerbated when Thor's fiancée develops an attraction to Zeb. Regardless of their differences, when Thor's mixed-race son marries Zeb's daughter and the young couple meet their untimely deaths, the two fathers are reunited through their mixed-race granddaughter.

The film opens with a black porter, George (McDaniel), making his way through the train as soldiers returning from World War I gamble in the narrow aisle to pass the time. At the very moment when the protagonist, Zeb (Burton), is introduced, George enters the scene—thus, the two characters are linked, and the porter's blackness becomes an extension of Zeb's Otherness. For example, Zeb is high strung, aggressive, defiant, impulsive, explosive, nonconformist, risk taking, hypersexualized, and unyielding—embodying many of the characteristics associated with the black stereotype in American society. Further indicative of Zeb's conformity to the black stereotype is the chastisement he receives from a fellow solider when Zeb engages in gambling and loses his money, a reprimand for his indulgence in a practice that the soldier regards as wasteful. The soldier criticizes Zeb for never being satisfied with what he has, to which Zeb responds, "You've got to reach for the sky even if you don't make it." Zeb is explicitly marked as Other through his behavior and his alignment with George. Although George does not appear on-screen again, his presence in these early moments of the film is significant because it establishes Zeb's Otherness as associated with the black stereotype.

At an Alaskan cannery, Zeb gains work in a menial position and develops a friendship with a Chinese immigrant, Wang (George Takei)—both of which link him to a second kind of Otherness. Zeb's Otherness is explicitly indicated not only through his characterization as Other relative to an Asian immigrant but also when Wang claims that he has never heard of a white man working in a cannery unless he has encountered trouble. In addition, Zeb signifies the Otherness that Wang embodies when he befriends him and engages in Asian cultural practices like eating pickled snake, which he then regurgitates once its origin is revealed. Rejecting the food represents an act of abjection since his expulsion of the food from his body becomes synonymous with the expulsion of his Otherness now infused in his body.

Zeb's Otherness is again affirmed when Wang falters in his productivity at the cannery and Zeb defends his Asian coworker to the company foreman. The two white men (Zeb and the foreman) engage in a dispute over Wang (the Asian Other), marking Zeb as Other—both because the dispute highlights Zeb's volatile disposition, aligning him with the black stereotype as established in the film's introduction to the protagonist, and because Zeb challenges his white boss in defense of an Asian immigrant, another Other. Zeb is "Not quite the Same, not quite the Other," as Trinh T. Minh-Ha suggests, even though he is marked as Other both for his conformity to the black stereotype and for his indoctrination into Asian culture.[12]

Evicted from the cannery, Zeb falls into the ocean but is miraculously rescued by ship captain Thor Storm. Recognizing Zeb's struggle for employment and quest for a post-military life—obstacles that again link Zeb to blackness—Thor offers Zeb work with his fishing outfit. During their journey, Thor reveals that his father was a missionary who migrated to Alaska, while Zeb makes it known that his father also sacrificed his life "for others" but was left "on a dark street bleeding." Zeb's background, thus, also links him to the black stereotype not only because he lacks a father figure but also because his father was murdered violently. When Thor takes Zeb under his wing, Thor then substitutes for Zeb's absent father. At this moment, Thor rescues Zeb not only physically but also psychologically, leading the two to become best friends. Unfortunately their relationship deteriorates when Thor's fiancée, Bridie Ballantyne (Carolyn Jones), develops an affection for the irresistible Zeb. Zeb, however, eager to finance his business venture with Thor, returns to Seattle and marries his former boss's daughter, Dorothy (Martha Hyer), to acquire the necessary financing, even though her father "detests that his icy daughter wants to be warmed in the Burton flame."[13] When Zeb returns to Alaska with a wife, Bridie admits to Thor her attraction to his friend; Thor subsequently abandons her and ends up living among Alaska Natives, identified in the film as Eskimos.[14]

Zeb works hard to expel his Otherness by ascending into white power and wealth; conversely, Thor now becomes the Other through his undesirability and his association with the Alaska Natives. Following his abandonment of Bridie, Thor travels to a remote part of Alaska, where he has an accident during a snowstorm and is rescued by a group of Eskimos. During his recovery, as J. E. Smyth explains, "two nude Eskimo women"—one of whom becomes Thor's wife—"warm the half-frozen Thor with warmth from their bodies."[15] Thor must restore his masculinity and achieves this through marrying an Alaska Native woman (an Other). According to Susan Courtney, "White men whose former states of privilege and idealization are now openly questioned in the exposure of profound weaknesses—social, psychic, and corporeal"—have to be resurrected. Thor's marriage to Una (Dorcas Brower) allows him to reclaim the masculinity and desirability denied.[16] In addition, his interracial marriage produces a mixed-race son, further affirming Thor's Otherness.

Zeb and Thor become diametrically opposed when Zeb's cannery business is transformed into a corporate enterprise that engages in environmentally unsafe practices and displaces local fishermen. In comparison, Thor is concerned with preserving the environment and supporting local fishermen. The divide between Thor and Zeb, however, escalates when their children, Christopher (Steve Harris) and Grace (Shirley Knight), respectively, become attracted to each other. Zeb insults Thor with the racially discriminatory warning to keep his "half-breed kid away" from his daughter. Their ongoing feud, rather than dividing Christopher and Grace, draws the young couple closer: they elope, flee to Christopher's childhood village, and conceive a child. Tragedy strikes, however, as the couple try to return home to birth their child; the only survivor is their newborn, the racially mixed Christine (Diane McBain). Zeb and Thor then fight for custody of the granddaughter they share, and, in the end, the court awards them joint custody.[17]

Christine's presence forces the two men to come to terms with her mixed-race ancestry and perhaps their own Otherness, which they have alternatively repressed, in the case of Zeb, and appropriated, in the case of Thor. Most exemplary of Zeb's transition into whiteness is his accusation against his granddaughter of fraternizing with Native Americans, Alaska Natives ("Eskimos"), "half-breeds," and any ethnicity other than "whites/whiteness." When Christine rejects his racialized views and threatens to attend the University of Alaska (an ethnic institution), he insists that she attend the University of Seattle (a nonethnic institution). Rejecting his proposition, Christine reminds her grandfather of her own mixed-race identity with the remark, "You seem to forget I am one-quarter Eskimo," to which he responds, "I am trying to forget." Attempting to erase her racial and ethnic identity while remaining oblivious to his own subject position as Other (since he previously conformed to the black stereotype), Zeb erases his Otherness/racialization through his transition into whiteness. His desire for whiteness is made glaringly apparent when he encourages his granddaughter to "pass as white"—as he himself has arguably done—for the purpose of becoming more "normalized" as white. Refusing her grandfather, Christine makes it clear that she has no intention to masquerade her identity and adamantly declares, "Prejudice is a cover for those who possess their own inferiorities." Zeb willingly uses his granddaughter for his own political and personal gain, and, considering his willingness to compromise his integrity for his own self-interests, he concludes the film aligned with the black stereotype that he began with, as identified by Sam McDaniel's presence on the train. Both of the film's protagonists, Zeb and Thor, are constructed as ambivalent Others—fluctuating between the polarities of not only white and black but also yellow (Chinese) and red (Native).

CONCLUSION

Double Indemnity and *Ice Palace* share in common the black presence that McDaniel provided—a presence deemed central to the films' development because it allowed white characters to appropriate blackness without being physically black. In other words, McDaniel's presence "darkened" the white protagonists who descend into immorality and allowed white characters to conform to the black stereotype psychologically if not physically. To render plausible the notion that black characters influenced the moral decline of the white protagonists as they descend into "darkness" in *Double Indemnity*, James M. Cain's 1936 novel on which the film was based references a range of racial or ethnic groups. Cain refers to the Spanish furniture and a Mexican rug that decorate the Nirdlinger (Dietrichson) home, and Huff (Walter) mentions a Chinese grocer Mr. Ling, a Filipino houseboy, and Lola's Italian boyfriend. However, while Cain mentions the garage attendant, porters, and redcaps, he does not specifically racially identify them. This omission lends credence to the position that when the novel was adapted for the screen, blackness was deliberately introduced to confirm that the white protagonists cross racial and ethnic borders.[18] The filmmakers thus double down on white immorality through the introduction of the black racial Other. As for *Ice Palace*, considering Edna Ferber's liberalism, it is conceivable that the race mixing woven into her novels could not have been effectively achieved on-screen without integrating persons of color into the film adaptations. Thus, when *Ice Palace* was transformed on-screen, McDaniel was strategically inserted into the film's beginning to prepare audiences for the film's race-mixing theme—a film that depicts white characters who are marked as ambivalent Others perhaps to allow white spectators to vicariously experience Otherness.

NOTES

1   Manthia Diawara, "*Noir* by *Noirs*: Toward a New Realism in Black Cinema," in *Shades of Noir: A Reader*, ed. Joan Copjec (London: Verso, 1993), 262.

2   Diawara, "*Noir* by *Noirs*," 262.

3   Eric Lott, "The Whiteness of Film Noir," *American Literary History* 9, no. 3 (1997): 547.

4   Lott, "Whiteness of Film Noir," 547.

5   Lott, "Whiteness of Film Noir," 546. For a discussion of the anklet, see Paula Rabinowitz, *Black & White & Noir: America's Pulp Modernism* (New York: Columbia University Press, 2002), 172.

6   Lott, "Whiteness of Film Noir," 551.

7   Lott, "Whiteness of Film Noir," 546.

8   E. Ann Kaplan, "'The Dark Continent of Film Noir': Race, Displacement and Metaphor in Tourneur's *Cat People* (1942) and Welles' *The Lady from Shanghai* (1948)," in *Women in Film Noir*, ed. E. Ann Kaplan (London: British Film Institute, 1998), 183.

9   J. E. Smyth, *Edna Ferber's Hollywood: American Fictions of Gender, Race, and History* (Austin: University of Texas Press, 2010), 233.

10   Smyth, *Edna Ferber's Hollywood*, 235, 238.

11   Vincent Sherman, *Studio Affairs: My Life as a Film Director* (Lexington: University Press of Kentucky, 1996), 271.

12   Trinh T. Minh-Ha, *When the Moon Waxes Red: Representation, Gender and Cultural Politics* (New York: Routledge, 1991), 74.

13   Richard L. Coe, "Epic of Alaska Finest Ferber," *Washington Post*, June 29, 1960, C10.

14   The use of the term "Eskimo" to describe Indigenous peoples of the Arctic region is pejorative. Indigenous peoples of Alaska are jointly called "Alaska Natives" and can be divided into five major groupings: Aleuts, Northern Eskimos (Inupiat), Southern Eskimos (Yuit), Interior Indians (Athabascans), and Southeast Coastal Indians (Tlingit and Haida).

15   Smyth, *Edna Ferber's Hollywood*, 257.

16   Susan Courtney, *Hollywood Fantasies of Miscegenation: Spectacular Narratives of Gender and Race, 1903–1967* (Princeton, NJ: Princeton University Press, 2005), 201.

17   It is important to note that Grace and Una die in childbirth and that their deaths can be interpreted as forms of punishment for women who produce mixed-race children. Courtney argues that the Other "often functions in these films to register possible challenges to the dominance of white male vision, only to then facilitate its restoration," which is made apparent in a reconstituted American identity. See Courtney, *Hollywood Fantasies*, 217.

18   David Bordwell suggested that I return to Cain's novel to determine if the garage attendant, porter, and red caps are racially identified; if they are not, this lends credence to the position that the filmmakers either consciously or unconsciously cast black actors in these roles—roles that blacks assumed off-screen.

15

INCURSIONS IN THE FORBIDDEN ZONE

GENRE AND THE BLACK SCIENCE FICTION FILM

Barry Keith Grant

Unsurprisingly, the representation of race in classical Hollywood science fiction cinema constitutes what Adilifu Nama calls a "structured absence" in the genre.[1] During the classical studio period, science fiction, like every other genre produced by Hollywood, presented a decidedly white (as well as masculine) world. The pioneering work of Laura Mulvey and Richard Dyer has shown how the normative Hollywood gaze is male, heterosexual, and white.[2] In white cultural representation, argues Dyer, white people are deracialized and speak for a universalized "human nature."[3] In the 1950s during the science fiction boom, studio-era movies about space exploration, like *Rocketship X-M* (Neumann 1950), *Destination Moon* (Pichel 1950), *Flight to Mars* (Selander 1951), and *Project Moonbase* (Talmadge 1953), typically featured all-white casts that, following Dyer, stand in for "humanity" or "the human race." Like the platoon in the World War II combat film, the rocket crew may have different ethnic and class identities, but they are almost always exclusively white.

To appreciate the extent to which whiteness prevailed in the Hollywood science fiction film, we need only think of one that was considered radical at the time of its release in 1984, John Sayles's independently produced *The Brother from Another Planet*, because it was the first science fiction feature to cast a black actor (Joe Morton) as a humanoid alien. It contrasted starkly with such preceding very white screen extraterrestrials as, say, Michael Rennie's Klaatu in *The Day the Earth Stood Still* (Wise 1951) or Jeff Morrow's Exeter from Metaluna in *This Island Earth* (Newman 1955). The very fact of the casting's unconventionality underscores how racially rigid such representations were. In the plot of Sayles's film, a black alien arrives on Earth in New York City and seeks refuge in Harlem, where he tries to survive, a stranger in a strange land. At the same time, he is hunted by two white extraterrestrial bounty hunters whose goal is to return him to slavery on their home world. The narrative unavoidably addresses historical racial oppression—especially of slavery in America and the Dred Scott laws that allowed escaped slaves to be returned to their owners in the South as "property"—which includes Hollywood's privileging of white representation.

Obviously, many science fiction films can be read—indeed, they invite such a reading—as metaphorically addressing issues of race. So, for example, Ed Guerrero describes the climax of Kurt Neumann's original version of *The Fly* (Neumann 1958) as yet another fearful expression of black male sexuality, as it involves a scientist who "emerges from an experiment with a monstrous Sambo-like, black fly's head, his compound eyes bulging and his erect, black, phallic arm jerking as he advances toward his screaming, white-clad wife."[4] Likewise, Charles Ramirez Berg has argued that the original *Terminator* films (1984 and 1991) reflect anxiety about Latino immigration, with Schwarzenegger's killer robot from the future embodying a fearsome bandito.[5] The most well-known example is the original *Planet of the Apes* series (1968, 1970, 1971, 1972, and 1973), in which the apes are widely understood to represent, as Guerrero puts it, "a sustained allegory not only for slavery but also the burdens of racial exploitation, the civil rights movement, and the black rebellion that followed it."[6]

Of course, science fiction movies with aliens commonly lend themselves to racialized readings. *Enemy Mine* (Petersen 1985) and *Alien Nation* (Baker 1988), obviously punning on the phrase "illegal alien," take the metaphor of the aliens' species difference as their explicit theme, an approach continued in the more recent *District 9* (Blomkamp 2009). These films make clear that, as with the genres of the Western and the horror film, the science fiction film comes with a built-in figure of the Other—the alien rather than Indians or monsters. In the genre's history aliens have been called upon to represent every anxiety felt by white patriarchal culture, including women, sexuality, children, communism, late capitalism, and racial difference—much the same list of bourgeois boogeymen that Robin Wood offered in his pioneering essay "An Introduction to the American Horror Film."[7]

Now, this clearly overdetermined whiteness in Hollywood science fiction, of which *The Brother from Another Planet* so powerfully reminds us, may seem somewhat curious given that the genre, by its very nature, allows for—or, more precisely—requires alternatives in its premises from the world as we know it. Yet the possible new worlds imagined by classic American science fiction cinema have avoided issues of race, implicitly, by omission, endorsing the genre's traditional white perspective, as if it were a Forbidden Zone, like that banned space in *Planet of the Apes* (Schaffner 1968) that contradicts the official worldview.[8] The recent film *Black Panther* (Coogler 2018) shows considerable progress in black representation within the American science fiction film, certainly. But *Black Panther* would not have been possible without a number of earlier films that sought to offer more progressive black representations within the constraints and conventions of the genre. In this chapter I look at two other Hollywood science fiction movies—*The World, the Flesh, and the Devil* (MacDougall 1959) and *The Meteor Man* (Townsend 1993)—that have addressed racial difference explicitly rather than metaphorically and how in earlier periods they negotiated the demands of genre in order to do so. Both engage with the genre's conventions and iconography to challenge its presumption of whiteness—an ideological constraint that has remained operative despite Hollywood's evolution from the classical to postclassical period.

Written and directed by Ranald MacDougall, a white filmmaker, *The World, the Flesh, and the Devil* rode the science fiction boom of the 1950s and a preceding cycle of prestige problem pictures about racism that included *Gentleman's Agreement* (Kazan 1947), *Pinky* (Kazan 1949), *Home of the Brave* (Robson 1949), and *Intruder in the Dust* (Brown 1949). Harry Belafonte, the film's star, produced it as the first film released through his company, Harbel Productions, along with MGM. Belafonte chose the project with the intent, as he declared, to "show Negroes as we are, as people with the same hopes and loves, weaknesses and problems as other people."[9]

The film's plot involves a Pennsylvania coal mine inspector, Ralph Burton (Belafonte), who survives a sudden nuclear war because the mine he was inspecting collapses before the outbreak of hostilities. At first Burton waits patiently to be rescued, but when the digging for him stops after several days, he rouses himself to action and manages to dig himself out, clawing dirt, lifting boulders and beams, and slogging through muck. When he gets to the surface, he discovers that he is the only survivor of a nuclear disaster. He heads for an eerily empty New York City, where he sets up living quarters in a luxury high-rise. Eventually he meets another survivor, a white woman, the blond Sarah Cardwell (Inger Stevens), who also has made her way to New York.

As time passes, Ralph and Sarah develop a close relationship but live in separate quarters, Ralph clearly uncomfortable with the prospect of a sexual relationship because of their racial difference. Then, a third survivor appears—another white man, Ben Thacker (Mel Ferrer), who immediately activates a masculine and racially fueled mortal contest by seeing Sarah as a prize to be fought over and won. In the climax Thacker stalks Burton through the concrete canyons of Manhattan in a private race war. But Burton refuses to resort to violence even as Thacker taunts him, and so, at the end, at the last moment, just as he is about to shoot Burton at point-blank range, Thacker has an improbable change of heart and lays down his weapon. In the end, the three characters walk off arm in arm to face a future free of racism—and, presumably, of the tyranny of heterosexual monogamy as well—as a title appears saying "The Beginning." As another contemporary review said, *The World, the Flesh, and the Devil* marched "steadfastly from a promising idea through the syrupy marshes of cliché." [10]

Generically, *The World, the Flesh, and the Devil* functions as a reply to earlier post-holocaust films, especially Arch Oboler's *Five* (1951). *Five* was the first postwar nuclear holocaust film, and it does have a black character as one of its five survivors. Unfortunately, though, not even dialogue provided by black writer James Weldon Johnson can save *Five* from its stereotyped and implicit racism, given its perhaps unexamined but fundamental assumption of a white perspective. In the film's plot, five people come together after surviving nuclear destruction: a rational and liberal white man; a pregnant white woman; a mountain-climbing racist; a dying banker deep in shock from what has happened; and Charles, the black man who tends him. Charles (Charles Lampkin), who worked in the bank in some unspecified but obviously menial position, readily assumes the chores for the group, even wearing an apron at one point as he cleans up in the kitchen. Once the banker dies from radiation poisoning, Charles is no longer necessary to the plot and so is conveniently dispatched by the white racist.

The macho Ben Thacker in *The World, the Flesh, and the Devil* seems clearly modeled on the racist adventurer, Eric (James Anderson), of *Five*. In both films, it is a white man who initiates the drive for masculine dominance; yet while in *Five*, although the more liberal white man, our figure of normative society, ends up with the white woman while the racist also dies of radiation poisoning, there is no questioning that it will be a white man who gets to sire the brave new world after the apocalypse. In *The World, the Flesh, and the Devil*, by contrast, it is the black character who is our figure of identification and who, unlike Charles, survives on equal footing with the two white characters, race no longer an issue in this future post-integration society.

Indeed, Burton is the main protagonist, the spectator's figure of identification throughout *The World, the Flesh, and the Devil*. Our narrative point of view is aligned with his. We never know more than he does. We remain trapped with him in the mine shaft, not knowing what is happening in the world outside until he does. Later, when Burton finds a radio station and listens to the final news broadcasts of the world dying, we experience it all entirely through an intense, lengthy close-up of Belafonte's face that lasts a full two minutes. It is a long take by any measure and a shot that, in mainstream cinema, perhaps at the time could only have been done with Belafonte, who was referred to then as "the first Negro matinee idol"[11]—the ideal of what Donald Bogle calls "the postwar sensitive good Negro"[12]—but that nevertheless was a kind of shot unprecedented in mainstream American cinema. This long take is a remarkable intervention not only within the specific genre of science fiction film but also transgenerically, across Hollywood's white male gaze more generally.

Two decades later, the 1990s witnessed a substantial shift in generic representation as profound as those initiated by the French New Wave in the 1960s and the New American Cinema in the 1970s. Spurred by the success of Spike Lee's *Do the Right Thing* in 1989 and Ridley Scott's *Thelma and Louise* two years later, these films launched new generic investigations of the

15.1. Harry Belafonte in *The World, the Flesh, and the Devil* (1959).

ideology and representation of race and gender. *Do the Right Thing* launched a cycle of Hollywood genre films made by black directors, including John Singleton's *Boyz n the Hood* (1991), Ernest Dickerson's *Surviving the Game* (1994), Lee's subsequent *Malcolm X* (1992) and *Get on the Bus* (1996), and Robert Townsend's *The Five Heartbeats* (1991) and *The Meteor Man* (1993). In Townsend's first film, *Hollywood Shuffle* (1987), which actually preceded *Do the Right Thing* by two years, Townsend satirically turns the limitations of the stereotypes and conventions of Blaxploitation into a virtue by making them the very subject of the film. Townsend plays Bobby Taylor, an aspiring actor who finds acting opportunities in Hollywood limited to pimps, drug dealers, and rapists. Taylor has a number of dreams in which he appears in various heroic movie roles such as Rambo. One of his dreams involves being a superhero, a fantasy that becomes the center of his later *Meteor Man*.

In *Meteor Man* Townsend plays the mild-mannered schoolteacher Jefferson Reed, whose Washington, DC, neighborhood is terrorized by a black gang known as the Golden Lords, who work for a white drug kingpin. One night the Golden Lords pursue Jeff, who hides in an alleyway dumpster. When he emerges later, he is severely injured by a glowing green meteorite that falls on him from the sky. Miraculously healed, Jeff soon discovers that the meteorite has given him superpowers. Jeff's parents urge him to use his powers to fight the Golden Lords and help the community. After initially resisting the idea, he defeats the gang and restores order to the hood by busting crack houses, thwarting robberies, and forcing both street gang and police to lay down their weapons and work together to rebuild the community.

Like *Do the Right Thing*, *Meteor Man* works to establish a black film aesthetic in part by providing a rich palette of black cultural iconography and references. In the opening scene alone, as Jeff gets ready for work, we see his Howard University jersey and a poster for a baseball game featuring the Baltimore Elite Giants, one of the teams in the old "Negro leagues." Jeff's dog is named Ellington, there is a breakfast discussion involving *Jet* magazine, and his neighbor Moses, played by iconic black actor James Earl Jones, is listening to Billie Holiday. The plethora of black iconography in the film, including many in the cast, works to establish and participate in a cultural history, like genre films themselves. Townsend's generic awareness is signaled immediately in the title of his production company in the opening credits: "A Tinseltownsend production." More than a mere pun, it refers to Townsend's attempt to work with a black sensibility within the Hollywood genre system.

15.2. Robert Townsend in *The Meteor Man* (1993).

This theme also is expressed by the way the film participates in the super-hero genre, at once fulfilling its conventions and poking fun at them. For example, the film's theme music recalls that for Richard Donner's *Superman* (1979). Like Superman's alter ego, Clark Kent, Jeff is exceedingly mild-mannered. And like the Man of Steel, Jeff can leap tall buildings in a single bound—although he gets stuck on top of a streetlamp when he first tries. The green meteorite that hits Jeff recalls Kryptonite, the one substance to which Superman is vulnerable, except here it provides strength rather than drains it. Jeff's parents urge him on for the common good, like the kindly Ma and Pa Kent.

Before Super Jeff takes a stand, when his father is about to stand up to the Golden Lords on the street, Moses tries to dissuade him: "When I want to see a hero, I'll rent *Rambo*." Townsend had already imagined himself as a black Rambo in *Hollywood Shuffle*, but the importance of this remark is fully illuminated by reference to another film, *White Man's Burden* (Nakano 1995), which presents an alternative United States where the actual power relations between blacks and whites are reversed. In one scene, a white factory worker, Louis (John Travolta), gives his son precious money to buy himself a birthday present. To Louis's dismay, his son chooses a black action figure, which is more expensive because it has greater cultural cachet than that of the white superhero. Louis tries to convince the boy to choose the less expensive white superhero, but his son remains adamant. The scene underscores how popular culture helps establish a sense of cultural identity—precisely what *Meteor Man* aims to do. Early in *Meteor Man*, one of Jeff's students gives him a comic book featuring a superhero named "The Faceless Crusader," whose racial identity is unclear on the comic's cover since he has no face. Jeff—and, by extension, Townsend—is seeking to fill in this blank in American popular culture. It is worth noting that the film succeeded in spawning a series of six Marvel comic books featuring the character Meteor Man, as well as an action figure, thus to some extent realizing Townsend's aim.

The science fiction films discussed here, like many black genre films, work in part by "signifying" upon their generic traditions, at once deploying and deflating generic conventions and iconography. According to Henry Louis Gates Jr., black writing is marked by a revision of—or "signifying" upon—texts in the Western tradition.[13] It is precisely in this play upon white texts, he argues, that black texts articulate their difference. So, for example, *Brother from Another Planet* signifies upon *Planet of the Apes*. In Sayles's film, the Brother first lands at Ellis Island, the place where so many teeming masses have entered America yearning, like the Brother, for freedom. When he first emerges from his ship, which has crashed in the harbor, the Brother is shown next to the Statue of Liberty, the same iconic statue that represents lost normative values in the famous twist ending of *Planet of the Apes*. One shot in *Brother* shows Liberty sharply in focus in the distance and then rack focuses suddenly as the Brother's head comes into the frame in the foreground of the image, so that the statue—and the democratic melting pot values it supposedly represents—suddenly seems to become unfocused, to lose definition, with the appearance of a black face and the challenge it represents to the lofty, universalized ideals ascribed to Liberty in *Planet of the Apes*.

These black science fiction films all employ the familiar images and conventions of the classic Hollywood science fiction film not to explore outer space but to make space for black American identity in the genre. Although science fiction, none of these films are set in a distant future, in an alternate universe, or on another world. Instead, they present familiar and recognizable American places, underscoring their aim of social critique. They signify on the genre's white texts by appropriating their generic conventions while challenging their traditional white way of seeing beyond the mere level of representation. Like the nameless narrator of Ralph Ellison's touchstone novel *Invisible Man* (1952), the protagonist of each of these films struggles to emerge from the darkness of oppression (in each, represented as a literal climbing out) into the light of cultural representation and identity. Despite the differences in the political and cultural discourses of their respective times, all three films examined in this chapter would seem to follow the same cinematic strategies called for earlier by feminist film critics such as Claire Johnston, whose notion of "counter-cinema" meant employing popular genres to challenge their traditional gender ideology.[14] Similar "counter-histories" can undoubtedly be traced in other mainstream genres. Thus, while it is true that the various Hollywood genres have been structured from a white perspective, a perspective that went almost entirely unchallenged during the studio era, Hollywood's genre system has at the same time provided potential space for marginalized voices subsequently to emerge.

NOTES

1   Adilifu Nama, *Black Space: Imagining Race in Science Fiction Film* (Austin: University of Texas Press, 2008), 2.

2   Laura Mulvey, "Visual Pleasure and Narrative Cinema," *Screen* 16, no. 3 (1975): 6–18; Richard Dyer, *White: Essays on Race and Culture* (New York: Routledge, 1997).

3   Dyer, *White*, 28.

4   Ed Guerrero, *Framing Blackness: The African American Image in Film* (Philadelphia: Temple University Press, 1993), 41–42.

5   Charles Ramirez Berg, "Immigrants, Aliens, and Extraterrestrials: Science Fiction's Alien 'Other' as (Among Other Things) New Latino Imagery," in *Film Genre Reader IV*, ed. Barry Keith Grant (Austin: University of Texas Press, 2012), 414–15.

6   Guerrero, *Framing Blackness*, 43.

7   Robin Wood, "An Introduction to the American Horror Film," in *Robin Wood on the Horror Film: Collected Essays and Reviews*, ed. Barry Keith Grant (Detroit, MI: Wayne State University Press, 2018), 73–110, especially 75–81.

8 One common tactic of ideological avoidance by mainstream science fiction cinema is to concentrate on class difference rather than race. Economic oppression, especially as the gap between rich and poor continues to grow, is a situation that potentially unites viewers across racial and ethnic lines. Movies such as *Total Recall* (Verhoeven 1990), *Elysium* (Blomkamp 2013), and *The Hunger Games* series (2012, 2013, 2014, and 2015), for example, following the lead of Fritz Lang's *Metropolis* (1927), emphasize class disparity in the future. Viewers of these films, regardless of race, especially in the era of Wall Street entitlement, appreciate these fantasy scenarios in which revolution by the underclass is usually successful. Dominant ideology, it would seem, has little difficulty in absorbing imaginary revolutions when they are set elsewhere and else when.

9 Daniel Leab, *From Sambo to Superspade: The Black Experience in Motion Pictures* (Boston: Houghton Mifflin, 1976), 220.

10 Quoted in Leab, *From Sambo to Superspade*, 219.

11 Quoted in Leab, *From Sambo to Superspade*, 219.

12 Donald Bogle, *Toms, Coons, Mulattoes, Mammies and Bucks: An Interpretative History of Blacks in American Films* (New York: Viking, 1973), 202.

13 Henry Louis Gates Jr., *The Signifying Monkey: A Theory of African-American Literary Criticism* (New York: Oxford University Press, 1988).

14 Claire Johnston, "Women's Cinema as Counter Cinema," in *Movies and Methods*, ed. Bill Nichols (Berkeley: University of California Press, 1976), 208–17.

VI

WOMEN AT WORK

16

DOING HER BIT

Women and Propaganda in World War I

Liz Clarke

Many of the gendered conventions of the Hollywood war genre that define the genre today—male strength in training, heroics on the battlefield, or the difficulties of returning home—arose in the 1920s and, by the 1940s, included the trope of the suffering yet strong wives and lovers of World War II soldiers. While these latter characters seem to be the most common type played by women in war films, such a view ignores the very active women of pre-1920s silent cinema. The war films of the 1910s offered a significantly different representation of war, particularly with regard to the use of female characters as central heroic protagonists. Straddling the periods of early cinema and studio-era Hollywood, the 1910s was a decade during which female characters dominated war adventure stories; Civil War girl spies and cross-dressing female soldiers were frequent characters of early narrative American films, and serial queen heroines proved to be very popular in films. It was in this context that heroic female characters were deployed in films that were either directly or indirectly about World War I. As the war genre emerged, changes to the American film industry stimulated changes to the war film's gendered representation of heroism and the genre's use in the promotion of patriotism. This chapter focuses on those films to better understand the possibilities of gender representation in the war genre in the early classical Hollywood era.

Prior to the genre's stabilization, active female protagonists appeared in melodramas and comedies, wherein they promoted patriotism for American efforts in World War I. World War I was used by filmmakers as a new subject through which the tried and tested formulas of the 1910s—the melodramas, the spectacle, the female heroine—could be shown anew. In *Reel Patriotism*, Leslie Midkiff DeBauche employs the term "practical patriotism" to describe the dual interests of those in the film industry to both support the nation and do good business. Patriotism was good for stars and good for ticket sales. These films played it safe: they drew from popular trends and included just enough war subject matter to allow the advertising and exhibition to exploit and promote interest in the war. Rather than staying home and depicting wartime service in industry—as did World War II's Rosie the Riveter—women in such films as *The Little American* (DeMille 1917), *Johanna Enlists* (Taylor 1918), *Joan of Plattsburg* (Goldwyn 1918), *Miss Jackie of the Army* (Ingraham 1917), *Her Country First* (Young 1918), *Arms and the Girl* (Kaufman 1918), and *Daughter of Destiny* (Irving 1917) were meant to inspire participation in the war effort by "doing their part" both on the battlefront and in active measures at home. For example, in *The Little American* and *Arms and the Girl*, the heroines find themselves caught up in the war in Europe and act as spies. In *Her Country First* and *Joan of Plattsburg*, the lead characters try to thwart foreign spies at home, all the while involved in makeshift military training.

One film that demonstrates the particularities of World War I–era film heroines from production to exhibition is *Joan the Woman* (1916). Produced by Famous Players-Lasky and released by Paramount Pictures in December 1916, several months prior to the United States' entry into the war in April 1917, the film continued to be exhibited throughout 1917. Yet *Joan the Woman*'s plot does not center on World War I so much as it uses the setting of the war as a frame for the telling of Joan of Arc's tragic story and to draw an analogy between characters in medieval France and modern England. In an early scene, British soldier Eric Trent (Wallace Reid) discovers a sword in the wall of a trench. His removal of the sword conjures a vision of its owner, Joan of Arc, and her telling of her life's story—which forms the majority of the film. At the end of his vision, Trent is inspired by Joan's heroism and death, and he volunteers to deliver a bomb, which results in his own death. His sacrifice parallels Joan's and, in the context of Paramount's eventual use of the film as a recruitment tool, may well have encouraged men in the audience to consider their own participation in the war. In this way, *Joan the Woman* may be seen as a film that was used to encourage enlistment in the US Army despite the plot's focus on Joan of Arc.

The prospect of enlistment in the US Army may well have been furthered by the status of *Joan the Woman* as an epic film: directed Cecil B.

DeMille from a scenario by Jeanie MacPherson, it featured a well-known female star (Geraldine Farrar), a large cast, and the sort of sprawling sets characteristic of spectacle pictures that were sweeping through Hollywood production at the time.[2] Indeed, the ongoing war in Europe was only of interest to filmmakers as subject matter inasmuch as it offered the possibility of an epic film with big sets, large battles, well-known stars, and other elements of spectacle. In her book, DeBauche provides numerous examples of letters between DeMille and producer Jesse Lasky in which they speculate about whether the war would still be occurring when the film was completed and released.[3] These letters demonstrate that making a film about World War I during the wartime years was not a motivating factor in producing the film; rather, World War I was a popular subject for films because its elements of spectacle entailed increased ticket prices and sales.

Ultimately, *Joan the Woman* is a unique example of a war film that was used as propaganda even though it was not made for that specific purpose. While Lasky and DeMille were focused on the cost of the production and the appeal of the film, after its release and the American entry into World War I, the use value of the film to promote patriotism and recruitment changed drastically. Almost immediately after the United States entered the war, Paramount's promotion for the film shifted to emphasize patriotism and heroism; for example, recruitment booths were set up at theaters showing the film. An additional, interesting example of how the film was repurposed for American recruitment transpired as a gimmick at a Chicago theater. Helen Ketchum, a "lobby girl" (female usher), dressed up as Joan of Arc in an attempt to ridicule "slackers"—a term that referred to the men who quickly married to avoid military service—and, thus, to convince them to enlist.[4] Additionally, decorations in the theater were both French and American themed. As one piece noted, while American patriotism was also on display, "the lobby decorations recall medieval France, and the program girls wear costumes suggested by Joan's armor, in the theater the boxes are draped with the American flag, and the national colors form the basis of the decorations."[5] The Colonial Theater's showing of the film included a prologue spoken by Grace Hickox, who ended "with a plea to the audience to consider Joan's patriotism when they are called on to serve their country."[6] During the same run, four of the lobby girls dressed themselves as Joan of Arc and drove through the city with recruiting officers while handing out flyers about enlistment. According to the reports, "Enthusiasm ran high, crowds were thick and enlistments came fast and furious."[7]

Lobby girls of the Colonial Theater, Chicago, aiding recruiting officers on the street.

16.1. "Theater Girls Aid Uncle Sam," *Motography* (April 1917). Courtesy of Media History Digital Library.

These publicity stunts in exhibition reveal a distinct turn from the celebration and promotion of the active female heroine that marked earlier film examples of melodramas to a focus on male heroics by shifting the emphasis onto enlistment. Recruitment was deemed a necessary objective at this time, and exhibitors and distributors alike were committed to helping the US government achieve its goal—but the active nature of the heroine, in this case Joan of Arc, was glossed over in these wartime promotions or served only the purpose of inspiring men to enlist. The popularity of Joan of Arc in wartime promotions was not as simple as the mere celebration of women's power. Robin Blaetz writes that the use of the figure of Joan of Arc for propaganda during World War I was indicative of the "uncertainty over the roles of the sexes in previously gender-specific arenas. Yet during the war, the freedom with which Joan of Arc was used (in comparison with her absence during the Second World War) suggests that the issue had yet to be recognized as a problem."[8] Within the Hollywood film industry, the role of women was prominent in the mid-1910s: female stars dominated and female heroics remained at the forefront of the burgeoning war genre. Films about war, much like the simultaneously emerging Western genre, were fertile ground for the character type of the woman who was as courageous, athletic, and patriotic as any man.[9] Arguably, Joan of Arc fit the bill for this type of athletic and battle-ready female heroine that dominated American film from the earliest series of Civil War "Girl Spy" films (the titular spy was played by Gene Gauntier) to the popular serial heroines played by Pearl White, Grace Cunard, and Helen Holmes.[10] Female heroines were a mainstay of the American film industry before and during the early Hollywood era.

Female-led films about the war continued into 1917 and 1918. Mary Pickford, Billie Burke, Mabel Normand, Emily Stevens, and Lillian and Dorothy Gish were just a handful of female actresses who starred in films about the war; they also "did their part" by appearing at various speeches, public events, and fundraising efforts in support of the war. These actresses were featured in films with female-centered narratives about American women at home or sometimes stranded in war-torn villages in Europe. The changing gender norms seen in the archetype of the New Woman were sublimated into participation in American military efforts. American-made films during World War I filtered the European conflict through American characters who exemplified this particular form of American femininity. For example, Mary Pickford plays a "little American" trapped in France during a German invasion in *The Little American*; Lillian Gish plays an American in a French village in *Hearts of the World* (Griffith 1918); and Billie Burke plays an American stranded in a Belgium village in *Arms and the Girl*. Home-front themes included women who shamed their husbands into enlisting, such as Emily Stevens in *The Slacker* (Cabanne 1917), and women who participated in military training, such as Mabel Normand in *Joan of Plattsburg* and Pickford in *Johanna Enlists*. DeBauche argues that the war "afforded stars, as it did the companies which employed them, the opportunity to increase their prestige with the American public."[11] In other words, by promoting the war, female stars proved patriotic to their country and simultaneously further developed their star personas in relation to American nationalism.

Of the abovementioned stars, Mary Pickford best illustrates the representation of women both on- and off-screen vis-à-vis World War I. She made the films *100% American* (Rosson 1918), *The Little American*, and *Johanna Enlists* at the same time as she appeared in public promoting the war effort. Pickford's efforts, as has been well documented and discussed, did not end with propagandistic film roles but also included promoting war bonds in speeches and even donating ambulances to the Red Cross and encouraging other stars to do the same.[12] In July 1917, Pickford's public appearance in San Francisco reportedly led the ten thousand people in attendance to purchase $2 million in Liberty Bonds.[13] Pickford's war films vary in subject matter, but all revolve around an American woman's participation—usually unwilling at first—in the war effort. Clémentine Tholas-Disset refers to Pickford's trilogy of war films as "an epic romance, a buffoonish comedy, and a semi-documentarian short advertising piece" that demonstrate how "the war film becomes then adaptable to address diverse audiences."[14] In *The Little American*, Pickford is an American in France who becomes a spy for the Allied forces. In *100% American*, she plays a woman at home doing her part to support the war—namely, by not spending money and, instead, buying Liberty Bonds. And *Johanna Enlists* features Pickford as a young farm girl who meets and encourages a regiment of soldiers who are staying on her family's farm before shipping overseas.

The Little American, directed by Cecil B. DeMille and written by Jeanie MacPherson, is more firmly entrenched in the narrative and generic patterns of the female melodramas typical to the DeMille-MacPherson team than it is dedicated to promoting war enlistment. In other words, if it is a war film, it is also a melodrama. As in the case of many filmmakers at the time, rather than use interest in the film to sell the war, DeMille and MacPherson used interest in the war to sell the film.

Films made during or close to the wartime era might be either propaganda or an exploitation of war for film promotion, or a combination of both. However, if we consider World War I's timing between early cinema and classical Hollywood, we can understand that these films belonged to trends from the 1910s: a growing reliance on spectacle, with the carryover interest in female heroines. If the codifying of particular genres within classical Hollywood style takes time to develop, I would argue that looking to the influences of popular trends prior to entrenchment in classical style can help us understand the early developments of popular genres. The war

16.2. "An American girl (Pickford) finds herself in France during a German invasion," *Motography* (July 1917). Courtesy of Media History Digital Library.

film drew from melodramatic modes—melodrama not meaning women's "weepies," as the term came to imply, but meaning the adventure pictures of the blood and thunder variety, which, as Ben Singer notes, came out of the popular theater tradition of the nineteenth century.[15]

DeBauche states, "In proportion to the number of films in release while the United States was involved in World War I, the number of films bearing any relation to the events of the war was small."[16] Studios and producers did not necessarily alter the production plans—which, according to DeBauche, could be six months for a feature film—to account for the war. Of the films made about the war, however, a fair number featured heroic female protagonists. Many of the studio films about World War I released during 1917 and 1918 used the war as subject while continuing to exploit the lasting popularity of the female heroine trope and the success of female stars of the day. If we look to the content of these films, we see that the war is used as a backdrop in already popular formulas of the period. But the promotion of these films also demonstrates how they are deployed to stir popular sentiment at the time of their release. The following promotion for *Joan of Plattsburg* suggests that women do not react to propaganda but, rather, hold strong in their beliefs:

> "Joan of Plattsburg," with a general appeal to both sexes, is directed nevertheless to the women of America. Men may react to false rumors, have their efficiency reduced through propaganda, but the faith of woman is endurable and constitutes an impregnable fortress in times of national trial, declares the Goldwyn statement.[17]

This statement reveals the uneasy relationship between popular film and the war as subject matter. The various war-related films in which female stars were featured—for timely, political, or simply financial reasons—not only served the purpose of defining women's part during war; these films also demonstrate the central role female stars and female heroics played in films of the 1910s.

Much work on early Hollywood and silent film has focused on women: these include studies of female audiences;[18] women stars; female characters;[19] and women as writers, directors, and other Hollywood creatives.[20] Research that shows how Hollywood began to masculinize in the late teens and 1920s continues to emerge.[21] Nonetheless, researchers should remain open to the idea that even the most masculine of genres—the war genre—historically featured far more female heroines than expected. We can find these women if we include Hollywood's emergence in our study rather than just focusing on the 1920s and onward.

NOTES

1   Leslie Midkiff DeBauche, *Reel Patriotism* (Madison: University of Wisconsin Press, 1997). Much of DeBauche's book explores the concept of "practical patriotism," with a preliminary definition on page xvi.

2   For more on the role of the epic and spectacle in *Joan the Woman*, see Sheldon Hall and Steve Neale, *Epics, Spectacles, and Blockbusters: A Hollywood History* (Detroit, MI: Wayne State University, 2010), 34–40. For a detailed analysis of preparation, production, promotion, and reception of the film, see DeBauche, *Reel Patriotism*, 5–28.

3   DeBauche, *Reel Patriotism*, 9.

4   "Lobby Girl Advertises Theater," *Motography*, April 21, 1917, 872.

5   "Presenting Geraldine Farrar Picture," *Motography*, April 21, 1917, 815.

6   "Presenting Geraldine Farrar Picture," 815.

7   "Theater Girls Aid Uncle Sam," *Motography*, April 21, 1917, 815.

8   Robin Blaetz, *Visions of the Maid: Joan of Arc in American Film and Culture* (Richmond: University of Virginia Press, 2001), 46.

9   See also Laura Horak's chapter, "Cowboy Girls, Girl Spies, and the Homoerotic Frontier," in *Girls Will Be Boys: Cross-Dressed Women, Lesbians, and American Cinema* (New Brunswick, NJ: Rutgers University Press, 2016), 54–89; and Rebecca Bell-Metereau's chapter, "Male Impersonation Before 1960," in *Hollywood Androgyny*, ed. Bell-Metereau, 2nd ed. (New York: Columbia University Press, 1993), 67–115.

10   Films in which Gauntier played Nan, the girl spy, include *The Girl Spy: An Incident of the Civil War* (Olcott 1909), *The Further Adventures of the Girl Spy* (Olcott 1910), and *The Girl Spy Before Vicksburg* (Olcott 1910).

11   DeBauche, *Reel Patriotism*, 34.

12   "Mary Pickford Starts Ambulance," *Motography*, July 28, 1917, 184.

13   "Mary Pickford Doing 'Bit.'" *Motography*, July 7, 1917, 33.

14   Clémentine Tholas-Disset, "Mary Pickford's WWI Patriotism: A Feminine Approach to Wartime Mythical Americanness," in *Heroism and Gender in War Films*, ed. Karen A. Ritzenhoff and Jakub Kazecki (New York: Palgrave Macmillan, 2014), 13.

15   Ben Singer, *Melodrama and Modernity: Early Sensational Cinema and Its Contexts* (New York: Columbia University Press, 2001), 37–58.

16   DeBauche, *Reel Patriotism*, 38.

17   "'Joan' Intended as Spy-Brake," *Motion Picture News*, May 18, 1918, 2944.

18   Shelley Stamp, *Movie-Struck Girls: Women and Motion Picture Culture after the Nickelodeon* (Princeton, NJ: Princeton University Press, 2000).

19   Laura Horak, *Girls Will Be Boys*; Maggie Hennefeld, *Specters of Slapstick and Silent Film Comediennes* (New York: Columbia University Press, 2018); Kristen Anderson Wagner, *Comic Venus: Women and Comedy in American Silent Film* (Detroit, MI: Wayne State University Press, 2018).

20   Mark Garrett Cooper, *Universal Women: Filmmaking and Institutional Change in Early Hollywood* (Urbana: University of Illinois Press, 2010); Karen Ward Mahar, *Women Filmmakers in Early Hollywood* (Baltimore, MD: Johns Hopkins University Press, 2006); Hilary A. Hallett, *Go West, Young Women! The Rise of Early Hollywood* (Berkeley: University of California Press, 2013);

Shelley Stamp, *Lois Weber in Early Hollywood* (Berkeley: University of California Press, 2015).

21   See Erin Hill, *Never Done: A History of Women's Work in Media Production* (New Brunswick, NJ: Rutgers University Press, 2016), for a revision of the long-told tale that women were pushed out of Hollywood as it standardized as an industry. Instead, Hill argues, women were pushed into invisible, below-the-line labor and clerical jobs.

17

GENRES OF PRODUCTION AND THE PRODUCTION OF GENRE

GENDER, GENRE, AND TECHNICAL LABOR IN THE ARTHUR FREED UNIT

Helen Hanson

It is a widely accepted notion in film history that the classical Hollywood cinema is *the* cinema of genre par excellence.[1] Genre criticism has been a key strand in analyzing Hollywood's "repertoire" of genres, their relationship with sociohistorical contexts, and the manner in which the representational codes created for, as well as the configurations of story offered to and recognized by, audiences form a meeting point between producers and consumers—what Steve Neale refers to as the "intertextual relay" of Hollywood genre.[2]

However, analyses of how notions of genre intersect with the processes of classical Hollywood production are far less common than criticism that examines the genre output of the major studios. In this chapter, I analyze how a notion of genre is "operational" in the production of the classical Hollywood musical. In the context of my argument, I take "operational" to mean a consensus among production workers of what kinds of work the production of the musical demanded, the shared knowledge of how these workers might produce the conventions of the musical, and, in a slightly widened context, how genre categorized and delimited the kinds of work that take place in production.

To focus my analysis, I will take a case study of a particular production context: the Arthur Freed Unit at MGM studios. Composer, songwriter, and producer Arthur Freed led the unit from 1944, overseeing the production of prestige budget musicals such as *Easter Parade* (Walters 1948), *An American in Paris* (Minnelli 1951), *Singin' in the Rain* (Donen and Kelly 1952), and

Gigi (Minnelli 1958), which are often taken to exemplify the musical and MGM's investment in production values at the musical's zenith.[3] Within this specific context I channel my analysis not "outward" from production to text; instead, by drawing on archival production sources, I try to trace the genres of labor that structure a particular case study, *Easter Parade*, giving particular attention to some of the routine, but essential, technical tasks in sound and music recording, editing, and postproduction that form the scaffolding in the production of musical numbers.

Writing in *Variety* in 1937, Denis Morrison asked rhetorically: "What makes the musical click?" His article explores the question, offering views of producers from the majors:

> Industry has toiled long and put out many millions in learning how to wrap up musical entertainment and peddle to the public. In the end the producers have, by and large, come back pretty close to the familiar formula of the old-time extravaganza, a sort of super-variety entertainment. Elements of girls, gags and tunes, with opinion almost, but not quite, unanimous in favor of sound story values as well. How to blend these elements most effectively, and where to find the talent to do it, have been the brain-fagging problems for the film impresarios.[4]

His article suggests a shared and operational understanding of genre production, as he notes: "Nowadays, when a major lot sets out to make a musical, the heads know exactly what has to be done, and the measure of success depends on how well-qualified are the experts who do the work."[5]

The "experts who do the work" in the musical were not only the producers, songwriters, composers, star performers, and choreographers—the "above-the-line" talent—but also the personnel who worked "below the line" in the craft and technical roles essential to seamlessly "blending" the "sound story values" that Morrison refers to.

ABOVE AND BELOW THE LINE IN CLASSICAL HOLLYWOOD'S PRODUCTION CULTURES

The production cultures of the classical Hollywood studio era were highly structured, and within these cultures work roles were hierarchically stratified. Writing in 1941, social theorist of Hollywood Leo Rosten distinguished

between the "anonymous movie workers" comprising thousands of craftspeople and the elite "movie makers" comprising the producers, directors,
and decision makers.[6] In more recent production studies, a number of critics
have pointed out how media industries delineate labor "above" and "below"
the line. Miranda Banks writes: "'Above-the-line' and 'below-the-line' are
industry terms that distinguish between creative and craft professions in
production." She notes that these forms of work are valued differently;
above-the-line labor is "evaluated . . . in terms of its imagination, artistry
and inventiveness," whereas "below-the-line practitioners are considered as
craftspeople or technicians . . . who work with their hands."[7] In Classical
Hollywood's production cultures, many below-the-line roles were filled by
women, and a growing area of new research into the studio system, such as
work by J. E. Smyth and Erin Hill, is uncovering and analyzing their contribution to filmmaking.[8]

This chapter traces the work of one woman at the Arthur Freed Unit:
Magdalene "Lela" Simone. She worked below the line in the role of music
coordinator for Freed from 1944 to 1957. German born and of Jewish
descent, Simone had studied music throughout her youth and was a distinguished and talented pianist. She immigrated to the United States in 1933
and, in February 1934, at the age of twenty-six, made her concert debut
with the Los Angeles Philharmonic Orchestra. Simone gradually moved
into motion picture work, first serving as an on-call recording pianist for
the MGM Music Department and then working in technical tasks—such
as music timing and editing—for the department from 1935 to 1944 before
her transfer to the Freed Unit. Simone is little known because she worked
behind the scenes but also because hers is the kind of work often pejoratively
labeled as "generic," in the sense that it was unexceptional compared to the
"talent" of stars or the "agency" of producers or directors.

Janet Staiger has outlined how work regimes within Hollywood's
producer-unit system were standardized and stratified, but, in her analysis of regimes of production, she notes that Hollywood's working cultures
did provide space for collaboration and for the exercise of shared values in
filmmaking:

> Hollywood's criteria of the quality film usually guided individual
> decisions, no matter what position or which workers have the power
> to make them. Together, groups of people worked on a film project,

collaborating on the commodity. Furthermore, Hollywood's mode of production, despite its modifications and minor variations through the 1930s and 1940s, continued to specialise the work tasks and to function with standardised production practices. Many workers felt positive about the collective work process.[9]

As music coordinator, Lela Simone worked below the line and predominantly in a technical role. But while the prevailing image of technical workers has typically been of "gadgeteers" operating complex apparatuses, a closer look at the kinds of tasks undertaken by technicians in this sphere of labor reveals that it demanded sophisticated and nuanced work, as I detail elsewhere.[10] Requiring absolute precision, sound and music production and postproduction demanded high-level, specialized knowledge that combined a command of the apparatus of sound recording and editing with a deep understanding of musical structure, timing, and mood.

Simone contributed to the majority of the Freed Unit films released between 1944 and 1958. The production roster of the unit was intensely busy, and it was usual for the unit to have several projects in production and postproduction simultaneously. Simone's day-to-day duties typically included tasks on different but concurrent films. For example, in the period in which she was working on *Easter Parade*, Simone was also undertaking postproduction for *The Pirate* (Minnelli 1948) and preproduction for *Words and Music* (Taurog 1948). With such a busy workflow, it is a challenge to encapsulate the varying aspects that came under the umbrella of Simone's job as music coordinator. However, we might usefully consider the ways in which she practiced different registers, or genres of work, such as organizational, technical, supervisory, creative, and administrative, although frequently she blended, or harmonized, different registers as necessary to the task.

Her organizational work required forward thinking and anticipatory vision; during preproduction for the Freed Unit films, she participated in the detailed technical planning for the musical numbers, overseeing prerecordings; coordinating recording schedules between the unit and the MGM Music and Sound Departments; managing, logging, and keeping track of the recordings; and supervising the recording sessions. These recording sessions, which were "talent facing," demanded tact and diplomacy; Simone frequently worked with Roger Edens (Freed's associate producer) to rehearse the talent in order to refine their performance for the prerecording.

The technical and supervisory registers of her work required minute attention to detail and demanded that she apply knowledge of musical timing to the processes of filmmaking. Simone's coordination is evident in the many tasks she performed to bring together the musical elements for each film as a whole—the production numbers, the sections of scoring, and the incidental "linking" music. Simone's command of technical detail is evident in documents in the Roger Edens Collection, which include her breakdowns for all the musical elements and setting the cues for the music: the tempo and the number of bars at which the music would come in or fade out. Her technical prowess is also amply demonstrated in her supervision of the many painstaking postproduction tasks she oversaw to finalize the music and sound for the Freed Unit films. Her supervision was sometimes hands-on; for example, as I discuss elsewhere, she was a key player in ensuring that Gene Kelly's "Singin' in the Rain" dance was synchronized with the appropriate sound textures to the tap sounds.[11] At other times, Simone attended review sessions with Freed and Edens and took notes about the tasks to be done to finish the sound and music. It was Simone's responsibility to correspond with the MGM Sound and Editorial Departments and her job to ensure that the notes were executed to Freed's satisfaction.

The administrative aspect of Simone's work included keeping track of the song properties used in the Freed Unit films and ensuring that the MGM Legal Department was updated in order to clear permissions to use them. While this aspect of her work may appear dry, it evidences her seat at the table for discussions among Freed, Edens, and their screenwriters and directors in the planning stages of the unit's films and for subsequent sessions where the producer and team reviewed the films in progress.

COORDINATING AND POLISHING *EASTER PARADE*

Arthur Freed began to develop the project of *Easter Parade* in June 1947. He held story conferences with screenwriting partners Frances Goodrich and Albert Hackett, encouraging them to spin their script around a simple story proposition: "A fella, who is dumped by his dancing partner, picks another girl and tries to build her into the exact duplicate of the first. The new act does badly, but when she displays her natural talent they take off."[12] Freed planned for the story to build into something special through its mode of presentation, the entertainment afforded by its period setting, and its roster of Irving Berlin songs. Gene Kelly was originally cast as Don Hewes, the "fella," and began rehearsing the dance numbers with Robert Alton (who directed the musical numbers for the film), but after Kelly broke his ankle, Freed replaced him with Fred Astaire.[13] Ann Miller played Nadine Hale—the dancing partner who dumps the fella—and Judy Garland played Hannah Brown—the girl whom Don Hewes tries to make over into a double of his partner. Peter Lawford played Don's best friend, Jonathan Harrow III, who falls in love with Hannah. All sixteen of the musical numbers were songs by Irving Berlin.

Analysis of production documents from the archive of Roger Edens permits the work of Simone to be traced. Simone had worked closely with Edens since she started at the unit. She shared with him a deep knowledge of music structure and timing; and, alongside him, she took on very precise technical tasks, such as producing musical breakdowns, working out the timings for musical numbers, and refining the blend of sound and music through the editing and postproduction phases. The film went into production in the second week of November 1947. Prerecording of the film's

17.1. Peter Lawford plays Jonathan Harrow III, the "The Fella with an Umbrella" who shelters Judy Garland in *Easter Parade* (1948).

musical numbers, which required liaison between the Freed Unit and the MGM Music and Sound Departments, was coordinated by Simone. Principal shooting on the film began on November 25, 1947; shooting was completed on February 9, 1948; the film was in postproduction through the spring and early summer; and it had its New York premiere on June 30, 1948.

Analyzing a sample of the production documents for *Easter Parade* illuminates the range of tasks that Simone executed. Simone's supervisory work on the film demonstrates that she had a voice and status in instructing different departments about the tasks needed as the film moved through production. In studying the flow of her communications during the production of *Easter Parade* we can gain a stronger sense of her agency, her ability to multitask, and her formidable oversight of a myriad of details. Simone's workflow intensified as the film entered the postproduction phase in February 1948.

A set of handwritten notes from a Freed Unit review screening of the film allows us to see how Simone generated and coordinated the different personnel and distinct tasks necessary in refining the film's sound and music. The notes are undated, but contextual information indicates that the review occurred close to the end of principal shooting. The notes record the comments of Freed and Edens about the requirements and refinements for sound and music editing. Against the review notes, Simone has written "Bud" (for Bud Cates of the MGM Editorial Department) and "Mike" (for Mike Steinore, sound effects editor for the MGM Sound Department), indicating the direction that she intended to channel her requests.[14] Further documents in the Edens Collection show how Simone followed up the tasks generated from the review notes. Her supervision covered three distinct areas in which her technical expertise intersected with the production of genre: first, her refinements to the musical timing of the picture, particularly smoothing the intros and outros to the musical numbers; second, her attention to the sound effects, ensuring that these connoted the appropriate mood or that they added verisimilitude to the picture; and third, her supervision of lines of wild or looped dialogue to ensure that all dialogue in the picture was intelligible.

Writing to Cates, Simone outlined required refinements to ensure the accurate musical timing and structuring for the numbers; she instructs him to "put in a start at the end of 'Beautiful Faces' just to re-do the applause. We will make this track with the six boys we are calling in for 'Steppin' Out With

My Baby.'"[15] She also asks him to "order two prints of orchestra track 'Steppin' Out With My Baby'" because "I want to elongate the ending to fit the picture." Simone also instructs him to check some cuts already made and to "check overlap in vaudeville montage from the end of 'Ragtime Violin' into 'Alabama Choo Choo.'"[16] At the end of the same week, Simone wrote to Jack McSweeney (Music Department), requesting the insertion of two new music cues in the picture, one to make space for a tune that Edens planned to play in the picture but that had not yet been selected.[17] These communications reveal Simone's careful supervision of the timings of the musical numbers, particularly at their start and finish, junctures at which the smooth movement between spoken and sung performance is crucial to the integration of the number into the larger storyline. At these points Simone's intervention is not simply "technical" but demonstrates how precise judgments about timing underpin the delicate integrative flow that is crucial to the classical Hollywood musical as a genre.

Simone's supervision of the sound effects and dialogue is also documented. She instructs Steinore on very precise requirements for sounds that tightly fit the verisimilitude of the story world and the tonal variations of the character interactions and situations at different junctures of the narrative. She requests that he refine the timbre of car sounds in the street at the beginning of Johnny's (Peter Lawford) romantic "Fella with an Umbrella" number, writing, "The automobile is passing, not starting as Peter runs to get umbrella." Simone also asks Steinore to "check everything in the rain sequence, voices for crowds, feet splashing in water, etc." Simone further instructs Steinore to create sounds of an audience for the end of the "Vaudeville Montage" sequence: "Make background chatter, laughter, etc., for ending of 'Alabama Choo Choo.'" The "Vaudeville Montage" comprises a sequence during which Hewes (Astaire) and Hannah (Garland) gradually find a fluency in their performance partnership. Up to this point in the story, Hewes has rigidly tried to coach Hannah into aping the performance style of his previous partner, Nadine (Miller). The "Vaudeville Montage" begins with Hewes finally allowing Hannah to "be natural" in her performance, and the segments of the montage sequence see their pairing gain charisma and comic vivacity, in successive appearances in front of larger and larger audiences, with their final appearance in the montage showing the pair auditioning for the renowned Mr. Ziegfeld. The extension of the background chatter and applause that Simone requests functions to round off more fully the montage and to give it closure.[18] A list of instructions for looped and wild lines of dialogue for each reel of the film is similarly detailed.[19]

Her administrative overview of the music is evident in the work she did at the preproduction and postproduction stages in helping to ensure MGM had the appropriate legal clearances in place for using the chosen Irving Berlin songs in the film. For example, before principal shooting began, George Schneider of the MGM Music Department, who specialized in legal work, wrote to Simone to check that Berlin's "Walking Up the Avenue"—one of the standout numbers in the final film—had been cleared to use.[20] As the picture was being finalized, from February through March 1948, Simone was in regular correspondence with Richard Powers (also of the MGM Music-Legal team) to ensure that the studio had cleared permissions for all the uses of Berlin's themes or songs in the film; this included instances of sung performances as well as themes adapted and woven into the fabric of the film's scoring and incidental music.[21]

CONCLUSION: THE "GIRL FOR EVERYTHING"

In her oral history interview, undertaken years after her retirement from motion picture work, Lela Simone reflected that at the Freed Unit her strong capabilities made her the person that others sought out for problem solving. She recalled, "I became [the] girl for everything."[22] It is evident from this brief case study of Simone's work that her input into the Freed Unit's production of genre was both significant, in terms of the intense workload that she sustained, and crucial, in terms of refining the Freed Unit films to a level of polished prestige. Production histories of classical Hollywood cinema have rarely taken account of the contribution that routine technical work, expertly executed, made to the films of the studio system. Simone's fine-grained refinements to sound effects, dialogue, musical cues, and timings demonstrate her command of genre production and her vision in tracking seemingly small details through production to put the jigsaw of a whole picture together. Freed recalled her skills with sound and music as follows: "Lela can do with a piece of soundtrack what a French chef can do with a piece of beef."[23] Through a study of the archival traces of Simone's labor, it is evident that she exercised and combined a formidable set of skills and knowledge and, by dividing her work into different types, or genres, that her special abilities were far from generic.

NOTES

1   Thomas Schatz, *Hollywood Genres: Formulas, Filmmaking and the Studio System* (Philadelphia: Temple University Press, 1981); Steve Neale, *Genre and Hollywood* (London: Routledge, 2000).

2   Neale, *Genre and Hollywood*, 2–3.

3   See, for example, Hugh Fordin, *The World of Entertainment! Hollywood's Greatest Musicals* (New York: Doubleday, 1975); John Kobal, *Gotta Sing, Gotta Dance: A History of Movie Musicals* (London: Hamlyn, 1983); Tino Balio, *MGM* (New York: Routledge, 2018), 76.

4   Denis Morrison, "What Is a Filmusical?," *Variety*, June 16, 1937, 3 and 10, reprinted in *Celluloid Symphonies: Texts and Contexts in Film Music History*, ed. Julie Hubbert (Berkeley: University of California Press, 2011), 235.

5   Morrison, "What Is a Filmusical?," 235.

6   Leo Rosten, *Hollywood: The Movie Colony and the Movie Makers* (New York: Harcourt and Brace, 1941), 32.

7   Miranda Banks, "Gender Below-the-Line: Defining Feminist Production Studies," in *Production Studies: Cultural Studies of Media Industries*, ed. Vicki Mayer, Miranda J. Banks, and John Thornton Caldwell (New York: Routledge, 2009), 89.

8   See J. E. Smyth, "Female Editors in Studio-Era Hollywood: Rethinking Feminist 'Frontiers' and the Constraints of the Archives," in *The Routledge Companion to Cinema and Gender*, ed. Patrice Petro, E. Ann Kaplan, Kristin Hole, and Dijana Jelaca (London: Routledge, 2016), 279–88; Smyth, "Organisation Women and Belle Rebels: Hollywood's Working Women in the 1930s," in *Hollywood and the Great Depression*, ed. Iwan Morgan (Edinburgh: Edinburgh University Press, 2016), 66–85; Smyth, "Barbara McLean: Editing, Authorship, and the Equal Right to Be the Best," *Cineaste* 42, no. 2 (2017): 20–23; Smyth, *Nobody's Girl Friday: The Women Who Ran Hollywood* (Oxford: Oxford University Press, 2018); Erin Hill, *Never Done: A History of Women's Work in Media Production* (New Brunswick, NJ: Rutgers University Press, 2016).

9   Janet Staiger, "The Producer-Unit System: Management by Specialization after 1931," in David Bordwell, Janet Staiger, and Kristin Thompson, *The Classical Hollywood Cinema: Film Style and Mode of Production to 1960* (London: Routledge, 1984), 320–29.

10   See Helen Hanson, *Hollywood Soundscapes: Film Sound Style, Craft and Production in the Classical Era* (London: British Film Institute, 2017).

11   Helen Hanson, "Looking for Lela Simone: *Singin' in the Rain* and Microhistories of Women's Sound Work Behind the Scenes and Below-the-Line in Classical Hollywood Cinema," *Women's History Review* 29, no. 5 (2020): 822–40, https://doi.org/10.1080/09612025.2019.1703537.

12   Fordin, *World of Entertainment*, 223.

13   Fordin, *World of Entertainment*, 226.

14   Handwritten Notes from Review Screening (undated), Roger Edens Collection, Easter Parade, Box 4, Folder 1418/1, Cinematic Arts Library, University of Southern California.

15   Interoffice Communication from Lela Simone to Bud Cates (Editorial), Subject: Easter Parade February 6, 1948. Roger Edens Collection, Easter Parade, Box 4, Folder 1418/1, Cinematic Arts Library, University of Southern California.

16   Interoffice Communication from Lela Simone to Bud Cates (Editorial), Subject: Easter Parade February 6, 1948. Roger Edens Collection, Easter Parade, Box 4, Folder 1418/1, Cinematic Arts Library, University of Southern California.

17   Interoffice Communication to Subject: EASTER PARADE, February 13, 1948. Roger Edens Collection, Easter Parade, Box 4, Folder 1418/1, Cinematic Arts Library, University of Southern California.

18   Typed Notes: Sound Effects, undated, 3 pages. Roger Edens Collection, Easter Parade, Box 4, Folder 1418/2, Cinematic Arts Library, University of Southern California.

19   Typed Notes: 'Loops, Wild Lines, Etc. for EASTER PARADE' undated, 1 page. Roger Edens Collection, Easter Parade, Box 4, Folder 1418/2, Cinematic Arts Library, University of Southern California.

20   Interoffice Communication from George Schneider (MGM Legal) to Miss Simone, Subject: Easter Parade, August 27, 1947. Roger Edens Collection, Easter Parade, Box 4, Folder 1418/1, Cinematic Arts Library, University of Southern California.

21   Interoffice Communications between Lela Simone and Richard Powers extend from February 9, 1948, to March 10, 1948. Roger Edens Collection, Easter Parade, Box 4, Folder 1418/1, Cinematic Arts Library, University of Southern California.

22   Oral History with Lela Simone, interviewed by Rudy Behlmer (1990), Academy of Motion Picture Arts and Sciences Oral History Program, Margaret Herrick Library, 15.

23   Arthur Freed, quoted in Fordin, *World of Entertainment*, 121.

18

GENE TIERNEY, "TROUBLED BEAUTY"

Star Labor, Mental Health, and Narratives of Recuperation

Will Scheibel

Following years of wartime promotion as a great beauty from the Twentieth Century-Fox lot—"the most beautiful woman in movie history," according to Fox's head of production, Darryl F. Zanuck[1]—Gene Tierney became one of the first major film stars to undergo treatment for mental illness publicly. In 1954, she suffered a nervous breakdown while rehearsing for an episode of the CBS anthology drama *General Electric Theater* and withdrew from the series. It was announced the she had a viral infection.[2] She then underwent an estimated total of thirty-two electroconvulsive treatment sessions, or ECTs, at Harkness Pavilion in New York City and the Institute of Living in Hartford, Connecticut, the experience of which she details in her harrowing autobiography, *Self-Portrait*, first published in 1978.[3] By the end of 1957, she had attempted suicide on the ledge of her mother's Manhattan apartment, and shortly thereafter her mother checked her into the Menninger Clinic, then located in Topeka, Kansas.[4]

This chapter examines Tierney's public image at the end of the 1950s to analyze the process of star rehabilitation within particular ideological determinants (discourses of female labor and mental health) at a particular historical moment (the last years of the classical Hollywood era, when studio-controlled publicity began to give way to star gossip). Richard Dyer has shown that Hollywood stars embody social contradictions in a way that seems to resolve them for the moviegoing public, who must negotiate these contradictions in their own lives:

> Stars frequently speak to the dominant contractions in social life—experienced as conflicting demands, contrary expectations,

irreconcilable but equally held values—in such a way as to appear to reconcile them. In part, by simply being one indivisible entity within an existence in the "real world," yet displaying contradictory personality traits, stars can affirm that it is possible to triumph over, transcend, successfully live out contradictions.[5]

The comeback narrative surrounding Tierney's first discharge from Menninger sought to recuperate her image by positing work as mental rehabilitation. I argue that the alignment of Tierney's image with professional acting—as opposed to the "natural" charisma of stardom—redefined social roles for women in the postwar era in terms alternative to the domestic sphere and yet reinscribed a traditional construction of femininity by attributing Tierney's illness to marital and maternal trauma, precipitating the need to get back to work. This reconciliation of work, on the one hand, and marriage and motherhood, on the other, masked a social expectation for women to "work through" illness to prove their professional capabilities, stabilizing Tierney's star image at a moment of potential disturbance.

Not until 1958 did Tierney's illness break in newspapers and magazines ranging from *Life* to *Modern Screen*. Upon her discharge, talk of future projects gave renewed attention to her career, which had been on hold since her last film, *The Left Hand of God* (Dmytryk 1955), but when she was admitted to Menninger again in 1959, she reemerged in the Topeka neighborhood of Westboro as a part-time salesgirl at Talmage's Ladies Apparel Shop. Working short, irregular hours, the star of *Laura* (Preminger 1944), *Leave Her to Heaven* (Stahl 1945), *The Ghost and Mrs. Muir* (Mankiewicz 1947), and thirty other feature films brought an upsurge in business to the chic local clothier.[6] As the ex-wife of Count Oleg Cassini, the renowned Hollywood costume designer who outfitted Tierney and launched his own designer fashion label in New York, Tierney had returned to a world she once knew, now a thirty-eight-year-old Menninger outpatient.

Tierney's illness would today be considered a bipolar disorder,[7] but the press described it vaguely and indirectly, opting instead to focus on its presumed causes and the optimism about her future, which she was said to have found in her return to Hollywood. With a headline that read "Gene Tierney Comes Home," an article in the December 1958 issue of the fan magazine *Modern Screen* illustrated the three-pronged approach that journalists took in accounting for the recent years in her life, identifying "a hopeless baby" (her daughter Daria, who was born in 1943 deaf and partially blind with a severe intellectual disability and spent her life in care facilities), "a hopeless marriage" (to Cassini, whom she divorced in 1952), and "a hopeless love" (to Aly Khan, the Muslim prince, who in 1954 supposedly called off their wedding).⁸ The tragic "Gene Tierney story" was already familiar to the public by the end of 1958, and in many ways this *Modern Screen* article was a summation of the yearlong series of interviews and reports of her treatment at Menninger that ran in national newspapers and general circulation magazines.

Journalistic attention to Tierney's treatment coincided with a larger American cultural interest in psychoanalytic therapy that gained ground in the press and peaked in the late 1950s, including discussions of psychoanalytic theories and practices as well as magazine features on "pop psychology" aimed at middle-class housewives. In her book *Couching Resistance*, Janet Walker explains that psychiatry expanded after World War II from servicemen to both male and female civilians. Walker claims that the "feminine adjustment" in postwar psychiatry, or the "process of fitting a woman into a rigid gender stereotype," emphasized women's roles as wives and mothers, which "often amounted to a prescription of exclusive domesticity"

18.1. "Gene Tierney Comes Home," *Modern Screen* (December 1958). Courtesy of Media History Digital Library.

authorized by the institution of "objective" medical science and promoted through mass culture to justify the social oppression of women.[9]

Although women's psychological problems dominated popular discourse on psychiatry, men equaled if not outnumbered women as psychiatric patients.[10] Veterans helped legitimize psychiatry for the public as "more deserving patients emerging from wartime experience" than the insane and the disenfranchised, but Walker points out that women's stories were more prominent for two reasons: the postwar bias against men's expressions of vulnerability or admission of illness and, more significantly, the way in which psychiatry reinforced society's assumption that "the problem of woman" is the only problem that cannot be disavowed.[11] Thus, while not discounting the actual mental illness of women or what she phrases the "very real adverse psychological effects of women's inequality," Walker makes clear that "certain psychiatric discursive practices themselves were motivated by and even contributed to the attribution of illness to women."[12]

Reading the commentary on Tierney, we can see little in the way of addressing her illness as an *illness* but, rather, as a gender-coded condition of individual problems. A September 1958 issue of *Life* featured a publicity story titled "Welcome for a Troubled Beauty," accompanied by photographs of Tierney embracing director George Cukor at Paramount and receiving a kiss on the cheek from Samuel J. Briskin, chief of studio operations at Columbia.[13] Other photographs depicted Tierney sitting in a camera operator's chair at Twentieth Century-Fox to observe a rehearsal for *The Sound and the Fury* (Ritt 1959) and visiting with the film's star, Joanne Woodward.[14] More revealing, though, is the information the article shares about the birth of Daria. We learn that her disability was caused by a case of rubella, also known as German measles, which Tierney contracted while entertaining troops at the Hollywood Canteen during her pregnancy. Unbeknownst to Tierney, a female Marine carrying the virus escaped quarantine to see her perform, and only after meeting the fan a year later did Tierney realize she was the source of the infection.[15] As much as the article served to publicize Tierney's Hollywood homecoming, it also made her mental illness legible by eliding the contradictory demands of women's work in the public sphere and motherhood in the private sphere, defining women's psychology exclusively within the realm of the maternal.

Domestic concerns of mother-daughter relationships were also coterminous with ideas about heteronormative romance in Tierney's star biography at the end of the 1950s. Until she turned twenty-one, her contract with Twentieth Century-Fox was to be not in her name but rather in that of Belle Tier Corporation, the holding company that her father, Howard, had set up for her (and had named after her mother, Belle Tierney) to administer her finances. Along with each member of her immediate family (her parents, brother, and sister), Gene Tierney allocated a quarter of her total earnings to Belle Tier, and the family shared the company's profits evenly. Each member of the family codirected the company, but Howard served as president. Unbeknownst to the rest of the family, he also held complete control of the company stock, as he retained 51 percent of the stock in his own name. After eloping with Cassini at the age of twenty, Tierney, as a married woman, was eligible to manage her own career, and Twentieth Century-Fox drew up a new contract. Howard still felt that Belle Tier was her rightful agent and issued a breach of contract suit, but it was supposedly thrown out of court.[16] Immediately after Howard and Belle divorced in 1942, he married a woman with whom he was having an affair, and Gene saw him for one of the last times in his life.[17]

New York Journal-American columnist Phyllis Battelle published a series of interviews with Tierney in November 1958. Describing her as Menninger's "most beautiful patient, but possibly one of their most emotionally repressed," Battelle reports that the doctors instructed Tierney to cry in order to confront memories from her past, ostensibly the root of her illness, beginning with her estrangement from her father.[18] According to Battelle, Tierney and Cassini were married until 1947, then remarried and divorced again, but in actuality the first divorce was never finalized.[19]

The Gene Tierney characterized in Battelle's series is a brokenhearted romantic, with her divorce from Cassini among the "tragic blows" in her life.[20] Tierney insisted that Cassini was not to blame for her illness, and Battelle goes as far as to refer to Cassini as "her first therapist" in that "he was someone to talk to and confide in" for Tierney at a young age.[21] In Battelle's configuration of the relationship, Cassini becomes a substitute for Tierney's father, but her divorce is therefore made doubly traumatic as it registers with the loss of her father that she already felt. Moreover, the comparison of Cassini to a therapist gives this story purchase not only in postwar ideologies of marriage but also in representations of psychiatry itself, which imagines women in need of and dependent on protection from patriarchal authority figures.

Prince Aly Khan had been romantically linked to Tierney in 1953, and rumors of their impending engagement provided grist for the Hollywood gossip mill following her divorce and his own divorce from another 1940s star, Rita Hayworth.[22] Refusing to blame Khan for her illness, Tierney later denied that they realistically planned to marry and called him a close friend who knew she was "in no [mental] state for an international social life."[23] Yet, the end of their royal affair was acknowledged as the last straw that broke the fragile Tierney, as if to narrativize her experience in the form of a fairy tale. A story in the *Los Angeles Examiner*, for example, included a photograph of the couple with the caption "Breakup of their romance left Gene Tierney despondent. Now the actress, ill, is confined and the dashing Aly Khan is long gone."[24] Other stories elaborated on the breakup, such as a *Los Angeles Times* item that commented on how Aga Khan, Aly's father, threatened to disinherit his son if he and Tierney were to wed.[25] Even upon Aly Khan's death in 1960, the fan magazine *Photoplay* turned to his breakup with Tierney once again and rehearsed the pitiable events in her life that were thought to have led to her psychiatric treatment, culminating in "the words, 'I cannot marry you.'"[26] The article recounted a night in which Tierney allegedly sat alone in a nightclub, dazed from his rejection; she deliberately removed long white gloves from her hands one finger at a time, then put them back on with equal care, and performed this ritual over and over again.[27] While the article claimed that Tierney first looked at her former lover's death as a bad omen, having been recently discharged from Menninger for the second time, it also reassured readers that she had discovered new love in Texas oil tycoon Howard Lee and a newfound sense of solace.

Despite the feminine domestic ideal we see in the maternal and romantic images of women promoted in American mass culture after World War II, Adrienne L. McLean and other film and cultural historians have shown that women did in fact work outside the home in the postwar era. Following the influx of women in the workforce during the war, women remained working at a gradual increase after the war even if they traded their "war jobs" for service or clerical positions.[28] However, as McLean elucidates in her book *Being Rita Hayworth*, star-making was based on "basic tenets of middle-class respectability," and for studios to market stars as ordinary, promotion and publicity demanded "that all stars *want* to be married and *should* be married because they are always so ordinary."[29] Female stars therefore modeled the problems of the middle-class wives and mothers who were still held to the standards of hegemonic domestic ideology in their pursuit of a career. Rita Hayworth, for instance, was forced to raise her children as a single mother after her divorce from actor and singer Dick Haymes. The press viewed her career as both an interference with her responsibilities as a mother and her only means with which to work as her family's provider. In other words, McLean argues, Hayworth was "urged to stay home and to stop working *at the same time* that her career is named as being all that she has left with which to support herself and her children."[30] With Tierney, we see repeated assertions of her status as a professional actor just as the press failed to recognize an identity independent from Daria, Oleg Cassini, and Aly Khan, but there is also an ambivalence over her work as a sign of her rehabilitation or another origin for her illness.

The "troubled beauty" whom we find in the pages of these newspapers and magazines implicitly creates a continuity with a range of "troubled beauties" Tierney had played on-screen, including jilted lovers (*Leave Her to Heaven, The Razor's Edge* [Goulding 1946]), women concerned with motherhood (*Dragonwyck* [Mankiewicz 1946]; *The Ghost and Mrs. Muir, Close to My Heart* [Keighley 1951]), and a housewife coping with a psychological disorder (*Whirlpool* [Preminger 1949]). As Dyer contends, "The star phenomenon depends upon collapsing the distinction between the star-as-person and the star-as-performer."[31] The historical reception of Tierney's purported comeback provides an example of this blurring between person and performer in the late studio era, showing how period discourse on women's labor served to recuperate the female star as worker by reconciling the contradictions between suffering and rehabilitation, the private and the public, and domestic and professional experiences.

NOTES

For access to primary research material, I wish to thank the Margaret Herrick Library of the Academy of Motion Picture Arts and Sciences in Beverly Hills, California, and the Billy Rose Theatre Division of the New York Public Library for the Performing Arts in New York, New York.

1   Richard Harland Smith, "Gene Tierney Biography," *Turner Classic Movies*, accessed June 30, 2016, https://www.tcm.com/tcmdb/person/191988%7C57782/Gene-Tierney#biography.

2   "Gene Tierney Collapses with Virus Infection," *Los Angeles Times*, September 22, 1954, Gene Tierney Clipping File, Margaret Herrick Library of the Academy of Motion Picture Arts and Sciences in Beverly Hills, CA (hereafter AMPAS).

3   Gene Tierney with Mickey Herskowitz, *Self-Portrait* (New York: Berkley Publishing, 1980), 179–86.

4   "Gene Tierney Again in Mental Hospital," *New York Journal-American*, January 21, 1958, Gene Tierney Clipping File, Billy Rose Theatre Division of the New York Public Library for the Performing Arts in New York, NY (hereafter NYPL).

5   Richard Dyer, "Four Films of Lana Turner," *Movie*, no. 25 (Winter 1977–78), 30.

6   Warren Hall, "New Saleslady in Town," *American Weekly*, December 13, 1959, Gene Tierney Clipping File, NYPL.

7   David Coleman, *The Bipolar Express: Manic Depression and the Movies* (Lanham, MD: Rowman & Littlefield, 2014), 98.

8   Doug Brewer, "Gene Tierney Comes Home," *Modern Screen*, December 1958, 44.

9   Janet Walker, *Couching Resistance: Women, Film, and Psychoanalytic Psychiatry* (Minneapolis: University of Minnesota Press, 1993), xvi, 8.

10 Walker, *Couching Resistance*, 8, 10.

11 Walker, *Couching Resistance*, 2, 12.

12 Walker, *Couching Resistance*, 12–13.

13 "Welcome for a Troubled Beauty: Long Ill, Gene Tierney Gets Back to Hollywood," *Life*, September 1958, 87, 88.

14 "Welcome for a Troubled Beauty," 88, 92.

15 "Welcome for a Troubled Beauty," 92.

16 Fox's biography outlined these events, estimating the suit at $90,000, and advised the press to "soft pedal" this story, "as Mr. Tierney is still boiling and would probably welcome a chance to sue somebody for something." Biography of Gene Tierney, 1943, Core Collection Files, AMPAS.

17 See Tierney with Herskowitz, *Self-Portrait*, 68–69, 72.

18 Phyllis Battelle, "The Long Road Back: 'Cry,' Clinic Doctors Told Gene Tierney," *New York Journal-American*, November 10, 1958, Gene Tierney Clipping File, NYPL.

19 Battelle, "The Long Road Back."

20 Battelle, "The Long Road Back."

21 Phyllis Battelle, "The Long Road Back: Gene Felt Like Broken Woman in Clinic," *New York Journal-American*, November 11, 1958, Gene Tierney Clipping File, NYPL.

22 "Gene Tierney 'Thinking Over,' Says He's Dear," *Los Angeles Herald-Examiner*, December 8, 1953; "Aly Khan Mum on Marrying," *Los Angeles Times*, May 6, 1953; "Should Gene Marry Aly? Tune in Next . . . ," *Los Angeles Daily News*, March 10, 1954; "Gene Tierney Admits She Loves Aly," *Los Angeles Times*, March 31, 1954; "Gene Tierney, Aly Here, Deny Stop for Wedding," *Los Angeles Times*, April 7, 1954. Gene Tierney Clipping File, AMPAS.

23 Battelle, "The Long Road Back."

24 "Gene Tierney Psychiatric Patient in Kansas Clinic," *Los Angeles Examiner*, January 22, 1958, Gene Tierney Clipping File, AMPAS.

25 "Gene Tierney Patient at Psychiatric Clinic," *Los Angeles Times*, January 22, 1958, Gene Tierney Clipping File, AMPAS.

26 Jim Hoffman, "Something Terrible's Going to Happen to Me—Again," *Photoplay*, October 1960, 86.

27 Hoffman, "Something Terrible's Going to Happen," 84.

28 Adrienne L. McLean, *Being Rita Hayworth: Labor, Identity, and Hollywood Stardom* (New Brunswick, NJ: Rutgers University Press, 2004), 17.

29 McLean, *Being Rita Hayworth*, 79.

30 McLean, *Being Rita Hayworth*, 102.

31 Dyer, "Four Films of Lana Turner," 30.

VII

CLASSICISM AFTER THE STUDIO ERA

19

MGM

LANDMARKS IN THE DECLINE OF A MAJOR HOLLYWOOD STUDIO

Tino Balio

MGM reigned supreme during the so-called studio era. No one would contest that assertion. MGM had its best year in 1944–45, but afterward MGM's earnings declined. Loew's Inc., MGM's parent company, was slow to react to postwar conditions. While the other members of the Big Five filed consent decrees to divorce their theater chains in accord with the *Paramount* antitrust case, Loew's stalled and was the last major to fall in line. During the rise of commercial television in the 1950s, Loew's stood on the sidelines, thinking that television would need Hollywood, and MGM in particular, not the other way around. While other studios dealt with the postwar box office slump by offering independent producers profit-sharing deals to strengthen their distribution rosters, MGM stayed pat with a central producer.

To turn the studio around, Loew's president, Nicholas Schenck, called for "a new Thalberg." Louis B. Mayer chose Dore Schary, former studio head at RKO. Under Schary's watch, MGM released a remarkable string of Arthur Freed musicals, among them Vincente Minnelli's *An American in Paris* (1951) and Stanley Donen and Gene Kelly's *Singin' in the Rain* (1952), and a range of hits like Minnelli's *Father of the Bride* (1950), Mervyn LeRoy's *Quo Vadis* (1951), and Richard Brooks's *Blackboard Jungle* (1955). But most of Schary's message pictures lost money. Mayer detested message pictures and resigned in protest in June 1951 when Schenck greenlighted Schary's *The Red Badge of Courage* (Huston 1951) over Mayer's objections. Loew's had come under withering criticism from Wall Street and dissident stockholders alike during Schary's rein, which led to Schenck's resignation in 1955 and Schary's ousting a year later.

During the rise of commercial television, dissident stockholders had demanded that MGM unload its film library to make a quick profit. But Arthur Loew, Schenck's successor, held firm. The wisdom of this decision became apparent immediately. In July 1956, MGM leased *The Wizard of Oz* (Fleming and Vidor 1939) to CBS TV for four showings at a total cost of $900,000. This was MGM's first sale to television. MGM's entry into television production was tentative like the other majors. Columbia's Screen Gems, MCA-Revue, Desilu, and other independent telefilm producers led the way. MGM finally became a player in the business beginning in the 1960s. Its first hits included *National Velvet* (1960–62), *The Asphalt Jungle* (1961), and *Dr. Kildare* (1961–66)—all inspired by older MGM features. *Dr. Kildare* was the most successful, lasting five seasons on NBC TV.

Loew's finally signed off on the *Paramount* case in 1959. The delay was caused in part by a group of dissident stockholders who insisted that MGM be split off from the company instead of the theaters. The dissidents contended that motion picture production was a losing business. But improved conditions convinced Loew's stockholders to accept management's plan to spin off the Loew's chain in 1959. At the 1960 annual meeting on February 25, 1960, Loew's Inc. changed its name to Metro-Goldwyn-Mayer, Inc.

MGM's move into independent production was cautious. It initially offered profit-participation deals to veteran in-house producers such as Pandro S. Berman, Joe Pasternak, and Arthur Freed but not to new talent. Berman and Pasternak were the most prolific, each producing over a dozen pictures for the studio. Berman, for example, produced Richard Thorpe's *Jailhouse Rock* (1957), starring Elvis Presley, and two big hits starring Elizabeth Taylor, Richard Brooks's *Cat on a Hot Tin Roof* (1958) and Daniel Mann's *Butterfield 8* (1960). Arthur Freed's first independent venture, *Gigi* (Minnelli 1958), was his biggest commercial hit and MGM's last great musical.

MGM entered the new era by signing outside independent producers in earnest beginning in the 1960s. The move introduced a period of relative prosperity with the release of two hits by Carlo Ponti—David Lean's *Doctor Zhivago* (1965) and Michelangelo Antonioni's *Blow-Up* (1966)—and Stanley Kubrick's *2001: A Space Odyssey* (1968). But by 1969, MGM hit the doldrums. It was not alone among the majors. Big-budget pictures were failing at the box office, and the networks ceased bidding on new movies for prime time. Hollywood was in the throes of a recession. In May 1969, MGM announced that its loss for the year could be as much as $19 million.

By year's end MGM posted a loss of $35.3 million. Nonetheless, MGM's extensive real estate holdings, film library, music publishing companies, and other assets made it an attractive takeover target.

Las Vegas casino operator Kirk Kerkorian was quick to take advantage of the opportunity and acquired operating control of the company in September 1969. This marked the start of a thirty-five-year period when Kerkorian would buy and sell the company three times. To turn MGM around, Kerkorian hired James Aubrey Jr., the former head of CBS TV. During his tenure from 1959 to 1964, CBS produced a string of smash "hick-coms" like *The Beverly Hillbillies* (1962–71), *Green Acres* (1965–71), *Gomer Pyle* (1964–69), and *Petticoat Junction* (1963–70). To reduce MGM's overhead, Aubrey relocated the company's corporate office from the MGM Building in New York to Culver City. In Culver City, he slashed the workforce and sold off two large back lots to real estate developers as well as a warehouse full of costumes and props—Judy Garland's ruby-red slippers included—to an auctioneer. Since Aubrey planned on making fewer films in the future, he downsized MGM's distribution arm by closing most of its domestic film exchanges. In England, Aubrey shuttered the Borehamwood Studio outside London. Later, in May 1972, MGM got out of the record business. Aubrey sold off MGM Records and its Los Angeles record pressing plant to Polygram Corp., a subsidiary of the Dutch-based Philips cartel. By 1971, Aubrey had done his job; he turned a $35 million loss in 1969 to a profit of $16.4 million and reduced MGM's bank debt from $80 million to $15 million.

Taking charge of production, Aubrey attempted to create a new image for the company by making low-budget pictures aimed at the youth audience. MGM released around eighteen such pictures a year under Aubrey, but only two could be considered hits: Gordon Parks's *Shaft* (1971) and Michael Crichton's *Westworld* (1973). The meager returns on these pictures and reduced production output led MGM to withdraw from film distribution in 1973. MGM wanted to be freed from the necessity of producing a full roster of pictures every year and from the burden of maintaining a worldwide distribution network. MGM thereupon sold off its seven remaining domestic branches and thirty-seven foreign branches and dismissed nearly two thousand employees. Without a distribution arm with the ability to market a picture worldwide, MGM reduced itself to second-tier status in the industry. To distribute its future lineup, MGM signed ten-year pacts with United Artists and Cinema International Corporation to handle its product worldwide. It was Kerkorian's, not Aubrey's, idea to withdraw from distribution. Kerkorian needed a cash infusion to finance the MGM Grand Hotel, which was under construction. Aubrey was overridden in the matter and resigned in October 1973.

The MGM Grand Hotel marked MGM's entry into the leisure-time field and was originally part of MGM's diversification strategy. The MGM Grand Hotel opened on December 5, 1973. The resort was an immediate success. Afterward, more money came from the hotel/ casino side than from the film/TV side. Kerkorian therefore decided in May 1980 to divide the company into two separate publicly held entities, Metro-Goldwyn-Mayer Film Co. and MGM Grand Hotels Inc. The move allowed Kerkorian to protect his hotel/casino interests from the more risky film production business. But the split left MGM a pure play company totally dependent on its film output.

By 1979, MGM could no longer afford to remain a second-tier film studio and decided to ramp up production. The decision was spurred in part by the arrival of two new distribution technologies—pay-TV and home video—that created two new lucrative ancillary markets for feature films. To head the film unit, Kerkorian chose David Begelman, the rehabilitated former head of Columbia Pictures who had been convicted of forgery and embezzlement. Next, he recaptured distribution by acquiring United Artists from Transamerica Corporation for $380 million in 1981 and forming a new company, MGM/UA Entertainment Company. But Begelman's expensive slate of pictures scheduled for 1981 turned out to be flops, and he was forced out of MGM in mid-1982.

MGM was burdened with debt from the purchase of United Artists and from a continual string of box office failures. Along came Atlanta broadcaster Ted Turner, who made a preemptive bid of $1.5 billion for the company in 1985. Turner basically wanted the MGM film library for his burgeoning WTBS cable network, and the deal called for him to sell back the United Artists component to Kerkorian for $470 million. To finance the acquisition, Turner turned to Drexel Burnham Lambert, the junk bond specialist. However, Drexel Burnham Lambert failed to arrange the necessary financing, and MGM agreed to reduce the terms of the deal by $200 million.

Turner took control of MGM/UA Entertainment on March 25, 1986. It was Turner, not Kerkorian, as some have maintained, who dismantled the studio. Acquiring a mountain of debt as a result of the takeover, Turner was forced to unload assets. Beginning in June 1986, he sold off MGM's remaining forty-four acres, including the Irving Thalberg Building, MGM's Metrocolor Film Laboratory, and twenty-four sound stages, to Lorimar-Telepictures for $190 million. Most of the fourteen hundred employees on the lot lost their jobs. Next, Turner sold back more assets to Kerkorian—the MGM studio, the Home Entertainment division, and the Leo the Lion trademark—which garnered him an additional $300 million. At the conclusion of the deal, Turner was left with the MGM film library and the smaller pre-1948 Warner Bros. and RKO film libraries. The residual assets sold back to Kerkorian were subsumed under a new corporate umbrella, MGM/UA Communications Co.

Having sold its historic studio to Turner, MGM/UA moved its operations across the street to the new Filmland Corporate Center, where it leased four floors of the eight-story building. Afterward, MGM was a revolving door of production chiefs who turned out far more misses than hits. Unlike the other majors, MGM did not or could not diversify to create "profit centers" to even out the risks of motion picture production. The *James Bond* films, which came with the United Artists acquisition, righted the ship more than once.

MGM still retained its allure, however, and attracted some unsavory characters, chief among them Italian financier Giancarlo Parretti. Parretti and his partners had extensive media holdings in Europe. He made his foray into Hollywood in 1987 when he acquired a controlling interest in Menachem Globus's Cannon Group, which he renamed Pathé Communications. He was backed by Crédit Lyonnais, the French state-owned bank. Parretti bid $1.2 billion for MGM in 1990, but he, too, had difficulty raising the money. He raised $325 million by somehow preselling the home video and television broadcast rights to MGM's film libraries before he took control of the studio. To close the funding gap, Parretti again turned to Crédit Lyonnais, which put up $1 billion. The deal closed on November 1, 1990, and marked the third time a Hollywood studio had been taken over by a foreign company. Parretti merged his Pathé Communications with MGM to form MGM-Pathé Communications. Having previously sold the ancillary rights to MGM's film libraries, Parretti had essentially mortgaged the company, leaving few assets to generate revenue.

A one-time waiter from Orvieto in Italy, Parretti had earlier been convicted seven times for passing bad checks and had been imprisoned for eleven months for making "false representation." At the time he made his bid for MGM, he was facing tax evasion charges in Rome and had been convicted of securities fraud in Naples. Why Crédit Lyonnais was willing to back a known crook was a mystery. After the takeover, *Fortune* magazine reported, "Parretti began looting the studio in earnest, firing most of the financial staff and naming his 21-year-old daughter, Valentina, to an important financial post. Various of Parretti's many women were seen entering his office suite each afternoon. Sounds of sex could be heard from behind closed doors."[1] MGM had reached its nadir.

After Parretti defaulted on his loans, Crédit Lyonnais deposed him and foreclosed on the company in May 1992. The bank renamed the studio Metro-Goldwyn-Mayer Inc. To recoup its investment, the bank installed a new management team and poured more money into the studio to kick-start production and prepare it for auction within five years to comply with American banking laws. The bank even revived the United Artists banner under the leadership of John Calley to increase market share. Metro-Goldwyn-Mayer Inc. was put up for auction in March 1996, but when the bids came in, Crédit Lyonnais lost any hope of recouping all of its $2.5 billion investment in the studio. Kirk Kerkorian's $1.3 billion bid won out. Kerkorian was joined in the bidding by Kerry Stokes's Seven Network Group, Ltd., the Australian media conglomerate.

Why Kerkorian wanted buy MGM a third time was open to speculation, but he no doubt smelled a bargain. Ever on the lookout for a good deal, Kerkorian acquired the film libraries of Orion Pictures, Samuel Goldwyn Pictures, and the PolyGram Filmed Entertainment to create the world's largest film vault. But as a pure play company, MGM lacked dedicated distribution outlets for its pictures. Kerkorian bought out Seven Network's stake in MGM in 1998 and set out to grow MGM into an entertainment conglomerate equal to Time Warner, Viacom, or News Corp. In the process, he repositioned United Artists under Bingham Ray to tap into the growing specialty market. Time Warner and the others had metamorphosed into completely integrated entertainment conglomerates with the distribution clout to tap every region of the world. MGM's big chance to become a major conglomerate occurred in 2003 when it entered a bidding war to acquire the ailing Vivendi Universal, but General Electric won out. Afterward, Kerkorian began to look for an exit strategy to cash out.

Suitors were soon at the door. In 2005, Kerkorian sold MGM a third time to a consortium of investors led by Sony Corporation of America in a leveraged buyout for $5 billion. Sony wanted MGM's library of four thousand films to help its Blu-ray technology win the DVD high-definition format war against HD DVD. Rather than purchase MGM outright, Sony took on Comcast, Providence Equity Partners, TPG Capital, and DLJ Merchant Banking Partners as equity partners and submitted the winning bid for the studio. At the conclusion of the buyout, Metro-Goldwyn-Mayer became a private company. To take ownership of MGM, the consortium formed MGM Holdings, Inc., on February 11, 2005. The new owners dismantled MGM's movie business and fired most of MGM's staff.

Cutting now to the bottom line, MGM Holdings, hobbled by debt from the 2005 buyout and declining DVD sales after 2009, filed for a prepackaged Chapter 11 bankruptcy in 2010. Afterward, MGM's creditors took control of the studio in exchange for debt forgiveness. In the process, Providence Equity and the other hedge fund partners saw their $1.6 billion stake wiped out. They became the latest casualties of the buying and selling of MGM. However, Sony's gambit worked. The MGM titles that Sony placed exclusively on Blu-ray helped it win the high-definition format war.

After the bankruptcy, Spyglass Entertainment, an independent production company founded in 1998 by veteran Hollywood producers Gary Barber and Roger Birnbaum, was brought in to run the company. Barber and Birnbaum set MGM on a new course. To freshen its catalog, MGM eschewed in-house production and entered into coproduction partnerships with other studios. They then refashioned the company as a worldwide television rights company and abandoned its domestic theatrical distribution operation. In the new scheme of things, film revenue ranked a distant third to international television sales and DVD and Blu-ray sales.

In September 2014, MGM expanded its television business by acquiring a majority stake in One Three Media and LightWorkers Media, owned by Hearst Productions and Emmy winners Mark Burnett and Roma Downey, and consolidated the entities into a new venture called United Artists Media Group. This was the third time MGM resurrected the United Artists banner. One Three Media produced the hit network reality shows *Survivor* (2000-present), *The Apprentice* (2004–17), *Shark Tank* (2009-present), and *The Voice* (2011-present). LightWorkers Media, the smaller of the two, produced scripted religious programming such as *The Bible* (2013), a History Channel ten-part miniseries.

MGM's business plan succeeded. MGM ended up as a hybrid—a company with a historic brand that owns a treasure trove of films containing mostly non-MGM titles and earns the lion's share of its revenue distributing reality television shows. MGM will remain a center of media attention because it holds rights to the *James Bond* films, which originated with United Artists. Its film library will be recycled on all the emerging platforms, and its motion picture output will comprise mostly remakes of old favorites.

Kerkorian bought and sold MGM three times, but he was not a builder like Steve Ross at Time Warner, Lew Wasserman at MCA, or Rupert Murdoch at News Corp. He was primarily an investor and a shrewd one at that. MGM forever lost its place in the Hollywood pantheon after Kerkorian bought the company in 1969. Aubrey turned MGM around mainly by selling off assets and retreating from distribution. But Kerkorian's decision to spin off his Las Vegas hotel from MGM sealed the film studio's fate. As a second-tier company, MGM had a future that would never be secure. But Kerkorian was not the only culprit in MGM's decline. It was Turner who dismantled the physical assets, and it was Parretti who plundered the remains and besmirched the company name. When Kerkorian's belated attempt to restore MGM's status as a major failed, he sold MGM a third time to the Sony consortium and cashed out his investment in the company. And, finally, it was the new MGM Holdings that reduced MGM to a hybrid on the periphery of Hollywood. Such is the coda of a great motion picture studio.

NOTES

1   David McClintick and Anne Faircloth, "The Predator: How an Italian Thug Looted MGM, Brought Credit Lyonnais to Its Knees, and Made the Pope Cry," *Fortune*, July 8, 1996, https://money.cnn.com/magazines/fortune/fortune _archive/1996/07/08/214344/.

20

RETHINKING ALTMAN AS ANTICLASSICAL

THE MODULATION OF CLASSICAL NARRATIVE NORMS IN *THE GINGERBREAD MAN* (1998) AND *GOSFORD PARK* (2001)

Lisa Dombrowski

The standard story advanced by critics and scholars positions Robert Altman's work as distinctly anticlassical, undermining or abandoning conventions designed to promote clarity, coherence, efficiency, and unity. Though Helene Keyssar notes that "Altman's films are usually more rigorously and tightly structured than we at first perceive,"[1] she largely mirrors Robert T. Self's later assessment that Altman's narration works in the tradition of art cinema as defined by David Bordwell, featuring delayed exposition, episodic plot construction, a loosening of casual structures, a reliance on chance encounters, open endings, and an objective approach to realism.[2] Robert Kolker also highlights the ways in which Altman deemphasizes clarity and coherence, arguing, "Events on the edges gain equal importance with events in the middle. More is seen and heard than one is accustomed to."[3] Focusing on Altman's fourteen multi-protagonist plots, Maria del Mar Azcona claims their abundance of characters unrelated to the plot, narrative pauses and digressions, leisurely pace, and fragmentary engagement with character subjectivity contradict the classical guidelines found in most writing manuals.[4]

The recurring stories Altman shared in interviews about his production process appear to provide evidence of why his films may so often abandon classical norms. One of his most frequent confessions—here made after completing *Gosford Park* (2001) but paraphrased in dozens of prior interviews—alludes to his resistance to utilizing the script as the blueprint of the film, a foundational tenet of the classical continuity system: "I don't learn the script. . . . I'm not trying to underscore the plot. I'm really interested in the behavior of the people."[5] Frank Caso picks up on this theme when he highlights Altman's allegedly contentious relationships with screenwriters and consistent use of improvisation, both key components of the director's biographical legend: "Altman had a tendency to view the script as a starting point from which to launch his (communally constructed) version of the story, this being in line with his philosophy of creating a film organically."[6] There is truth in this account—Altman *was* interested in behavior and *did* allow improvisation on set—yet it elevates his collaboration with actors at the expense of contributions provided by other colleagues, including the screenwriters who laid the foundation for his films' narrative structures and the producers and executives who provided notes along the way.

This chapter engages the existing conversation regarding Altman's alleged resistance to classical narrative norms, extending a reassessment initiated by Mark Minett's work on Altman's early 1970s films.[7] Production papers held in the Robert Altman Archive at the University of Michigan provide extensive evidence of the director's script development and production process and complicate the standard story. These documents shed light on the relationship between Altman and his collaborators, their shared or competing goals, and how the process of collaboration impacted Altman's narrational preferences and produced completed works that were closer to or further from classical conventions. Two case studies from Altman's late era are particularly intriguing—*The Gingerbread Man* (1998) and *Gosford Park*—as both tackle seemingly un-Altman-like generic material: a John Grisham thriller and an English upstairs-downstairs murder mystery. *The Gingerbread Man*, Altman's only late-period film to focus on a single protagonist, finds the director in a tug-of-war with both his source material and production and distribution executives, who consistently pull the film toward classical and generic norms. Yet Altman's supervision of script revisions and the production process enables him to muddy the "white knight" protagonist and increase ambiguity in a manner that challenges generic and classical expectations without completely undermining them. *Gosford Park* develops more as a pas de trois between Altman, actor/writer/producer Bob Balaban, and screenwriter Julian Fellowes. Though *Gosford Park* is an elaborate multi-protagonist film, Fellowes's understanding of Altman's aesthetic preferences and their shared desire for authenticity result in an exceedingly tight narrative structure that utilizes classical techniques to maintain clarity, coherence, and unity. These case studies illustrate the necessity of understanding Altman's relationship to classicism as on a spectrum and the utility of considering the varying influence of Altman's many collaborators on his work.

Altman came on board *The Gingerbread Man* after Island Pictures acquired the film rights to John Grisham's only original screenplay in the hopes of repeating the blockbuster success of the first three legal thrillers adapted from Grisham novels: *The Firm* (Pollack 1993), *The Pelican Brief* (Pakula 1993), and *The Client* (Schumacher 1994). Although Altman said he thought Grisham's script for *The Gingerbread Man* was "dreadful," [8] Kenneth Branagh, hired to play the lead, recalled, "It was much more structured than Bob might normally allow and he was excited by that." [9] Altman recruited Clyde Hayes—an actor with two writing credits—to revise Grisham's screenplay; Hayes wrote five subsequent drafts over approximately seven months under Altman's supervision. Though Grisham had no role in the script development process, the fundamental plot structure he created remained consistent through each revision: an aggressive lawyer, Rick Magruder, agrees to assist an attractive woman in need, Mallory Doss, with getting a court order to commit her abusive father to psychiatric evaluation. What emerges, however, is that Rick has been set up by femme fatale Mallory and her not-quite-ex-husband, who seek to inherit her father's land. Script drafts and notes reveal that Altman and Hayes alter character traits and motivations as well as the rhythm and content of individual acts, shifting the emphasis of the narrative *away* from clear exposition and redundant plot points that build toward Rick learning a life lesson and *toward* delayed plot advancement, narrative suppression, and a greater emphasis on Rick's loss of control and power. At the same time, distribution executives pushed back against the many changes to Grisham's formula, ultimately removing Altman from the editing of the film in a last-ditch effort to create a more commercial product. The end result is a fascinating amalgam of generic and "Altmanesque" elements that bend classical norms but do not entirely break them.

Grisham's original script, dated September 8, 1995, closely adheres to generic and classical conventions in its approach to character and plot structure. The script introduces Rick taking a series of work-related phone calls while at the circus with his two kids, immediately defining his central character trait: he is a lawyer who has sacrificed his family in pursuit of success. After introducing Rick's inattentiveness to his family in the first

20.1. Robert Downey Jr., Daryl Hannah, Robert Altman, and Kenneth Branagh on the set of *The Gingerbread Man* (1998). Courtesy of Special Collections Research Center, University of Michigan Library.

two scenes, the Grisham script unveils Mallory and her case in the third scene, thereby establishing the initial situation clearly and efficiently. Mallory provides heightened and redundant information regarding the danger of her father, Dixon Doss, that motivates Rick to take the case. His subsequent actions progress in a clear, causally linked fashion toward Doss's commitment at the end of the first act, which is accomplished on page 30 of the 120-page script. In a classically conventional manner, Rick's professional plotline—the Doss case—becomes entwined with his personal plotline—his estrangement from his wife and kids—as the action is complicated and develops. It is only when his work on the case directly endangers his children that Rick realizes the need to change his ways. Once Rick has figured out the double cross by Mallory, the final act of the script features explicit revelations that clarify both the nature of Mallory's plan and the manner in which Rick figures it out, ensuring the viewer's understanding of the plot. At the conclusion of the script, Rick's loss of his law license after shooting Doss in self-defense functions as an opportunity for him to reinvest in his family. Grisham emphasizes the cathartic nature of the conclusion by having Rick's ex-wife and children reunite with him at the courthouse as Rick extends profuse apologies. The script thus provides closure to Rick's personal journey; he ends the film in a fundamentally different place than where he started, having solved his "problem" and become a changed man.

Altman's take on *The Gingerbread Man* completely abandons the inciting incident and character arc found in Grisham's script, delays causally driven plot development, and withholds narrative information; the result upends viewer expectations for a canonical Grisham hero and requires more work to understand character motivations and events. From the start, Altman and Branagh both agreed to craft Rick (Branagh) as, in Altman's words, "a Clinton-like figure who couldn't keep his dick out of trouble."[10] In Hayes's revised drafts, Rick has sex with Mallory (Embeth Davidtz) before he knows about her father (Robert Duvall) or even learns her name; his pursuit of her case and his subsequent hoodwinking are entirely motivated—as secondary characters repeatedly reinforce—by his unwise sexual behavior, complicating viewer alignment with his character. By crafting a morally ambiguous protagonist who receives a well-deserved comeuppance, Hayes and Altman undercut the conventional pleasure of rooting for a clearly defined hero who triumphs over his adversary and is positively transformed. Additionally, the setup of the initial situation in Hayes's drafts and the final film is less efficient and causally driven than in Grisham's script. Episodically linked scenes elongate the first act and direct attention to character development, emphasizing Rick's routines and personality traits rather than advancing the plot. In a memo to Altman discussing the third draft of Hayes's script, Island Pictures executives questioned the diffusion of the plot, starting with the opening scene: "Do we want to open our movie with a six-page scene that . . . doesn't serve to move the story forward, it only serves to establish Rick as a shark?" Altman wrote his succinct response in the margin of the memo: "Yes."[11] While the plot becomes more causally driven once Rick offers to assist Mallory, the lengthy first act (43 of 114 minutes in the film) delays the process of hypothesis formation and creation of suspense that typically drive a legal thriller. Finally, whereas Grisham's script explicitly and redundantly lays out for the viewer Rick's process of deducing Mallory's plan and the fact that she knows that he knows all about it, Hayes's revision withholds pertinent causal information, even in the climactic final act. One of Altman's producers, David Levy, expressed concern in a memo that the script was leaving too much to chance: "It would seem as though there are just too many variables in place for the conspirators to think their plan will work." [12] In the finished film, Altman relies on camerawork, particularly slow zoom-ins to Rick, to suggest his thought process without explicitly clarifying exactly *what* he thinks. The most revealing clues regarding Mallory's double cross are provided through the improvisation of Robert Downey Jr. (playing Rick's investigator), as he describes her early on as a "Pandora's box" and pointedly asks, following the death of Doss at Rick's hands, "Who started this party?"

Though Altman's most proximate collaborators—including Hayes, Levy, and Island Pictures executives—undoubtedly shaped the direction of the film, perhaps none did so more than the collaborator Altman never met: John Grisham. The final cut of *The Gingerbread Man* is an atmospheric blend of the classically driven Grisham story integrated with formal elements more frequently associated with Altman, including a focus on character behavior, delayed exposition, and narrative suppression. While the film contains none of the digressions scholars often attribute to Altman's work and progresses in a causally driven, goal-oriented fashion following the introduction of the case, the transformation of Rick's character complicates the viewer's ability to root for him and the plot structure postpones the process of investigation and frustrates the viewer's understanding of the double cross. Test screenings consistently revealed audiences complaining about a slow pace and long length, a hard-to-follow narrative, a lack of suspense, and a lack of resolution in the ending, prompting the distributor to challenge Altman's final cut and sharply reduce prints and advertising for the film. [13] Yet many of the same elements that test audiences found perplexing were described as refreshing by critics resistant to the facile pleasures of the Grisham formula; more than three-quarters of major-market reviews were positive or mixed. [14] The hybrid nature of *The Gingerbread Man* highlights the strategies utilized by Altman to harness classical and generic conventions and steer them to his own ends.

Gosford Park originated in a pitch made by actor/writer/producer Bob Balaban, a longtime Altman friend, who suggested the two team up to make an Agatha Christie–style country house murder mystery. Altman and Balaban asked Eileen Atkins and Jean Marsh, who created *Upstairs, Downstairs* (1971–75), to draft the initial script; after finding it unsuitable they turned to Julian Fellowes, an actor who was just getting into writing. Fellowes, determined to make the most of the opportunity, consciously crafted what he thought Altman would like: an anthropological study of English life in the 1930s. He said of Altman in an interview, "I knew that he was happiest in the genre of multi-arc, multi-strand storytelling where you have stories that go right through the movie, others with less overreaching spans, and some quite short that would be told in two or three scenes." [15] Fellowes wrote nine drafts of the script over an eleven-month period, remaining in constant contact with Balaban and Altman. The overarching situation as well as most of the thirty primary characters in the finished film are in place from Fellowes's first complete draft: new money magnate Sir William McCordle and his snobbish wife, Sylvia, host three couples, assorted guests, and their servants at a country estate for a weekend shooting party, but on the second night McCordle is killed. Revelations ensue. Altman and Balaban offered key additions and revisions throughout the script development and shooting process, including removing elements of nostalgia, deemphasizing the murder mystery, and eliminating overt explanations in favor of suggestion. Yet Altman's interest in character behavior meshed effectively with Fellowes's careful attention to motivation and causality, resulting in a completed film that combines Altman's propensity for expansive ensembles and improvisation with a tightly woven plot rife with classical technique.

In keeping with Altman's predilections, several key changes to the plot structure occurred during script development that shifted the narrative away from more generically conventional territory and toward a critique of the interwar British class system. Fellowes's initial partial draft of March 2000, titled *The Back of the Tapestry*, opens in the present with Mary, a former lady's maid, returning to what remains of a country estate she first visited while in service during the 1930s. Fellowes writes the opening scene as a mournful ode to a glamorous lost world—a tone not at all in keeping with Altman's taste but later foundational to Fellowes's highly successful television series *Downton Abbey* (2011–15)—and the sequence does not survive initial feedback. [16] More significantly, the importance of the murder mystery to the plot is gradually lessened over the course of script revisions. The partial draft and the first full draft, dated May 2000, locate McCordle's murder at the midpoint of the film after dinner on the second day; the latter half of the script is then given over to the investigation and character discussions regarding its consequences. The narrative resolves after Mrs. Wilson, the housekeeper, walks Mary step-by-step through how and why she framed Sylvia for the murder, an explanation made even more explicit through the use of a flashback. Beginning with the second full draft of July 2000, the murder is delayed past the midpoint, the scapegoat plot as well as the flash-back are dropped, and the investigation becomes a farcical subplot that is never officially resolved. Instead of progressing in a generic fashion toward a climactic character convergence as the inspector reveals who killed William McCordle in the study with poison (and a knife), the plot quickly exposes the inspector as a bumbling fool completely incapable of solving the crime. As the murder mystery shifts into the background, the role of Mary as a tour guide and an investigator of Gosford Park's secrets moves to the fore.

Although Fellowes's revisions challenge the expectations of an Agatha Christie–style murder mystery, they nevertheless rely heavily on classical techniques to organize the more than fifteen plotlines that weave through the film, thereby maintaining clarity and coherence. In doing so, both the scripts and the completed film illustrate many of the same strategies Kristin Thompson highlights in *Storytelling in the New Hollywood* as indicative of classically constructed multiple-protagonist plots, particularly those in which the characters cross paths and impact each other's causal chains.[17] In *Gosford Park*, the daily rhythm and rituals of life in the house over the four days of the shooting party motivate the scene order, while meals and events such as the hunt and the murder provide opportunities for character convergences that link the many subplots together. Upstairs characters are defined by their relationships to McCordle and, typically, their need for his money. The requirements of labor or the temporary escapes of gossip or pleasure (sex, smoking, music) motivate servant actions. Characters with defined goals initiate causal chains that often involve deadlines, such as Lt. Commander Anthony Meredith, who confides to his wife on the first night that during the visit he needs McCordle to commit to remaining invested in his business scheme. Dialogue hooks and dangling causes, including the story told by Mrs. Croft, the head cook, regarding McCordle's history of seducing his female employees, cue the viewer to anticipate and recognize connections between different characters and plots. The three sisters upstairs and the three female servants downstairs who have personal (and often sexual) connections to McCordle also form parallels that encourage viewers to compare and contrast different life choices and attitudes toward him. Along with Mary's investigation into the occupants of Gosford Park and the murder of McCordle, these techniques unify the narrative and develop the film's class critique, highlighting the false promises of noblesse oblige and the ways in which the strictures of service rob staff members of control over their lives and their families.

Even Altman's tendency to "create a film organically" on set does not challenge the classical foundation of the script. Fellowes played an unusually active role compared to most screenwriters on a Robert Altman film, not only creating the primary characters and structuring the plot but also utilizing his knowledge of English upstairs-downstairs life to ensure all the period details were correct. To that end, Altman allowed Fellowes to be on set nearly every day. As producer David Levy noted, this enabled Fellowes to attempt to maintain control over the script not only during the revision process but also during production: "Bob would scribble in the morning and try to change things and Julian worked very, very hard . . . to take whatever changes there were and incorporate them officially and formally and get those to be the words the actors did say on the day."[18] The film's continuity script (created by the script supervisor for the editor and noting all changes in dialogue and blocking during production) reveals that this process even included Fellowes writing brief summaries of conversation topics for the actors to ad-lib during the scene depicting the first day's initial gathering in the saloon. This structured improvisation develops key character traits, suggests past alliances and conflicts, and initiates new relationships, thereby clarifying the presentation of characters and causal chains beyond that found in the shooting script.[19]

Though the continuity script also reveals that some actors occasionally or even regularly ad-libbed in place of scripted lines during production, particularly Balaban (playing the visiting Hollywood producer Weissman, whose phone calls to studio executives are largely improvised) and Emily Watson (playing the head housemaid Elsie, who tweaked her lines with offhanded quips), the improvisation that most significantly impacted the plot was the result of collaborative problem-solving by Balaban, Altman, Fellowes, and actors Helen Mirren and Eileen Atkins. In an undated letter written by Balaban to Altman that focuses on script suggestions, Balaban recommends that the housekeeper, Mrs. Wilson (Mirren), explain in a final monologue her relationship to the cook, Mrs. Croft (Atkins), so as to motivate their oft-referenced rivalry.[20] But the rivalry remained unmotivated in the script until shortly after production started, when Altman first saw Mirren and Atkins together in costume over lunch and realized how similar they looked. Altman later relayed, "Julian was at another table. I said right then, 'Let's make them sisters who hate each other.' And this whole thing was done over pudding!"[21] Though Fellowes quickly wrote the sister plot, Mirren and Atkins improvised all but the opening line of its climactic scene—eight brief sentences that clarified their characters' relationship, provided an understated reconciliation between the two, and allowed Mrs. Wilson an uncharacteristically emotional outburst, punctuating both her motivation for poisoning McCordle (to kill him before her abandoned son did) and the nature of her conflict with her sister (unlike Mrs. Wilson, Mrs. Croft did not give up her son by McCordle and suffered for it). Rather than serving the digressive function often cited by scholars, here improvisation retroactively clarifies character traits and goals, motivates action, unifies the plot, and provides closure; the result is one of the most emotionally devastating moments in the film and boldly underlines its major themes.

20.2. Robert Altman, actress Kelly Macdonald, and script supervisor Penny Eyles on the set of *Gosford Park* (2001). Courtesy of Special Collections Research Center, University of Michigan Library.

Gosford Park more seamlessly integrates the influence of its collaborators than *The Gingerbread Man*, as Balaban and Fellowes tailored their work toward Altman's narrative preferences—though Fellowes's obsessive attention to detail allegedly annoyed Altman at times.[22] The film consistently employs classical strategies to organize and unify the many characters and plotlines, thereby developing larger themes, while even the on-set addition of a major plot point increases narrative coherence. Critics heralded *Gosford Park* as a return to form for the director, celebrating the film's subversion of genre for the purpose of social critique. Some critics, particularly those of *Sight and Sound*, applauded what they saw as freewheeling improvisation,[23] while others expressed relief that Altman had a proper script and seemed to adhere to it.[24] Stephen Holden in the *New York Times* explained the apparent contradiction: "Almost every sentence conveys crucial information, but in a deceptively off-hand style that's so light it feels like casual banter."[25] The ability of Altman and his collaborators to create a tightly plotted ensemble film that feels spontaneous and thus quintessentially "Altmanesque" illustrates yet another way classicism can function in Altman's films—not as a structure that can bind but as a set of tools that can liberate.

These brief analyses of *The Gingerbread Man* and *Gosford Park* reveal the importance of considering the impact of Altman's collaborators—particularly his screenwriters and producers—when exploring the relationship between classicism and the "Altmanesque." The creators of the initial screenplays for each film provided a classically constructed foundation that shifted and reformed during script development and production, focusing more on character behavior and culture than on adhering to generic conventions and moving away from explicit narrative revelation and toward suggestion. Yet even as the films rely on the viewer to piece the plot threads together, *The Gingerbread Man* retains much of its large-scale classical structure, while *Gosford Park* utilizes classical techniques to promote clarity and unity throughout. *The Gingerbread Man* and *Gosford Park* demonstrate the merit in revisiting Keyssar's claim that "Altman's films are usually more rigorously and tightly structured than we at first perceive,"[26] encouraging us to take a closer look at the range of ways classical techniques can play a role in organizing his narratives. Altman had a long and diverse career, and the pendulum swings between adherence to classical or art cinema conventions in his films can be quite broad; a more nuanced look at the variations within his filmmaking, particularly after his much-analyzed "peak" years in the

1970s, is in order. Such an effort will enlarge our understanding not only of Altman's authorship but also of the enduring presence of classicism within even the "maverick" corridors of American independent film.

NOTES

Many thanks to Kira Newmark and Benjamin Yap for their research assistance.

1   Helene Keyssar, *Robert Altman's America* (New York: Oxford University Press, 1991), 16–38.

2   Robert T. Self, *Robert Altman's Subliminal Reality* (Minneapolis: University of Minnesota Press, 2002), 47–53.

3   Robert Kolker, *A Cinema of Loneliness: Penn, Stone, Kubrick, Scorsese, Spielberg, Altman* (New York: Oxford University Press, 2000), 346.

4   Maria del Mar Azcona, "A Cinema of Plenty: Robert Altman and the Multi-Protagonist Film," in *Robert Altman: Critical Essays*, ed. Rick Armstrong (Jefferson, NC: McFarland, 2011), 140–53.

5   David Thompson, ed., *Altman on Altman* (London: Faber and Faber, 2006), 199.

6   Frank Caso, *Robert Altman: In the American Grain* (London: Reaktion Books, 2015), 11.

7   Mark Minett, *Robert Altman and the Elaboration of Hollywood Storytelling* (New York: Oxford University Press, 2021), 33–76.

8   Thompson, *Altman on Altman*, 181.

9   Mitchell Zukoff, *Robert Altman: The Oral Biography* (New York: Knopf, 2009), 457.

10 Thompson, *Altman on Altman*, 182.

11 Island Pictures to Robert Altman memorandum, December 23, 1996, *The Gingerbread Man* Script Notes, Robert Altman Archive: Projects—1990s, University of Michigan Library (Special Collections Research Center).

12 David Levy to Robert Altman memorandum re: 10/16/96 script draft, November 4, 1996, *The Gingerbread Man* Script Notes, Robert Altman Archive: Projects—1990s.

13 Kevin Yoder, National Research Group, to Peter Graves, Polygram Pictures, memorandum, June 13, 1997, *The Gingerbread Man* Test Screenings Results and Correspondence, Robert Altman Archive: Projects—1990s.

14 Joshua Astrachan to Robert Altman memorandum, April 6, 1998, *The Gingerbread Man* Press Reaction Correspondence, Robert Altman Archive: Projects—1990s.

15 Giulia D'Agnolo Vallan, "An Interview with Julian Fellowes," in *Altman*, ed. Kathryn R. Altman and Giulia D'Agnolo Vallan (New York: Harry N. Abrams, 2014), 283.

16 In the pre-title sequence of *The Back of the Tapestry*, Fellowes highlights the "hideous carpets and cheap furniture" at the present-day Gosford Park, a nursing home, and its gardens, which "display that heartless municipal lack of humor so ubiquitous today." A split screen contrasts the opulent past with the drab present: "a blazing fire instead of some ill-made, dusty paper flowers, rich carpets instead of linoleum, fine portraits on the walls staring haughtily down. It is gone." *The Back of the Tapestry* screenplay, March 2000, *Gosford Park* Scripts, Robert Altman Archive: Projects—2000s.

17 Kristin Thompson, *Storytelling in the New Hollywood: Understanding Classical Narrative Technique* (Cambridge, MA: Harvard University Press, 1999), 248–334.

18 Zukoff, *Robert Altman*, 475–76.

19 In his analysis of *McCabe and Mrs. Miller* (Altman 1971), Minett discusses how Altman's use of improvisation often functions to add texture and depth to the world of the film. See Minett, *Robert Altman and the Elaboration of Hollywood Storytelling*, 223–37.

20 Bob Balaban to Robert Altman, undated, *Gosford Park* Production and Post-Production Correspondence, Robert Altman Archive: Projects—2000s.

21 Thompson, *Altman on Altman*, 203.

22 Zukoff, *Robert Altman*, 475.

23 Geoffrey Macnab, "Gosford Park," *Sight and Sound* 12, no. 2 (2000): 45–46.

24 See Marcus Berkmann, "The Servants Have It," *The Spectator*, February 2, 2002, 43; Kirk Honeycutt, "Gosford Park," *Hollywood Reporter*, November 8, 2001, 10, 18.

25 Stephen Holden, "Full of Baronial Splendor and Hatefulness," *New York Times*, December 26, 2001, E1.

26 Keyssar, *Robert Altman's America*, 16.

21

SCRIPTING PROTOCOLS AND PRACTICES

SCREENWRITING IN THE PACKAGE-UNIT ERA

Janet Staiger

One of the issues for classical Hollywood cinema studies is the extent to which a film is considered "classical" or not. The answer to this issue hinges on four features: industrial structure, mode of production, narrative forms, and stylistic choices. David Bordwell, Kristin Thompson, and my initial 1985 project, *The Classical Hollywood Cinema*, was to describe and explain the relationships among these features during 1915–60, now referred to as the "studio era."[1] We did gesture to post-1960, and all three of us have discussed continuities and differences from the "studio" years.

This chapter will focus on recent developments in analyzing screenwriting practices (including debates about describing the script as a "blueprint") and the need to retain awareness of how the mode of production affects screenwriting practices. As an example, I will consider how independent contracting of screenwriting labor in the package-unit system since the 1970s has simultaneously produced demands for greater rigidity and yet "violations" in scripting protocols and practices since screenwriters now have to expect that a script will circulate among many potential readers. This situation becomes an impetus in screenwriting advice to ensure that potential buyers read at least the start of the "spec" script.

First, though, a comment about terminology. Unfortunately, I do not have space here to discuss this, but I distinguish among notions related to the industry, to film form and style, and to systems of production. I would mark out one factor of *form and style*—continuity—as prevalent from about 1915 to present. As Bordwell has argued, circa the mid-1970s to 1980s, "intensified continuity" also developed as a bounded stylistic option in the classical cinema. I will leave it to others to argue whether such a form and style as "postclassical" exists, but I am not convinced it does, or, at least, "postclassical" is not a very good term for it. I do believe that in the United States, besides its avant-garde and documentary practices, an indie film style appears in its first wave about 1960 with the prototypical film *Shadows* (Cassavetes 1959).[2]

Those observations are about film form and style. For *systems of production*, I differentiate between the studio era (about 1915 through about 1960) and the post-studio era (about 1960 to present day) when the management-labor organization shifts primarily to the package-unit system and the physical locales for filmmaking spread.[3] Both large firms and independent companies utilize the variety of systems of production.[4] Finally, I note that during both the studio and post-studio eras, scripts were developed in three ways: hired writers; group writing (which continues in series writing today); and spec scripts—scripts brought to the attention of decision makers, after 1915 usually via agents.

RECENT DEVELOPMENTS IN ANALYZING SCREENWRITING PRACTICES

Ever since people began writing about films, individuals have looked at screenwriters and screenwriting practices.[5] Since 2006, an organized group of scholars, led by Ian Macdonald, has focused on this area.[6] The Screenwriting Research Network is a large and active organization with annual conferences and in 2009 began the *Journal of Screenwriting*. For an understanding of the future direction of scholarship on screenwriting, scholars should look there.

One of the debates that has developed is whether it is appropriate to use the term "blueprint" for a script. Steven Maras introduces this question in his book *Screenwriting* (2009). While criticizing isolating the script from the production process, he notes that the blueprint metaphor can too easily produce the wrong idea that "conception" is isolated from "execution," that the script "controls" the production. He does recognize value in the metaphor, however, noting the invocation of composing and building processes for making films and the industrial context. Maras advocates using the term "notation" instead.[7] Steven Price in *The Screenplay* (2010) argues that "the screenplay is not so much a blueprint as an enabling document, necessary for the production but transformed by directors, actors, vagaries of the weather, and a multitude of other factors." Price's critique also includes suggesting that the term "blueprint" "compromises the aesthetic and thematic seriousness of the text because it ascribes to the screenwriter a bathetic non-imagination."[8]

I am unsure where I picked up (or made up) the analogy between blueprints and scripts.[9] I appreciate the potential for conceptual abuse of the term, but I think that anyone who has built a house knows that blueprints are a starting point, not an inviolate instruction. Moreover, I have emphasized that other paper records are important parts of the planning and execution processes. "Blueprint" seems a beneficial description of the functions that document serves for the production process. It is, however, also the case that the blueprint analogy now shows up in trade discourse, as I mention below. So, first of all, making distinctions about who is using the term and its connotations is necessary.

A second point worth noting is that if one is considering the conceptualizing processes of the writer or writers, archives now provide not only drafts of scripts but also many other fascinating documents that materialize thinking and planning.[10] Also to be consulted are all of the paper and audio records of actors' and other workers' comments on scripts that indicate their interpretations and plans. While the discussion about whether *scholars* should continue to use the analogy of the script as blueprint deserves consideration, the widening of documents available to reveal conceptualization and actions is heartening.

THE PACKAGE-UNIT SYSTEM AND CURRENT SCREENWRITING PRACTICES

Thompson, in *Storytelling in the New Hollywood*, observes: "With the rise of package production since the 1970s . . . freelance scriptwriting has enjoyed a resurgence, and a flood of manuals has appeared to cater to aspiring authors."[11] Although writing for series retains the features of the hired-employee, studio-department system,[12] the current scheme of the package-unit system for making many individual films has altered the situation for freelance screenwriters. Rather than proving oneself to be a good team member within a studio department, the writer needs to gain attention from numerous gatekeepers to access those with the power to approve financial support for a project.[13]

This independent purchasing of scripts and individual contracting of labor for specific projects have produced minor changes (and "violations") from the earlier scripting protocols. Now the screenwriter has to prepare a spec script to circulate among many potential buyers.[14] This creates writing requirements for branding personal authorship through "originality" and for attracting immediate attention to the script and holding it. These present conditions of precarious labor result in culture-of-production discursive guidance that screenplays need both to adhere to supposed "rules" and also to find novel ways to grab and maintain the reader's interest. For screenwriters, manuals, professional columns, and industry seminars advocate, for instance, *rigidity*[15] (e.g., the rule of a first-act plot point occurring somewhere on pages 25–30 of a 120-page manuscript; no camera directions; Courier not Helvetica font) and *visualization* (e.g., "action" writing, rhythm writing, symbolic descriptive settings). Here I want to review this contemporary advice and summarize its logic both aesthetically and industrially.

In my "Considering the Script" essay, I point out that the package-unit system has maintained many of its features for screenwriters from the earlier production systems that developed for "the purposes of saving costs and controlling quality." Today, "writers have encountered specific demands on their production planning. . . . These newer demands include [1] budgeting considerations such as product placement, fan satisfaction and the author-function; [2] contemporary theories about storytelling; [3] cultivation of franchises through sequels and serial storytelling; and [4] multiple platforms for the narrative universe."[16] As John Caldwell puts it, "All screenplays are also business plans."[17] Despite these newer demands, the advantages of the scripting formats developed during the studio era remain. Scripts have a particular and learned format so that everyone in the labor process can easily read the directions. Thus, freelance writers hoping to land a spec script must learn and follow certain rules to look as if they are professionals.

Both eras have gatekeepers who also work within a very articulated and rigorous production culture. During the studio era, department heads and producers ran the production process. During the post-studio/package-unit era, a hierarchy of script readers toss out or retain scripts to move them up the chain of decision makers. Both eras provide massive amounts of guidance to budding writers (an industry in itself). These books, newsletters, and advice columns express and reenforce the aesthetics of the classical Hollywood cinema. For example, in a January 2018 advice column in *Script*, the author (a script reader) writes, "Now it's time to look at the narrative's structure—specifically does the story have a solid beginning, middle, and end? . . . Yes, I believe in the three-act structure and believe that all successful dramatic narratives adhere to it, whether knowingly or unknowingly." [18] The author also goes on to write that the story must have a goal-seeking protagonist and an antagonist.

While I might survey numerous guidelines about character development, genre, story structure, and so forth, I want to focus here on the logic of two features of this advice. One is the expressed reasoning for following certain "rules." The other is rather fascinating work-arounds to one of the cardinal sins: providing camera and other directions that are considered within the work functions of other members of the production staff.

RULES AND RIGIDITY

From the point of view of efficiency, having a set of guiding principles about screenplays saves readers a lot of time. As well, if a reader is used to a set of rules, standardized formatting makes for a more pleasurable (and, thus, friendlier) read. Hence, the maxim that one page of script equals one minute of film is a very handy imperative for someone picking up a new spec script. Possibly the most prominent of the current advice givers, Syd Field, states in his 1982 manual, *Screenplay*: "The standard screenplay is approximately 120 pages long, or two hours long. It is measured at one page per minute. It does not matter whether your script is all dialogue, all action, or both. The rule holds firm—one page of screenplay equals one minute of screen time." [19] Field continues that while the initial readers expect a script to "grab" them within 30 pages, the next person up the line will likely "scan the first few pages himself [or herself], ten pages, to be exact." [20] William Packard echoes this prescription: "A word about length—screenplays should be 120 pages long, no more, and rarely less. That is the standard rule in the film industry." [21] Not just length but also format matters. Dave Trottier notes, "You should write in short, visual sentences, avoiding more than three sentences in a descriptive paragraph or heavy dialogue. Avoid the temptation to give camera angles or direction to the actors. A script is simply a blueprint for a director, actors, costume designer, set designer, cinematographer, etc." [22]

Advice givers do attempt to explain why these rules exist. Hillis Cole and Judith Haag point out: "There are many reasons for adhering strictly to a consistent standard format. A given script must serve as a basic tool which is used by many hands."[23] Second, "author" scripts differ from "production"/ shooting scripts; if the spec script is purchased, other workers will turn an author script into a shooting script.[24] In other words, advice givers are saying that writers have a specific position and function within a divided labor system; they should stay out of the work roles of others.

A third reason articulated for the rules involves the effects of the widespread acceptance of the rules (a case of circularity). As Trottier writes, "Knowing how to format a screenplay is critical for executives to feel confident you can write professionally. When a writer deviates from industry standard formatting, a reader will quickly lose interest and most likely stop reading, thinking the story will be as amateur as the flawed formatting."[25] An MGM story editor summarizes her rules: "What kinds of things turn a reader off a script right off the bat? Having character names that can't be pronounced. Seeing a page count that's way over the standard length. A poorly typed script, or one that's in an improper format. Cover art or embossed titles that suggest a snow job. Excessive stage directions. Those will all trigger an immediate negative reaction."[26]

These rules, however, raise a contradictory problem for the spec writer. A company script reader will need more than bland description and dialogue to begin to sense that the project is worth pursuing. Thus, the contrary goal to format standardization is to make the script vivid and unique. And "visualization"—turning words into pictures in the script reader's mind—must be accomplished without impinging significantly on the rules of little or no camera instruction or other such directions and, thus, taking over the prerogatives of the other skilled workers.

VIOLATIONS AND VISUALIZATION

As Caldwell puts it, "Mainstream screenwriters . . . are restricted in formatting to spare storytelling and simple descriptions only, and few producers will even read scripts that include anything more than this spare format, which should never include directorial comments, thematic interpretations, or camera instructions. Only 'amateurs' add those elements."[27] While Caldwell is basically right, the advice givers provide all sorts of suggestions as to how to finesse or even cheat on that rule.

For example, Robin Russin states that since the writer's goal is to make the reader see the story, the writer should use a "descriptive noun [or] juicy metaphor or simile [that] would enliven the description rather than bog it down."[28] In fact, stereotypes might be justified. Adrian Laudermilk recommends to writers: "Rely on clichés and general assumptions to build pictures in the reader's mind rather than bog down your first ten pages."[29]

Right after warning that "an abundance of CAMERA angles like long shots, close shots, instructions about zooms, pans, and dollies immediately revealed a novice screenwriter who didn't know what he or she was doing," Field does acknowledge a writer can make minor "suggestions" about stage directions and music and sound and then supplies twelve terms to replace "CAMERA" such as "angle on," "pov," "reverse angle," "moving shot," and "insert."[30]

Additionally, advice givers explain how to use aspects of the standard format to advantage. Alex Southey points out that for a scene in the script of *Raiders of the Lost Ark* (Spielberg 1981), Lawrence Kasdan shortened the blocks of description to make the reading pace on the page faster, attempting to match the pace of the scene's action.[31] In another example of this trick, the author provides methods to "turn words into pictures," including "set[ting] a [reading] rhythm to match the action," and offers the following illustration: "Shane Black sets a staccato, hard-hitting tempo to match the intensity of his shoot-/em-up, THE LAST BOY SCOUT." In the scene starting with "Cole's fingers paw the cold earth," each line is one sentence, which keeps the reader moving down the page. The author concludes, "As you write action, keep in mind that you want the reader to 'see' the film as clearly as you do. An economy of words, all chosen with deliberate care, structured into sentences that match the tempo of the scene, will go a long way toward bringing your script off the page and into the mind's eye of the reader."[32]

While noting that the script is a "blueprint," Russin extends the commentary: "It may sound strange, but well-written description . . . is a lot like poetry—it demands not only economy, but also precise choices: the specificity of choosing exactly the right words and rhythms to conjure the desired images and emotions."[33]

CONCLUSION

Not surprisingly, screenwriters have "heroes" who both follow and break the rules successfully. My screenwriting colleagues at the University of Texas promptly offered Black as an example of this.[34] Their immediate illustration is the opening of Black's first produced film, *Lethal Weapon* (Donner 1987).

```
SUPER MAIN TITLES.

TITLES END, as we --

SPIRAL DOWN TOWARD a lush, high-rise apartment complex.
The moon reflected in glass.

CAMERA CONTINUES TO MOVE IN THROUGH billowing curtains,
INTO the inner sanctum of a penthouse apartment, and
here, boys and girls, is where we lose our breath,
because --

spread-eagled on a sumptuous designer sofa lies the
single most beautiful GIRL in the city.
Blonde hair. A satin nightgown that positively  glows.
Sam Cooke MUSIC, crooning from five hundred dollar
SPEAKERS.

PASTEL colors. Window  walls.  New  wave  furniture  tor-
tured into weird shapes.  It looks like robots live here.

On the table next to the sleeping Venus  lies  an  open
bottle of pills ... next to that, a mirror dusted with
cocaine.

She rouses herself to smear some powder  on  her  gums.
As she does, we see from her eyes that she is thoroughly,
completely whacked out of her mind...

She stands, stumbles across the room, pausing to glance
at a photograph on the wall:

Two men.  Soldiers.  Young, rough-hewn, arms around each
other.

The Girl throws open the glass doors ... steps out onto a
balcony, and there, beneath her, lies  all  of  nighttime
L.A.  Panoramic splendor.  Her hair flies, her expression.
rapt, as she stands against this sea of technology.  She
is beautiful.
```

21.1. First page of *Lethal Weapon* (1987), written by screenwriter Shane Black.

Here is an example of a writer who flirts with the standard format and rules but whose narrational voice insists on picture making and whose manipulation of the format swiftly carries the reader along. Thus, Black establishes a strong authorial style, which helps explain his success within the package-unit system. It is hardly surprising that Black's work is looked to as a place for illumination and for imitation.[35] It is also a fine instance of when both the rigidity of rules and the directives to visualize make for not only a blueprint but also an excellent, indeed poetic, read.

NOTES

Special thanks to my University of Texas colleagues Stuart Kelban, Richard Lewis, and Cindy McCreery, who are always exceptionally helpful in letting me know about practices and resources in screenwriting.

1   David Bordwell, Janet Staiger, and Kristin Thompson, *The Classical Holly-wood Cinema: Film Style and Mode of Production to 1960* (London: Routledge, 1985).

2   See Janet Staiger, "Proto-Indie: 1960s 'Half-Way' Cinema," in *A Companion to American Indie Cinema*, ed. Geoff King (Oxford, UK: Wiley-Blackwell, 2017), 209–32.

3   Petr Szczepanik and Patrick Vonderau summarize three critiques of my 1985 formulation of the "mode of production" in their "Introduction," in *Behind the Screen: Inside European Production Cultures*, ed. Szczepanik and Vonderau (New York: Palgrave Macmillan, 2013), 1–9. I appreciate these criticisms.

4   "Indie" is a form and style; "independent" refers to an industrial structure. While occasionally linked, they are not necessarily connected.

5   See Richard Corliss, *Talking Pictures: Screenwriters in the American Cinema* (New York: Penguin Books, 1974); Edward Azlant, "The Theory, History, and Practice of Screenwriting, 1897–1920," PhD diss., University of Wisconsin-Madison, 1980; Tom Stempel, *FrameWork: A History of Screenwriting in the American Film*, exp. ed. (New York: Continuum, 1991); Kevin Alexander Boon, *Script Culture and the American Screenplay* (Detroit, MI: Wayne State University Press, 2008); Claus Tieber, *Schreiben für Hollywood: Das Drehbuch im Studiosystem* (Berlin: Lit Verlag, 2008); and Steven Maras, *Screenwriting: History, Theory and Practice* (London: Wallflower Press, 2009), 187n4.

6   *Screenwriting Research Network*, accessed April 2, 2018, https://screenwritingresearch.com/about-us/.

7   Maras, *Screenwriting*, 22, 117–29.

8   Steven Price, *The Screenplay: Authorship, Theory and Criticism* (Houndmills, UK: Palgrave Macmillan, 2010), xi, 46.

9   See, in particular, Janet Staiger, "Blueprints for Feature Films: Hollywood's Continuity Scripts," in *The American Film Industry*, ed. Tino Balio, 2nd ed. (Madison: University of Wisconsin Press, 1985), 173–92.

10 For a discussion and illustrations of this, see Janet Staiger, "Considering the Script as Blueprint in 2012," *Northern Lights* 10 (2012): 75–90.

11 Kristin Thompson, *Storytelling in the New Hollywood: Understanding Classical Narrative Technique* (Cambridge, MA: Harvard University Press, 1999), 11.

12 John Thornton Caldwell, *Production Culture: Industrial Reflexivity and Critical Practice in Film and Television* (Durham, NC: Duke University Press, 2008), 211–16.

13 In a recent excellent and depressing book, Angela McRobbie analyzes the politics and costs of creative labor in the new culture industries. McRobbie, *Be Creative: Making a Living in the New Culture Industries* (Cambridge, UK: Polity, 2016).

14 I am dealing here with the situation for noncommissioned work.

15 A nicer term would be "standardization."

16 Staiger, "Considering," 75.

17 Caldwell, *Production Culture*, 232.

18 Ray Morton, "Meet the Reader: The Six Axes of Screenplay Analysis, Part I," *Script*, January 5, 2018, accessed January 9, 2018, http://www.scriptmag.com. Thompson argues against the three-act structure as what is actually occurring in classical Hollywood films in *Storytelling*, 22–26, 364; however, her analysis has not influenced the articulated advice in Hollywood script-writing culture or practices by Hollywood script readers.

19 Syd Field, *Screenplay: The Foundations of Screenwriting*, exp. ed. (New York: Dell, 1982), 8.

20 Field, *Screenplay*, 67.

21 William Packard, *The Art of Screenwriting: Story, Script, Markets* (New York: Paragon House, 1987), 116.

22 Dave Trottier, "Why Is Proper Script Writing Format Important?" *Script*, accessed January 8, 2018, http://www.scriptmag.com.

23 Hillis R. Cole Jr. and Judith H. Haag, *The Complete Guide to Standard Script Formats, Part 1—Screenplays* (North Hollywood, CA: CMC, 1994), 1.

24 Cole and Haag, *Complete Guide*, 1; Rick Reichman, *Formatting Your Screenplay* (New York: Paragon House, 1992), xv–xvi.

25 Trottier, "Why." As a former Hollywood story reader explained to me, "Anyone who regularly reads screenplays knows there's a very strong correlation

between non-standard formatting and bad writing . . . it is a clear indication that a painful read is most likely ahead." Richard Lewis, email to Janet Staiger, February 9, 2018.

26 "Interview: MGM Story Editor Catherine Tarr," *Hollywood Scriptwriter*, June 1988, 8.

27 Caldwell, *Production Culture*, 233.

28 Robin Russin, "You're Writing a Picture: So Use Picture-Making Words," *Script*, March–April 2004, 28.

29 Adrian Loudermilk, "Hollywood Insider," *Hollywood Scriptwriter*, December 2000, 12.

30 Field, *Screenplay*, 167, 171–72.

31 Alex Southey, "How to Write Action Description," *Creative Screenwriting*, April 12, 2017, accessed January 9, 2018, https://creativescreenwriting.com/action-description/.

32 "It's Called Action for a Reason! Turning Your Action Descriptions into Moving Pictures," *Hollywood Scriptwriter*, February 1994, 5–7.

33 Russin, "You're Writing," 28.

34 The term "hero" applies to Black as a writer not as a person.

35 This said, the final script is a product of multiple rewrites and feedback from executives.

VIII

NEW APPROACHES

22

THE TRADE PAPERS AND CULTURES OF 1920s HOLLYWOOD

Eric Hoyt

The migration of American motion picture production to Southern California, and the construction of permanent studio facilities in and around Los Angeles, was largely a movement of the 1910s.[1] However, the advent of "Hollywood" as a culture and community—detached from the rest of society within its own "colony" and associated with movies, money, sex, sun, and busloads full of aspiring actresses—only truly took form during the 1920s.[2] As film historians have shown, newspapers and fan magazines both played important roles in disseminating the ideas and imagery of what constituted Hollywood.[3] What has received less attention is how the industry's Los Angeles trade papers participated in the ways in which movie workers conceived of themselves as belonging to and participating within this community. The *Hollywood Reporter* (established in 1930) and *Daily Variety* (established in 1933) are the film industry's two best-known and longest-running trades. Yet contrary to the *Hollywood Reporter*'s self-serving claim that "no one had ever published a trade paper from Hollywood before [it],"[4] at least eleven trade papers had emerged in Hollywood before the *Reporter* arrived on the scene. The Media History Digital Library has digitized many of these forgotten Los Angeles trade papers, and they are now freely accessible online to anyone who wants to read them.[5]

This chapter analyzes three especially significant 1920s Los Angeles trade papers, highlighting the ways they contributed to early Hollywood. *Camera!*, the *Film Mercury*, and the *Film Spectator* all spoke to Los Angeles–based communities of creative workers, as well as many readers who wanted to break in. In analyzing the trade papers, I pay particular attention to questions of change and continuity. What assumptions about the motion picture and publishing industries guided the trade papers' editors? Which of the strategies they employed continue with us to the present? And which strategies were abandoned?

Collectively, the Hollywood trade papers participated in the creation and maintenance of industry cultures. Consequently, we need to understand the Hollywood trade papers as vehicles for maintaining cultures and communities just as much as we see them as vessels for disseminating the news. In his landmark essay "A Cultural Approach to Communication," communications theorist James W. Carey contrasted two frameworks for understanding communication: the transmission view and the ritual view. As Carey writes, "If one examines a newspaper under a transmission view of communication, one sees the medium as an instrument for disseminating news and knowledge"; in contrast, a ritual view of communication will understand "newspaper reading less as sending or gaining information and more as attending mass, a situation in which nothing new is learned but in which a particular view of the world is portrayed and confirmed."[6] As Carey points out, "A ritual view does not exclude the processes of information transmission or attitude change," but it insists that these occur within a broader cultural framework. Carey defines communication as "a symbolic process whereby reality is produced, maintained, repaired, and transformed."[7] What is remarkable is how consistent this view is with the entertainment industry's own thinking. "Perception is reality" has become a commonplace adage in today's Hollywood, an example of what John Thornton Caldwell calls "industry self-theorizing."[8] Many creative workers in 1920s Hollywood assumed this to be the case as well, and the advertising managers of *Camera!*, the *Film Mercury*, and the *Film Spectator* were happy to take their money for the opportunity to achieve new realities.

CAMERA! AND THE EMERGENCE OF AN ADVERTISING BASE

Camera! was the film industry's first weekly trade paper to publish consistently from Los Angeles, and it proved that a sufficient advertising base could sustain such a paper. Yet when *Camera!* began publishing in 1918, it did not arrive sui generis. *Camera!* very much modeled itself on the entertainment industry trade publications published in New York City. The *New York Clipper*, the *New York Dramatic Mirror*, the *Morning Telegraph*, and *Variety* all covered the intertwined industries of legitimate theater, vaudeville, and motion pictures (the Cincinnati-based *Billboard* was also an active participant in these markets). Additionally, *Moving Picture World* and *Motion Picture News* were the two leading film-specific trade publications, covering the film industry in depth from their New York offices through a network of correspondents (including representatives based in Los Angeles). These entertainment trade papers all reported on industry trade developments, reviewed new productions, and offered editorial "thought leadership" on pressing issues. They were also filled with advertisements. The economic significance of those advertising pages is important to understand. The cost of producing a trade paper far exceeded the revenue obtained from subscriptions. Typically, subscriptions only generated between 10 and 20 percent of a publication's revenue. In many ways, paid subscriptions were more important as evidence that the right readership wanted to receive the paper than they were as a source of income. Without advertising revenue, the trade papers could not exist.

Yet advertising posed risks. Selling ads could damage a trade paper's perceived independence and integrity. Some of the advertisers were important theater and vaudeville producers, such as the Schuberts and the Keith-Albee circuit, or motion picture distributors, such as Universal or Famous Players-Lasky. Skeptical readers might reasonably wonder whether the reviewer of a new Universal feature pulled his punches after taking a look at his publisher's balance sheet. Another approach to advertising was selling directly to actors and other industry workers. This was far more common for the theater and vaudeville papers, which had a large readership of performers, than it was for *Motion Picture News* and *Moving Picture World*, which had a readership primarily composed of film exhibitors. However, the practice of cultivating actors as both readers and advertisers also provoked controversies.

Camera!'s success in navigating these waters may have stemmed from the fact that its business manager, Raymond Cannon, was a working actor. He understood very well the desires of actors seeking to gain notice, shape their perception, and secure employment. In 1919, a year in which Cannon was consistently listed as *Camera!*'s business manager, he was also credited as an actor in no fewer than five films, including D. W. Griffith's *True Heart Susie* (1919).[9] We can speculate that working simultaneously in acting and in industrial publishing may have been good for business on both fronts. Being on movie sets and interacting with cast and crew members provided opportunities for Cannon to solicit gossip, news items, and advertisements. Meanwhile, *Camera!* elevated Cannon's own status and visibility within the industry. In the age of the silent movie, it is unlikely that any other character actor of his status possessed such a loud voice.

Camera! provided industry news alongside the advertisements that promoted actors, writers, and directors. The "Pulse of the Industry" section tracked active studio productions, and a column titled "Where to Sell Your Scenario?" pointed aspiring screenwriters toward potential buyers (interestingly, this column was discontinued early on; perhaps the industry was moving toward the "no unsolicited submissions" policy that governs contemporary Hollywood).[10] One consistent theme, across both news items and opinion pieces, was the address toward the film colony as a particular community with shared interests. *Camera!* bristled at the ways in which Southern California's elite institutions discriminated against the industry (e.g., banning movie people from the Wilshire Country Club).[11] Yet the trade paper also insisted that the movie industry was special; it needed to be treated differently than other commercial enterprises when it came to taxation and other select business matters.[12] Most of all, *Camera!*'s editorials opposed all forms of external regulation. The industry community was in the best position to govern itself.[13]

The author of most of these editorials was twenty-year-old Franchon Royer, the wife of Raymond Cannon. Like her spouse, Royer came to the trade paper from acting. Just a year earlier, in 1919, she had taken out an advertisement in *Camera!* promoting herself as "a versatile ingénue."[14] Over the next three years, Royer would indeed prove herself versatile. Her editorials sometimes performed the voice of the stern trade paper "thought leader," a position that Chicago-based publisher Martin Quigley had come to embrace around the same time. But in her best writing, Royer drew from her own experiences to contribute a nuanced understanding of the industry that was missing elsewhere. In her remarkable 1921 editorial "Pictures and the Girl Question," Royer sketched out a middle ground between the discourses of Hollywood as a den of sin or the land of milk and honey: "The girls who wait on us over counters, wires, and tables are those who having learned about the law of averages are making the best of it." And she explained that, while "some impressionable souls" had been led to disillusionment, other women had moved West to escape repressive, dysfunctional, or abusive family situations. No, they had not become the next Mary Pickford, but in many cases, waiting tables in Los Angeles brought far more joy and freedom than the life they had known before in Wichita or Grand Rapids.[15] This was *Camera!* at its best—reminding us of the unexpected ways in which human lives become intertwined and transformed within the industry.[16]

THE *FILM MERCURY* AND THE INDUSTRY THAT MIGHT HAVE BEEN

A number of small, competing trade papers soon joined *Camera!* on the West Coast. Most of them attempted to carve out some sort of niche. *Hollywood Filmograph* (established in 1922) spoke to the community of Hollywood actors, and its editor, Harry Burns, supported Equity's attempt to gain a foothold on the West Coast. Harry Tullar, on the other hand, focused his address to exhibitor communities. Tullar promoted his reviews of short films as the distinguishing feature of *Tullars Weekly* (established in 1922). *Wid's Weekly* (established in 1923) also emphasized reviews, alongside the fiction that Hollywood's elite were all devoted readers of the paper. Editor Wid Gunning, who had previously created the New York–based *Wid's Daily* (which became the *Film Daily*), took the hard-sell approach in lecturing aspiring actors and screenwriters as to why they should buy ads: "Wid has never claimed or expected that everyone will always agree with his opinions. The important thing from the viewpoint of the advertiser is that every important personage in the film industry—executive, director, author, player, technical artists and theater owners—does read carefully what he has to say. It is your job to sell yourself. . . . WHAT'S YOUR NAME WORTH?"[17] Like *Camera!* before it, *Wid's Weekly* conceived of Hollywood as a community invested in taste, gatekeeping, and self-promotion.

Tamar Lane's *Film Mercury* (established in 1924) shared many of the features of *Camera!* and its theatrical trade paper predecessors. The *Film Mercury* included news items about the studios, reviews of new movies, and editorials addressing industry problems. And it was advertisements purchased by aspiring actors—along with ads for the vendors who serviced them, such as drama teachers and plastic surgeons—that made Lane's publication possible. Yet within this familiar framework, Lane pushed the *Film Mercury* in a distinctive, innovative direction. The result may be Hollywood's first and last avant-garde trade paper.

One year before creating the *Film Mercury*, Lane had published a scathing book of film criticism. Titled *What's Wrong with the Movies?*, Lane's book provided several answers to this central question, with each chapter offering an indictment of a different sector within the industry. However, Lane was able to convey his core thesis in a mere seven words: "The photoplay is an art without artists." [18] The potential of a remarkable art form, in Lane's estimation, was being utterly squandered. In the *Film Mercury*, Lane offered weekly updates on this same general theme.

Lane did not arrive on these views within a vacuum. Lane's taste sensibility combined two critical frameworks of his day: Mencken-esque cynicism and modernist theories of film art. Because the combination of these critical frameworks tells us something about 1920s Hollywood culture, each of these traditions merits a brief unpacking. In *The Decline of Sentiment: American Film in the 1920s*, Lea Jacobs details how H. L. Mencken and a coterie of other critics in the late 1910s and 1920s established new values for taste culture and the evaluation of literature, film, and art. Mencken's magazine, the *American Mercury*, panned sentimental novels and films, dismissing them with the pejorative label "hokum." As these taste assumptions spread among film critics at other publications, they resulted in the critics imagining American audiences as bifurcated between sophisticated urban viewers and small-town moviegoers who clung onto old-fashioned conventions. Jacobs notes the strong degree to which *Variety*'s film reviewers in New York City adopted this disdain for hokum. [19] However, Tamar Lane embraced the sensibility just as vociferously from his office on Hollywood and Vine. In 1925, Lane editorialized:

> The general public has a right to demand hokum entertainment if that is the sort of silent drama it prefers—and judging from the films that are flooding the theatres of the country the public is getting its belly full. To say, however, that every film must be made in accordance with the mentalities of the morons and nit-wits that make up most of our theatre audiences is nonsense. . . . It is quite possible for an institution to be both popular entertainment and art. [20]

As the above passage makes clear, Lane shared Mencken's contempt for most of the American public, who bore considerable responsibility for "what's wrong with the movies." But what separated the two writers, at least from Lane's perspective, were their theories about the potential of film as an art form. Mencken primarily concerned himself with writing and language.

From the *Film Mercury*'s perspective, Mencken had only "contempt for the lowly movie" and "disdain for most of those connected with it."[21] Lane, on the other hand, believed that cinema was "the greatest instrument for stimulating emotion yet born."[22] Few truly great movies had been produced, in Lane's estimation, but there were many films with "scenes which expressed beauty, mood, and imagination," and those scenes held the promise for the brilliant artworks that would one day be made.[23]

The *Film Mercury* participated in a global theorizing of film as a medium and art. Lane considered his critical peers to be not the other ink-stained trade paper editors in Los Angeles and New York but rather a group of avant-gardists publishing their ideas of cinema from Europe. In 1928, Lane promoted his trade paper within the pages of *Close Up*, a film journal that today is far better remembered than the *Film Mercury*.[24] An English-language periodical that was published in Switzerland, *Close Up* was a forum for energetic debates about the nature of cinema and manifestos imagining new forms of filmmaking and spectatorship. The magazine published articles by filmmakers such as Sergei Eisenstein and female literary modernists such as H. D. and Gertrude Stein.[25] Lane contributed to the advertising base of this organ for film theory, purchasing full-page ads promoting the *Film Mercury* as "the most fearless and feared film paper published in America."[26]

Lane's conviction that the Los Angeles film community and European intelligentsia would both find value in the *Film Mercury* speaks to a particular moment in Hollywood history—one in which it was possible to believe that a large-scale avant-garde film movement might be commercially viable within the United States. No, Lane did not assume that the nation's "morons and nit-wits" would abandon their appetite for hokum, but he did believe that a more discerning audience existed and that this audience could be further cultivated. How best to serve the audiences of refined taste? Lane advocated for the creation of a parallel system of distribution and exhibition. As the 1920s continued, Lane praised the development of art house theaters and networks—such as Symon Gould's Little Theatre Movement—even though they never reached the stature and scale that he imagined.

Whereas Lane believed in a bifurcation among exhibitors—separating the art theaters from the hokum houses—he was less rigid in his thinking about filmmakers and production personnel. Many directors, screenwriters, and actors held the capacity to create screen art. D. W. Griffith directed the overly sentimental *Orphans of the Storm* (1921), but he had also made

Broken Blossoms (1919), which Lane considered to be one of the greatest films ever produced. Lane imagined a system in which the talent, technology, and production resources—all clustered in Los Angeles—would make films to satisfy the discerning theaters and audiences across the country and, more broadly, the world. And, yes, the movie colony would continue making schmaltz and hokum, too.

Lane's assumptions about the industry's fluidity seemed viable in the 1920s. In his history of the Los Angeles avant-garde, film historian David James has detailed that "through the 1920s stylistic innovations, production personnel and methods, and career opportunities crossed with no great difficulty between the studios and artisanal practices outside them, between the film industry and the avant-garde."[27] When the *Film Mercury* suspended publication in 1931, the Great Depression was at its height, and the resources required to achieve the ideal of a fluid production sector and flourishing art exhibition sector no longer seemed possible. But for a time, industry news, actor self-promotion, and theories of film art could all coexist within the same magazine. The commercial avant-garde had a Hollywood trade paper, even if it never fully materialized within the studio system.

THE *FILM SPECTATOR* AND ITS PARTISAN READERS

The most significant trade paper in 1920s Hollywood also experienced the most unexpected trajectory. Founded in 1926, the *Film Spectator* emerged as a magazine primarily devoted to craft-oriented film criticism. However, it exploded in popularity when its editor shifted the paper's incisive criticism away from individual movies and toward the producers, studios, and industry structure that manufactured them. The rise of this particular trade paper can tell us much about Hollywood's culture—which simultaneously identified as a single community ("picture people") yet bore deep partisan fault lines between management and creative workers.

The *Film Spectator*'s founder and editor, Welford Beaton, shared many of Tamar Lane's cinematic tastes. Beaton loved the German Expressionist films that had reached American screens, and he detested stale stories. However, Beaton's method of expressing his tastes and observations differed from Lane's. Beaton's prose was loose and conversational. He viewed his magazine as an ongoing conversation with filmmakers who wanted to improve their craft and improve the medium as a whole. He was the hardware store owner, leaning over the counter, offering pointers to the carpenters who came in for supplies.

In the summer of 1927, the significance of the *Film Spectator* fundamentally changed. The industry was abuzz over the issue of budgets, with producers insisting that a salary cut was necessary for all writers, directors, and actors. Beaton framed himself as an objective outsider—a "spectator," one might say—to the whole matter. He wrote, "I must admit that to one like myself, sitting on the sidelines and with no material interests at stake, the whole affair is so amusing that it is difficult to discuss it with so much gravity that the chuckles will not show through." Yet he was unequivocal and unrelenting in his placement of blame, decrying how "producers have brought about the present situation." [28] For Beaton, the poor management of producers was largely responsible for the poor quality of the pictures he reviewed. He declared, "The artistic emancipation of the screen waits upon its economic reformation, for perfect examples of screen art can be produced only by following perfect scripts." [29] He pointed out that film budgets would decline if productions followed the script and avoided filming superfluous shots and scenes. [30]

Beaton argued that the producers were wrong and that Hollywood's creative workers were right. Empowering screenwriters, not slashing their salaries, was the key to improving the film industry. And the best strategy for screenwriters to achieve this new level of power—and then make those better movies—was for creative workers to organize. "I do not believe in unions, but I do believe in waging a fight with the most potent weapon," wrote Beaton. "Only an organized movement will set matters right; consequently I am glad to see both the actors and writers organizing to present a united front." [31] When the Academy of Motion Pictures Arts and Sciences stepped in to help mediate the contentious salary cut debates, he dismissed the newly formed organization as a "catspaw to pull the producers' chestnuts from the fire." [32]

The response among Hollywood's creative community was electric. The *Film Spectator* became essential reading overnight. Screenwriters, actors, directors, and other craftspeople subscribed in droves. Here was a trade paper that validated their resentments and attacked their opponents. The *Film Spectator* was only published once every two weeks, so the creative community did not rely on it for the latest breaking news about negotiations with the producers. Instead, they read it to feel their anger affirmed, to connect with others in their community, and to relish in seeing Beaton tear apart their enemies with such forcefulness and wit. Hundreds of exhibitors, and most likely a large number of producers and studio executives, also subscribed in order to follow along.

When the *Film Spectator* published its "second birthday" issue in March 1928, Welford Beaton reflected on the unexpected turning point in his journal's young life:

> For the first eighteen months apparently I was the only one who took [the *Film Spectator*] seriously. Then the salary cut crisis arose, and I wrote an open letter to Jesse Lasky. It acted like an explosion with an element of humor in it. Within thirty days the circulation of The Spectator more than doubled, and it has turned over a couple of times since. I think it now has twice the combined circulation of all the other film papers published in Hollywood.[33]

Beaton credited his success to his policy of "absolute honesty." He believed that "honest opinions in a paper are like honest emotions on the screen."[34] But it requires a viewing audience to observe, interpret, and feel those emotions. And it took a community of creative workers, who felt under attack, to respond to Beaton's opinions and elevate the *Film Spectator* into becoming the most important trade paper for the Los Angeles film industry of the late 1920s.

CONCLUSION

While the Hollywood studios were engaged in the production of *The Covered Wagon* (Curtiz 1923), *The Big Parade* (Vidor 1925), and other silent features, the Los Angeles trade papers that chronicled those films and studios were participating in the production of Hollywood's cultures and communities. The plural—*cultures* and *communities*—is important here. In the late 1910s and early 1920s, *Camera!* distinguished between Los Angeles's community of movie people and the city's elites. But, within a few years, the *Film Mercury* and the *Film Spectator* had found new fault lines to conceive of Hollywood—between artists and hokum merchants, between creatives and producers. And all of these trade papers, including *Camera!*, depended upon a community of actors, writers, and directors seeking upward mobility within the industry as their advertising base. This was a community premised upon aspiration—buying space for their faces and names to appear in front of the influential community that they desperately wanted to join.

Today, the Hollywood trade papers continue to exhibit many of the same cultural features as their 1920s counterparts. Industry workers still use *Variety* and the *Hollywood Reporter* to try to position themselves and their projects favorably. Tamar Lane's vision of a second commercial film industry—premised upon a commitment to artistic filmmaking and an infrastructure of devoted theaters—did not take hold in the late 1920s and 1930s in the way that he had imagined. But distributors such as A24, exhibition chains such as Landmark, and the hybrid trade-fan website *Indiewire* are the descendants of Lane's ideals (even if the cynical side of Lane would still have much to find fault with in all of them). Most significantly, the *Film Spectator's* model for meteoric growth—a young publication skyrocketing in circulation by siding with creatives during a dispute with management—was replicated by the *Hollywood Reporter* in 1933 and *Deadline Hollywood* during the 2007 Writers Guild of America strike. In 2007, the striking writers and their allies found their Beaton-esque champion in Nikki Finke, a seasoned entertainment journalist who unapologetically took their side, reported dispatches from the front lines, and called out studio executives as greedy and incompetent. Her blog, *Deadline Hollywood*, became the industry's essential trade sheet, and the strike dealt a blow to *Variety's* and the *Hollywood Reporter's* print subscriptions, which never recovered (both *Variety* and the *Hollywood Reporter* are now read primarily on the web, and their famous daily print editions have ceased publication).

Ironically, the same technologies at the center of so many of contemporary Hollywood's upheavals—including digital production and distribution—have allowed for online access to the Los Angeles film communities' earliest trade papers. The digitization of *Camera!*, the *Film Mercury*, and the *Film Spectator* has given the voices of Franchon Royer, Tamar Lane, and Welford Beaton the power to speak to us again. As film researchers, we are cheating ourselves if we only scour these pages for reviews, news items, and other pieces of historical evidence that fit neatly within a footnote. These sources need to be understood for the complex roles they played in the development and maintenance of Hollywood's cultures. There has never been a better time to revisit Royer, Lane, and Beaton and to think critically—as they did—about gender, artistry, and ownership in Hollywood.

NOTES

1   Richard Koszarski, *An Evening's Entertainment: The Age of the Silent Feature Picture, 1915–1928* (New York: Scribner, 1990).

2   Jan Olsson, *Los Angeles before Hollywood: Journalism and American Film Culture, 1905 to 1915* (Stockholm: National Library of Sweden, 2008); Leo Braudy, *The Hollywood Sign: Fantasy and Reality of an American Icon* (New Haven, CT: Yale University Press, 2011).

3   Kathryn H. Fuller, *At the Picture Show: Small-Town Audiences and the Creation of Movie Fan Culture* (Charlottesville: University of Virginia Press, 2001); Anthony Slide, *Inside the Hollywood Fan Magazine* (Jackson: University of Mississippi Press, 2010).

4   Tichi Wilkerson and Marcia Borie, *Hollywood Reporter: The Golden Years* (New York: Arlington House, 1986), 5.

5   See the Media History Digital Library's Hollywood Studio System collection, http://mediahistoryproject.org/hollywood.

6   James W. Carey, *Communication as Culture: Essays on Media and Society* (New York: Routledge, 1988), 20.

7   Carey, *Communication as Culture*, 20.

8   John Thornton Caldwell, *Production Culture: Industrial Reflexivity and Critical Practice in Film and Television* (Durham, NC: Duke University Press, 2008), 15.

9   "Raymond Cannon," in *Early Cinema History Online* (ECHO), https://echo.commarts.wisc.edu/.

10   "The Pulse of the Studio," *Camera!*, April 13, 1919, 8; "Where to Sell Your Scenarios," *Camera!*, April 13, 1919, 13.

11   "Another Social Break," *Camera!*, May 1, 1920, 5.

12   "In Regard to the Income Tax," *Camera!*, May 8, 1920.

13   Franchon Royer, "The Censors Differentiate," *Camera!*, December 3, 1921.

14   Lisle Foote, "Fanchon Royer," in *Women Film Pioneers Project*, ed. Jane Gaines, Radha Vatsal, and Monica Dall'Asta (New York: Columbia University Libraries, 2013), https://wfpp.cdrs.columbia.edu/pioneer/fanchon-royer/.

15   Franchon Royer, "Pictures and the Girl Question," *Camera!*, April 16, 1921, 3.

16   For a valuable history of *Camera!* during the period after Cannon and Royer's leadership of the trade paper, see Peter Lester, "'Why I Am Ashamed of the Movies': Editorial Policy, Early Hollywood, and the Case of Camera!," *Moving Image* 18 (Spring 2018): 48–66.

17 "They May Not Always Agree—But They Do Read Wid's," *Wid's Weekly*, October 6, 1923, 1.

18 Tamar Lane, *What's Wrong with the Movies?* (Los Angeles: Waverly, 1923), 13.

19 Lea Jacobs, *The Decline of Sentiment: American Film in the 1920s* (Berkeley: University of California Press, 2008), 1–78.

20 Tamar Lane, "Are the Movies Art or Entertainment?" *Film Mercury*, May 22, 1925, 3.

21 Anabel Lane, "Anabel Lane Says," *Film Mercury*, July 29, 1927, 15; see also "Mr. Mencken Pays Tribute to the Film Mercury," *Film Mercury*, December 17, 1926, 3.

22 Lane, *What's Wrong with the Movies?*, 12.

23 Lane, *What's Wrong with the Movies?*, 12.

24 *Film Mercury* Advertisement, *Close Up*, June 1928, n.p.

25 For more on *Close Up*, see James Donald, Anne Friedberg, and Laura Marcus, *Close Up (1927–1933): Cinema and Modernism* (Princeton, NJ: Princeton University Press, 1998).

26 *Film Mercury* Advertisement, *Close Up*, June 1928, n.p.

27 David E. James, *The Most Typical Avant-Garde: History and Geography of Minor Cinemas in Los Angeles* (Berkeley: University of California Press, 2005), 22.

28 Welford Beaton, "Writers and Actors Should be Organized," *Film Spectator*, July 23, 1927, 3.

29 Welford Beaton, "How Not to Make a Picture," *Film Spectator*, June 25, 1927, 5.

30 Welford Beaton, "Some Day Will Be Much Better," *Film Spectator*, June 25, 1927, 5.

31 Beaton, "Writers and Actors Should be Organized," 3.

32 Welford Beaton, "Academy Becomes Tool of Producers," *Film Spectator*, August 20, 1927, 3.

33 Welford Beaton, "Spectator Celebrates Its Second Birthday," *Film Spectator*, March 3, 1928, 3.

34 Beaton, "Spectator Celebrates Its Second Birthday," 3.

23

THE VIDEO ESSAY AND CLASSICAL HOLLYWOOD STUDIES

Patrick Keating

Classical Hollywood films are both systematic and strange. They combine well-constructed plots with nonsensical musical numbers, unobtrusive cinematic technique with stylistic flourish, boy-next-door relatability with otherworldly glamour. For the scholar, it can be difficult to capture this peculiar mix, explaining how classical films work while acknowledging the peculiarity of the tradition's most memorable characters and scenes. Recently, the video essay has emerged as a tool that can address this perennial problem. At its best, the video essay balances two opposing tendencies—the explanatory and the poetic.[1] This makes the video essay an ideal form for the scholar who seeks to convey the systematic nature of studio-era film construction without losing sight of the tradition's enduring power to surprise us. Combining audiovisual precision with creative expression, the video essay allows the scholar to describe classical films with exceptional clarity and simultaneously to evoke the essayist's personal, affective responses to the films' idiosyncrasies and achievements.

Video essays are short movies about movies, typically made by editing together clips from DVDs and/or online sources, often paired with a scripted analysis delivered via the author's recorded voice-over or via on-screen text. Also known as videographic or audiovisual criticism, the video essay takes advantage of digital editing tools to produce a new genre of original scholarship. Championing the form's contributions to scholarship, the leading practitioner Catherine Grant has proposed the term "practice-led research."[2] Rather than use digital clips to illustrate a preexisting argument, the video essayist allows the practical, creative labor of digital editing to lead the research; ideally, the creative work of putting one clip next to another enables the scholar—and the viewer—to make unanticipated discoveries about the films in question. Such a methodology encourages the essayist to remain open to each film's nuances and textures.

As the form has developed over the last decade, theorists of the video essay have identified two distinct approaches, which may be combined productively. On one side of the spectrum, some video essays are *explanatory*, relying on a voice-over to make a precise argument over a series of shots; on the other side, some works are *poetic*, juxtaposing clips in a less linear way to open up a wider range of associations. A key purpose of drawing this distinction is to show how many of the leading practitioners draw inspiration from both trends. For instance, Christian Keathley contrasts the explanatory and the poetic mode, only to insist that images remain "mysterious and poetic" even when they illustrate an otherwise expository voice-over track.[3] Similarly, Cristina Álvarez López and Adrian Martin contrast the tradition of the "pedagogical demonstration—an enhanced form of the illustrated lecture"—with the tradition of the "cine-poem," while noting that both forms rely on montage, a "charged activity" that produces new and often surprising meanings through juxtaposition.[4] They encourage video essayists to avoid the twin dangers of excessive homogeneity, where every shot contributes to a single line of argument, and excessive heterogeneity, where bad matches fail to produce a meaningful connection. An effective video essay may be thought to include elements of both approaches.

Even the most explanatory features can slip into the poetic mode—and vice versa. For instance, an essayist's recorded voice-over would appear to be the defining feature of the "explanatory" video, laying out a carefully scripted argument that relegates the image track to a supporting role. But a good voice-over inevitably adds an affective layer to each video, because a vocal performance may convey feelings not articulated by written words alone. Does the essayist like the movie or hate it? Is the essayist confident about the film or puzzled by it? Was this movie surprising on first viewing, and is it still surprising now? Depending on how it is performed, a voice-over may communicate personality, interest, puzzlement, delight, or passion, or maybe all of the above. In so doing, the technique may remind us that scholarly inquiry often begins with a sense of wonder at a film's mysterious complexity.

Thinking about the productive tension between the explanatory and the poetic is useful for anyone working in audiovisual criticism, but the issue holds special relevance to the essayist studying classical Hollywood cinema. *The Classical Hollywood Cinema*, by David Bordwell, Janet Staiger, and Kristin Thompson, is a masterpiece of explanatory scholarship that famously defined the tradition as an "excessively obvious cinema."[5] Such excessive obviousness may pose an obstacle for those seeking to recover the poetic strangeness of each work, but the video essay allows scholars to evoke personal or poetic responses to each film without diluting explanatory ambition. For instance, "Observations on Film Art No. 12: *Brute Force—The Actor's Tool Kit*," produced by the Criterion Channel and presenting an analysis by David Bordwell, seems to me to achieve the difficult balance that Keathley, Álvarez López, and Martin have endorsed.[6] On the one hand, the essay fits squarely into the explanatory mode, relying on carefully crafted exposition (sometimes delivered in voice-over and sometimes on camera) to list the tools that Hollywood actors deployed to express their characters' goals and emotions. The results are as clear and cogent as anything in *The Classical Hollywood Cinema*. On the other hand, Bordwell's enthusiastic performance, combined with the loving choice of clips, conveys something else: an abiding fascination in the sheer physicality of Burt Lancaster's performance in *Brute Force* (Dassin 1947). The essay is a cine-poem just as much as it is a powerful piece of pedagogy.

Other scholars may approach the classical Hollywood cinema from a different direction and produce works with the same delicate balance of the systematic and the surprising. Laura Mulvey's *"Gentlemen Prefer Blondes* (remix remixed 2013)" initially seems to belong firmly to the poetic mode.[7] Working without a voice-over, Mulvey takes a short clip from the film and deforms it by using freeze-frames and slow motion. The result is a brilliant piece of film analysis, using images, sounds, and editing to foreground the nuance and control of Marilyn Monroe's dance performance. Her character enacts certain gestures of disorder, as when she mimes the fixing of a shoulder strap, but those movements seem intriguingly "at odds with the mechanical precision of this and each gesture."[8] Although Mulvey remains skeptical of Hollywood's narrative pleasures, she has written optimistically about the power of digital tools to recover hidden moments, even in Hollywood films.[9] Rashna Wadia Richards situates this turn in Mulvey's scholarship within the context of a revived culture of cinephilia. "These cinephiliac interruptions," Richards explains, "run counter to the flows of narrative development."[10] The *Gentlemen Prefer Blondes* (Hawks 1953) remix begins by playing the clip uninterrupted for about ten seconds, allowing us to register a sense of linear development, but then the bulk of its running time consists of a series of variations, allowing us to be jolted anew by the performer's distinctive body, movement, and voice. For Catherine Grant, the result is simultaneously "analytic and affectual."[11]

Many of my favorite video essays on classical Hollywood are works of close analysis, in which the creator takes a short scene and breaks it down into parts to show how it works. See, for instance, "Pass the Salt," by Christian Keathley; "Opening Choices: *Notorious*," by John Gibbs and Douglas Pye; and "The Thinking Machine 13: Between Two Plot Points," by Cristina Álvarez López and Adrian Martin.[12] The goal of each analysis is explanation, but these videos remind us that analysis often starts with something more personal, such as curiosity, engagement, or wonder, contributing to the culture of cinephilia that Richards and others have described. For instance, Keathley has championed the value of studying individual scenes in seemingly unremarkable Hollywood films because the scenes contain "moments that strike us, that perplex us, that gently call our attention to the fact that they are *like that*."[13] Álvarez López and Martin explicitly state that their study of a Howard Hawks scene is a study of an intriguing contradiction: Hawks is both a master of classicism, always keeping the plot moving forward, and an artist who delighted in "easy-going character interaction," developed between plot points.[14] Not only do these essayists manage to combine the explanatory and the poetic in a creative way, but they do so in order to address a paradox at the heart of classicism itself, whereby a carefully managed industrial system managed to turn out films that still provoke and delight us today.

At the 2018 "Classical Hollywood Studies in the 21st Century" conference, I premiered "Dietrich Lighting: A Video Essay."[15] When I started making the essay, my ambitions were purely explanatory. Director Josef von Sternberg liked to joke that he did not care about narrative, but I hoped to show that many of his films used lighting in a surprisingly classical way, modulating the highlights and shadows to amplify the dramatic arc of each story. By experimenting with a perspective filter available on Adobe Premiere, I was able to suggest how lamps were arranged in three-dimensional space. However, as I edited the essay, another aspect of the films came to the fore. Watching the clips over and over, I came to appreciate Marlene Dietrich's contributions to the lighting effects, not because she personally lit the films but because her movements and gestures as a performer brought those effects to life, creating suspense by forcing us to wait for the revelatory moments when her eyes captured the light. As in Bordwell's analysis of Burt Lancaster in *Brute Force* and Mulvey's analysis of Marilyn Monroe in *Gentlemen Prefer Blondes*, my analysis of the Dietrich films came to center on the physical movements of a star. The argument about classicism remained in place, but that argument gained in richness when I acknowledged this additional layer of cinephiliac suspense.

Choices about sound pushed this explanatory video further into the poetic mode. Having produced three video essays already, I worried that my vocal performances had become dull and predictable, and I forced myself to deliver my reading with more vocal modulation and quicker pacing, to better convey my genuine pleasure in these films. Similarly, I changed my approach to the video's musical score. On previous videos, I had opted for slower, ambient music tracks, both to ensure the dominance of my voice track and to capture the sad mood of films like *Sunrise* (Murnau 1927) or *The Magnificent Ambersons* (Welles 1942).[16] On the Dietrich video, I used a more upbeat musical track by Chris Zabriskie, a talented composer who makes works available for fair-use purposes through freemusicarchive.org. Although this track's delightful beat threatened to overwhelm my voice-over, the risk was worth it because the new score better expresses what it feels like to watch these strange, wonderful films.

However much I continue to admire the artistry and efficiency of studio filmmaking, classical Hollywood films remain worth studying because they remain powerfully affective, with stories that can still grip us and stars that can still astonish us. Combining the explanatory with the poetic, the video essay has emerged as an ideal tool for classical Hollywood scholars because it allows them to explain the nuances of how Hollywood films work while conveying a more personal sense of why these nuances still matter.

NOTES

1   Christian Keathley, "*La caméra-stylo*: Notes on Video Criticism and Cinephilia," in *The Language and Style of Film Criticism*, ed. Alex Clayton and Andrew Klevan (London: Routledge, 2012), 181.

2   Catherine Grant, "Dissolves of Passion: Materially Thinking through Editing in Videographic Compilation," in *The Videographic Essay: Criticism in Sound*

and Image, ed. Christian Keathley, Jason Mittell, and Catherine Grant, 2nd ed. (Montreal: caboose books, 2019), 65, http://videographicessay.org/works/videographic-essay/dissolves-of-passion-1?path=contents.

3   Keathley, "*La caméra-stylo*," 181.

4   Cristina Álvarez López and Adrian Martin, "The One and the Many: Making Sense of Montage in the Audiovisual Essay," in *The Audiovisual Essay: Practice and Theory of Videographic Film and Moving Image Studies* (September 2014), http://reframe.sussex.ac.uk/audiovisualessay/Frankfurt-papers/cristina-alvarez-lopez-adrian-martin/.

5   David Bordwell, Janet Staiger, and Kristin Thompson, *The Classical Hollywood Cinema: Film Style and Mode of Production to 1960* (New York: Columbia University Press, 1985), 3.

6   "Observations on Film Art No. 12: *Brute Force*—The Actor's Tool Kit," Criterion Channel (October 2017), https://www.criterionchannel.com/brute-force-the-actor-s-toolkit.

7   Laura Mulvey, "Gentlemen Prefer Blondes (remix remixed 2013)," *[in]Transition: Journal of Videographic Film & Moving Image Studies* 1, no. 1 (2014), http://mediacommons.org/intransition/2014/03/04/intransition-editors-introduction.

8   Laura Mulvey, *Death 24x a Second: Stillness and the Moving Image* (London: Reaktion Books, 2006), 172.

9   Mulvey, *Death 24x a Second*, 147.

10   Rashna Wadia Richards, *Cinematic Flashes: Cinephilia and Classical Hollywood* (Bloomington: Indiana University Press, 2013), 17.

11   Catherine Grant, "Star Studies in Transition: Notes on Experimental Videographic Approaches to Film Performance," in *The Videographic Essay*, ed. Keathley, Mittell, and Grant, 104, http://videographicessay.org/works/videographic-essay/star-studies-in-transition?path=contents.

12   Christian Keathley, "Pass the Salt," 2006, https://vimeo.com/23266798; John Gibbs and Douglas Pye, "Opening Choices: *Notorious*," *Movie: A Journal of Film Criticism* 7 (May 2017), http://www2.warwick.ac.uk/fac/arts/film/movie; Cristina Álvarez López and Adrian Martin, "The Thinking Machine 13: Between Two Plot Points," *De Filmkrant* (October 2017), https://filmkrant.nl/rubriek/the-thinking-machine-13/.

13   Christian Keathley, "Otto Preminger and the Surface of Cinema," *World Picture* 2 (Autumn 2008): 3. Keathley is discussing a conversation between Stanley Cavell and Andrew Klevan.

14   Álvarez López and Martin, in a short note accompanying the video cited above.

15   Patrick Keating, "Dietrich Lighting: A Video Essay," *Movie: A Journal of Film Criticism* 8 (2019): 72, https://warwick.ac.uk/fac/arts/film/movie/movie_journal_8.pdf. Most of the clips in the video are from von Sternberg's *Morocco* (1930), *Dishonored* (1931), *Shanghai Express* (1932), *Blonde Venus* (1932), *The Scarlet Empress* (1934), and *The Devil Is a Woman* (1935).

16   See, for instance, Patrick Keating, "A Homeless Ghost: The Moving Camera and Its Analogies," *[in]Transition: A Journal of Videographic Film & Moving Image Studies* 2, no. 4 (2016), http://mediacommons.futureofthebook.org/intransition/issue-2-4; and Patrick Keating, "The Strange Streets of a Strange City: The *Ambersons* Montage," *NECSUS: European Journal of Media Studies* (Spring 2018), https://necsus-ejms.org/the-strange-streets-of-a-strange-city-the-ambersons-montage/.

24

INSTITUTIONS OF THE MODE OF PRODUCTION AND *THE CLASSICAL HOLLYWOOD CINEMA* IN CONTEMPORARY MEDIA STUDIES

Paul Monticone

Three and a half decades on from the publication of *The Classical Hollywood Cinema: Film Style and Mode of Production to 1960* (CHC), David Bordwell, Janet Staiger, and Kristin Thompson's text continues to be generative of research that details the formal system and production practices of the mid-century film industry in the United States and extends the authors' powerful explanatory framework beyond that study's temporal limits. The "Classical Hollywood Studies in the 21st Century" conference and this collection of essays evince the continued vitality of this research project. But *CHC*'s influence has exceeded the authors' original project, and with the dust settled on the "paradigm wars," the study's title has become the standard term for an object of study—the popular cinema of the mid-1910s to 1960—within the field of film and media studies.[1] *CHC* has lent its name to conferences, numerous monographs, edited collections, and a recently formed scholarly interest group—many of which are and include work distinct from Bordwell, Staiger, and Thompson's project in their foci and methods, as is also the case in many of these collected proceedings. *CHC* now, in the twenty-first century, encompasses much else besides the original authors' inquiry into a mode of film practice mutually determined by both stylistic norms and production practices.

Over the same period of time that "classical Hollywood cinema" ceased to specify only Bordwell, Staiger, and Thompson's project and became accepted as the term for that object of study, the broader academic field continued to grow and transform, and today it is considerably different than that which existed when *CHC* arrived and "invigorated" "scholarship on studio-era filmmaking."[2] In 2002, the Society of Cinema Studies was rechristened the Society of Cinema and Media Studies (SCMS), reflecting the increasing breadth of audiovisual forms investigated by the society's ever-expanding membership. This expansion has, unsurprisingly, been accompanied by fragmentation or balkanization: the annual conference has ballooned from forty-five panels in 1985 to nearly ten times that in 2020, necessitating nearly two dozen concurrent sessions and leading to a multiday conference that is often experienced as a series of discrete conversations. The rapid proliferation of new subfields is evidenced by the founding, between 2005 and 2015, of nearly three dozen Scholarly Interest Groups (SIGs). Perhaps lulled into complacency by the relatively central place in the field their object of study had long enjoyed, the classical Hollywood studies community was late to avail itself of this institutional form and only established its own SIG just five years ago.

Among the rationales for the formation of the Classical Hollywood SIG was the sense that the community of scholars researching this object could no longer assume that its relevance was obvious to a broader community of film and media scholars who think of the Hollywood studio era less as an ongoing research concern and more as a topic that must be covered in their survey courses after the annual conference concludes. Such a SIG, according to the group's mission statement, can provide a place where "the rich, long-standing tradition of classical-cinema scholarship" can meet "the new challenges and opportunities that the contemporary media landscape presents."[3] So, too, does an edited collection, and the conveners of the conference that originated this volume asked contributors to assess "where academic inquiry on classical Hollywood cinema has gone, where it is now, and—most importantly—where it is going."[4] Below, I argue that both the recent research inspired by *CHC* and the too-long-overlooked contributions of Bordwell, Staiger, and Thompson's original text have much to offer the contemporary field of cinema and media studies.

Although classical Hollywood studies is not reducible to *CHC*, I focus on it here because it continues to offer valuable agenda-setting methodological insights that can help secure the study of this cultural institution a place in today's rapidly expanding and diversifying field. The following is structured around a challenge posed—or opportunity presented—to classical

Hollywood studies that was implicit in the formation of another scholarly interest group within SCMS. Recent and forthcoming work on classical Hollywood's mode of production attests to the fact that *CHC* continues to be generative of research projects that complement emergent research agendas in the broader field; moreover, *CHC* offers conceptual tools that scholars of classical Hollywood should find valuable in solving methodological problems and cohering our diverse studies of industry institutions around more than a shared period or general subject heading.

"MATTER MORE": HOLLYWOOD'S INSTITUTIONS AND MODE OF PRODUCTION

A long-standing objection to *CHC* was the supposed autonomy of Bordwell, Staiger, and Thompson's model of the classical Hollywood cinema, and, as the field's methodological pluralism makes a minority practice of textual analysis of any sort, *CHC* likely remains suspicious to many on these grounds. The consolidation of a "nontheatrical cinema" research project, through its own dedicated SIG founded in 2007, and three major edited collections focusing on industrial, educational, and generally "useful" cinema, published between 2009 and 2012, is a notable expansion in the scope of media history to which scholars of classical Hollywood should see their work contributing.[5] Films sponsored by government agencies, businesses, schools, nonprofit organizations, and myriad other institutions might well have outnumbered (in titles, screening locations, and feet of celluloid) the modes of cinematic practice that have most often attracted the attention of film scholars: films either made for mass entertainment or that are more easily classified as art. Charles Acland and Haidee Wasson, introducing one of these collections, advertise the promise of this research agenda to integrate "moving-image culture into a fuller spectrum of historical analysis . . . to reveal the intricate relations among films, institutions, and exhibition locations."[6] Acland and Wasson's ambition for the study of "useful cinema" is, self-consciously, a bid for a "cinema history that matters more," as Richard Maltby put it in a 2007 polemic.[7] Maltby's work is, of course, much closer to the familiar ground of Hollywood history, but he likewise encourages scholars to look beyond Hollywood films themselves: cinema history, to Maltby, "matters more" the further it gets from "an aesthetic history of textual relations between individuals or individual objects"—that is, the "Film Style" that makes up the first half of *CHC*'s subtitle.

Maltby, and much of the subsequent work in "new cinema history," locates the social process and cultural function of cinema largely in the study of audiences, moviegoing, the everyday consumption of Hollywood's products, and other such topics in broader movie cultures, areas of inquiry that are bracketed off from Bordwell, Staiger, and Thompson's inquiry in opening pages and that have become an important branch of classical Hollywood studies.[8] But Maltby's essay advocates a "cinema history" that is equally "engaging with economic, industrial, and institutional history" in order to specify "how the commercial institution of cinema operated."[9] Institutional history is not a historiographical approach equivalent to any of Robert Allen and Douglas Gomery's classic models of historical inquiry and determination—that is, aesthetic, technological, economic, and social history—but, depending on the institution under consideration, institutional history cuts across these categories.[10] Instead, institutional history is loosely defined as the selection of an object (a discrete organization) and the primary sources from which the historian constructs her account: these studies are "grounded in the minutiae of memos, letters, the minutes of board meetings, financial records and the proceedings of Court cases and Congressional hearings."[11] Ruth Vasey, in a historiographic survey of approaches to the Hollywood industry history, identifies a model of such work in Tino Balio's study of United Artists, which "counters melodramatic histories founded on memory and anecdote with solid data that enables Balio to place the company in its corporate and social contexts," thereby improving on histories written outside—or before the ascendancy of—academic film studies.[12] Vasey's rather minimalist definition of this body of literature—taking its sources and narrative mode as constitutive—notes the tendency of historians to place their objects of study into "contexts" but their potential to integrate social determinants into cinema history.

Here, I find it useful to return to *CHC*, specifically the sections named for the "Mode of Production" half of that project's subtitle. As a delineation of industrial practices of a commercial cinema, Staiger's account of the mode of production is, of course, central to Bordwell, Staiger, and Thompson's project of describing how a mode of film practice (or group style) emerges and is sustained by a commercial art industry. For Staiger, the production practices and ideological/signifying practices that characterize the classical

Hollywood cinema are located primarily in the division of labor, and Staiger's chapters in *CHC* on the mode of production are given over to delineating the organization of the Hollywood studios' labor force across several decades and the mechanisms by which one detailed division of labor replaced another. The adoption of successive arrangements of production practices was neither wholly the result of profit maximization nor solely the result of "a *Zeitgeist* or immaterial forces."[13] Rather, these practices were "discuss[ed], describ[ed], and validat[ed]" through specific, material sites, "industrial mechanisms . . . which facilitated standardization."[14] Staiger divides these into three subcategories: "advertising practices, industrial interest groups, and institutions adjacent to but not directly part of the industrial structure."[15]

Staiger's brief profiles of these industry and industry-adjacent institutions, covering in total eleven pages of *CHC*'s text,[16] have provided a research program for scholars of classical Hollywood cinema, and, reading these pages today, one cannot get through a paragraph without thinking of several recent studies that continue to build upon this work.[17] A 1993 special issue of *Film History* focusing on "institutional histories" was edited by Thompson and featured research not only on filmmaking practices but also on early advertising practices, interest in aspects of which continues.[18] Industrial interest groups and labor and craft associations, touching as they do on a well-established subdiscipline in history and some of the most dramatic moments in Hollywood's history, made early appearances in accounts of the industry's labor strife and purges, but, more recently, individual institutions, such as the Writers Guild of America and the American Society of Cinematographers, have merited monograph-length studies.[19] Of the film industry's professional and technical associations, the Research Council of the Academy of Motion Picture Arts and Sciences and the Society of Motion Picture Engineers received the most attention in *CHC*, important as they are to technological standardization, and these have been taken up as the focus of several recent projects.[20] Slightly further removed from the studios and their employees are Joseph Turow's concepts of auxiliaries and facilitators, such as talent agents and entertainment attorneys, which recent scholarship has found contributed to the operation of the mode of production even during this period of relative centralization.[21] As for Staiger's adjacent institutions, there is a rapidly expanding literature, increasingly fueled by the digitization of printed material from the period, on handbooks and correspondence courses, fan magazines, college courses and programs, and the trade press.[22]

Scholars working on such topics unpack the histories of industry sites that Staiger's text has only the space to identify and briefly explain. These scholars, of course, do the ordinary historian's work of telling us more about how these entities work—that is, providing the chronicles of foundings, publications, activities, and organizational structures—but they also locate their film industrial institution within multiple contexts: its functional place not only in the Hollywood system as a standardizing mechanism that shaped what the classical Hollywood cinema was (as concerned *CHC*) but also in the broader social context of which the given institution is a part. That is, for example, technical associations located within the context of East Coast technology manufacturing firms; college film courses within the early twentieth-century university; or trade papers and fan magazines within business and popular publishing. In so doing, Hollywood historians, building on Staiger's analysis of the mode of production, have increasingly integrated "moving-image culture into a fuller spectrum of historical analysis" and revealed "the intricate relations" between the most historically dominant form of moving image culture in the United States—that is, the classical Hollywood cinema—and the broader form of American business and industry.[23]

CLASSICAL HOLLYWOOD AND MEDIATING INSTITUTIONS

As classical Hollywood scholars write histories of industrial institutions that extend the reach of film history into Acland and Wasson's "fuller spectrum," we encounter a centrifugal force that scatters classical Hollywood studies among a range of subdisciplines in cultural history—from labor and gender to technology and business, and many more when we consider work of scholars of circulation, reception, stardom, and fandom of classical Hollywood. The shared object of study, the midcentury American film industry, does not ensure legibility across the variegated terrain of the classical mode; historians of technology may have more use for a film history detailing the development of sound technology than a film historian concerned with women's work in the film industry. Mileage may vary as to whether this is a desirable state of affairs, but *CHC* shows us that it is not necessary and, moreover, provides a model for integrating studies of the various aspects of the mode of production considered above. Beyond highlighting topics for further research—certainly one of *CHC*'s legacies—Bordwell,

Staiger, and Thompson sensitize us to questions of how the institutions of and adjacent to Hollywood's mode of production regulate the influence of transformations in the broader social history of the United States in mid-twentieth century on the film industry. Such institutions look not only beyond the Hollywood system but also in toward it.

The central feature of *CHC* is neither its description of an aesthetic system and mode of film practice, the classical style that so shaped *CHC*'s early reception, nor its description of the mode of production, which, as I have outlined above, so many young scholars are continuing to research. Rather, joining the two in an explanatory framework shows how a central industrial and economic function (the drive to organize production to maximize profits) and an aesthetic function (the production of films that adhere to classicism's aesthetic norms) are mutually reinforcing, the former consisting of the most "proximate and pertinent institution for creating, regulating, and maintaining those norms."[24] The interlocking nature of these systems—industrial and aesthetic—developed, in debates over *CHC* and Bordwell's subsequent work, into an account of the relationship of the institution of cinema to broader social and cultural forces and institutions, which Bordwell, drawing on Marxist social theory, later termed "mediations."[25] In his study of Yasujiro Ozu, Bordwell bridges the distance between Ozu's films and cultural norms associated with Zen Buddhism and traditional Japanese aesthetics by positing that the filmmaker's work occupies the center of a series of concentric circles, with "the broad and general features of Japanese society or history" occupying the outermost circle. Between these two, Bordwell sketches three mediating variables—the mode of production and consumption within which Ozu worked, the formal norms of his filmmaking practice, and the specific cultural milieu in which Ozu lived and worked—that "warped, refracted, or transformed" the "broad social forces."[26] These mediating variables shape the relationship between the two spheres, making the large-scale social forces meaningful determinants on the features of particular films. We might see a similar process occurring within the various material sites that make up the mode of production and conceive of each as a borderline institution that converts broader social formations into proximate determinations of the Hollywood studio system.

A rich body of scholarship already suggests the details of this process, which we might see occurring among other components of the mode of production. The most closely studied institution that mediates between

American entertainment cinema and the broader society has, of course, been the Production Code Administration (PCA), which remains the most thoroughly chronicled of Hollywood's non-studio institutions—little wonder, given the PCA's vast archive and its staging of a clear confrontation of Hollywood's storytelling and stylistic conventions with a host of broad cultural concerns. The most detailed of these institutional histories have interpreted the reorganization of the Studio Relations Committee into the PCA in 1934 not as a radical break with the earlier period but as a continuation with the so-called pre-Code era. Lea Jacobs, most notably, traces an ongoing process whereby self-regulation was increasingly integrated into the mode of production. Matters over which Code administrators and producers would negotiate, and the terms of those negotiations, gradually shifted,[27] as the Code administrators became more fully integrated participants in the studios' production processes; they thus became able to make the cultural concerns that attracted the attention of censors legible and meaningful to production personnel. Strong self-regulation is, in such accounts, the result of a gradual institutionalization of a more formalized relationship between producers and PCA personnel—in other words, their integration into the mode of production as opposed to a switch to be flipped "on" or "off"—though the Motion Picture Producers and Distributors of American (MPPDA) loudly promoted this "apocalyptic" account in order to enjoy the maximum public relations value from the change in policy.[28]

My own work on the MPPDA, the organization of which the PCA was a part, views the institution through two lenses: on the one hand, as a cooperative institution like others in broader American society, a trade association, and thus part of a history of American business; and, on the other hand, as an institution unique to the film industry, which brought together a unique range of film industry participants.[29] While the former is necessary to understand the MPPDA as a societal institution, the latter pertains to how the organization translated broader developments in American business into determinants of cooperative action within the Hollywood system. As my interest is in the MPPDA as a form of industrial organization that encompassed content regulation, I consider initiatives quite distant from the site of production and as diverse as institutional advertising campaigns, public relations, lobbying efforts, and the registration of intellectual property. At this level of analysis, the MPPDA is not the borderline institution between cultural concerns of censors and public pressure groups, on the one hand,

and films and their production, on the other. Instead, it is the mediating institution between the sector of broader American business communities typified by cooperative organizations of major firms in any major industry and a culture industry that sought to behave cooperatively. The range of proximate determinants pertinent to such an analysis is obviously not the group style or division of labor but instead the occupational identities and managerial cultures of film industry workers and entrepreneurs.[30]

The MPPDA was a site where two quite different groups of social actors—trade association staffers and the businesspeople who led or worked for individual companies—came together to effectuate some change in the operation of the industry. Will H. Hays, recruited from the Harding Administration to run the association, was famously attractive to industry leaders precisely because of his distance from the industry—a respected outsider hired to clean up the industry just as Judge Kenesaw Mountain Landis had done for Major League Baseball—and by the 1930s the MPPDA boasted a full-time and salaried staff of over one hundred, the vast majority of whom came from backgrounds and professions not only distinct from the day-to-day operations of the film or amusement industry but also beyond the realm of the field of business management. They provided the benefit of integrating the industry with the increasingly elaborate institutional environment in which business existed, but they also introduced what Louis Galambos characterizes as an ideological fissure between the association and its membership: such staffers were "closer to professional managers than entrepreneurs philosophically."[31] Their "philosophical" affinities may have aligned more closely with professional management than amusement industry entrepreneurs, but, also like Hays, these trade association workers were connected as well to many other social communities and occupational identities, ranging from political organizations and religious denominations to civic groups and educational societies.

The divergence in these backgrounds and managerial cultures could result in clashes between well-educated and well-connected association professionals, who discerned industry trends in relation to their long-term impacts on the status of the industry among important social groups, and workers in the member firms, whose attention was fixed on the immediate needs and problems in the production and sale of cultural goods. Such was the case with the decade-long struggle to implement an effective system of content and advertising self-regulation. As has been rehearsed by many scholars, Hays's efforts to placate the industry's critics, who were increasingly becoming his own, were stymied by the incompatibility of associational and member perspectives, until the combination of a financial crisis, public pressure, and a boycott (fomented by employees of the association) brought those viewpoints into alignment.[32] From this perspective, the Code story is a dramatic episode that typifies, in admittedly spectacular fashion, the more persistent feature of the organization. The differences in managerial cultures within the association's sphere extended down from the board of directors and the Hollywood production executives to the MPPDA's standing and special committees, on which lower-level industry workers and association employees served. Entertainment lawyers' understanding of effective lobbying shaped how the industry would respond to congressional investigations; studio publicity directors' routines for dealing with fan magazines and press agents would affect how the industry sought to manage press scrutiny; and advertising executives' proclivity for ballyhoo shaped how the industry would tout its wartime service in public relation campaigns. In tracing these mediations between business lobbying, press relations, and institutional advertising, I have found the conceptual tools offered by *CHC*'s analysis of standardizing mechanisms, proximate determinants, and mediations valuable for writing cultural and social history that trace back into the history of cinema. There is no doubt that classical Hollywood studies continues to be a robust research tradition, continuously nourished by the digitization of heretofore unavailable primary sources or the reassessment of underappreciated or overlooked production workers, but *CHC*, thirty-five years on, remains a study that can invigorate that tradition.

NOTES

1 Jane Gaines, ed., *Classical Hollywood Narrative: The Paradigm Wars* (Durham, NC: Duke University Press, 1992).

2 "Description and Objectives," *Classical Hollywood Studies in the 21st Century*, accessed April 12, 2020, https://conferences.wlu.ca/classical-hollywood -studies-2018/description-and-objectives/.

3 "Mission Statement," *SCMS Classical Hollywood SIG*, accessed April 12, 2020, https://scmsclassichollywood.wordpress.com/mission/.

4 "Description and Objectives."

5   Vinzenz Hediger and Patrick Vonderau, eds., *Films That Work Industrial Film and the Productivity of Media* (Amsterdam: Amsterdam University Press, 2009); Charles Acland and Haidee Wasson, eds., *Useful Cinema* (Durham, NC: Duke University Press, 2011); Devin Orgeron, Marsha Orgeron, and Dan Streible, eds., *Learning with the Lights Off: Educational Film in the United States* (New York: Oxford University Press, 2012).

6   Acland and Wasson, "Introduction: Utility and Cinema," in *Useful Cinema*, 13.

7   Richard Maltby, "How Can Cinema History Matter More?" *Screening the Past* 22 (2007), http://www.screeningthepast.com/issue-22-tenth-anniversary/how-can-cinema-history-matter-more/.

8   "Certainly conditions of consumption form a part of any mode of film practice. . . . This history, as yet unwritten, would require another book, probably as long as this." David Bordwell, Janet Staiger, and Kristin Thompson, *The Classical Hollywood Cinema: Film Style and Mode of Production to 1960* (New York: Columbia University Press, 1985), xiv.

9   Elsewhere Maltby notes, "There are fewer published book-length business histories of Hollywood than there are biographies of Louise Brooks or analyses of *His Girl Friday* (Hawks 1940). Instead of the comparative analyses of distribution practice and the detailed studies of executive decision-making in the studios that may eventually comprise this ordinary cinema history, film studies to date has far more frequently echoed Hollywood's own use of the past as a form of source material to be adapted to an established set of commercial and ideological conventions"; Maltby, "How Can Cinema History Matter More?"

10   For an overview of Allen and Gomery's four approaches, see Robert C. Allen and Douglas Gomery, *Film History: Theory and Practice* (New York: McGraw-Hill, 1985), 65–190.

11   Ruth Vasey, "The Hollywood Industry Paradigm," in *The Sage Handbook of Film Studies*, ed. James Donald and Michael Renov (Thousand Oaks, CA: Sage, 2008), 300–301.

12   Vasey, "The Hollywood Industry Paradigm," 301. In this respect, Vasey's characterization of the approach aligns with Maltby's criticism of Hollywood history generally and Code histories specifically: they seem under the obligation to write "entertainin'" history that conforms to the narrative patterns of the entertainment they write about. See Richard Maltby, "The Production Code and the Mythologies of 'Pre-Code' Hollywood," in *The Classical Hollywood Reader*, ed. Steve Neale (London: Routledge, 2012), 240–43.

13 Bordwell, Staiger, and Thompson, *Classical Hollywood Cinema*, 89.

14 Bordwell, Staiger, and Thompson, *Classical Hollywood Cinema*, 97.

15 Bordwell, Staiger, and Thompson, *Classical Hollywood Cinema*, 97.

16 Bordwell, Staiger, and Thompson, *Classical Hollywood Cinema*, 97–108.

17 Some of Staiger's own work elaborates on the mechanisms described in *The Classical Hollywood Cinema*. See, for example, Janet Staiger, "Standardization and Independence: The Founding Objectives of the SMPTE," *SMPTE Journal* 96, no. 6 (1987): 532–37; and Janet Staiger, "Announcing Wares, Winning Patrons, Voicing Ideals: Thinking about the History and Theory of Film Advertising," *Cinema Journal* 29, no. 3 (1990): 3–31.

18 See Charlie Keil "Advertising Independence: Industrial Performance and Advertising Strategies of the Independent Movement, 1909–10," *Film History* 5, no. 4 (1993): 472–88; Ben Singer, "Fiction Tie-Ins and Narrative Intelligibility 1911–18," *Film History* 5, no. 4 (1993): 489–504.

19 See Miranda J. Banks, *The Writers: A History of American Screenwriters and Their Guild* (New Brunswick, NJ: Rutgers University Press, 2015); Patrick Keating, *Hollywood Lighting from the Silent Era to Film Noir* (New York: Columbia University Press, 2010). See also Monica Sandler, "PR and Politics at Hollywood's Biggest Night: The Academy Awards and Unionization (1929–1939)," *Media Industries Journal* 2, no. 2 (2015).

20 Luci Marzola, "A Society Apart: The Early Years of the Society of Motion Picture Engineers," *Film History* 28, no. 4 (2016): 1–28; Dawn Fratini, "Better the 'Devil' You Know: The Motion Picture Research Council, 3-D, and the Hollywood Studio System," *Spectator* 38, no. 2 (2018): 31–39. See also Luci Marzola, *Engineering Hollywood* (Oxford University Press, forthcoming).

21 See, for example, Tom Kemper, *Hidden Talent: The Emergence of Hollywood Agents* (Berkeley: University of California Press, 2010); Pete Labuza, "When a Handshake Meant Something: The Emergence of Entertainment Law and the Constitution of Hollywood Artists, 1944–1967," PhD diss., University of Southern California, 2020. On Turow's "power roles" framework, see Joseph Turow, *Media Systems in Society: Understanding Industries, Strategies, and Power*, 2nd ed. (New York: Longman, 1997).

22 See, for example, Anne Morey, *Hollywood Outsiders: The Adaptation of the Film Industry, 1913–1934* (Minneapolis: University of Minnesota Press, 2003); on fan magazines, see Tamar Jeffers McDonald and Lies Lanckman, eds., *Star Attractions: Twentieth-Century Movie Magazines and Global Fandom* (Iowa City: University of Iowa Press, 2019); on universities and the film industry,

see Peter Decherney, *Hollywood and the Culture Elite: How the Movies Became American. Film and Culture* (New York: Columbia University Press, 2005); and on the trade press, see Daniel Biltereyst and Lies Van de Vijver, eds., *Mapping Movie Magazines: Digitization, Periodicals and Cinema History* (London: Palgrave Macmillan, 2020).

23 Acland and Wasson, "Introduction: Utility and Cinema," 13.

24 Bordwell, Staiger, and Thompson, *Classical Hollywood Cinema*, 9.

25 Though the concept is perhaps most familiar in film and media studies through Raymond Williams's discussion of the term, which centers on the relationship between reality and art, Bordwell instead draws on Eric Olin Wright's work, which attends to more the concrete categories of state structure and state intervention. See Wright, *Class, Crisis and the State* (London: NLB, 1978), 23–29.

26 David Bordwell, *Ozu and the Poetics of Cinema* (Princeton, NJ: Princeton University Press, 1988), 17.

27 Lea Jacobs, *The Wages of Sin: Censorship and the Fallen Woman Film, 1928–1942* (Berkeley: University of California Press, 1997), especially chapters 2 and 5.

28 Richard Maltby, "More Sinned against Than Sinning: The Fabrications of Pre-Code Cinema." *Senses of Cinema* 23 (2003), accessed 23 April 2020, http://sensesofcinema.com/2003/feature-articles/pre_code_cinema/.

29 Paul Monticone, "For the Maintenance of the System: Institutional and Cultural Change within the Motion Picture Producers and Distributors of America, 1922–1945," PhD diss., University of Texas–Austin, 2019.

30 Derek Johnson, Derek Kompare, and Avi Santo, eds. *Making Media Work Cultures of Management in the Entertainment Industries* (New York: NYU Press, 2014).

31 Louis Galambos, *Competition and Cooperation: The Emergence of a National Trade Association* (Baltimore, MD: Johns Hopkins University Press, 1966), 111.

32 Richard Maltby has shown that the Legion of Decency campaign was encouraged in "almost constant conspiratorial correspondence" from Joseph Breen, which was encouraged by Hays, who sought "to outmaneuver the MPRC, independent exhibitors, and other groups still demanding federal regulation" of trade practices. See Richard Maltby, "The Production Code and the Hays Office," in *Grand Design: Hollywood as a Modern Business Enterprise, 1930–1939*, ed. Tino Balio (Berkeley: University of California Press, 1996), 59–62.

25

NEW CINEMA HISTORY AND THE CLASSICAL HOLLYWOOD CINEMA

Richard Maltby

In a number of previous essays, I have proposed a distinction between film history and cinema history: that is, between an aesthetic history of textual relations among individuals and individual objects and the social history of a cultural institution.[1] Film history, the history of textual relations and stylistic influence, borrows its methods and rationale from the practices of art and literary history. It is predominantly a history of production and producers, concerned with issues of intention and agency underpinning the process of cultural production, often at the level of the individual, less frequently at the level of the institution, and it is relatively little interested in anything, other than aesthetic influence, that happens beyond the point of production.

By contrast, writing the social history of cinema is a project engaging, on the one hand, with elements of economic, industrial, and institutional history in accounts of how the commercial institution of cinema operated and, on the other, with the sociocultural history of its audiences. These two histories are far more closely bound together than either of them is to a film history of textual relations. For the past decade, much of the work in this territory, particularly in Europe, has traveled under the description of the "new cinema history."[2] Centering its concerns on the social experience of cinema, new cinema history is likely to pay more attention to questions of circulation than production and of brokerage than authorship; to consider cinema as experience rather than film as apparatus; and to examine the heterogeneity and social construction of cinema audiences rather than the textual construction of spectatorship. This is not to say that its interests are limited to audiences, their experiences, and their behaviors, but the perspective from the audience informs the manner of its engagement with industrial and aesthetic histories of cinema.

In one sense, this opposition does no more than make a functional distinction, using different words to refer to different things: considering cinema as events, experiences, and the conditions that bring them into being and considering films as works, texts, and the conditions that bring them into being. Recognizing that "much belongs to the history of cinema . . . that does not involve actual films," Thomas Elsaesser has argued that "the film/cinema distinction" raises the questions, "Does the cinema provide goods or services? Do we pay for a product or an experience?"[3] Such questions are clearly not susceptible to resolution through an examination of individual films or clusters or indeed genealogies of them. They are questions about cinema as a commercial and experiential system: questions about its processes rather than its products.

From the General Film Company's description of its "complete service" to exhibitors to the identification of the movies as one of the new "mass service" industries by the President's Committee on Recent Economic Changes in 1929, exhibitors, distributors, and analysts emphasized cinema as a service, or what the authors of a 1927 theater management manual called the business of "selling *happiness.*"[4] The Standard Exhibition Contract, the most ubiquitous document of the classical Hollywood cinema, allowed distributors to change the films covered by any contract and explicitly excluded any guarantee that the distributor would actually release the product announced in their annual production schedules, on which the exhibition contracts were based.[5]

As with other branded goods, the reliable interchangeability of product was a guarantee of quality in the delivery of this service to its consumers. Paramount's national advertising throughout the 1920s declared, "If it's a Paramount Picture, it's the Best Show in Town." Ethnohistorical research into audiences' experiences reinforces the understanding of cinema as service. Oral histories consistently demonstrate the primacy of participants' recollection of the routines and rituals of cinemagoing as a public event—of "who sat where each week, and with whom, and what they wore"—to the extent that if "interviewees recall specific movies at all, they do so largely in order to tell stories about the community."[6] The local rhythms of moviegoing were place specific, shaped by the continuities of life in the family, the workplace, and the neighborhood. The resilient parochialism of individuals and communities incorporated and accommodated the passing content that occupied their screens to their local concerns and community experiences.

Stories that cinemagoers recall return repeatedly to the patterns and highlights of everyday life, its relationships, pressures, and resolutions. Only the occasional motion picture proves to be as memorable, and it is as likely to be memorable in its fragments as in its totality and is most often memorable for the conditions of its viewing. Although these accounts may sometimes underestimate the impact of particular movies on individuals or audiences at the time of viewing, they remind us that the vast majority of films do not seek out landmark status for themselves. Rather, like individual dreams that may be briefly vivid and impressive on waking, most films fade back into the overall field of our cultural experiences.

This culturally normative process of forgetting and moving on parallels the rapid cycling of movies through theaters and in doing so acknowledges the deliberately engineered ephemerality of cinema's products as a property of their commercial existence. Moviegoing offered its audiences an everyday encounter with the extraordinary—encapsulated in the advertising for *Only Angels Have Wings* (Hawks 1939), which offered "Each Day a Rendezvous with Peril! Each Night a Meeting with Romance!"—but their everyday occurrence rendered these extraordinary encounters customary.⁷ Like the leopards breaking into the temple in Kafka's parable, when the extraordinary events of the movies were repeated so often that they could be reckoned on in advance, they became part of the ritual, part of what Juri Lotman called "the poetics of the everyday."⁸

As Robert Allen has argued, film history's assumptions have typically inverted the accounts of popular memory, reducing the experience of cinema to an abstracted, uneventful, individual act of textual engagement. Substituting theories of spectatorship for social histories, film studies "has invested a great deal in conceptualizing what was involved aesthetically, ideologically and sexually in playing the role of spectator" but has left largely unexplored the social preconditions that determined any instance of that role: how attendance at this or that cinema defined a class or caste identity or how a racial or religious affiliation determined access to the apparent democracy of entertainment through social negotiations that took place outside the theater as well as inside it.⁹

Moviegoing may have been advertised as classless, but like all forms of consumption, it also acted as a source of social fragmentation, providing new opportunities for discrimination, exclusion, and distinction. Cinema attendance was locally specific. For much of its history it involved the cultivation of highly parochial habits of loyalty exercised within a very small territory of choice, in ways that were nevertheless critical to the survival of the industry as a whole. The sociality of this experience was at no stage meaningfully separate from other locally prevailing patterns of social segmentation, and the cultural boundaries that these conventions of social geography constructed were more than strong enough to determine the parameters of a leisure activity such as cinemagoing. The picture show provided an occasion on which existing social, economic, and religious distinctions could be projected onto the informal social segregation of cinema seating arrangements.

Historical investigations that explore such occasions are, of necessity, microhistories: studies of particular situations, often over relatively short periods of time and defined by the specific local conditions under examination. What would connect these histories to the established concerns of film studies is a more extensive understanding of the commercial history of the industry: of who sold what to whom and on what terms. By comparison to what we know of the minutiae of films' production processes, we know hardly anything about the processes of their circulation. Distribution, the least examined sector of the cinema system, was the component that made classical Hollywood's oligopoly and all that flowed from it possible. Distribution controlled exhibitors'—and therefore audiences'—access to films as well as producers' access to exhibition venues and audiences. It served as the means by which revenue was allocated to industry sectors, and the industry's trade practices—its typology of theatrical venues, its differentiated systems of release, its programming of films into its run-clearance system in each of its geographical zones, its deployment of percentage and fixed-price rental rates and the Standard Exhibition Contract—all existed primarily to enable the distribution of revenue within the system.

And yet we know so little about distribution, either as "the physical task" that General Counsel Charles Pettijohn of the Motion Picture Producers and Distributors of America (MPPDA) quantified in 1940 as "the physical task of distributing 25 to 30 thousand miles of film every day to 16,500 theaters located in 9,187 cities, towns, villages, and hamlets" or as the financial and logistical strategizing involved in ensuring that the most commercially successful films were shown on the most profitable screens for the highest number of occasions using the minimum number of prints of each film.[10] The zones, runs, and clearances of classical Hollywood's distribution system served primarily to maintain product differentiation within a geographical market, with the clear purpose of differentiating between theaters and the different levels of service they offered. For the majors, who had constructed their expansion around the social differentiation provided by deluxe first-run theaters, the maintenance of social hierarchies through the exhibition system was necessary to their return on investment. One purpose of the system was to maintain a hierarchy of culturally and socially safe spaces for its various audiences. The social safety of each space was determined, in substantial part, by the sociality of its particular audience, and that in turn was conditioned by the social—class—environment of the theater. But according to Assistant Attorney General Russell Hardy, who prosecuted the federal government case against Warner Bros., Paramount, and RKO in St. Louis in 1935, this system was also "a great generic conspiracy . . . a long continuing oppressive and coercive action . . . committed by the large companies . . . on hundreds . . . of smaller" competitors.[11] Classical Hollywood cinema endured for the life of that conspiracy.

How this system determined the commercial aesthetics of classical Hollywood is a question of significance—as yet largely unpursued—for classical Hollywood studies. For example, the increasingly widespread adoption of double billing as an exhibition practice after 1933 was widely agreed, within the industry and among its consumers, to have deleteriously affected picture quality. It generated a vicious circle in which the belief that the studios did not produce enough high-quality product for a single feature to sustain an evening's program reinforced exhibitors' arguments that they needed "to give their long-suffering patrons quantity instead of quality" because of "the tremendous amount of trash pictures turned out by Hollywood."[12] Faced with the volume of demand from double billing, studios had to calculate what volume of production they required to maintain their control of distribution and how thinly they had to spread their production budgets to do this. *Newsweek* suggested that two-thirds of Hollywood's output in 1936 had been "Class B pictures."[13]

David Palfreyman, the head of the MPPDA's Department of Theatre Service, observed that "pictures with very little entertainment value or quality are made profitable to the producing and distributing company by this sort of an operating policy," but that "jamming them down the throats of the theatre patrons tends to drive away patronage from the theatres."[14] In February 1937, exhibitor J. H. Thompson called double features "an Octopus Strangling Quality and Receipts" and "a Frankenstein slowly crushing its creators to death," and he urged exhibitors to recognize that "the more we play double features, the more and worse pictures the producers are going to put out."[15]

For audiences, exhibitors, and producers alike, double billing represented a trade-off between quality and duration. One respondent to a 1937 Kansas City newspaper poll complained, "We go to the movies to be entertained, not detained."[16] A year later, a *Fortune* survey found only one in ten participants willing to say that movies "gave the public what they wanted."[17] But the persistence and ubiquity of double billing in the second half of the 1930s suggest that duration won out over both quality and convenience. What drove the decisions involved was the majors' need to maintain their control over distribution's system of circulation.

The history of that system is the history of the motion picture industry's constant engagement with the antitrust laws. Court decisions shaped the industry from the Motion Picture Patents Company onward, and as the *Paramount* case made clear in 1948, the existence of the classical Hollywood cinema depended upon a particular interpretation of those laws. The question at issue was whether the major distributor-exhibitors conspired to restrain the trade of independent producers and exhibitors or merely exercised the strategic advantages they possessed by virtue of the scale and scope of their activities. This ought to have been a political question, to be finally determined by the passage of legislation. But because such legislation was never created at a federal level, the question was addressed through the application of existing legislation by the courts. And the answers given by the courts equivocated over a twenty-year period from 1927 to 1948, while the political conditions under which the question was asked oscillated from the very high level of support afforded the majors under the National Recovery Administration (1933–35) to the opposite extreme of Attorney General Thurman Arnold's vigorous campaign of antitrust enforcement, which began in 1938.

Until the *Paramount* suit, all these cases—from *Binderup v. Pathé Exchange* through *Paramount Famous Lasky v. US* to the *Youngclaus, Quittner, Perelman, Rembusch*, and *Robison* cases and *US v. Warner Bros.*—addressed individual aspects or instances of the overall protection system; none of them challenged the basic, vertically integrated structure of the industry. Judgments in these cases, including some of those that reached the Supreme Court, were often ambiguous and occasionally contradictory. The majors either ignored unfavorable decisions or circumvented them through a revised strategy. They pursued their concentration of economic power and profit under the expectation that these activities were defensible at law and that, as and when they were deemed to have overstepped the law, a renegotiation of the offending practice would be both possible and appropriate. That expectation was, indeed, ful-filled as late as the 1940 consent decree in the Paramount case, which rep-resented a complete reversal of the Department of Justice's previously firm position and a return to conditions almost as favorable to the majors as had applied under the National Recovery Administration. The consent decree, which the *University of Chicago Law Review* described as "a blue-print of industrial cartelization," was a product of election-year politics and the gov-ernment's need for the industry's cooperation in the coming war effort, but it was only a temporary measure, nominally in place for three years.[18] When it expired in 1944, the Department of Justice and the industry began discussing a replacement, but negotiations broke down over the government's insistence on the divorcement of exhibition, and the case returned to trial in October 1945, reaching the Supreme Court in May 1948.[19] The Court's decision was both the most systemic and the most severe verdict on the classical Hollywood system of film circulation since its inception, going significantly further than the trial court in identifying "the vertical combination of producing, distrib-uting, and exhibiting motion pictures" that sustained classical Hollywood as an illegal conspiracy intended "to substitute monopoly for competition" and in requiring the divorcement of theaters from production and distribution in order to "undo . . . what the conspiracy achieved."[20]

Despite the fact that legislative acts and court decisions determined the conditions under which the industry operated, we have as yet no compre-hensive legal and legislative history of the American motion picture indus-try. The fragmentary parts of this history that do exist have been written almost entirely by scholars in disciplines far removed from the conventional concerns of film studies and published in journals of law or economics.[21] But cinema history ought to provide the overarching context for such a history, an account that traces the history of disputations over the protection system rather than focusing on the legal significance of this or that decision for the history of antitrust in general. Constructing that history, along with the history of Hollywood's system of circulation, is a critical task for classical Hollywood studies in the twenty-first century.

NOTES

1   Richard Maltby, "On the Prospect of Writing Cinema History from Below,"
    Tijdschrift voor Mediageschiedenis 9, no. 2 (2006): 74–96; "How Can Cinema

History Matter More?," *Screening the Past* 22 (December 2007), http://www .screeningthepast.com/issue-22-tenth-anniversary/how-can-cinema-history -matter-more/; "New Cinema Histories," in *Explorations in New Cinema History: Approaches and Case Studies*, ed. Richard Maltby, Daniel Biltereyst, and Philippe Meers (Malden, MA: Wiley-Blackwell, 2011), 3–40.

2 Daniel Biltereyst, Richard Maltby, and Philippe Meers, eds., *Cinema, Audiences and Modernity: New Perspectives on European Cinema History* (London: Routledge, 2011); Judith Thissen and Clemens Zimmerman, eds., *Cinema Beyond the City: Small-Towns & Rural Film Culture in Europe* (London: British Film Institute, 2016); Daniella Treveri Gennari, Danielle Hipkins, and Catherine O'Rawe, eds., *Cinema Outside the City: Rural Cinema-Going from a Global Perspective* (New York: Palgrave, 2018); Daniel Biltereyst, Richard Maltby, and Philippe Meers, eds., *The Routledge Companion to New Cinema History* (London: Routledge, 2019).

3 Thomas Elsaesser, "Is Nothing New? Turn-of-the-Century Epistemes in Film History," in *A Companion to Early Cinema*, ed. Nicolas Dulac, André Gaudreault, and Santiago Hidalgo (Oxford: Blackwell, 2012), 601, 603, 605.

4 Committee on Recent Economic Changes of the President's Conference on Unemployment, *Recent Economic Changes in the United States* (New York: McGraw Hill, 1929), xvi–xvii; John Francis Barry and Epes Winthrop Sargent, *Building Theatre Patronage; Management and Merchandising* (New York: Chalmers, 1927), 436.

5 Paramount Exhibition Contract, 1939, reproduced in *Motion-Picture Films (Compulsory Block Booking and Blind Selling), Hearing before the Committee on Interstate and Foreign Commerce*, U.S. House of Representatives, 76th Congress, 3rd Session (Washington, DC: Government Printing Office, 1940), 235 (hereafter *Hearings*, 1940). See also Mae D. Huettig, *Economic Control of the Motion Picture Industry: A Study in Industrial Organization* (Philadelphia: University of Pennsylvania Press, 1944), 121.

6 Nancy Huggett and Kate Bowles, "Cowboys, Jaffas and Pies: Researching Cinema in the Illawarra," in *Hollywood Abroad*, ed. Melvyn Stokes and Richard Maltby (London: British Film Institute, 2005), 68, 75.

7 Poster for *Only Angels Have Wings* (Hawks 1939), reproduced in Rick Altman, *Film/Genre* (London: British Film Institute, 1999), 5.

8 Franz Kafka, "Leopards in the Temple," in *Parables and Paradoxes* (New York: Schocken, 1961), 93; Juri Lotman, "The Poetics of Everyday Behaviour in Russian Eighteenth-Century Culture," in *The Semiotics of Russian Culture*, ed.

Juri Lotman, Boris A. Uspenskij, and Ann Shukman (Ann Arbor: University of Michigan Press, 1984), 231–56.

9   Robert C. Allen, "Reimagining the History of the Experience of Cinema in a Post-Moviegoing Age," in *Explorations in New Cinema History*, ed. Maltby, Biltereyst, and Meers, 53.

10 *Hearings*, 1940, 462.

11 Quoted in *Harrison's Reports*, March 7, 1936, 39. For a more extensive account of classical Hollywood's distribution system, see Richard Maltby and Ruth Vasey, "A Great Generic Conspiracy: Classical Hollywood's Protection System," *Participations* 16, no. 2 (2019), https://www.participations.org/.

12 Chris. G. Holmes (Manager, Alhambra Theatre, Toronto), "That Continuous Performance Double Bill Factor," *Motion Picture Herald*, May 19, 1934, 25–26.

13 "Screen Fans Organize to Bite Hand That Feeds Them Double Features," *Newsweek*, October 4, 1937, 25.

14 David Palfreyman, memo to Will Hays, November 30, 1938. Record 1181, MPPDA Digital Archive, Flinders University, accessed August 16, 2018, https://mppda.flinders.edu.au/records/1181.

15 *Motion Picture Herald*, February 13, 1937, 70.

16 *Motion Picture Herald*, March 13, 1937, 30.

17 Quoted in Susan Ohmer, *George Gallup in Hollywood* (New York: Columbia University Press, 2012), 147.

18 "Notes: The Sherman Act and the Motion Picture Industry," *University of Chicago Law Review* 13, no. 3 (1946): 349.

19 For an account of the Paramount case, see Giuliana Muscio, *Hollywood's New Deal* (Philadelphia: Temple University Press, 1997), 143–95.

20 *United States v. Paramount Pictures, Inc.* (1948), 334 U.S. 131, 141, 149, 171.

21 See, for example, William F. Whitman, "Anti-Trust Cases Affecting the Distribution of Motion Pictures," *Fordham Law Review* 7, no. 2 (1938): 189–202, accessed August 16, 2018, http://ir.lawnet.fordham.edu/flr/vol7/iss2/3; "Notes: The Sherman Act and the Motion Picture Industry," *University of Chicago Law Review* 13, no. 3 (1946): 346–61; David A. Butz and Andrew N. Kleit, "Are Vertical Restraints Pro- or Anticompetitive? Lessons from Interstate Circuit," *Journal of Law and Economics* 44, no. 1 (2001): 131–59; and Alexandra Gil, "Breaking the Studios: Antitrust and the Motion Picture Industry," *NYU Journal of Law & Liberty* 3, no. 1 (2008): 83–123.

SELECTED BIBLIOGRAPHY

Altman, Rick. *The American Film Musical*. Bloomington: Indiana University Press, 1987.

———. *Film/Genre*. London: British Film Institute, 1999.

Alton, John. *Painting with Light*. Berkeley: University of California Press, 1995.

Ames, Christopher. *Movies About the Movies: Hollywood Reflected*. Lexington: University Press of Kentucky, 1997.

Anderson, Christopher. *Hollywood TV: The Studio System in the Fifties*. Austin: University of Texas Press, 1994.

Andrew, Geoff. *The Films of Nicholas Ray: The Poet of Nightfall*. London: British Film Institute, 2008.

Bacher, Lutz. *Max Ophuls in the Hollywood System*. New Brunswick, NJ: Rutgers University Press, 1996.

Balio, Tino, ed. *The American Film Industry*. 2nd ed. Madison: University of Wisconsin Press, 1985.

———. *Grand Design: Hollywood as a Modern Business Enterprise, 1930–1939*. Berkeley: University of California Press, 1993.

———. *MGM*. New York: Routledge, 2018.

———. *United Artists: The Company Built by the Stars*. Madison: University of Wisconsin Press, 1979.

Barrier, Mike. *Hollywood Cartoons: American Animation in Its Golden Age*. New York: Oxford University Press, 2003.

Basinger, Jeanine. *The Star Machine*. New York: Knopf, 2007.

———. *The World War II Combat Film: Anatomy of a Genre*. Middletown, CT: Wesleyan University Press, 2003.

Belton, John. *American Cinema/American Culture*. 5th ed. New York: McGraw-Hill, 2017.

———. *Widescreen Cinema*. Cambridge, MA: Harvard University Press, 1982.

Berenstein, Rhona. *Attack of the Leading Ladies: Gender, Sexuality and Spectatorship in Classic Horror*. New York: Columbia University Press, 1996.

Bernstein, Matthew, ed. *Controlling Hollywood: Censorship and Regulation in the Studio Era*. New Brunswick, NJ: Rutgers University Press, 1999.

———. *Walter Wanger: Hollywood Independent*. Berkeley: University of California Press, 1994.

Blanke, David. *Cecil B. DeMille, Classical Hollywood, and Modern American Mass Culture: 1910–1960*. London: Palgrave MacMillan, 2019.

Bogle, Donald. *Bright Boulevards, Bold Dreams: The Story of Black Hollywood*. New York: Ballantine Books, 2005.

———. *Toms, Coons, Mulattoes, Mammies and Bucks: An Interpretative History of Blacks in American Films*. New York: Viking, 1973.

Boon, Kevin Alexander. *Script Culture and the American Screenplay*. Detroit, MI: Wayne State University Press, 2008.

Bordwell, David. *Narration in the Fiction Film*. Madison: University of Wisconsin Press, 1985.

———. *Reinventing Hollywood: How 1940s Filmmakers Changed Movie Storytelling*. Chicago: University of Chicago Press, 2017.

Bordwell, David, Janet Staiger, and Kristin Thompson. *The Classical Hollywood Cinema: Film Style and Mode of Production to 1960*. New York: Columbia University Press, 1985.

Braudy, Leo. *The Hollywood Sign: Fantasy and Reality of an American Icon*. New Haven, CT: Yale University Press, 2011.

Brunovska Karnick, Kristine, and Henry Jenkins, eds. *Classical Hollywood Comedy*. New York: Routledge, 1995.

Cagle, Chris. *Sociology on Film: Postwar Hollywood's Prestige Commodity*. New Brunswick, NJ: Rutgers University Press, 2017.

Caldwell, John. *Production Culture: Industrial Reflexivity and Critical Practice in Film and Television*. Berkeley: University of California Press, 2008.

Cavell, Stanley. *Pursuits of Happiness: The Hollywood Comedy of Remarriage*. Cambridge, MA: Harvard University Press, 1981.

Chung, Hye Seung. *Hollywood Asian: Philip Ahn and the Politics of Cross-Ethnic Performance*. Philadelphia: Temple University Press, 2006.

———. *Hollywood Diplomacy: Film Regulation, Foreign Relations, and East Asian Representations*. New Brunswick, NJ: Rutgers University Press, 2020.

Clark, Danae. *Negotiating Hollywood: The Cultural Politics of Actors' Labor*. Minneapolis: University of Minnesota Press, 1995.

Cohan, Steven. *Incongruous Entertainment: Camp, Cultural Value, and the MGM Musical*. Durham, NC: Duke University Press, 2005.

———. *Masked Men: Masculinity and the Movies in the Fifties*. Bloomington: Indiana University Press, 1997.

Cooper, Mark Garrett. *Universal Women: Filmmaking and Institutional Change in Early Hollywood*. Urbana: University of Illinois Press, 2010.

Courtney, Susan. *Hollywood Fantasies of Miscegenation: Spectacular Narratives of Gender and Race, 1903–1967*. Princeton, NJ: Princeton University Press, 2005.

Crafton, Don. *The Talkies: American Cinema's Transition to Sound, 1926–1931*. Berkeley: University of California Press, 1999.

Cripps, Thomas. *Making Movies Black: The Hollywood Message Movie from World War II to the Civil Rights Movement*. New York: Oxford University Press, 1993.

———. *Slow Fade to Black*. New York: Oxford University Press, 1993.

Davis, Blair. *The Battle for the Bs: 1950s Hollywood and the Rebirth of Low-Budget Cinema*. New Brunswick, NJ: Rutgers University Press, 2012.

Decherney, Peter. *Hollywood and the Culture Elite: How the Movies Became American*. New York: Columbia University Press, 2005.

Dimendberg, Edward. *Film Noir and the Spaces of Modernity*. Cambridge, MA: Harvard University Press, 2004.

Dixon, Wheeler, ed. *American Cinema of the 1940s: Themes and Variations*. New Brunswick, NJ: Rutgers University Press, 2005.

Doane, Mary Anne. *Desire to Desire: The Woman's Film of the 1940s*. Bloomington: Indiana University Press, 1987.

Doherty, Thomas. *Hollywood's Censor: Joseph I. Breen and the Production Code Administration*. New York: Columbia University Press, 2007.

———. *Pre-Code Hollywood: Sex, Immorality, and Insurrection in American Cinema, 1930–1934*. New York: Columbia University Press, 1999.

———. *Show Trial: Hollywood, HUAC, and the Birth of the Blacklist*. New York: Columbia University Press, 2019.

Dombrowski, Lisa. *The Films of Samuel Fuller: If You Die, I'll Kill You*. Middleton, CT: Wesleyan University Press, 2008.

Dyer, Richard. *Stars*. London: British Film Institute, 1979.

Fischer, Lucy, ed. *American Cinema of the 1920s: Themes and Variations*. New Brunswick, NJ: Rutgers University Press.

Flinn, Caryl. *Strains of Utopia: Genre, Nostalgia, and Hollywood Film Music*. Princeton, NJ: Princeton University Press, 1992.

Gaines, Jane, ed. *Classical Hollywood Narrative: The Paradigm Wars*. Durham, NC: Duke University Press, 1992.

Gates, Philippa. *Criminalization/Assimilation: Chinese/Americans and Chinatowns in Classical Hollywood Film*. New Brunswick, NJ: Rutgers University Press, 2019.

Giovacchini, Saverio. *Hollywood Modernism: Film and Politics in the Age of the New Deal*. Philadelphia: Temple University Press, 2001.

Glancy, Mark. *When Hollywood Loved Britain*. Manchester, UK: Manchester University Press, 1999.

Gledhill, Christine, ed. *Home Is Where the Heart Is: Studies in Melodrama and the Woman's Film*. London: British Film Institute, 1987.

Glitre, Kathrina. *Hollywood Romantic Comedy: States of the Union, 1934–65*. Manchester, UK: Manchester University Press, 2006.

Gomery, Douglas. *The Coming of Sound: A History*. London: Routledge, 2005.

——. *The Hollywood Studio System: A History*. London: British Film Institute, 2005.

——. *Shared Pleasures: A History of Movie Presentation in the United States*. Madison: University of Wisconsin Press, 1992.

Grieveson, Lee, and Haidee Wasson, eds. *Inventing Film Studies*. Durham, NC: Duke University Press, 2008.

Guerrero, Ed. *Framing Blackness: The African American Image in Film*. Philadelphia: Temple University Press, 1993.

Hallett, Hilary A. *Go West, Young Women! The Rise of Early Hollywood*. Berkeley: University of California Press, 2013.

Hanson, Helen. *Hollywood Heroines: Women in Film Noir and the Female Gothic Film*. London: I. B. Tauris, 2007.

——. *Hollywood Soundscapes: Film Sound Style, Craft and Production in the Classical Era*. London: British Film Institute, 2017.

Hark, Ina Rae, ed. *American Cinema of the 1930s: Themes and Variations*. New Brunswick, NJ: Rutgers University Press, 2007.

Higgins, Scott. *Harnessing the Technicolor Rainbow: Color Design in the 1930s*. Austin: University of Texas Press, 2007.

Hilmes, Michele. *Hollywood and Broadcasting: From Radio to Cable*. Urbana: University of Illinois Press, 1990.

Horak, Laura. *Girls Will Be Boys: Cross-Dressed Women, Lesbians, and American Cinema*. New Brunswick, NJ: Rutgers University Press, 2016.

Houston, Penelope. *Keepers of the Frame: The Film Archives*. London: British Film Institute, 1994.

Jacobs, Lea. *The Decline of Sentiment: American Film in the 1920s*. Berkeley: University of California Press, 2008.

——. *Film Rhythm after Sound: Technology, Music, and Performance*. Berkeley: University of California Press, 2014.

——. *The Wages of Sin: Censorship and the Fallen Woman Film*. Berkeley: University of California Press, 1997.

Jancovich, Mark. *Rational Fears: American Horror in the 1950s*. Manchester, UK: Manchester University Press, 1996.

Jenkins, Henry. *What Made Pistachio Nuts? Early Sound Comedy and the Vaudeville Aesthetic*. New York: Columbia University Press, 1992.

Jewell, Richard B. *The Golden Age of Cinema: Hollywood, 1929–1945*. Malden, MA: Blackwell, 2007.

———. *RKO Radio Pictures: A Titan Is Born*. Berkeley: University of California Press, 2012.

Kalinak, Kathryn. *Settling the Score: Music and the Classical Hollywood Film*. Madison: University of Wisconsin Press, 1992.

Keating, Patrick. *The Dynamic Frame: Camera Movement in Classical Hollywood*. New York: Columbia University Press, 2019.

———. *Hollywood Lighting from the Silent Era to Film Noir*. New York: Columbia University, 2009.

Kemper, Tom. *Hidden Talent: The Emergence of Hollywood Agents*. Berkeley: University of California Press, 2009.

Klinger, Barbara. *Melodrama and Meaning: History, Culture, and the Films of Douglas Sirk*. Bloomington: Indiana University Press, 1994.

Knight, Arthur. *Disintegrating the Musical: Black Performance and American Musical Film*. Durham, NC: Duke University Press, 2002.

Konzett, Delia Malia Caparoso, ed. *Hollywood at the Intersection of Race and Identity*. New Brunswick, NJ: Rutgers University Press, 2019.

Koppes, Clayton R., and Gregory D. Black. *Hollywood Goes to War: How Politics, Profits, and Propaganda Shaped World War II Movies*. London: The Free Press, 1987.

Koszarski, Richard. *An Evening's Entertainment: The Age of the Silent Picture Feature, 1915–1928*. Berkeley: University of California Press, 1992.

———. *Hollywood on the Hudson: Film and Television in New York*. New Brunswick, NJ: Rutgers University Press, 2008.

Kozloff, Sarah. *Invisible Storytellers: Voice-Over in American Fiction Film*. Berkeley: University of California Press, 1989.

Krutnik, Frank, Steve Neale, Brian Neve, and Peter Stanfield, eds. *"Un-American" Hollywood: Politics and Film in the Blacklist Era*. New Brunswick, NJ: Rutgers University Press, 2007.

Kuhn, Annette, ed. *Queen of the Bs: Ida Lupino Behind the Camera*. New York: Praeger, 1995.

Lastra, James. *Sound Technology and the American Cinema: Perception, Representation, Modernity*. New York: Columbia University Press, 2000.

Leab, Daniel. *From Sambo to Superspade: The Black Experience in Motion Pictures.* Boston: Houghton Mifflin, 1976.

Leff, Leonard. *Hitchcock and Selznick: The Rich and Strange Collaboration of Alfred Hitchcock and David O. Selznick in Hollywood.* Berkeley: University of California Press, 1999.

Leslie, Esther. *Hollywood Flatlands: Animation, Critical Theory and the Avant-Garde.* London: Verso, 2002.

Lev, Peter. *The Fifties: Transforming the Screen, 1950–1959.* Berkeley: University of California Press, 2006.

Lewis, Jon. *American Film: A History.* 2nd ed. New York: Norton, 2007.

Mahar, Karen Ward. *Women Filmmakers in Early Hollywood.* Baltimore, MD: Johns Hopkins University Press, 2006.

Maltby, Richard. *Hollywood Cinema.* 2nd ed. Malden, MA: Blackwell, 2003.

Marchetti, Gina. *Romance and the "Yellow Peril:" Race, Sex, and Discursive Strategies in Hollywood Fiction.* Berkeley: University of California, 1993.

McBride, Joseph. *How Did Lubitsch Do It?* New York: Columbia University Press, 2018.

McElhaney, Joe, ed. *Vincente Minnelli: The Art of Entertainment.* Detroit, MI: Wayne State University Press, 2009.

McGilligan, Patrick. *Backstory 1: Interviews with Screenwriters of Hollywood's Golden Age.* Berkeley: University of California Press, 1988.

——. *Backstory 2: Interviews with Screenwriters of the 1940s and 1950s.* Berkeley: University of California Press, 1991.

McLean, Adrienne L. *Being Rita Hayworth: Labor, Identity, and Hollywood Stardom.* New Brunswick, NJ: Rutgers University Press, 2004.

Melnick, Ross. *American Showman: Samuel "Roxy" Rothafel and the Birth of the Entertainment Industry, 1908–1935.* New York: Columbia University Press, 2012.

Monaco, James. *The Sixties: 1960–1969.* Berkeley: University of California Press, 2003.

Morgan, Iwan, and Philip John Davies, eds. *Hollywood and the Great Depression: American Film, Politics, and Society in the 1930s.* Edinburgh: Edinburgh University Press, 2016.

Munby, Jonathan. *Public Enemies, Public Heroes: Screening the Gangster from Little Caesar to Touch of Evil.* Chicago: University of Chicago Press, 1999.

Muscio, Giuliana. *Hollywood's New Deal.* Philadelphia: Temple University Press, 1997.

Naremore, James. *More Than Night: Film Noir in Its Contexts.* Updated and expanded ed. Berkeley: University of California Press, 2008.

Neale, Steve. *Genre and Hollywood.* London: Routledge, 2000.

————. *Screening the Stage: Case Studies of Film Adaptations of Stage Plays and Musicals in the Classical Hollywood Era, 1914–1956*. New Barnet, UK: John Libbey, 2017.

Nielsen, Mike. *Hollywood's Other Blacklist: Union Struggles in the Hollywood System*. London: British Film Institute, 1996.

Orgeron, Marsha. *Hollywood Ambitions: Celebrity in the Movie Age*. Middletown, CT: Wesleyan University Press, 2008.

Petty, Miriam J. *Stealing the Show: African American Performers and Audiences in 1930s Hollywood*. Berkeley: University of California Press, 2016.

Phillips, Alastair, and Ginette Vincendeau, eds. *Journeys of Desire: European Actors in Hollywood*. London: British Film Institute, 2008.

Platte, Nathan. *Making Music in Selznick's Hollywood*. New York: Oxford University Press, 2018.

Polan, Dana. *Power and Paranoia: History, Narrative, and the American Cinema, 1940–1950*. New York: Columbia University Press, 1985.

————. *Scenes of Instruction: The Beginnings of the U.S. Study of Film*. Berkeley: University of California Press, 2007.

Pomerance, Murray, ed. *American Cinema of the 1950s: Themes and Variations*. New Brunswick, NJ: Rutgers University Press, 2005.

Pravadelli, Veronica. *Classic Hollywood: Lifestyles and Film Styles of American Cinema, 1930–1960*. Translated by Michael Theodore Meadows. Urbana: University of Illinois Press, 2015.

Price, Steven. *A History of the Screenplay*. Basingstoke, UK: Palgrave Macmillan, 2013.

Ray, Robert. *A Certain Tendency of Hollywood Cinema, 1930–1980*. Princeton, NJ: Princeton University Press, 1985.

Richards, Rashna Wadia. *Cinematic Flashes: Cinephilia and Classical Hollywood*. Bloomington: Indiana University Press, 2013.

Roddick, Nick. *A New Deal in Entertainment: Warner Brothers in the 1930s*. London: British Film Institute, 1983.

Rodriguez, Clara. *Heroes, Lovers, and Others: The Story of Latinos in Hollywood*. New York: Oxford University Press, 2008.

Rubin, Martin. *Showstoppers: Busby Berkeley and the Tradition of Spectacle*. New York: Columbia University Press, 1993.

Rybin, Steven. *Gestures of Love: Romancing Performance in Classical Hollywood Cinema*. Albany: SUNY Press, 2018.

Salt, Barry. *Film Style and Technology: History and Analysis*. 3rd ed. London: Starword, 1992.

Schaefer, Eric. *Bold! Daring! Shocking! True! A History of Exploitation Films, 1919–1959*. Durham, NC: Duke University Press, 1999.

Schatz, Thomas. *Boom and Bust: American Cinema in the 1940s*. Berkeley: University of California Press, 1999.

———. *The Genius of the System: Hollywood Filmmaking in the Studio Era*. New York: Henry Holt, 1996.

———. *Hollywood Genres: Formulas, Filmmaking and the Studio System*. Philadelphia: Temple University Press, 1981.

Schauer, Bradley. *Escape Velocity: American Science Fiction Film, 1950–1982*. Middletown, CT: Wesleyan University Press, 2017.

Scott, Ellen C. *Cinema Civil Rights: Regulation, Repression, and Race in the Classical Hollywood Era*. New Brunswick, NJ: Rutgers University Press, 2015.

Shiel, Mark. *Hollywood Cinema and the Real Los Angeles*. London: Reaktion Books, 2012.

Sikov, Ed. *Laughing Hysterically: American Screen Comedy of the 1950s*. New York: Columbia University Press, 1996.

Siomopolous, Anna. *Hollywood Melodrama and the New Deal: Public Daydreams*. New York: Routledge, 2012.

Slide, Anthony. *Inside the Hollywood Fan Magazine: A History of Star Makers, Fabricators, and Gossip Mongers*. Jackson: University of Mississippi Press, 2010.

Slowik, Michael. *After the Silents: Hollywood Film Music in the Early Sound Era, 1926–1934*. New York: Columbia University Press, 2013.

Smoodin, Eric, ed. *Looking Past the Screen: Case Studies in American Film History and Method*. Durham, NC: Duke University Press, 2007.

———. *Regarding Frank Capra: Audience, Celebrity, and American Film Studies, 1930–1960*. Durham, NC: Duke University Press, 2004.

Smyth, J. E. *Edna Ferber's Hollywood: American Fictions of Gender, Race, and History*. Austin: University of Texas Press, 2010.

———. *Nobody's Girl Friday: The Women Who Ran Hollywood*. Oxford: Oxford University Press, 2018.

———. *Reconstructing American Historical Cinema: From Cimarron to Citizen Kane*. Lexington: University Press of Kentucky, 2006.

Snead, James. *White Screens, Black Images: Hollywood from the Dark Side*. New York: Routledge, 1994.

Sobchack, Vivian. *Screening Space: The American Science Fiction Film*. New Brunswick, NJ: Rutgers University Press, 1997.

Spadoni, Robert. *Uncanny Bodies: The Coming of the Sound Film and the Origins of the Horror Genre*. Berkeley: University of California Press, 2007.

Spring, Katherine. *Saying It with Songs: Popular Music and the Coming of Sound to Hollywood*. New York: Oxford University Press, 2013.

Stamp, Shelley. *Lois Weber in Early Hollywood*. Berkeley: University of California Press, 2015.

———. *Movie-Struck Girls: Women and Motion Picture Culture after the Nickelodeon*. Princeton, NJ: Princeton University Press, 2000.

Stempel, Tom. *FrameWork: A History of Screenwriting in the American Film*. Expanded ed. New York: Continuum, 1991.

Taylor, John Russell. *Strangers in Paradise: The Hollywood Emigres, 1933–1950*. London: Faber & Faber, 1983.

Telotte, J. P. *The Mouse Machine: Disney and Technology*. Urbana: University of Illinois Press, 2008.

Thomson, David. *Warner Bros: The Making of an American Movie Studio*. New Haven, CT: Yale University Press, 2017.

Vasey, Ruth. *The World According to Hollywood, 1918–1939*. Exeter, UK: University of Exeter Press, 1997.

Wagner, Kristen Anderson. *Comic Venus: Women and Comedy in American Silent Film*. Detroit, MI: Wayne State University Press, 2018.

Wallin, Zoë. *Classical Hollywood Film Cycles*. New York: Routledge, 2019.

Weisenfeld, Judith. *Hollywood Be Thy Name: African American Religion in American Film, 1929–1949*. Berkeley: University of California Press, 2007.

Wexman, Virginia Wright. *Hollywood's Artists: The Directors Guild of America and the Construction of Authorship*. New York: Columbia University Press, 2020.

White, Patricia. *Uninvited: Classical Hollywood Cinema and Lesbian Representability*. Bloomington: Indiana University Press, 1999.

CONTRIBUTORS

TINO BALIO is Emeritus Professor of Film Studies in the Department of Communication Arts at the University of Wisconsin-Madison. He is the author and editor of numerous books and articles on the American film industry, including *United Artists: The Company Built by the Stars* (1975), *The American Film Industry* (ed., 1976), *United Artists: The Company That Changed the Film Industry* (1987), *Hollywood in the Age of Television* (ed., 1990), *Grand Design: Hollywood as a Modern Business Enterprise, 1930–1939* (1993), *The Foreign Film Renaissance on American Screens: 1946–1973* (2010), *Hollywood in the New Millennium* (2013), and, most recently, *MGM* (2018), the inaugural volume of the Routledge Hollywood Centenary Series. Balio served as the director of the Wisconsin Center for Film and Theater Research (1966–83) and was the 2001 recipient of the inaugural Academy Film Scholar Grant from the Academy of Motion Picture Arts and Sciences.

DAVID BORDWELL is Jacques Ledoux Professor Emeritus at the University of Wisconsin-Madison. He has received the Chancellor's Award for Teaching, an honorary doctorate from the University of Copenhagen, and fellowships from the Fulbright and Guggenheim foundations and the US Library of Congress. He is the author of several books on film history and aesthetics, including *Narration in the Fiction Film* (1985), *On the History of Film Style* (1997), *The Way Hollywood Tells It* (2006), *Poetics of Cinema* (2007), *The Rhapsodes: How 1940s Critics Changed American Film Culture* (2016), and *Reinventing Hollywood: How 1940s Filmmakers Changed Movie Storytelling* (2016). With Kristin Thompson he has written two textbooks, *Film Art: An Introduction* and *Film History: An Introduction*. He collaborated with Thompson and Janet Staiger on *The Classical Hollywood Cinema: Film Style and Mode of Production to 1960* (1985). He and Thompson blog regularly at www.davidbordwell.net.

CHRIS CAGLE is Associate Professor of Film History and Theory in the Film and Media Arts Department at Temple University in Philadelphia. His research interests include classical Hollywood, cinematography, documentary, and social theory. His book, *Sociology on Film: Postwar Hollywood's*

Prestige Commodity (2016), examines the 1940s social problem film as both a form of popular sociology and a strain of middlebrow "prestige" cinema. Additionally, he has published essays in *Cinema Journal, Screen,* and *Quarterly Review of Film and Video* and in a number of edited volumes, including, most recently, *Cinematography* (ed. Patrick Keating, 2014) and *Middlebrow Cinema* (ed. Sally Faulkner, 2016). His forthcoming book, *The Film Festival Documentary,* is an examination of an international "festival film" style in contemporary documentary.

LIZ CLARKE is Assistant Professor in the Department of Communication, Popular Culture and Film at Brock University, Canada. Her research is focused on feminist media history, including women in silent American film, women screenwriters, and women showrunners in American television. She has published articles in *Camera Obscura, Feminist Media Histories, Literature/Film Quarterly,* and the *Journal of Popular Film and Television,* as well as chapters in the edited anthologies *New Perspectives on the War Film* (2019) and *Martial Culture, Silver Screen: War Movies and the Construction of American Identity* (2020). Her forthcoming book, titled *The American Girl Goes to War: Women, National Identity and U.S. Silent Film,* examines female heroines in American film from 1908 to 1919 and is under contract with Rutgers University Press.

STEVEN COHAN is Dean's Distinguished Professor Emeritus in English at Syracuse University and a past president of the Society for Cinema and Media Studies. He has taught and lectured on multiple aspects of classical Hollywood. His books include *Screening the Male: Exploring Masculinities in Hollywood Cinema* (1993), *Masked Men: Masculinity and the Movies in the Fifties* (1997), *Incongruous Entertainment: Camp, Cultural Value, and the MGM Musical* (2005), *CSI: Crime Scene Investigation* (2008), *The Sound of Musicals* (2010), *Hollywood by Hollywood: The Backstudio Picture and the Mystique of Making Movies* (2018), and *Hollywood Musicals: Routledge Film Guide Book* (2019). In addition to his essays in numerous collections, his work has appeared in *Screen, Camera Obscura, Celebrity Studies,* and *Cinema Journal.*

BLAIR DAVIS is Associate Professor of Media and Cinema Studies in the College of Communication at DePaul University in Chicago. His books include *The Battle for the Bs: 1950s Hollywood and the Rebirth of Low-Budget Cinema*

(2012), *Movie Comics: Page to Screen/Screen to Page* (2017), and *Comic Book Movies* (2018); his essays appear in anthologies including *Reel Food: Essays on Film and Food* (2004), *Horror Film: Creating and Marketing Fear* (2004), *American Horror Film: The Genre at the Turn of the Millennium* (2010), *Recovering 1940s Horror Cinema* (2014), and the Eisner-Award–winning *The Blacker the Ink: African Americans and Comic Books, Graphic Novels and Sequential Art* (2015). He edited an "In Focus" section for a 2017 issue of *Cinema Journal* on *Watchmen*; has written articles for the *Washington Post, USA Today,* and *Ms.* magazine; and appeared on two episodes of AMC's *James Cameron's Story of Science Fiction.*

LISA DOMBROWSKI is Professor in the College of Film and the Moving Image at Wesleyan University. She is the author of *The Films of Samuel Fuller: If You Die, I'll Kill You!* (2008), editor of *Kazan Revisited* (2011), and coeditor of *ReFocus: The Later Films and Legacy of Robert Altman* (with Justin Wyatt, 2021). She has contributed chapters to *United Artists: Hollywood Centenary* (2020); *Independent Female Filmmakers: A Chronicle through Interviews, Profiles, and Manifestos* (2018); *Silent Features: The Development of Silent Feature Films, 1914–1934* (2018); *Behind the Silver Screen: Cinematography* (2014); and *Widescreen Worldwide* (2010). Her articles have also appeared in *Film History, Film Quarterly, Film Comment,* the *New York Times,* and the Criterion Collection, among others. She is currently completing a book on Robert Altman and American independent cinema in the 1990s and 2000s.

KYLE EDWARDS is Associate Professor of Film at Oakland University in Rochester, Michigan, where he teaches courses in film history and theory, genre studies, and transmedia. His research on the industrial history of Hollywood studios and film genres has appeared in a variety of academic journals, including *Cinema Journal* and *Film History,* and several edited collections. He is currently at work on a manuscript on the Hollywood B-film that examines US producers' strategies with respect to the feature film category from the 1930s through the 1950s. He also serves as associate editor of Routledge's *Creative Industries Journal.*

RYAN JAY FRIEDMAN is Professor of English and Film Studies at The Ohio State University. He specializes in early African American film and the racial politics of classical Hollywood, while teaching courses and writing on a range of other topics, including African American literature, film theory, and American film's social histories. He is the author of *Hollywood's African American Films: The Transition to Sound* (2011) and *The Movies as a World Force: American Silent Cinema and the Utopian Imagination* (2019). He has also contributed to the collections *Early Race Filmmaking in America* (ed. Barbara Lupack, 2016), and *Hollywood at the Intersection of Race and Identity* (ed. Delia Malia Caparoso Konzett, 2020).

PHILIPPA GATES is Professor of Film Studies at Wilfrid Laurier University, Canada. She is the author of *Criminalization/Assimilation: Chinese/ Americans and Chinatowns in Classical Hollywood Film* (2019), *Detecting Women: Gender and the Hollywood Detective Film* (2011), and *Detecting Men: Masculinity and the Hollywood Detective Film* (2006), as well as the coeditor of *Transnational Asian Identities in Pan-Pacific Cinemas* (with Lisa Funnell, 2012) and *The Devil Himself: Villainy in Detective Fiction and Film* (with Stacy Gillis, 2002). She is also the recipient of several research grants from the Social Sciences and Humanities Research Council of Canada and a Faculty of Arts Teaching Scholar Award from Wilfrid Laurier University. Her current book project explores the representation of Chinese immigrants in classical Hollywood Westerns.

BARRY KEITH GRANT is Professor Emeritus of Film Studies and Popular Culture at Brock University in Ontario, Canada. An Elected Fellow of the Royal Society of Canada, he is the author or editor of many books, including *100 Science Fiction Films* (2013), *Invasion of the Body Snatchers* (2010), *The Dread of Difference: Gender and the Horror Film* (1996, 2015), *Shadows of Doubt: Negotiations of Masculinity in American Genre Films* (2011), *Monster Cinema* (2018), *The Twilight Zone* (2020), and the forthcoming *100 American Horror Films* (2021). His work has appeared in numerous anthologies and journals, and he has lectured around the world on film and popular culture. He is also the editor of the Contemporary Approaches to Film and Media (including TV Milestones) series for Wayne State University Press.

HELEN HANSON is Associate Professor in Film History at the University of Exeter. She has written widely on classical Hollywood cinema and its history. She is the author of *Hollywood Soundscapes: Film Sound Style, Craft and Production in the Classical Era* (2017) and *Hollywood Heroines: Women* *in Film Noir and the Female Gothic Film* (2007) and the coeditor of *The Femme Fatale: Images, Histories, Contexts* (with Catherine O'Rawe, 2010) and *A Companion to Film Noir* (with Andrew Spicer, 2013). She is currently researching women's work behind the scenes and below the line in the classical Hollywood studio system.

SCOTT HIGGINS is Charles W. Fries Professor of Film Studies, Curator of the Reid Cinema Archive, and Director of the College of Film and the Moving Image at Wesleyan University, where he teaches and studies film history, genre, and aesthetics. Higgins has written about film technology and style, action film, melodrama, serial storytelling, color cinema, and 3D. His books include *Harnessing the Technicolor Rainbow* (2007), *Arnheim for Film and Media Studies* (2011), and *Matinee Melodrama: Playing with Formula in the Sound Serial* (2016). He has contributed to *Serial Narrative* (2017), *Behind the Silver Screen: Editing and Special Effects* (2016), and *The Ultimate Stallone Reader* (2014). He is currently at work on a study of film style and perceptual engagement in the films of Vincente Minnelli.

ERIC HOYT is the Kahl Family Professor of Media Production in the Department of Communication Arts at the University of Wisconsin–Madison. He is the author of *Hollywood Vault: Film Libraries before Home Video* (2014), which explores how the Hollywood studios exploited their old movies across new markets and technologies from the 1910s through the 1960s, and coeditor of *Hollywood and the Law* (2015) and *The Arclight Guidebook to Media History and the Digital Humanities* (2016). In addition to publishing about Hollywood history, Hoyt has been a leader in enabling broad access to historical sources and in building digital tools to help us better understand them. Hoyt directs the Media History Digital Library, which has scanned over 2.5 million pages of books, magazines, and trade papers related to film and broadcasting history for broad public access. He is currently completing a book about the history of Hollywood's trade press.

KATHRYN KALINAK is Professor of English and Film Studies at Rhode Island College. She is the author of *Settling the Score: Music and the Classical Hollywood Film* (1992), *How the West Was Sung: Music in the Westerns of John Ford* (2007), and *Film Music: A Very Short Introduction* (2010), which has been translated into Hungarian, Italian, Albanian, Greek, and Arabic with Chinese forthcoming. She has edited two anthologies, *Music and the Western: Notes from the Frontier* (2012) and *Sound: Dialogue, Music, Effects* (2015). Her latest book, with Nico de Villiers and Asing Walthaus, is *Richard Hageman: From Holland to Hollywood* (2020). In 2011 she was named the Mary Tucker Thorp Professor of Rhode Island College.

PATRICK KEATING is Professor of Communication at Trinity University in San Antonio, where he teaches courses in film studies and video production. His first book, *Hollywood Lighting from the Silent Era to Film Noir* (2009), won the Best First Book Award from the Society of Cinema and Media Studies. The Academy of Motion Picture Arts and Sciences named him an Academy Film Scholar in support of his research on camerawork, which led to his most recent book, *The Dynamic Frame: Camera Movement in Classical Hollywood* (2019). He is the author of several essays on Hollywood film, including two contributions to *The Classical Hollywood Reader* (2012), and the editor of *Cinematography*, a contribution to Rutgers's Behind the Silver Screen series. His video essays can be found on Vimeo.

CHARLIE KEIL is Principal of Innis College and Professor in the Cinema Studies Institute and the Department of History at the University of Toronto. He is the author or editor of seven books, including *Early American Cinema in Transition: Story, Style and Filmmaking, 1907–1913* (2001), *American Cinema's Transitional Era: Audiences, Institutions, Practices* (with Shelley Stamp, 2004), *Cinema of the 1910s: Themes and Variations* (with Ben Singer, 2009), *Funny Pictures: Animation and Comedy in Studio-Era Hollywood* (with Daniel Goldmark, 2011), *Editing and Special/Visual Effects* (with Kristen Whissel, 2016), *A Companion to D. W. Griffith* (2018), and *Oxford Handbook of Silent Cinema* (with Rob King, forthcoming). He is the 2019 recipient of the SCMS Distinguished Pedagogy Award and 2014 recipient of the University of Toronto's Faculty of Arts & Science Outstanding Teaching Award.

RICHARD MALTBY is the Matthew Flinders Distinguished Emeritus Professor of Screen Studies at Flinders University and a Fellow of the Australian Academy of the Humanities. He has coedited eight books on the history of cinema audiences, exhibition, and reception, including *Going to the Movies: Hollywood and the Social Experience of Cinema* (2007), *Explorations in New Cinema History* (2011), and *The Routledge Companion to New Cinema History* (2019).

His other books include *"Film Europe" and "Film America": Cinema, Commerce and Cultural Exchange, 1925–1939* (1999), *Hollywood Cinema* (2003), and *Decoding the Movies: Hollywood in the 1930s* (2020). He is the series editor of *Exeter Studies in Film History* and is currently writing a history of Warner Bros. for the Routledge Hollywood Centenary series.

DENISE MCKENNA is Lecturer in the Cinema Program at Palomar College. Her research explores the gender and class politics of the early American film industry's social and economic integration with Los Angeles and Hollywood's emergent studio culture. Her work on film extras, gender, and labor stratification and the class politics of editorial cartoons in early film journals has been published in *Film History* and *Early Popular Visual Culture*, and she has edited a special issue on labor for *Feminist Media Histories*. Her current book project, coauthored with Charlie Keil, is a history of Hollywood's institutional and ideological consolidation during the 1910s and 1920s.

PAUL MONTICONE is Assistant Professor in the Radio, Television, and Film Department at Rowan University. His book project examines the Motion Picture Producers and Distributors of America as a business cultural institution, tracing its efforts to negotiate the competing interests of its member firms and to forge and channel "industry interests," the precondition for the collusive activities for which this trade association is known. In addition to his work on industry institutions of the classical Hollywood era, he has published in *Cinema Journal*, the *Quarterly Review of Film and Video*, and the *Editing and Special/Visual Effects* volume of Rutgers's Behind the Silver Screen series, writing about Hollywood genre cycles and transformations in the postwar years, industrial films during the 1920s consolidation of the studio system, and the norms and work practices of studio-era editing departments.

CHARLENE REGESTER is Associate Professor in the Department of African, African American and Diaspora Studies and Faculty Affiliate with the Global Cinema Studies Minor at the University of North Carolina–Chapel Hill. She is the author of *African American Actresses: The Struggle for Visibility, 1900–1960* (2010), which was nominated for an NAACP Image Award. She is the coeditor of *Intersecting Aesthetics* (forthcoming 2021) and *The Josephine Baker Critical Reader* (2017). Her essays have appeared in the anthologies *Hollywood at the Intersection of Race and Identity* (2020), *African American Cinema through Black Lives Consciousness* (2019), *Hollywood Renaissance* (2018), *Early Race Filmmaking in America* (2016), and *New Approaches to "Gone with the Wind"* (2015). Regester serves on the editorial boards of the *Journal of Film and Video* and *Choice Reviews* for academic libraries. She has been featured in documentaries such as *How It Feels to Be Free* (2021) and *Birth of a Movement* (2017).

BRADLEY SCHAUER is Associate Professor in the School of Theatre, Film and Television at the University of Arizona. He is the author of *Escape Velocity: American Science Fiction Film, 1950–1982* (2017) and has published chapters in edited volumes including *Cinematography* (ed. Patrick Keating, 2015), *Make Ours Marvel* (ed. Matt Yockey, 2017), and *The Oxford Handbook of New Science Fiction Cinemas* (forthcoming, Oxford University Press). His work has appeared in journals such as *Film History*, the *Quarterly Review of Film and Video*, and the *Velvet Light Trap*. Aside from classical Hollywood cinema, his research interests include the contemporary film industries, cult film and television, and the American comic industry.

WILL SCHEIBEL is Associate Professor of Film and Screen Studies in the Department of English at Syracuse University. His research focuses on the relations between classical Hollywood film aesthetics and the culture of modernity at the middle of the twentieth century, particularly surrounding issues of authorship, stardom and performance, genre, and representation. With Julie Grossman, he is the coauthor of a volume on *Twin Peaks* in the TV Milestones series (2020). He is also the author and coeditor, respectively, of two books on director Nicholas Ray: *American Stranger* (2017) and *Lonely Places, Dangerous Ground* (with Steven Rybin, 2014). Currently, he is writing a book on Gene Tierney.

KATHERINE SPRING is Associate Professor in the Department of English and Film Studies at Wilfrid Laurier University. She is the author of *Saying It With Songs: Popular Music and the Coming of Sound to Hollywood Cinema* (2013). Her scholarship on film sound and music of the studio era has appeared in the periodicals *Cinema Journal*, *Film History*, and *Music and the Moving Image* and in the anthologies *Sounds of the Future: Essays on Music in Science Fiction Film* (ed. Matthew J. Bartkowiak, 2010) and *Palgrave*

Handbook of Sound Design and Music (ed. Liz Greene and Danijela Kulezic-Wilson, 2016). The recipient of multiple research grants from the Social Sciences and Humanities Research Council of Canada, as well as a Faculty of Arts Teaching Scholar Award from Wilfrid Laurier University, Spring is currently working on a book project about the history of electronic music in American cinema.

JANET STAIGER is William P. Hobby Centennial Professor Emeritus in Communication and Women's and Gender Studies at the University of Texas. She particularly attends to questions about situated and historical authorship, audiences and reception, and positionalities of gender and sexuality. Among her books are *The Classical Hollywood Cinema: Film Style and Mode of Production to 1960* (coauthored, 1985), *Interpreting Films* (1992), *Bad Women: Regulating Sexuality in Early American Cinema* (1995*), Blockbuster TV: Must-See Sitcoms in the Network Era* (2000), *Perverse Spectators* (2000), *Authorship and Film* (coedited, 2002), *Media Reception Studies* (2005), and *Political Emotions* (coedited, 2010).

KIRSTEN MOANA THOMPSON is Professor of Film Studies and Director of the Film Program at Seattle University. She researches and writes on animation, color studies, and material culture, as well as American cinema and Pacific studies. Her publications include *Animation and Advertising* (coedited with Malcolm Cook, 2019), *Apocalyptic Dread: American Cinema at the Turn of the Millennium* (2007), *Crime Films: Investigating the Scene* (2007), and *Perspectives on German Cinema* (coedited with Terri Ginsberg, 1996). She is currently working on three new books: *Animated America: Intermedial Promotion from Times Square to Walt Disney*; *Color, Visual Culture and American Cel Animation*; and *Bubbles*.

INDEX